THE NEW BOOK OF KNOWLEDGE ANNUAL

THE NEW BOOK OF KNOWLEDGE ANNUAL

The Young People's Book of the Year

Grolier Incorporated, Danbury, Connecticut

1988

Highlighting Events of 1987

ISBN 0-7172-0619-X
ISSN 0196-0148
The Library of Congress Catalog Card Number: 79-26807

STAFF

EDITORIAL DIRECTOR	**BERNARD S. CAYNE**
EXECUTIVE EDITOR	**FERN L. MAMBERG**
ASSOCIATE EDITOR	**SARA A. BOAK**
ART DIRECTOR	**MICHÈLE A. McLEAN**

YOUNG PEOPLE'S PUBLICATIONS

EDITOR IN CHIEF	**JEAN E. REYNOLDS**
ART DIRECTOR	**NANCY HAMLEN**
MANAGING EDITOR	**DORIS E. LECHNER**
EDITORS	**GRACE F. BUONOCORE** **ELAINE HENDERSON** **JULIA M. MARKL** **VIRGINIA QUINN McCARTHY** **BARBARA WIESE McKINNEY** **JEROME NEIBRIEF**
CHIEF, PHOTO RESEARCH	**ANN ERIKSEN**
PHOTO RESEARCHER	**PAULA J. KOBYLARZ**
MANAGER, PICTURE LIBRARY	**JANE H. CARRUTH**
INDEXER	**JILL SCHULER**
PRODUCTION EDITOR	**DIANE L. GEORGE**
STAFF ASSISTANTS	**JENNIFER PICKETT VOGT** **MAUREEN C. HAUGHT**

MANUFACTURING

DIRECTOR OF MANUFACTURING	**JOSEPH J. CORLETT**
PRODUCTION MANAGER	**MARILYN SMITH**
PRODUCTION ASSISTANT	**ELIZABETH A. HULL**

CONTENTS

CONTRIBUTORS

BADDERS, Donald
President, National Foundation for Consumer Credit; Chairman of the Board, International Credit Association

CREDIT CARDS

BICKFORD, Maggie
Brown University, Assistant Professor of Art; Rhode Island School of Design Museum of Art, Curator of Asian Art; author, *Bones of Jade, Soul of Ice, the Flowering Plum in Chinese Art*

CHINESE ART

CASSEDY, Sylvia
Author, *In Your Own Words: A Beginner's Guide to Writing; Behind the Attic Wall; M. E. and Morton; Roomrimes*

COMPOSITIONS

DEWAR, Ken
Art Gallery of Ontario, Education Services, Education Officer

CANADIAN ART AND ARCHITECTURE

ENGLISH, Paul W.
University of Texas at Austin, Chairman, Department of Geography; author, *World Regional Geography: A Question of Place;* co-author, *Man, Space, and Environment: Concepts in Contemporary Cultural Geography*

CONTINENTS

FREEDMAN, Russell
Author, *Animal Instincts; Tooth and Claw; How Animals Learn; Growing Up Wild; Getting Born; How Animals Defend Their Young; Animal Architects; The Brains of Animals and Man; How Birds Fly; Animal Superstars; Children of the Wild West; Immigrant Kids; Cowboys of the Wild West*

WHO NOSE?

GOLDBERG, Hy
Sports journalist; former co-ordinator of sports information, NBC sports

SPORTS, 1987

HACKER, Jeffrey H.
Editor, *The Olympic Story;* author, *Carl Sandburg; Franklin D. Roosevelt; Government Subsidy to Industry; Spectator's Guide to the 1984 Olympics*

THE AMERICA'S CUP
SHERLOCK HOLMES—STILL ALIVE AT 100
FOLLOWING THE LIGHT

HAHN, Charless
Stamp editor, *Chicago Sun-Times;* co-author, *British Pictorial Envelopes of the 19th Century*

STAMP COLLECTING

JONES, Lucy E.
Brooklyn Botanic Gardens, Director of educational programs

BOTANICAL GARDENS

LAUBER, Patricia
Author, *Journey to the Planets; Get Ready for Robots; Dinosaurs Walked Here and Other Stories Fossils Tell; Volcano: The Eruption and Healing of Mount St. Helens* (1987 Newbery Honor Book); *Tales Mummies Tell* (1986 New York Academy of Sciences Honor Book)
URANUS
NEPTUNE

MANTEL, Linda H.
City College of New York, Professor of Biology; co-author, *The Balance of Living—Survival in the Animal World;* editor, *The Biology of Crustacea,* vol. 5
CRUSTACEANS

ORR, Lynn Boak
Law Clerk, United States Court of Appeals for the 10th Circuit
INTERPRETING THE CONSTITUTION

PASCOE, Elaine
Author, *The Horse Owner's Preventive Maintenance Handbook; South Africa: Troubled Land; Racial Prejudice*
AROUND THE WORLD
OLYMPIC EQUINES

SHAW, Arnold
University of Nevada—Las Vegas, Director, Popular Music Research Center; author, *A Dictionary of American Pop/Rock; The Jazz Age: Popular Music in the 1920's; Black Popular Music in America; Honkers and Shouters; 52nd St.: The Street of Jazz; The Rockin' 50's; The World of Soul*
THE MUSIC SCENE

SHOEMAKER, Earl A.
Krause Publications (*Numismatic News*); University of Wisconsin, History Lecturer
COIN COLLECTING

SILVERSTEIN, Alvin
SILVERSTEIN, Virginia
Authors, *Circulatory Systems; Heart Disease: America's #1 Killer*
CIRCULATORY SYSTEM

SKODNICK, Ruth
Statistician
INDEPENDENT NATIONS OF THE WORLD

STAINES, David
University of Ottawa, Professor of English; Editor, *The Canadian Imagination: Dimensions of a Literary Culture; The Forty-Ninth and Other Parallels: Contemporary Canadian Perspectives*
CANADIAN LITERATURE

TESAR, Jenny
Designer, computer programs; series consultant, *Wonders of Wildlife;* author, *Introduction to Animals* (Wonders of Wildlife series)
CD-ROM: SHARING INFORMATION
A NEW WAY
CAREERS IN COMPUTERS

TOSH, Nancy
Editor, *Crafts 'n Things* magazine
POPULAR CRAFTS

IN THE PAGES OF THIS BOOK...

How closely did you follow the events of 1987? Do you remember the people who made news during the year? What about the trends—what was in and what was out? Who won in sports? What were the top songs, films, and television shows? What important anniversaries were celebrated? All these things helped make up your world in 1987—a year that was like no other.

Here's a quiz that will tell you how much you know about your world—about what took place during the past year and about other things as well. If you're stumped by a question, don't worry: You'll find all the answers in the pages of this book. (The page numbers after the questions will tell you where to look.)

October 19, 1987, went down in history as "Black Monday." What economic crisis occurred on that day? (*35;50*)

Robots are all the rage these days. But a robot would have to be controlled by a computer "brain" as big as (a Cadillac/Texas/the Empire State Building) to be as intelligent as the human brain. (*121*)

What famous document—which George Washington didn't think would last more than 20 years—celebrated its 200th anniversary in 1987? (*32;191;192*)

In 1987, the "Great One" led the _____ to their third Stanley Cup in four years. (*178*)

A brilliant detective celebrated the 100th anniversary of his literary debut in 1987. Who is this fictional sleuth, who still receives letters at his 221B Baker Street address? (*204*)

And what fictional girl detective, who's been around since the 1930's, startled readers when she started wearing jeans, going to rock concerts, and driving a Mustang convertible? (*234*)

In April, the U.S. Patent and Trademark Office announced that it would allow scientists to patent new forms of animal life created by _____. (*23*)

In May a 19-year-old West German pilot caused a flap when he landed his small plane in front of (the White House/Buckingham Palace/the Kremlin). (*67*)

What huge creatures emerged from the past to appear in games and books, on T-shirts, as dolls, and even as a kind of spaghetti? (*81;135*)

1987 was an especially dreadful year for triskaidekaphobes. Why were they so nervous in February, March, and November? (*133*)

Under Soviet leader Mikhail Gorbachev's policy of *glasnost,* dramatic reforms were being made affecting the Soviet system of government, the economy, and human rights. *Glasnost* means (openness/awareness/democracy). (*54;56*)

Early in 1987, *Stars & Stripes* defeated *Kookaburra III,* and the United States regained the _____, sailing's most prestigious racing trophy. (*164*)

Scientists have recently announced breakthroughs in research into unusual materials that do away with the phenomenon of electrical resistance. What are these amazing materials called? (*98;104*)

In April, a new museum opened in Washington, D.C., devoted to the art of (children/American Indians/women). (282)

What purrfectly adorable animal became the most popular pet in the United States for the first time? (77)

Early settlers of this city outlawed theaters! But _____ became the motion picture capital of the world and celebrated its 100th birthday in 1987. (208)

Canadians have new dollar coins, which are expected to replace their paper dollar bills by 1989. The design on the new coin depicts (a maple leaf/a hockey puck/a loon). (157)

Some called him a renegade, others called him a hero. But everyone agreed that Marine Lieutenant Colonel _____ captured the public's attention during the Iran-contra hearings. (43)

What's the name of the exciting new technology that allows a library of information to fit onto a small round disc? (126)

What great entertainer, known for his dazzling dancing and debonair demeanor, died in June? (27)

Light from an explosion that had occurred 160,000 years ago was seen by astronomers in February. What they were viewing was (a quasar/a supernova/the formation of a new planet). (18;119)

It was the year of the _____ in the animal world. These large, cuddly visitors from China made the rounds in New York, Florida, and California during 1987. (75)

For the first time since baseball's World Series began in 1903, each of the final seven games in 1987 was won by the home team. Which home team won the Series? (167)

In May, a U.S. Navy frigate, the Stark, was hit while on patrol in the Persian Gulf, resulting in the deaths of 37 sailors. Missiles from an (Iranian/Iraqi/Italian) warplane were said to have been fired accidentally. (25;46)

What Irish rock group was hailed as "the rock phenomenon of 1987"? (262)

In August, the Great Basin National Park, in _____, was dedicated as the 49th national park in the United States. (30)

In September, the Soviets launched a monkey named Yerosha into space. The monkey lived up to its name by freeing one of its paws and playing with anything it could reach—including the control panel. Yerosha means (navigator/curious/troublemaker) in Russian. (115)

People thought Walt Disney was mad when he made _____, the first feature-length animated cartoon. It went on to become one of the most popular movies of all time and celebrated its 50th birthday in 1987. (258)

(Biological rhythms/diseases/environmental threats) are so widespread among plants and animals that a new branch of science has evolved called chronobiology. (100)

1987 marked the 50th anniversary of one of aviation's most puzzling events. While attempting a round-the-world flight, _____ disappeared over the Pacific Ocean, leaving no clues behind. (222)

Sunflowers set a record in March, and Irises broke that record in November. Why were these flowers by Vincent van Gogh in the news? (21;37)

In 1987, tennis veteran Martina Navratilova was aced out of the top spot by 18-year-old _____ of West Germany. (182)

In October, the U.S. Senate voted 58 to 42 not to confirm strongly conservative Supreme Court nominee (Douglas Ginsburg/Oliver North/Robert Bork). (28;64)

Why was it a "first" when Marlee Matlin won the 1987 Academy Award as best actress? (278)

1987 marked the 100th anniversary of a sport once referred to as "kitten ball." Name the sport. (187)

THE WORLD IN 1987

Iranian women, cloaked in the traditional veil called the chador, walk past a mural depicting Iranian soldiers and their leader, Ayatollah Ruhollah Khomeini. In 1987, Iran's continuing war with neighboring Iraq threatened major oil supply routes in the Persian Gulf. And Iran's growing militancy throughout the Middle East seemed to be threatening world stability.

THE YEAR IN REVIEW

International tensions were balanced by new prospects for world peace in 1987. While war and terrorism continued in the Middle East and in other parts of the world, the United States and the Soviet Union worked toward a new arms control agreement. And Central American countries developed a plan they hoped would end several long-running conflicts in their region. But the year was also marked by economic worries and, in the United States, a scandal in government.

At a historic summit meeting in December, U.S. President Ronald Reagan and Soviet leader Mikhail Gorbachev signed the first treaty reducing the size of their countries' nuclear forces. The agreement was the product of two years of negotiations, and it still required ratification by the U.S. Senate. It called for both countries to destroy within three years all their intermediate-range nuclear missiles (missiles with ranges of 300 to 3,400 miles, or 480 to 5,470 kilometers). And it set up a system of inspections to ensure that the destruction would be carried out. At their three-day summit meeting in Washington, D.C., Reagan and Gorbachev also discussed reductions in other nuclear weapons, including long-range missiles.

In Central America, five countries—El Salvador, Nicaragua, Costa Rica, Honduras, and Guatemala—were in the process of implementing a plan designed to end several civil wars in the region. The most serious of these conflicts were in El Salvador, where the government was fighting leftist rebels backed by Nicaragua and Cuba, and in Nicaragua, where the leftist government was pitted against rebels backed by the United States. The peace plan called for a halt in the fighting and for the governments involved to release political prisoners, declare amnesty for the rebels, and take steps to increase democracy in their countries.

In the Middle East, however, the outlook for peace seemed dim. Iran's long war with Iraq continued, threatening shipping in the Persian Gulf. Because the Gulf is an important route for oil tankers, the United States became involved. U.S. forces conducted minesweeping operations in the Gulf and provided naval escorts for Kuwaiti tankers traveling through the embattled region, and as a result they exchanged fire with Iranian forces. And 37 U.S. sailors were killed when a Navy frigate, the *Stark*, was accidentally hit by an Iraqi missile. Meanwhile, other Middle Eastern problems—Lebanon's civil war, terrorism, the question of a homeland for displaced Palestinian Arabs—also remained unsolved.

The conflicts in Central America and the Middle East figured in a scandal that shook the United States government in 1987. The outlines of the affair had first been revealed late in 1986: Members of the Reagan administration had sold weapons to Iran, in direct violation of U.S. policy and an arms embargo against the country. Their goal appeared to have been to gain the release of American hostages being held by Iranian-backed terrorists in Lebanon. They had then used the profits from the arms sales to supply military equipment to the rebels in Nicaragua, during a time when Congress had barred such aid. In 1987, several investigations revealed the details of the operation. In November, a Congressional panel issued a report that was highly critical of the administration's actions, and it was widely expected that several key figures in the affair would be charged with having broken laws.

The year also saw hints of greater freedom in the major Communist countries. In the Soviet Union, the government relaxed some controls and permitted more open criticism of its actions. It also took steps toward economic reform, moving away from strict central planning and government control, and it seemed ready to allow more political freedom. In China, which began economic reforms several years ago, new leaders who were committed to change came to power. But in both countries, the rulers made it clear that political freedom would still be limited and that they would block any changes that went too far.

For one non-Communist country, however, the year's events showed that greater democracy alone wasn't a quick solution to problems. In the Philippines, Corazon Aquino had become president in 1986, ending the repressive rule of Ferdinand Marcos. But coup attempts, a Communist rebellion, and continuing economic problems troubled the new president during her first year in office.

Where worldwide economic issues were concerned, the year ended on an uncertain note. In October, the New York Stock Exchange and other major world stock markets suffered their greatest losses since the Depression of the 1930's. While the world economy showed many healthy signs, investors lost billions of dollars, and there were fears that the crash would touch off a recession. Analysts pointed to two major concerns that appeared to be behind the crash: the mounting annual U.S. federal budget deficits, and the fact that the United States had developed an enormous trade deficit by importing more goods than it exported. The U.S. government began work on plans to correct these deficits, and it called for international cooperation to restore confidence in the world economy.

1 People in the United States began to celebrate 1987 as the Year of the Reader—a time to stress the importance of reading. National, state, and local projects were organized across the country to encourage people to read more and to make reading a more valued activity.

A disastrous New Year's Eve fire at a luxury hotel in San Juan, Puerto Rico, killed 96 people and injured more than 140 others. Investigators found that the fire had been deliberately set, and three hotel employees were arrested and charged with the crime.

READ

and The Force is with you.

1987 was proclaimed the Year of the Reader, and posters, banners, bookmarks, calendars, bumper stickers, shopping bags, and buttons carried the message. Throughout the United States, programs and events were organized to encourage people to read more.

In January, slipping on the ice was common in Paris and in most other cities throughout Europe. A severe cold spell swept across the continent and resulted in more than 260 deaths.

4 A high-speed Amtrak passenger train collided with a Conrail train of three locomotives near Baltimore, Maryland. Sixteen people were killed and more than 170 were injured in what was the worst accident in Amtrak's fifteen-year history.

15 Ray Bolger, the American actor and dancer, died at the age of 83. A stage, screen, and television star, Bolger was best known for his role as the rubber-legged Scarecrow in the 1939 film *The Wizard of Oz*.

16 In China, Hu Yaobang was forced to resign as Communist Party leader, the most important political office in the country. He had held the post since 1981. Premier Zhao Ziyang was appointed to replace him. (Zhao also retained the premiership.)

31 During the month, Europe experienced one of its worst cold spells on record. Freezing temperatures and heavy snows resulted in more than 260 deaths across the continent. Hardest-hit was the Soviet Union, where temperatures fell below $-30°$F ($-34°$C).

FEBRUARY

2 In the Philippines, a huge turnout of voters overwhelmingly approved a new constitution. The vote was seen as an important sign of confidence in President Corazon Aquino and her year-old government. In 1986, Aquino had ended the repressive rule of Ferdinand Marcos, who had been president for twenty years.

4 Liberace, the American pianist and entertainer, died at the age of 67. Born Wladziu Valentino Liberace, he was best known for his dazzling showmanship, lavish costumes, and the giant candelabra that adorned his piano.

The U.S. *Stars & Stripes* beat Australia's *Kookaburra III* in a four-race sweep and won the America's Cup, the international yachting trophy. The United States had lost the prestigious Cup to Australia in 1983, after having held it for 132 years.

17 In national elections in Ireland, the Fianna Fail party won the most seats in parliament. Charles J. Haughey, the party's head, became prime minister. He succeeded Garret FitzGerald, who had held the position since 1982. Haughey had previously been prime minister from December, 1979, to June, 1981, and during part of 1982.

22 Andy Warhol, the American artist, died at the age of 58. Warhol was one of the founders of the Pop Art ("popular art") movement of the 1960's. He was most famous for his multiple-image paintings and prints of celebrities, such as Marilyn Monroe, and commonplace items, such as Campbell's soup cans.

24 Astronomers at a University of Toronto observatory in the mountains of Chile announced that they had discovered a huge supernova, or exploding star. The supernova was about 160,000 light years from Earth. (In other words, the light reaching Earth was generated by an explosion that occurred 160,000 years ago. A light year is the distance light travels in one year—about 6 trillion miles.) It was the closest and brightest supernova to be seen since 1604. By observing it, astronomers expected to learn a great deal about these explosions, their origins, and their role in the evolution of the universe.

Pop artist Andy Warhol died in February. Warhol was best known for his 1960's prints showing repeating images of famous people and commonplace things—such as Campbell's soup cans.

3 Danny Kaye, the American comedian, died at the age of 74. A star of stage, screen, television, and radio, the versatile entertainer appealed to audiences of all ages. Among his best-known films were *The Secret Life of Walter Mitty, Hans Christian Andersen,* and *The Court Jester.* In recent years, Kaye entertained children in many countries on behalf of the United Nations Children's Fund (UNICEF), earning the title "ambassador to the world's children."

5–6 A series of earthquakes struck the northeastern jungle region of Ecuador, causing massive mudslides and flooding. More than 300 people were killed, and another 4,000 were missing. An estimated 20,000 people were left homeless.

Sunflowers, by Vincent van Gogh, was sold for a record $39.9 million. The painting was one of a series of seven that the artist had done in 1888–89, in Arles, France.

This rock painting of a diprotodon was found in Australia. Diprotodons were the largest of all the marsupials and have been extinct for about 6,000 years. This was the first rock painting of an Ice Age animal ever found outside Europe.

6   A British passenger-and-auto ferry, *Herald of Free Enterprise,* capsized shortly after leaving Zeebrugge, Belgium, en route to Dover, England. Of the 543 people aboard, 188 lost their lives. It was the worst peacetime disaster in the history of English Channel shipping.

30   *Sunflowers,* a painting by Dutch artist Vincent van Gogh (1853–90), was sold for $39.9 million. The price was the highest ever paid for a painting at auction. The previous record price was $10.4 million, paid in 1985 for Andrea Mantegna's *Adoration of the Magi.*

31   Researchers reported the discovery of the first rock painting of an Ice Age animal to be found outside Europe. The painting was discovered in Queensland, Australia. It shows a diprotodon, a rhinoceros-sized marsupial that became extinct about 6,000 years ago. The rock painting seems to show ropes around the diprotodon, suggesting to some scientists that the animal may have been domesticated.

6 U.S. President Ronald Reagan and Canadian Prime Minister Brian Mulroney ended a two-day meeting in Ottawa, Canada. It was their third annual summit meeting. Their talks focused on acid rain and economic issues.

27 The U.S. Justice Department placed Austrian President Kurt Waldheim on a list of people barred from entering the United States. The action was taken because Waldheim was believed to have been involved in Nazi war crimes during World War II. It was the first time that such an action was taken against the leader of a friendly nation. (On April 28, Prime Minister Brian Mulroney said that Waldheim wouldn't be welcome in Canada.)

30 Harri Holkeri became premier of Finland, heading a four-party coalition government. The coalition was formed when national elections held six weeks earlier resulted in no party winning a majority in parliament. The new government was Finland's first conservative one since World War II. Holkeri succeeded Kalevi Sorsa, who had been premier since 1982.

On April 5, a bridge on the Governor Thomas E. Dewey Thruway, near Albany, New York, collapsed. Several cars and a truck plunged into the Schoharie Creek below, and ten motorists were killed. Experts speculated that floodwaters from a recent storm had carried away gravel and silt around the footings of the bridge, thereby weakening the bridge's supports. The accident was the latest in a series of bridge collapses around the United States. And studies indicated that nearly half the bridges in the country were structurally deficient.

Strawberry plants in California are sprayed with genetically altered bacteria.

THE DEBATE OVER GENETIC ENGINEERING

New debate over genetic engineering emerged in the United States in April. In genetic engineering, or gene-splicing, scientists alter the hereditary traits of living things by making changes in their genes, the units of protein inside each cell that control such traits. For instance, by splicing genes from one animal into the genetic material of another, they can give the second animal traits that it would not naturally have.

Two events fueled the debate. On April 16, the U.S. Patent and Trademark Office said it would allow scientists to patent new forms of animal life that were created by gene-splicing. The office had previously allowed patents for plants and microbes (such as bacteria) created by gene-splicing. Some people hailed the new ruling. They said it would encourage people to use gene-splicing to improve livestock—creating, for example, cows that give more milk. Other people were concerned about moral questions and wondered if, someday, people would be allowed to patent new human traits. As the debate continued, Congress threatened to pass a law banning animal patents, and the Patent Office held off granting any.

Meanwhile, on April 24, genetically altered bacteria were legally released outdoors for the first time. The bacteria, designed to protect crops from frost damage, were sprayed on strawberry plants in California in an experiment. Some people said that this, too, was an important step for agriculture. But others feared that the altered bacteria would have unforeseen harmful effects on the environment.

MAY

9 In national elections in Malta, an island nation in the Mediterranean, the conservative Nationalist Party won a majority of seats in parliament. Eddie Fenech Adami, the party's leader, thus became prime minister. He succeeded Carmelo Mifsud Bonnici of the Labor Party, who had been prime minister since December, 1984.

Fireworks, a parade of ships, a 50-gun salute, and other festivities marked the 50th anniversary of the Golden Gate Bridge on May 24. The bridge, which spans San Francisco Bay, was considered an engineering marvel when it opened in 1937 and is still famous for its beauty. During the anniversary celebrations, some 250,000 people crowded onto it—so many that their weight briefly flattened the normal arch of the bridge deck.

The U.S.S. *Stark*, a jagged hole in its hull, limps toward Bahrain. The Navy frigate was struck by Iraqi missiles while on patrol in the Persian Gulf, resulting in the deaths of 37 sailors.

14 Rita Hayworth, the American film star, died at the age of 68. Hayworth's career reached its peak in the 1940's, when her legendary glamour and beauty made her Hollywood's "love goddess." She appeared in more than 40 movies, including *Cover Girl* (1944) and *Gilda* (1946).

In Fiji, Prime Minister Timoci Bavadra, who had been in office only one month, was ousted in a military coup. The leader of the coup, Sitiveni Rabuka, took control of the country. The coup was the first in this Pacific island country, which had a democratic parliamentary government ever since its independence from Britain in 1970.

17 The U.S.S. *Stark*, a Navy frigate on patrol in the Persian Gulf, was struck by missiles fired by an Iraqi warplane. Thirty-seven American sailors were killed in the attack, which Iraq said was accidental. It was the first serious attack on American forces in the Persian Gulf since the start of the war between Iran and Iraq in 1980.

JUNE

1 Lebanon's Premier Rashid Karami was assassinated when a bomb exploded aboard the helicopter in which he was traveling. Karami, 65, had been premier ten times since 1955. Selim al-Hoss was named to succeed him.

Errol W. Barrow, prime minister of Barbados, died at the age of 67. Barrow had led the Caribbean island country to independence from Britain in 1966. Since that time, he served four terms as prime minister. Barrow was succeeded by Erskine Sandiford.

2 Andrés Segovia, the Spanish classical guitarist, died at the age of 94. Segovia enriched classical guitar technique, revived interest in the instrument, and taught and performed all over the world. His transcriptions of music written for other instruments make up a large part of today's music for the classical guitar.

3 Canadian Prime Minister Brian Mulroney and the premiers of the Canadian provinces signed an agreement bringing Quebec under the Constitution. The Constitution had been adopted in 1982. But Quebec, where the majority of people speak French, had refused to sign, fearing it would lose its special identity. The agreement granted wider powers to all the provinces and recognized Quebec as a "distinct society," with the right to pass laws protecting its identity. The agreement would be incorporated into the Constitution after approval by the Canadian Parliament and the provincial legislatures.

11 In national elections in Britain, the Conservative Party won a majority of seats in Parliament. Margaret Thatcher, the party's head, became the first British leader in 160 years to be elected to a third consecutive term as prime minister.

18 In Vietnam, Vo Chi Cong was named president, and Pham Hung was named premier. They succeeded Truong Chinh and Pham Van Dong, the last founders of the Vietnamese Communist Party still in power. Chinh had held office since 1981; Dong, since 1955.

22 Fred Astaire, the American dancer and actor, died at the age of 88. Astaire starred in more than 30 musical comedies between 1933 and 1968, in which he was noted for his debonair style and his sophisticated, inventive dancing.

24 Jackie Gleason, the American comedian and actor, died at the age of 71. Known as the "Great One," Gleason is best remembered for his portrayal of blustering bus driver Ralph Kramden, in the 1950's television series "The Honeymooners." The series is considered a TV classic, and the reruns are still viewed by millions of people.

Karoly Grosz was named premier of Hungary. He succeeded György Lazar, who had held the position since 1975.

 Justice Lewis F. Powell, Jr., retired from the Supreme Court. A member of the Court since 1971, Powell was considered a moderate in his views. He was the "swing vote" on many recent Court decisions, providing the critical fifth vote needed for a majority.

Fred Astaire, one of the all-time great entertainers, died in June. In top hat and tails, Astaire dazzled audiences with seemingly effortless dance steps performed with spontaneity and elegance.

1   U.S. President Ronald Reagan nominated Robert H. Bork to the Supreme Court. Bork, a judge of the Court of Appeals for the District of Columbia, was named to succeed Lewis F. Powell, Jr. (On October 23, the Senate voted not to confirm Bork.)

5   An African river barge carrying 470 people hit a sandbar, capsized, and sank in the Luapula River between Zaïre and Zambia. About 400 passengers lost their lives.

TITANIC TREASURES

On July 26, a French underwater expedition retrieved dishes from the wreckage of the *Titanic*—the first objects ever recovered from the luxury ocean liner that hit an iceberg and sank on its maiden voyage in 1912. The wreckage lies on the floor of the Atlantic Ocean, several hundred miles south of Newfoundland. It was located by a team of French and American researchers in 1985. In 1986, the U.S. researchers explored the *Titanic* but brought up no artifacts, urging instead that future explorers leave the ship undisturbed "as a memorial to deep-water exploration." Despite the pleas to leave the ship untouched, the French decided to carry out their salvage operation. By the time the 46-day project ended on September 8, the team had retrieved about 300 artifacts—including more dishes, a pair of gold spectacles, a silver ladle, and some money and jewels.

A set of dishes from the *Titanic*, shown just as they were discovered.

Iranian protestors (*above*) stormed the Saudi Arabian embassy in Teheran, the capital of Iran. The rampage came in the aftermath of violent clashes between police and Iranian Muslims in Saudi Arabia's holy city of Mecca.

13 Giovanni Goria, a member of the Christian Democratic Party, was named premier of Italy by President Francesco Cossiga. The Christian Democrats had won the largest percentage of votes in general elections held in June. The formation of the new government ended a political crisis that had begun when Bettino Craxi resigned as premier on March 3.

Kim Chung Yul was named premier of South Korea. He succeeded Lee Han Key, who resigned after less than two months in office.

Ramaswamy Venkataraman was chosen president of India. He succeeded Zail Singh, who had held the position since 1982.

25 U.S. Secretary of Commerce Malcolm Baldrige died in a horseback riding accident at the age of 64. Baldrige had been a member of President Ronald Reagan's Cabinet since 1981.

31 In Mecca, Saudi Arabia, more than 400 people died when fighting broke out between Saudi riot police and Iranian Muslims who were staging a political demonstration. Mecca is Islam's holiest city, and hundreds of thousands of Muslim pilgrims from many countries had gathered there on the eve of the annual pilgrimage, or *hajj,* which marks the high point of the Islamic year. The Saudi government doesn't allow political demonstrations in Mecca during the *hajj,* but the Iranians ignored the ban.

AUGUST

10 President Ronald Reagan nominated C. William Verity, Jr., as U.S. Secretary of Commerce. He would succeed Malcolm Baldrige, who had died in July. (On October 13, the Senate confirmed the nomination.)

15 The Great Basin National Park, in eastern Nevada, was dedicated as the 49th national park in the United States. Covering 77,109 acres of deserts and mountains, it was the first new national park in the 48 contiguous states in fifteen years. The park includes Wheeler Peak (which has the southernmost glacier in the United States) and Lehman Caves (which is the largest limestone cavern in the West).

17 Rudolf Hess, onetime deputy to Nazi German dictator Adolf Hitler, died at the age of 93. Hess was the last survivor of the nineteen German officials convicted in the Nuremberg war crimes trials in 1946. He had been an inmate of Spandau Prison in West Berlin since 1947—the only inmate there for the last 20 years. The United States, France, and Britain had urged that he be released for humanitarian reasons, but the Soviet Union wouldn't agree.

24 Marine Sergeant Clayton J. Lonetree, a former guard at the U.S. embassy in Moscow, was sentenced to thirty years in prison for spying for the Soviet Union. He had been court-martialed on charges that, while serving in Moscow from 1984 to 1986, he had developed a relationship with a Soviet agent and had received

Spectacular limestone formations are a major feature of the Great Basin National Park.

The brother of one of the victims of the Northwest Airlines plane crash.

THE OVERCROWDED SKIES

On August 16, a Northwest Airlines plane crashed onto an interstate highway soon after takeoff from a Detroit airport, killing 153 people on the plane and 3 people on the ground. The only survivor aboard the plane was a 4-year-old girl from Arizona. The accident was the second deadliest in U.S. aviation history. It was also the worst U.S. aviation incident in a year filled with problems. There were more than 400 near midair collisions involving passenger planes, and serious errors by air-traffic controllers were at an all-time high. Poor service was another issue, as passengers complained about crowded airports, delayed flights, lost baggage, and shoddy in-flight facilities. Much of the problem was due to the great increase in air traffic. There was an average of 140,000 commercial and private flights daily in the United States, with some 400 million travelers taking to the skies each year.

money for passing secrets to the Soviets. Several other Marine guards had been similarly charged, but most of the charges were dropped for lack of evidence. The investigations prompted wide concern about the security of U.S. embassies.

 John Huston, the American film director and actor, died at the age of 81. The first picture Huston directed was *The Maltese Falcon* (1941), one of the best detective thrillers ever made. He went on to direct some forty more films, including *The Treasure of the Sierra Madre* (1948), for which he won best-writer and best-director Academy Awards, and *The African Queen* (1951).

3 Jean-Baptiste Bagaza, president of Burundi since 1976, was overthrown in a military coup. Army major Pierre Buyoya assumed the presidency.

14 Elizabeth Hanford Dole announced that she would resign as U.S. Secretary of Transportation. (On October 8, President Ronald Reagan nominated James H. Burnley IV to succeed Dole. On November 30, the Senate confirmed Burnley's nomination.)

15 The 42nd annual session of the United Nations General Assembly opened at U.N. headquarters in New York City. Peter Florin of East Germany was elected to serve as assembly president for one year.

16 Twenty-four nations, including the United States and Canada, signed a treaty designed to protect the ozone layer in the Earth's atmosphere. Ozone, a form of oxygen, absorbs much of the sun's harmful ultraviolet radiation. For many years, scientists have warned that the ozone shield was being destroyed by chlorofluorocarbons (CFC's). These industrial chemicals are used in refrigerants, solvents, foam insulation, and as propellants in aerosol sprays. Few steps were taken in response to the scientists' warnings, although several nations banned CFC's in aerosol propellants. Recently, however, scientists discovered severe thinning of the ozone layer over the Antarctic and also a thinning of the ozone layer worldwide. Under the terms of the treaty, CFC production would be reduced 50 percent by 1999. The treaty marked the first time that the world's nations agreed to cooperate on an environmental problem.

17 With parades, fireworks, the ringing of bells, and other festivities, Americans celebrated the 200th anniversary of the signing of the U.S. Constitution.

20 Pope John Paul II ended an eleven-day tour of North America that included stops in nine U.S. and two Canadian cities. At masses and meetings with church leaders, the Pope affirmed the church's official position on moral issues. And he stated that dissent from church doctrine wasn't compatible with being a good Catholic.

30 In India, months of extreme weather conditions resulted in great devastation. The month of September brought heavy rains and severe flooding to eastern and northern sections, killing more than 1,200 people and leaving over a million homeless. In July and August, India's worst drought in a century had caused many deaths and extreme hardship. (In Bangladesh, India's neighbor to the east, a month of severe rains and flooding in August had resulted in the deaths of nearly 1,000 people and destroyed $1.3 billion worth of crops and property.)

Pope John Paul II, wearing a fringed vestment, emerges from a ceremonial teepee in Fort Simpson, Northwest Territories. He later said mass for 4,000 Indians at this old trading and missionary post in Canada's far north.

OCTOBER

1   A severe earthquake followed by numerous aftershocks hit the Los Angeles area. The quake, the strongest to hit the area since 1971, caused seven deaths and many injuries. Property damage was estimated at more than $200 million.

3   The United States and Canada agreed on a comprehensive trade pact. The most significant aspect of the pact is the elimination, before 1999, of all tariffs between the two nations. (Tariffs are taxes on goods imported to a country.)

9   Clare Boothe Luce, the American writer and public official, died at the age of 84. Luce was a journalist and author of several successful plays before entering politics in the 1940's. She served in the House of Representatives from 1943 to 1947, and she was later appointed Ambassador to Italy—the first American woman ever to hold a major diplomatic post.

A severe earthquake shook the Los Angeles area on the morning of October 1. Buildings collapsed, glass was torn from skyscrapers, and cars were jolted on freeways. Seven people died in the disaster.

15 William E. Brock announced that he would resign as U.S. Secretary of Labor. (On November 3, President Ronald Reagan nominated Ann Dore McLaughlin to succeed Brock. On December 11, the Senate confirmed McLaughlin's nomination.)

Thomas Sankara, president of Burkina Faso since 1983, was killed during a military takeover of the country. Blaise Compaore assumed the presidency.

19 The day became known as "Black Monday," as the U.S. stock market had its worst day in history. The Dow Jones industrial average, the major indicator of changes in the level of stock prices, fell 508 points. More than 604 million shares were traded. The frantic trading and plunging prices were followed by similar events on stock markets elsewhere in the world.

29 President Ronald Reagan nominated Douglas H. Ginsburg to the U.S. Supreme Court. Ginsburg, a judge on the Court of Appeals for the District of Columbia, was Reagan's second nominee, to succeed Lewis F. Powell, Jr. (On November 7, Ginsburg withdrew as nominee, following disclosures that he had smoked marijuana in the past.)

THE 1987 NOBEL PRIZES

Chemistry: Donald J. Cram and Charles J. Pedersen of the United States and Jean-Marie Lehn of France, for pioneering a field of chemistry that involves the creation of artificial molecules that can perform the same functions as molecules produced by living cells.

Economics: Robert M. Solow of the United States, for his contributions to the theory of economic growth, including the development of a mathematical model showing that long-term growth depends on technological progress.

Literature: Joseph Brodsky, an exiled Russian who is now a U.S. citizen, for his essays and poetry, which were cited for their "clarity of thought and poetic intensity."

Peace: Oscar Arias Sánchez, president of Costa Rica, for working out an accord, signed by five Central American countries, that might bring "stability and peace" to their region.

Physics: K. Alex Müller of Switzerland and J. Georg Bednorz of West Germany, for their discoveries that led to great advances in the field of superconductivity—the ability of certain materials to carry electric current with no loss of energy.

Physiology or Medicine: Susumu Tonegawa of Japan (the first Japanese to win the prize), for his discoveries of how the human body can produce millions of different kinds of antibodies to fight germs.

1 Deng Xiaoping, the chief architect of sweeping economic changes in China and the nation's paramount leader since 1979, resigned from all but one of his leadership positions in the Communist Party. The resignation of Deng and other aging members of the party opened the way for a younger generation of leaders. (On November 24, Li Peng was named premier of China. He succeeded Zhao Ziyang, who retained his position as leader of the Communist Party.)

Mahmoud Zubi became premier of Syria. He succeeded Abdel Raouf al-Kassem, who had resigned after eight years in office.

4 It was announced that scientists had identified fossils of the largest seabird ever known. The fossils, discovered in an excavation made in 1984 in Charleston, South Carolina, were in rock dated at about 30 million years old. The creature was a member of the extinct family *pseudodontorn* ("bony-toothed bird"). Its jaws were lined with rough, bony structures that looked somewhat like teeth. It had a wingspan of more than 18 feet (5.5 meters)—in comparison, the largest living seabird, the albatross, has a wingspan of 11 feet (3.4 meters).

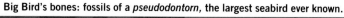

Big Bird's bones: fossils of a *pseudodontorn*, the largest seabird ever known.

Vincent van Gogh's *Irises* was sold for $53.9 million, the highest price ever paid for a work of art. It was painted in 1889, a week after the artist had committed himself to a mental asylum in France.

5 Caspar W. Weinberger announced his resignation as U.S. Secretary of Defense. President Ronald Reagan nominated Frank C. Carlucci to succeed Weinberger. (On November 20, the Senate confirmed Carlucci's nomination.)

6 Noboru Takeshita was elected premier of Japan by the nation's parliament. Takeshita succeeded Yasuhiro Nakasone, who had been premier since 1982.

7 In Tunisia, President Habib Bourguiba was ousted in a coup. Zine el-Abidine Ben Ali, the country's premier, assumed the presidency. Bourguiba, 84, had led Tunisia for 31 years, since it had gained independence from France.

10 Seyni Kountche, president of Niger since 1974, died at the age of 56. He was succeeded by Ali Seybou.

11 *Irises*, a painting by Dutch artist Vincent van Gogh (1853–90), was sold for $53.9 million. The price was the highest ever paid for a painting at auction. The previous record price was $39.9 million, paid in March for van Gogh's *Sunflowers*.

President Reagan nominated Anthony M. Kennedy to the U.S. Supreme Court. Kennedy, a judge on the Court of Appeals for the Ninth Circuit in San Francisco, was Reagan's third choice to fill the seat left vacant by the resignation of Lewis F. Powell, Jr.

37

DECEMBER

1 James Baldwin, the black American writer who was a prominent leader in the civil-rights movement of the 1950's and 1960's, died at the age of 63. Baldwin wrote novels, plays, and essays that eloquently described racial discrimination in America. These included *Go Tell It on the Mountain* (1953), *Notes of a Native Son* (1955), and *The Fire Next Time* (1963).

5 In Fiji, Sitiveni Rabuka, who had seized power in May, appointed Ratu Sir Penaia Ganilau president. He also appointed Ratu Sir Kamisese Mara as prime minister. Mara had been prime minister for seventeen years prior to being defeated in national elections in April. His defeat had served as the main reason for Rabuka's coup.

10 Jascha Heifetz, the Russian-born violinist who became an American citizen in 1925, died at the age of 86. Heifetz, one of the greatest violinists of all time, was a child prodigy—he played for the first time at the age of 3 and won wide acclaim while still in his teens.

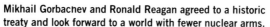

Mikhail Gorbachev and Ronald Reagan agreed to a historic treaty and look forward to a world with fewer nuclear arms.

THE SUMMIT MEETING

December 8, 1987, marked a historic first in relations between the United States and the Soviet Union: the signing of the first treaty between these countries reducing the size of their nuclear arsenals. The signing took place in Washington, D.C., during three days of meetings between U.S. President Ronald Reagan and Soviet leader Mikhail Gorbachev.

The treaty set up a three-year schedule for eliminating intermediate-range nuclear missiles—those with ranges of 300 to 3,400 miles. In recent years the Soviet Union had installed many such missiles within range of targets in Europe and Asia. The United States had countered by setting up intermediate-range missiles in Western European countries that were members of the North Atlantic Treaty Organization (NATO), within range of targets in the Soviet Union and Eastern Europe.

The treaty called for all these missiles to be crushed, burned, blown up, or otherwise destroyed. Teams of inspectors from each country would visit the other country's missile sites to ensure that the destruction was actually carried out, and each country would have the right to inspect the other's missile sites on short notice for thirteen years after the treaty took effect.

Before it could take effect, however, the agreement required the approval of the U.S. Senate. Some senators had reservations about it, and a few opposed it strongly. They worried that the inspection procedures wouldn't really be able to prevent cheating, and that Western Europe would be left poorly defended against the threat of an invasion by the Soviet Union. Still, it was expected that the treaty would be ratified.

The meeting between the U.S. and Soviet leaders gave people in the United States their first close-up look at Gorbachev, who had come to power in 1985 and had pressed for many changes in his country. More importantly, the talks gave Reagan and Gorbachev an opportunity to discuss plans to eliminate more nuclear weapons, including long-range missiles, bombs, and weapons with very short ranges. (The intermediate-range missiles that would be eliminated represent only about 3% of the U.S.-Soviet nuclear arsenal.) A major roadblock to further discussions was Reagan's proposal to create a space-based missile defense system (the Star Wars plan), which the Soviets said would violate the Antiballistic Missile Treaty that the two countries had signed in 1972. But despite this disagreement, the summit meeting produced hope around the world that the threat of nuclear war could be reduced and that relations between the two superpowers would improve.

17 In Czechoslovakia, Milos Jakes was named general secretary of the Communist Party. He succeeded Gustav Husak, who resigned after 18 years in office. Husak remained as president.

20 A Philippine passenger ferry collided with an oil tanker about 100 miles (160 kilometers) south of Manila. More than 1,600 people drowned as a result of the accident.

23 Three Soviet cosmonauts launched aboard a Soyuz spacecraft docked with the Mir space station. Two remained at the station, replacing the two-man crew of Yuri Romanenko and Aleksandr Aleksandrov. (On December 29, the other cosmonaut returned to Earth with Romanenko and Aleksandrov. Romanenko had spent a record-breaking 326 days in orbit.)

A scandal swirled around the White House in 1987 over the secret sale of arms to Iran and the diversion of funds from this sale to Nicaraguan rebels called the contras. Investigations into the Iran-contra affair created a crisis for President Ronald Reagan.

THE IRAN-CONTRA AFFAIR

Late in 1986, the U.S. government made a startling admission: It had secretly sold weapons to Iran, a country that promoted international terrorism. The sales were in direct contradiction to U.S. policy, and they also appeared to violate an arms embargo against Iran that has been in effect since 1980. The news took many people by surprise, but it was only the tip of the iceberg. A preliminary investigation into the sales turned up an even stranger twist: Profits from the arms sales had been used to provide military aid for the Nicaraguan rebels called the contras—during a time when Congress had specifically forbidden such aid.

The scandal surrounding these events captured the country's attention for much of 1987. The Iran-contra affair, as the events became known, brought about separate investigations by the Justice Department, a presidential commission (the Tower Commission), Congress, and an independent counsel appointed by a federal court. Each of these investigations sought the answers to some important questions: Who was responsible for setting up these secret policies? Could the policies be justified? Had laws been broken and, if so, by whom?

The Iran-contra affair prompted concern about the U.S. government's standing and credibility in the eyes of the world. It also raised questions about the way the government was supposed to work. Many of these questions couldn't be answered easily. But as the investigations continued, a rough outline of the affair emerged.

THE SECRET OPERATION

According to testimony before the various investigators, the arms sales to Iran were set up by officials of the National Security Council (NSC)—an executive body that advises the president on foreign policy and national security matters. The NSC officials began the operation in mid-1985, channeling the arms through Israel and a network of private arms dealers. The main figures were National Security Advisor Robert C. McFarlane; his successor, Vice Admiral John M. Poindexter; and their assistant Oliver L. North, a Marine lieutenant colonel. These officials gained the approval of President Ronald Reagan for the shipments, over the objections of the Secretary of State and the Secretary of Defense.

Although the arms sales were originally proposed as a way of improving relations with Iran, the main goal seemed to have been the chance of obtaining the release of a number of Americans being held hostage by terrorists in Lebanon. In exchange for the arms, Iran was to have used its influence with the terrorists. The sales continued through October, 1986, and during that time three hostages were released. But the rest weren't freed, and one was killed. And three more Americans were kidnapped.

The money received from the sales was deposited in Swiss bank accounts set up for the operation. Part of the money went to reimburse the U.S. government for the cost of the weapons. But the profits—about $16 million—weren't turned over to the government. What happened to all this money wasn't known. But it was certain that some of it was used to provide military aid to the contras. Until mid-1984, the United States had openly supported these rebels, who were fighting the Communist government of Nicaragua. But many people had questioned whether the United States should be involved in a civil war in another country, and Congress had banned military aid to the contras. (The ban was lifted in mid-1986.)

Again, NSC officials, chiefly North, directed the operation. North also appeared to have been involved in efforts to obtain aid for the contras from private individuals and from other countries. This kind of aid wasn't banned by Congress. But Congress had barred U.S. officials from directly soliciting aid for the contras.

The investigations examined some unusual sidelights to the affair. One was a secret trip by McFarlane, North, and other U.S. officials, who flew to Teheran, Iran's capital, in May, 1986, hoping for the release of all the American hostages. No hostages were released, however, and they left. In another twist, a $10-million contribution from the Sultan of Brunei, earmarked for nonmilitary aid to the contras, was lost. At first

At a January press conference, Iranian officials display a Bible signed by President Reagan. It had been delivered to Iranian officials as a goodwill gesture during secret meetings in which the White House sought to establish contact with Iran.

the money was thought to have been spent on arms. But later it was found to have been deposited in the wrong Swiss account.

Besides piecing together the events, the investigations sought to determine who was responsible for the affair. President Reagan claimed that the arms sales to Iran were more an attempt to improve relations with that country than a deal to free the hostages. He also said that he hadn't known about the diversion of funds to the contras. Poindexter backed him up, claiming that he alone had approved the contra aid. But polls showed that a majority of Americans thought Reagan must have known of it.

The Tower Commission report accepted Reagan's statement that he didn't know of

Several investigations tried to unravel the Iran-contra affair. Here, Oliver North, a key figure in the affair, is sworn in prior to testifying before a Congressional committee.

the contra aid but criticized him for having too little control over his assistants. The Congressional report was harsher: It said that Reagan had failed in his constitutional duty to see that the law was upheld, and that he bore the "ultimate responsibility" for the affair. "If the President did not know what his national security advisers were doing," the report said, "he should have."

One unanswered question was the role of the director of the Central Intelligence Agency, William Casey. Like many other top figures in the Reagan Administration, Casey claimed that he hadn't known of the diversion of funds to the contras. North, on the other hand, said Casey had both known and approved of it. But Casey died in May, leaving his true role a mystery.

WIDER QUESTIONS

The Iran-contra affair raised important concerns about U.S. foreign policy. Iran was involved in a war with Iraq, and the United States had officially taken a neutral position in the war. But by selling weapons to Iran, the United States seemed to take the Iranian side. The investigations also turned up the fact that the United States had given distorted intelligence reports to both countries.

Also troubling to many people was the fact that the weapons sales to Iran appeared to have been part of an arms-for-hostages trade. The United States had previously said that it wouldn't negotiate with terrorists in any way. It had banned arms sales to Iran in 1980, after Iranians had stormed the U.S. embassy in Teheran, their capital, and held more than 50 Americans hostage for over a year. And it had urged other countries to do the same.

The events raised questions, too, about the way the U.S. government was supposed to work. In their reports, the Tower Commission and the Congressional panel expressed concern that the policies behind the Iran-contra affair had been developed secretly by a few people. Many important Administration officials and a Congressional committee set up to oversee secret operations had been kept in the dark. When the story came out, documents were shredded and memos were altered to hide the details.

The last investigation, still to be con-

OLIVER NORTH: RENEGADE OR HERO?

The Congressional hearings on the Iran-contra affair were broadcast live by the major television networks. Of all those who appeared, the person who made perhaps the biggest impression on the public was Marine Lieutenant Colonel Oliver L. North. As a National Security Council aide, North had played a key role in both the arms sales to Iran and the diversion of profits to the contras. He had been fired by President Reagan late in 1986, after the diversion of funds came to light.

North's friends described him as hard-working, dedicated, intelligent, and ambitious. His critics described him as a renegade who had taken U.S. foreign policy into his own hands and liked to exaggerate his importance and his closeness to the president. In his five years with the NSC, North had been closely involved in planning other undercover government actions. These included the U.S. invasion of Grenada in 1983, the mining of three harbors in Nicaragua in 1984, the interception of an Egyptian airliner that carried terrorists who had hijacked a cruise ship in 1985, and the bombing of Libya in 1986. Beginning in 1983, he had also been involved in Central Intelligence Agency operations to supply the contras with arms.

Testifying before the Congressional committee, North defended his actions in the Iran-contra affair. He said that he firmly believed he had the approval of his superiors and that the diversion of funds to the contras was in the best interests of the United States. He also openly admitted shredding documents relating to the affair to keep them from investigators.

Appearing before the panel in full military uniform, North gave testimony that was often highly emotional. He was perceived by many people as a hero, and he received hundreds of telegrams and letters expressing support. Other people, however, were disturbed by what they saw as North's cocky manner and defiant attitude. And as later witnesses contradicted some of North's testimony, some of his supporters had second thoughts about his role in the affair.

Along with his superior, Vice Admiral John M. Poindexter, North was granted limited immunity for his testimony before the Congressional panel. That is, he couldn't be prosecuted on the basis of anything he said to the panel. But if the independent counsel investigating the Iran-contra affair found separate evidence that he had broken the law, he might be charged.

cluded, was that of the independent counsel, Lawrence E. Walsh. His job was to determine whether anyone might have broken the law, either by taking part in the affair or by covering up after it.

But beyond the question of individual responsibility, the Iran-contra affair seemed certain to have some long-range effects. Reagan's image had been hurt, and this seemed likely to reduce his effectiveness as president. It also raised the hopes of the Democrats for a win in the 1988 presidential election.

Meanwhile, the image of the United States had been hurt abroad—many foreign governments said they had lost faith in U.S. foreign policy. And a tough question remained: how foreign policy could be conducted so that similar events wouldn't happen in the future.

Signs of the coming Olympic Games were evident everywhere in South Korea. But the country was in the news for another reason in 1987: Its people were demanding greater freedom.

SOUTH KOREA: STEPS TOWARD DEMOCRACY

In 1988, South Korea will be the site of the Summer Olympic Games. But in 1987 the eyes of the world were on this Asian country for another reason. As South Korea prepared to host the Games, it was rocked by confrontations between government forces and demonstrators demanding greater freedom. As a result, the country saw its first direct presidential election in years.

A DIVIDED LAND

South Korea has had special importance to Western countries since the end of World War II. Until that time, Korea was a single country that encompassed the Korean Peninsula, which extends from the Chinese coast. But in 1945, Communists took over the northern part of the peninsula, and the country was divided. The boundary between Communist North Korea and the republic of South Korea was set in 1948.

In 1950, Communist forces invaded the south, setting off the Korean War. Forces from the United Nations and the United States fought on the side of South Korea for three years. But neither side won a total victory, and the country remained divided. Since that time, both sides have maintained large armies, ready for further conflict. U.S. forces are also stationed in South Korea.

Although South Korea is a republic with an elected government, the country has in fact enjoyed little democracy. The South Korean government has said that controls are needed to keep the country united against the threat from the north. Thus the election system has been set up to ensure that one party, the Democratic Justice Party, wins. Civil liberties, such as freedom of speech and of the press, have been limited. Early in 1987 an estimated 1,900 people were in jail on political charges. And reports of torture were common.

Meanwhile, South Korea's economy has boomed. The ruling Justice Party is closely allied with the army and with business groups, and it has encouraged economic growth. Since the Korean War, South Korea has rapidly changed from a farming society to an industrial one. It is now a major exporter of products like cars, ships, computers, and television sets.

With economic growth have come new problems. Millions of people have moved to the cities, straining housing and social services. Many have done well and enjoy a better life than ever before. But others remain poor, and the gap between rich and poor has grown. This has helped create new political tensions. And as South Korea has changed, its people have increased their calls for greater freedom.

These calls first came from students, church leaders, and labor groups. But gradually, the middle class began to chafe under the government's restrictions. The government responded by relaxing some of its tightest controls and agreeing to discuss political reform. But for many South Koreans, these changes were too little.

EVENTS OF 1987

As 1987 began, the government was discussing changes in the election system. President Chun Doo Hwan had announced that he would step down early the next year, so elections for his successor were scheduled for December. Under the existing system, the next president would be picked by an electoral college, and the Justice Party was all but guaranteed a victory. Opposition groups wanted the system changed, to permit a direct vote.

Then, in April, the government abruptly cut off the discussions. It described opposition leaders as "radicals" and brought criminal charges against some of them. All debate on the election system was put off until 1989. The reason the government gave for its action was that the country couldn't afford the disunity provoked by the debate, especially with the Olympics coming up.

Instead of promoting unity, however, the government's action set off protests. Students took to the streets in demonstrations that turned violent when the police attempted to stop them. And for the first time, the students were joined by people from many walks of life, including members of the middle class.

On June 10, the Justice Party announced that Roh Tae Woo was its choice for president (and would thus automatically succeed Chun). New rioting broke out immediately. Then, suddenly, the government made an abrupt about-face: It announced that it would support direct elections and other democratic reforms.

Several factors led to the government's decision. The demonstrations—both their strength and the widespread support they received—were the major one. Government leaders said they feared that if the rioting continued, the army might step in and take over the country. But they were also aware that in 1986, such demonstrations had driven President Ferdinand Marcos of the Philippines from power. And the image of riot police firing tear gas at demonstrators wasn't the one that South Korea wanted to present to the world in the coming Olympic year. The United States, South Korea's close ally and supporter, was also pressuring the government for democratic reforms.

Thus on December 17, South Korea held its first direct presidential election since 1971. Roh, the government candidate, received about 40% of the vote, while over half the voters chose the opposition. But because the opposition's votes were split among several candidates, Roh won. Opposition leaders accused the government of vote fraud. But opposition's failure to pick just one candidate was judged a key factor in their defeat. Although protests followed the election, South Korea seemed to have taken the first steps toward democracy.

Angry students protest the government's decision to cancel discussions about changes in the election system.

The seven-year war between Iran and Iraq has threatened shipping in the Persian Gulf, an important route for oil tankers. In 1987, Iran began to place mines in the gulf, further endangering shipping.

THE MIDDLE EAST

For a world dependent on oil from the Middle East, 1987 was a year of concern. The widening war between Iran and Iraq threatened to involve nearby countries and drew U.S. forces into the Persian Gulf to protect shipping lanes. Elsewhere, terrorism and conflict between the region's many religious and political groups continued.

The Middle East has long been a troubled region. Israel, created in 1948 as a Jewish homeland, has fought several wars with neighboring Arab countries that refuse to recognize its existence. Territorial disputes and the question of a homeland for displaced Palestinian Arabs remain unsolved. In Lebanon, a civil war has raged since the mid-1970's. But in 1987, it was the Persian Gulf that captured most of the world's attention.

THE GULF WAR

The war between Iran and Iraq began as a territorial dispute in 1980. At first, Iraq had some major victories and made inroads into Iran. But Iran drove the Iraqis back in a series of offensives. By 1987, the Iranians had succeeded in winning some territory in southern Iraq. And early in the year, in another major offensive, they nearly captured the southern Iraqi city of Basra but were driven back.

The war has taken a heavy toll on both countries, and it has also threatened the world's oil supply. Countries in the Persian Gulf area provide a large share of the oil used around the world, and the gulf itself is an important route for oil tankers. Iran and Iraq have each attacked shipping and offshore oil platforms in the gulf; while Iraq has focused on attacking Iranian installations, Iran has also attacked ships of neutral countries and mined the waters of the gulf.

Thus the gulf has become increasingly dangerous for all ships. On May 17, a U.S. Navy frigate, the *Stark,* was hit by an Iraqi missile. Thirty-seven sailors aboard the ship were killed, and the *Stark*'s failure to defend itself led to an inquiry. The Iraqis said the attack was a mistake.

Kuwait, which lies just south of Iraq and has supported that country in the war, has been especially threatened by Iranian attacks. Early in 1987, Kuwait asked for help from the United States. And in July, the United States placed eleven of Kuwait's oil tankers under U.S. registry and began providing them with naval escorts. After a U.S.-registered tanker struck a mine, U.S. forces also began to sweep for mines in the gulf. Britain, France, and Italy joined in the minesweeping, although they were reluctant at first. These moves were designed to keep oil flowing and to block Soviet influence in the region—Kuwait had also asked Soviet tankers and escorts to ship its oil. But the moves were sharply debated in the United States, where many people feared being drawn into the Persian Gulf conflict.

Also in July, the United Nations Security Council passed a resolution calling for a cease-fire and talks to end the war. But after a brief respite, attacks on shipping resumed in August. And it wasn't long before the United States became more involved.

At first there was a series of small incidents. The United States captured an Iranian boat that was believed to be sowing mines, seized two Iranian military speedboats, and sank a third. Then, in October, the Iranians launched a missile attack on a U.S.-registered tanker in Kuwaiti waters. The United States responded with attacks on Iranian oil platforms that had been used to stage military operations in the gulf; Iran hit back by attacking a Kuwaiti offshore oil-loading facility. As violence and tension mounted in the gulf, the chances for peace seemed more and more remote.

VIOLENCE IN MECCA

The events in the Persian Gulf weren't the only violent incidents to involve Iran during the year. In July, at the high point of the annual Muslim pilgrimage known as the *hajj*, more than 400 people were killed when violence broke out between Iranian pilgrims and Saudi Arabian police in the holy city of Mecca.

Mecca, which is in western Saudi Arabia, is considered the birthplace of Islam. Each year thousands of Muslims from all over the world travel to the shrine there during the *hajj*. The 1987 clashes reflected deep reli-

More than 1.5 million Iranian and Iraqi soldiers have been killed or wounded in the long, bitter conflict. Here, *Chador*-clad Iranians are being trained to fight.

Thirty-seven American sailors were killed in May, when an Iraqi missile mistakenly hit a U.S. Navy frigate, the *Stark,* in the Persian Gulf.

gious and political divisions in the Muslim world. The Saudis, like the majority of Muslims, belong to the conservative Sunni sect. The Iranians belong to the more radical Shi'ite sect, which preaches revolution. In an effort to keep peace during the holy season, the Saudis had banned political demonstrations. But the Iranians demonstrated anyway, chanting slogans such as "Death to America!" and waving pictures of their leader, Ayatollah Ruhollah Khomeini.

Iran said that the Saudis had opened fire on a peaceful crowd, and they called for the immediate overthrow of the Saudi ruling family. But the Saudis said the demonstrators had rioted, burned cars, fought with other pilgrims, and attacked police with knives. They claimed that no shots were fired and that the deaths had been caused by trampling.

The incident was seen by many people as part of an Iranian policy to bring disruption to the Middle East. In this way, Shi'ite groups might gain power, just as Shi'ite clerics had seized control of Iran in a revolution in 1979. Iran was backing radical Muslim terrorist groups in several countries; both Egypt and France broke off relations with Iran in 1987 over the terrorism issue. But Iran's hand was seen at work most clearly in Lebanon.

LEBANON AND TERRORISM

Shi'ite Muslims have been just one of many groups involved in Lebanon's long civil war—Palestinian Arab refugees, Maronite Christians, Druses (another Muslim sect), and others have been involved. The war began as a fight between Christians, whose strongholds are mainly in East Beirut and the north, and Muslims. At various times, both Syria and Israel have sent troops into the country to control the situation.

Early in 1987, the latest attempt at a cease-fire between the warring factions broke down. Shi'ite fighters attacked Palestinians, besieging them in the refugee areas of West Beirut. The Shi'ites were in turn attacked by Druse militia forces, who were backed by Sunni groups. To stop the fighting Syria sent more than 7,000 troops into Beirut. The situation in Beirut calmed down, although terrorists killed Lebanese Premier Rashid Karami (a pro-Syrian Sunni Muslim) in June.

But fighting continued in southern Lebanon, where Shi'ite and Palestinian fighters were involved in clashes with Israel and Israeli-backed forces as well as with each other. The Shi'ites and the Palestinians agreed to a cease-fire in September. But fresh fighting then broke out in the north, between Syrian and Christian forces and between various Christian factions.

These events were played out against a backdrop of terrorism conducted by various shadowy groups, many of which were thought to be supported by Iran and Libya. One of their tactics was to kidnap foreigners and hold them as hostages. In November, 1987, two French hostages were released. But the terrorists were still holding 21 hostages, including eight Americans.

Some of the kidnappers remained silent, but others stepped forward and made demands for their captives' release. Officially, the United States, France, Britain, and most other countries whose citizens have been seized have refused to negotiate with terrorists, on the grounds that this would only encourage more kidnappings. Privately, this policy has been undercut several times when countries have made deals with terrorists. Perhaps the most serious of these incidents was a U.S. plan, revealed late in 1986, to win the release of hostages by sellings arms to Iran. The secret policy was unproductive: For every American released, another was kidnapped.

THE WEST BANK

Ever since Israel seized the West Bank from Jordan in 1967, this strip of occupied territory has been a trouble spot. Israel has sought to secure its hold by establishing settlements there, and this has led to clashes between Arabs and Jews. The West Bank has also been proposed as a site for a Palestinian homeland. But the Israelis and the Palestinians have refused to negotiate directly with each other on the issue.

In 1987, hope for a solution seemed as far away as ever. Jordan proposed an international conference that would involve both the United States and the Soviet Union. This plan, however, didn't win support from the other countries and groups involved, including Israel and the Palestine Liberation Organization (PLO), which is the main Palestinian group. And the West Bank continued to be troubled by clashes between Arabs and Israeli police.

Late in 1987, clashes also broke out in the Gaza Strip, which Israel had seized from Egypt in 1967. A number of demonstrators were killed as Palestinian youths battled Israeli police. In late December the unrest spread, and protests and strikes were staged by Arabs throughout Israel as well as in the occupied territories.

But there were some encouraging signs in the Middle East, too. In 1979, Egypt had signed a peace treaty with Israel, and most other Arab countries had promptly ended relations with Egypt. In 1987, Iraq, Saudi Arabia, and most other Arab countries restored diplomatic ties with Egypt, and they toned down their usually harsh statements about Israel. One reason was thought to be their desire to stand united against Iran.

Early in 1987, Syria sent troops into West Beirut to restore order among the rival factions. Organizing a clean-up operation, the Syrians ordered that all political posters and slogans be removed from city walls, including this one of Iranian leader Ayatollah Khomeini.

THE STOCK MARKET CRASH

On October 19, 1987, stock prices on the New York Stock Exchange took their biggest plunge since World War I. The Dow Jones industrial average—the major indicator of the health of the stock market—dropped a record 508 points, losing 22.6 percent of its value in a single day. More than 600 million shares of stock changed hands as frenzied sellers tried to unload their investments. And stock markets in London, Frankfurt, Tokyo, and other cities around the world quickly followed suit.

Black Monday, as the day quickly became known, recalled another dark day 58 years earlier: October 29, 1929, the day of the stock market crash that heralded the Great Depression of the 1930's. In fact, the market actually lost a greater percent of value in the 1987 crash than it had in 1929.

Investors lost millions of dollars—but they weren't the only ones to be concerned. There were fears that the effects of the crash would affect every aspect of the world's economy. As stock prices continued to fluctuate widely in the days after the crash, two important questions were being asked: What had caused these events? And was the world headed for another depression?

THE STOCK MARKET

A share of stock represents a share of ownership in a company. In theory, people who buy stock in a company will see their investment grow if the company makes money—and shrink if the company does poorly. In practice, many other factors affect the price of stock. A rosy economic forecast may send stock prices up. Threat of war or political turmoil can send them down. People who believe stock prices will go up—"bulls"—buy stocks hoping to sell them later at a profit. People who believe the prices will go down—"bears"—may stay out of the market or sell their shares.

In 1987, the stock market was at the peak of a five-year-long bull market. Stocks had soared to unheard-of levels. Then several factors combined to burst the bubble.

Some of these factors involved the market itself. For one, stock prices had risen so high that in many cases they had little relationship to the underlying worth of the companies they represented. They were overvalued. For another, many large investors—pension funds, institutions, and investment firms—traded in huge blocks. When a number of such firms decided to sell, millions of shares were dumped on the market at once, sending prices down. And as small investors saw prices drop dramatically, they panicked and sold their shares, too.

In fact, panic was a major factor in the crash. To many people, the massive selling seemed unwarranted: Even though many stocks were overvalued, U.S. business was healthy. Corporate profits were up. Unemployment was low. But panic alone didn't create the crash of '87. Despite the health of the economy, there were warning signs of trouble ahead. These warning signs pointed to two serious problems for the United States: its trade deficit and the federal budget deficit.

THE TRADE DEFICIT

Americans are in love with imports (foreign goods). And this has caused a problem: For the past few years, the United States has been buying more abroad than it sells. Consumer goods such as cars and television sets are just part of the problem; there are other factors, such as government spending. Together, they have helped create an enormous trade deficit, or gap between imports and exports. In 1987, that gap was expected to be more than $160 billion.

The trade deficit worries economists. When U.S. consumers buy U.S. products, the money they spend remains in the country. It pays salaries and keeps businesses running. But when U.S. consumers buy foreign goods, the money goes abroad and no longer helps the U.S. economy. And as the country as a whole continues to buy more than it produces, it must borrow from abroad to make up the difference.

The deficit is new—until the 1980's, the United States generally exported more than it imported. Then, in 1981–82, the world suffered a recession, or economic decline. The United States was one of the first countries to recover. That meant that people in the United States had more money to spend, and they went shopping. In many cases, they found that imported goods were a good buy.

Consumers weren't the only ones creating the deficit. In 1986 alone, the U.S. government purchased more than $9 billion of military equipment from foreign producers. Meanwhile, sales of U.S. goods abroad were sluggish. The economies of other countries weren't growing as fast as the U.S. economy, so U.S. exports didn't find ready markets. And U.S. manufacturers charged that some countries traded unfairly: They exported goods to the United States at little or no profit, to win customers. But they placed tariffs (entry charges) and other restrictions on U.S. exports, making the U.S. goods more expensive in their countries.

The United States debated various strategies to bring imports and exports into balance. One was to impose new trade restrictions and tariffs, especially against countries that traded unfairly or ran large trade surpluses. But this policy of protectionism, as it was called, had dangers. U.S. consumers would have fewer goods to choose from if imports were kept out. Prices might rise across the board, for domestic products as well as imports. And by closing off its markets to trade, the United States might hurt countries that depended on exports to survive and touch off a worldwide recession.

President Ronald Reagan promised to veto bills that imposed too strong restrictions.

Meanwhile, in 1987, the U.S. government temporarily placed high tariffs on certain Japanese products, in retaliation for what it saw as unfair trade practices. But it signed a new agreement with Canada, its largest trading partner, to reduce trade barriers.

Other proposals focused on making U.S. exports more competitive in world markets. Among these plans were government support for job training and technical research, to help U.S. industries be more efficient.

Another approach to the trade deficit had to do with currency exchange. In early 1985, the U.S. dollar was at a record high against the Japanese yen—it took about 260 yen to equal one dollar. The dollar was also high in relation to other currencies. This had the effect of making imports cheap in the United States—because the strong dollar could buy more. Then the U.S. government decided to let the dollar fall in value. (Exchange rates among the world's free countries aren't rigidly controlled. Instead, governments can use various methods to try to influence them.) By early 1987, it took only about 150 yen to equal one dollar.

The idea behind the dollar's fall was to make foreign goods more expensive in the United States, so that people would buy fewer of them. But this didn't happen im-mediately. Some foreign manufacturers simply cut their profits, so they could continue to keep their prices low. And even when import prices rose, many Americans seemed willing to pay a premium for the imported products they had grown to love. Although the volume of imports dropped, the dollar amount of the trade deficit continued to rise. This discouraging news was one of the factors that set off the stock market crash.

THE BUDGET DEFICIT

Adding to the worry over the trade deficit was the fact that the federal government was borrowing huge sums of money each year to cover its budget deficit, the gap between the amount it spent on various programs and the amount it took in from taxes and other revenues. The U.S. budget deficit had begun to grow in the recession of the early 1980's, as the government cut taxes and spent money in efforts to stimulate the economy. When the economy began to recover from the recession, the government was unwilling to trim the deficit by raising taxes or cutting spending, for fear that this would halt the recovery. By 1986, the federal budget deficit had topped $220 billion.

As it borrowed more and more to cover its yearly deficit, the United States became one

This cartoon takes a humorous look at one of the events surrounding the stock market crash of 1987. To help the U.S. balance of trade, the dollar was allowed to decline in value compared to the Japanese yen and other currencies. Both the trade deficit and the dollar's decline worried investors.

"I don't care how far the dollar declines... you're not getting your allowance in yen!"

of the world's largest debtors. And that posed serious dangers. Much of the borrowed money came from abroad. The borrowed money—and the interest on it—would have to be paid back. That would add to the trouble created by the trade deficit by taking still more funds out of the country.

The budget deficit also tended to drive interest rates on loans up. As its borrowing requirements grew, the United States competed with other borrowers—businesses and individuals—for the funds that were available. Coupled with this increased competition was the drop in the value of the dollar. As the dollar decreased in value, foreign investors might be less willing to buy dollar investments (such as U.S. Treasury bonds). Thus, in order to borrow enough money to cover its budget deficits, the United States would have to pay higher interest rates to attract foreign investors.

In fact, these factors did drive interest rates up in 1987. And that helped create fears of another recession: Consumers would spend less, and businesses wouldn't be able to expand, if they couldn't afford the high cost of loans.

Late in 1985, Congress had passed a law that set limits on the budget deficits. But the government didn't meet the 1986 target and seemed likely to miss 1987's goal, too. Congress and the Reagan administration argued over how to cut spending and whether taxes should be raised, with President Reagan continuing to insist that raising taxes would do more harm than good.

In August, 1987, many investors seemed to despair of the government's finding solutions to the budget and trade deficits. Stock prices began to retreat from their record highs. And in October, investor panic and other factors chipped in to turn this retreat into a rout.

THE EFFECTS OF THE CRASH

The greatest concern after the crash was that it would bring on a recession. During the long bull market, many people had made money in the stock market. Even those who hadn't were affected—the rising stock prices gave the impression of economic good times. Thus people had been willing to spend money, and this helped businesses expand and grow. And businesses were able to raise money for expansion by selling stock to investors.

When stock prices plunged, many people lost large amounts of money. And again, even those who didn't lose directly were affected—the news of the crash seemed to indicate that hard times were on the way. This, it was feared, would make consumers less willing to spend. And as companies saw the worth of their stock shrink, they might be less willing to expand. Thus the fear of recession, which had helped set off the stock market crash in the first place, might actually help create a recession.

In fact, there were enough parallels between 1929 and 1987 to make some people fear a second Great Depression. Both crashes came after astonishing stock-market booms. Both came at a time when debts were high and trade relations were strained, with protectionism growing.

But most analysts thought a depression could be averted in 1987 because, after the 1929 crash, certain safeguards had been built into the economic system. For example, a major factor in the Great Depression had been the failure of many banks—people had lost their savings. After that, the government regulated banks more closely and insured bank deposits. Brokerage accounts were also insured, and unemployment insurance and other social programs were in place to help people who lost their jobs.

In 1929, too, the U.S. government had raised interest rates after the crash, which helped push the country into the Depression. In 1987, one of the government's first moves was to lower interest rates. By making it easier to borrow money, it was hoped, low rates would help head off a recession.

The United States also allowed the dollar to slide in value still more, in a further effort to correct the trade imbalance. And Reagan and other administration officials met with congressional leaders to work out a solution to the budget problem. The United States also called on other countries to lower interest rates and stimulate their economies.

These moves were watched carefully around the world. Decisive government action and international cooperation, it was felt, would be the best way to restore confidence in the world economy and prevent a repeat of the Great Depression.

IS COMMUNISM CHANGING COURSE?

Nearly a third of the world's people live under Communism, which ranks among the most restrictive systems of government. Traditionally, governments in the Communist countries have sought to control all aspects of life, from the goods factories produce to the television programs people watch and the opinions they express. In 1987, however, change was evident in the world's two major Communist powers, the Soviet Union and China. Since relations between the Communist powers and the Western democracies are a critical factor in world peace, people everywhere watched these changes closely.

In the Soviet Union, the government seemed to be relaxing some of its controls. The relaxation could be seen mostly in the Soviet economic system, but it extended at times to politics and to human rights as well. Many smaller Communist countries take their cue from the Soviets, so some people wondered if the new Soviet attitude would lead to greater openness in Communist societies throughout the world.

That hope was shaded with caution, however. And people also watched events in China. There, the government has introduced many reforms since the late 1970's.

But in 1987, the Chinese seemed to be pulling back from those reforms and making some aspects of their society more restrictive.

CHANGE IN THE SOVIET UNION

Since the 1930's, the Soviet economic system has depended on the idea of central planning. In this system, the state owns all the factories and other means of production. Planners in the government decide the type and quantity of goods that are produced and also set prices for them. Workers are assigned jobs at fixed wages. Thus free enterprise—the idea of going into business for oneself—has been just about unknown.

Over the years, the system hasn't worked very well. The planners tended to concentrate on heavy industry and military equipment. Consumer goods were often produced in quantities that were too small to meet demand. And even when the planners called for consumer items, factories often turned out shoddy goods or didn't produce the amounts called for—since workers were guaranteed jobs at fixed wages, they had no incentive to produce more or better goods.

Wage levels were low, so that a pair of shoes might cost the average Soviet worker

Soviet leader Mikhail Gorbachev explains his policy of *glasnost* ("openness") to residents of a collective farm in Estonia. Dramatic reforms being made under this policy are affecting the Soviet system of government, the economy, and human rights.

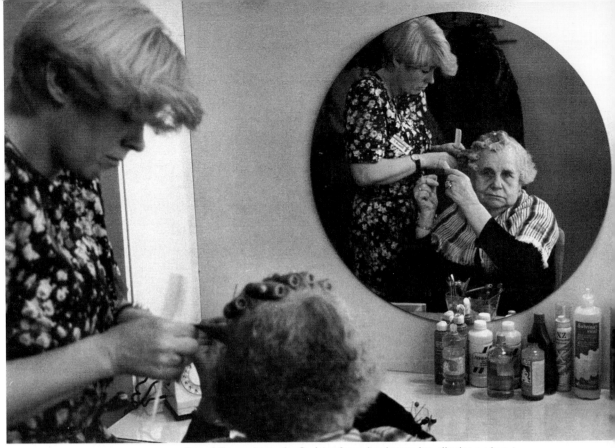

One of the most popular Soviet reforms has been a law allowing workers to operate small businesses—such as hairdressing salons—outside their regular jobs.

nearly a week's salary. The government subsidized prices for certain goods, particularly basic foodstuffs. But the results of the price subsidies often made no sense. It was cheaper for a Soviet farmer to feed bread to pigs, for example, than to feed the pigs the grain that bread was made from.

As it struggled with these problems, the Soviet Union gradually slipped further and further behind the West in its economic growth and standard of living. But in 1985 a new leader, Mikhail S. Gorbachev, came to power in the Soviet Union. He began to call for changes in the system.

In 1987, Gorbachev called for the most radical changes yet: higher rates of pay and other incentives for workers who produced more and better goods, less central planning, a complete restructuring of the price system. One of the most popular reforms was a law that allowed Soviet citizens to open small businesses—as hairdressers, taxi drivers, or whatever—while moonlighting from their regular jobs.

There were potential risks as well as benefits to these reforms. With less government planning, factories and businesses would be left to compete for sales. Those that couldn't compete might fail, and workers might lose their jobs. These were problems that the Soviets had long boasted troubled only Western countries. But, Gorbachev announced, "We cannot put up with the lag in community and consumer services."

Meanwhile, reform seemed to be spreading into other areas of Soviet life. The Soviet Union has only one political party, the Communist Party. No one suggested that that should change. But Gorbachev proposed new policies—secret balloting and a choice of candidates in elections for Party officials. In an experiment in June, 1987, Soviet voters were for the first time offered a choice of candidates for local office.

Gorbachev also called for more open debate on public issues. This was a breakthrough in a country where criticizing the government had meant risking a prison term.

Will China's Great Wall become a Great Mall? This cartoon spoofs China's recent economic reforms, which include more free enterprise and increased trade with the West.

Now even the government-controlled press began to openly criticize inefficiency in government—although the criticism didn't extend to high-ranking officials.

There were also gains in human rights. Andrei Sakharov, a Soviet scientist who had been exiled to a remote city for criticizing the government, was allowed to return to his home in Moscow. Many other dissidents were released from jails and labor camps. And the government began to allow more people, including many Jews, to emigrate.

The Soviets used the word *glasnost,* or "openness," to refer to this new official attitude. As *glasnost* spread, books, films, and works of art that had once been banned were allowed to appear. These included novels such as *Dr. Zhivago,* by Russian author Boris Pasternak, which had been published in the West to great critical acclaim. And for the first time in seven years, the Soviets stopped jamming, or blocking the signal of, the U.S. radio station Voice of America.

People in the West welcomed these changes—but they did so cautiously. It was unclear how sincere or far-reaching the reforms truly were. While many dissidents were released, no one knew how many remained behind bars. In the fall, a leading advocate of free debate was dismissed as a leader of the Moscow city Communist Party. And the government cracked down on some unofficial political groups.

One thing was clear: The Communist Party remained firmly in control of Soviet life. And many of the reforms faced great resistance from Party officials who were secure in their positions and opposed change. If this group were to gain power, the reforms might vanish overnight.

CHANGE IN CHINA

Just such a struggle between Party officials seemed to be behind changes in China during the year. Deng Xiaoping, the country's 82-year-old leader, had introduced many economic reforms, including greater free enterprise and increased trade with the West. He had also allowed greater freedom of expression than the country had known under its first Communist leader, Mao Zedong. It was widely expected that Deng would soon retire and be succeeded by Hu Yaobang, the general secretary of the

Chinese Communist Party, who was also a reformer. But in January, 1987, Hu was forced to resign.

Observers in the West weren't sure what led to Hu's resignation. But it followed a six-week period of increasing protests by students, who demanded more Western-style freedoms. And it came together with official attacks on democratic ideas. Free speech was curbed, and a number of officials and important figures—including a leading newspaper editor who had exposed government corruption—were denounced and expelled from the Party. It seemed that Party officials had decided that reform had gone too far, and that it was time to tighten up.

Once before, in the 1950's, China's Communist leaders had allowed a period of freedom of expression. That period was followed by the Cultural Revolution, one of the most repressive times in the country's history. But in 1987, Chinese leaders said that no such drastic crackdown was planned—the economic reforms of recent years would be retained, even if the government became stricter about politics. In fact, Hu was temporarily replaced by Zhao Ziyang, who had been behind many of the economic changes.

As the year wore on, it seemed that a power struggle was underway between reformers and conservatives within the Party. Conflicting statements, for and against reform, appeared at various times in the official press. And other events made the future of the country seem unclear. In late September and early October, Tibet, a region that had been taken over by China in 1950, was wracked by violence. Tibetans who demonstrated against Chinese control were harshly suppressed.

But in November, Zhao was confirmed as general secretary of the Communist Party. At the same time, Deng stepped down from the Party's ruling committee (although it was expected that he would still influence government policies). Many other older officials, including some who had opposed change, also stepped down. And new reforms, including a plan to let Chinese farmers own rights to land, were proposed.

Although the outlook was still uncertain, the changes that had come to both China and the Soviet Union were encouraging. Smaller Communist countries, too, were reforming their economic systems and permitting greater political freedom. Thus there was hope that the trend toward greater openness would continue.

China's reforms, however, didn't extend to Tibet. There, the worst unrest in decades occurred in 1987, as Tibetans protested Chinese control of their region.

AROUND THE WORLD

A new plan for peace in Central America and a desert war between Chad and Libya were among the events that made headlines in 1987. The following is a roundup of these and other developments around the world.

CENTRAL AMERICA

Since the late 1970's, Central America has been among the world's most troubled regions. Conflict has been sharpest in two countries, El Salvador and Nicaragua.

In Nicaragua, leftists took power in 1979, following a civil war. Their government became increasingly restrictive—censoring the press, limiting political opposition—and allied itself more and more with the Soviet bloc. This brought opposition from many Nicaraguans and from the United States, which

In 1987, Nicaragua agreed to negotiate indirectly with the contra rebels, shown here along the Honduran border.

began to support rebel fighters called the contras. Military aid to the contras has been controversial in the United States, where many people fear being drawn into the conflict. From late 1984 to mid 1986, Congress barred such aid. And a scandal erupted in the United States when it was learned that the Reagan administration had provided the aid anyway, using profits from secret arms sales to Iran.

In El Salvador, a moderate government was elected in 1984 and is supported by the United States. However, leftist guerrillas have been fighting the government, while right-wing "death squads" have been accused of kidnapping and killing their opponents. The government managed to control the right-wing extremists to a degree, but the civil war continued. Many people believed that Nicaragua was supporting and supplying the Salvadoran leftist rebels.

Besides these conflicts, there were smaller rebellions in Guatemala and Honduras. And over the years, various plans have been proposed to end the Central American fighting, largely without success. But in August, 1987, hopes for peace were buoyed when five countries—El Salvador, Guatemala, Honduras, Nicaragua, and Costa Rica—signed a peace agreement. The peace plan had been developed by Costa Rican President Oscar Arias Sánchez, who won the 1987 Nobel Peace Prize for his efforts.

The agreement, which took effect in early November, called on the groups involved in the fighting to negotiate cease-fires as the first step in ending their wars. The various governments were also to grant amnesty to political prisoners, take steps to increase political freedom and democracy, and encourage the return of refugees and political exiles who had fled the fighting. And the governments were required to cut off aid to outside rebel groups and to forbid these groups to use their territory in fights with neighboring countries.

Not everyone was happy with the plan. President Ronald Reagan objected to it because, he said, it included no way of enforcing the provisions and didn't safeguard democracy and U.S. interests. Nicaragua at first refused to negotiate with the contras, saying that the United States, which wasn't part of the accord, should speak for them. But slowly, the countries began to take steps toward peace. When Salvadoran rebels broke off talks with the government in late October, the government said it would observe a cease-fire anyway. It also announced amnesty for political prisoners and refugees, and it loosened political controls. And in early November, Nicaragua finally agreed to negotiate indirectly with the contras, through mediators.

Violence continued, however, and Nicaragua and Honduras especially seemed to be dragging their feet as they moved to put the peace plan into effect. And underlying the conflicts in Central America were problems of poverty and land ownership that remained unsolved. The region's leaders agreed to meet again early in 1988 to evaluate their progress.

HAITI

In Haiti, the first presidential elections in 30 years, scheduled for November, were abruptly canceled when bands of armed attackers massacred voters on their way to the polls.

From 1957 to 1986, Haiti had been ruled by dictators: François (Papa Doc) Duvalier and, later, Jean-Claude Duvalier, his son. The Duvaliers held power through terror and used their secret police, the Tontons Macoute, to eliminate their opponents. But in 1986, after a series of riots and demonstrations, Jean-Claude Duvalier fled the country. A military junta took over and promised elections in 1987.

In March, 1987, Haitian voters approved a new constitution. Then the presidential campaign began. From the start, it was marked by violence—one candidate was even shot dead. Under the new constitution, former Duvalier aides were barred from running, and they were thought to be behind the violence. The Haitian government, meanwhile, did little to halt it.

On election day, November 29, armed bands attacked Haitians as they went to vote, killing at least two dozen and wounding many more. Observers said that government troops stood by during the attacks and sometimes even took part. The government halted

A MAN OF PEACE

Costa Rican President Oscar Arias Sánchez emerged as a peacemaker in troubled Central America in 1987. His efforts were behind an accord designed to end the civil wars in Nicaragua and El Salvador and bring greater liberty throughout the region. And as a result, he won the 1987 Nobel Peace Prize.

Arias, 46, studied law and economics in college and began his government career as an economic adviser. He won a seat in the Costa Rican Congress in 1978, and a year later he became leader of the National Liberation Party. As his party's candidate in the presidential election of 1986, he was considered a long shot, but he won on a platform that stressed the danger of war in Central America and called for international efforts for peace.

That issue was especially important in Costa Rica, the most democratic of the Central American countries. Costa Rica has no army and has tried to steer a neutral course in the region's various conflicts. But its location south of Nicaragua had made it a staging ground for Nicaraguan rebels.

One of Arias' first acts as president was to bar rebels from using Costa Rica for their operations. He then set to work on the peace plan, winning the agreement of the leaders of Nicaragua, El Salvador, Honduras, and Guatemala in long, tough negotiations. Although the United States had reservations about the accord that emerged, it won the enthusiastic support of Central Americans and many people elsewhere.

With cunning strategy, Chadian military forces staged a series of attacks and managed to push Libyan troops from nearly all of Chad. The victories also helped to unite Chad's ethnic and political groups.

the voting, and it promised that new elections would be held. But the United States, which had pressed for democracy in Haiti, canceled military and some economic aid to the country because of the government's failure to keep order.

CHAD AND LIBYA

From 1983 until late in 1986, Chad was virtually split in two. The government controlled the southern half of this North African desert country, which is among the world's poorest. Rebels controlled the north, with the help of Libyan forces. Then the picture changed: The rebels split with the Libyans and decided to side with the government. And in a series of attacks in 1987, Chadian forces managed to push the Libyans from nearly all of Chad.

France (Chad's former colonial ruler) provided support in the form of supplies and air strikes against Libyan positions. But credit for the victories went to the cunning strategies of the Chadian military. The Chadians staged carefully planned lightning attacks, streaking across the desert in jeeps and light

trucks to knock out heavy Libyan tanks and armored personnel carriers before they could react. Their weapons were no match for the Libyans', but speed and surprise gave them the advantage. In January, Chad took back the desert town of Fada; in March, Wadi Doum (where the Libyans had built an air base). Along the way, they captured or killed a third of Libya's forces in Chad and seized millions of dollars worth of military equipment.

The Libyans were pushed into the Aozou strip, a band of territory along the Libya-Chad border that is rich in uranium and other minerals. Libya claims this territory, but most of the world recognizes it as part of Chad. Early in August, Chad captured the town of Aozou, the main settlement in the strip. The Libyans retook it later the same month. Chad retaliated by capturing and demolishing an air base in Libya that had been used to stage attacks on Chadian forces. At the urging of the Organization of African Unity, the two sides accepted a cease-fire on September 11 and agreed to let the OAU mediate in their territorial dispute.

Besides regaining territory, Chad won another benefit in its war with Libya: The victories helped unite the country's ethnic and political groups, which have been quarreling almost since Chad gained independence from France in 1960. Chadian President Hissen Habré added to the unity by bringing former rebel leaders into his government, rather than punishing them.

SRI LANKA

During 1987, ethnic violence flared in Sri Lanka, an island country off the coast of India that was formerly known as Ceylon. Two groups were involved: the Sinhalese, who form the majority and control the government, and the Tamils, who are the largest minority group and live mostly in the north. The groups speak different languages and follow different religions (the Sinhalese are Buddhists, and the Tamils are Hindus). Since Sri Lanka won independence from Britain in 1948, disputes have broken out repeatedly between them. In the 1980's, the disputes became more intense, with some rebel Tamil groups demanding independence and clashing with government troops.

Early in 1987, the Tamils rejected a proposal that would have given them greater self-government in the north. In response, government forces closed in on rebel strongholds and made some gains. Then the worst violence erupted: On April 17, Tamil guerrillas ambushed a bus and other vehicles along a jungle road and killed 127 Sinhalese civilians. A few days later, a bomb believed to have been placed by Tamils exploded at a bus station in Colombo, the capital, during rush hour. At least 110 people died.

The government responded with bombing raids and, in May and June, major offensives on rebel bases. India, where many Tamils also live, sent food and medical supplies to those living in the north as the government forces closed in, and the two sides fought to a stand-off. Then Sri Lanka asked India to help negotiate a truce with the Tamils. An agreement was reached in July.

Under the truce, the Tamils were to abandon their fight for independence and surrender their weapons. In return, the Tamils would have more self-government. The Sri Lankan government asked Indian troops to be sent in to enforce the truce.

But some Tamils refused to turn in their weapons. And some Sinhalese objected to the agreement and rioted; there was even an assassination attempt against President Junius Jayewardene. Thus the Indian force was increased from 3,000 to almost 30,000 troops, and they found themselves in action in both the north and the south. In October, as the level of violence increased, they fought a major offensive in the north, gaining control of the city of Jaffna. But many Tamil rebels escaped. And violence continued in the south, where on November 9 a bomb exploded in Colombo and killed at least 32 people.

FIJI

To many people, Fiji has long seemed like a quiet tropical paradise. But in 1987, ethnic

Violence in Sri Lanka between the Sinhalese and the Tamils left the country in turmoil. Here, a soldier pours out a helmet full of grain for a Tamil villager.

violence and two military takeovers troubled this Pacific Island nation.

At the heart of the trouble was friction between two ethnic groups: Fijians and Indians, who first came to the island in the late 1800's and are now mainly prosperous merchants. The Indians outnumbered the Fijians by a small margin. And in 1987, a predominantly Indian government was voted in in parliamentary elections. (Since gaining independence from Britain in 1970, Fiji had been ruled by a democratic parliamentary government. It retained a governor-general, who represented Britain but whose position was largely ceremonial.)

Fijians demonstrated to show their opposition to the new government. And on May 14, the military staged a coup and imprisoned the new government leaders. The coup's leader, Lieutenant Colonel Sitiveni Rabuka, released them a week later after a power-sharing arrangement was worked out with the governor-general. A temporary ruling council was set up.

But in September, just before a new, bipartisan government was to be formed, Rabuka seized power again. He abolished the constitution and said that a new one would be drawn up to ensure that Fijians held power. The British governor-general resigned, and Britain gave up its last claim to sovereignty in Fiji. In December, Rabuka appointed the former governor-general (Ratu Sir Penaia Ganilau) the first president of the new republic of Fiji.

THE PHILIPPINES

In 1986, Corazon Aquino became president of the Philippines after Ferdinand Marcos, who had ruled for twenty years, was forced by public pressure to resign. It was hoped that this turn of events would lead to greater freedom and democracy. But in 1987, Aquino found herself beset by troubles on all sides. The year's developments were watched anxiously in the United States, which once controlled the Philippines and still has close ties and important military bases there.

The troubles began in January, when a group of soldiers attempted to take control. They were foiled by loyal soldiers, but there were rumors that more coup attempts were planned. The figures behind these plans were said to be Marcos, who was living in exile in Hawaii, and Juan Ponce Enrile, a former defense minister who had supported Aquino at first but had broken with her late in 1986.

Fijians read about the conflict in their country as they wait for the results of a meeting between the military and government leaders. The tropical island in the Pacific experienced ethnic violence and military takeovers during the year.

Philippines President Corazon Aquino, who had ended the long, repressive rule of Ferdinand Marcos, was herself beset by major problems in 1987. By the end of the year, the continuing unrest raised questions about the future of her leadership.

Some of the military had been unhappy with Aquino's handling of an eighteen-year-old Communist rebellion. The new president had declared a cease-fire with these rebels late in 1986 and had opened talks with them. But the talks made no progress. And, not long after the military rebellion was put down, the Communists broke off the discussions and ended the cease-fire. Acknowledging that peace efforts had failed, Aquino ordered the army to fight them.

In February, Filipinos showed wide support for Aquino in a vote to adopt a new constitution. She also won support in congressional elections in May. Meanwhile, she worked on plans to redistribute land, since most of the country's good farmland was held by a few wealthy families. But these families resisted changes, while many of Aquino's opponents said her efforts didn't go far enough.

In August, labor unions and leftists staged a one-day strike to protest price increases.

And in the same week, right-wing dissident soldiers rebelled again, seizing a television station and key points in Manila, the capital. Again, the rebellion was put down, and Aquino weathered the storm. In response to some of her critics, she re-arranged her cabinet and dropped one of her less popular advisers. But the continuing unrest raised questions about the future of her leadership. Vice-President Salvador Laurel, who was also foreign secretary, resigned his cabinet post in a split with the president. (He remained vice-president.)

The Communist rebels stepped up their attacks in the fall. And in November, three American servicemen stationed in the Philippines were killed. Communist rebels took responsibility for the killings, and they warned Americans that they were targets for attack. Aquino's troubles seemed to be only just beginning.

ELAINE PASCOE
Author, *South Africa: Troubled Land*

NEWSMAKERS

When **Robert H. Bork** was nominated to fill an empty seat on the U.S. Supreme Court in July, 1987, he immediately became a focus of controversy. Bork had a strong record as a scholar (he had taught at Yale) and a jurist (he was a judge on the U.S. Court of Appeals in Washington, D.C.). But his outspoken criticism of past Supreme Court decisions promoting privacy and civil rights caused concern. Although Bork had the support of the Reagan Administration, the Senate voted 58 to 42 not to confirm him—the largest margin by which the Senate had ever rejected a Supreme Court nominee.

From 1981 to 1987, **Terry Waite**, a British church worker, made four trips to the Middle East as the special envoy of the Anglican Church. His goal was to negotiate with the terrorists for the release of hostages, and he had often succeeded. But in January, 1987, on his fifth mission, Waite himself disappeared in Lebanon, and it was believed that he, too, had been taken hostage by terrorists. By year's end, there was still no official word about him. (Below, Waite is seen with bodyguards and reporters on his 1987 trip.)

Hulda Crooks, 91 years old, reached a peak in 1987—the peak of Mt. Fuji, Japan's highest and most famous mountain. She thus became the oldest woman to reach the top (a 99-year-old man had climbed the peak in 1986). Crooks, from Loma Linda, California, has been a climber for about 50 years. She said she made this climb to make a point: that people can remain active and vigorous in old age.

The case of **Bernard Goetz**, which touched off a national debate on self-defense, continued in 1987. In 1984, Goetz had shot four young men on a New York City subway train. He said he had acted because the youths were about to rob him and that he had a right to defend himself, even though he had no permit for his gun. The youths said that they had been panhandling. In June, 1987, after a seven-week trial, a jury acquitted Goetz of attempted murder and other charges relating to the shooting. But he was convicted of illegally possessing a concealed pistol, and he was sentenced to six months in prison.

A tiny child known as **Baby M** was the center of a major controversy in 1987. Two New Jersey couples, **William and Elizabeth Stern** (*right*) and **Richard and Mary Beth Whitehead** (*left*), sought custody of the child in a case that was the first court test of the concept of surrogate motherhood. The story began in 1985. The Sterns wanted a child, but because Elizabeth Stern had multiple sclerosis, they decided that pregnancy would be too risky. Mary Beth Whitehead agreed to act as a surrogate mother: She would bear William Stern's child in exchange for $10,000, and she signed a contract to that effect. But after the baby was born in March, 1986, she changed her mind, refused the money, and fled to Florida with the baby. The Sterns obtained a court order for the return of the child, whom they had named Melissa, and the case went to court early in 1987. Whitehead argued that she should have custody of the baby, whom she called Sara, because she was her natural mother. The Sterns said that they had an equal right to the child because William Stern was the father. The judge ruled in their favor, finding that the contract Whitehead had signed was binding and that the Sterns could provide a better home. Nationwide, more than 500 babies have been born through similar surrogate arrangements, and the ruling was expected to have an effect on disputes that might arise in the future.

In May, 1987, **Mathias Rust**, a 19-year-old West German pilot, took off from Helsinki, Finland, crossed 500 miles (805 kilometers) of Soviet territory, and landed his single-engine plane in front of the Kremlin in Moscow. Rust's ability to make the flight without being challenged or stopped embarrassed the Soviet armed forces and led to the abrupt dismissal of several top officials. The pilot said he had flown to Moscow as a peace gesture and had hoped to meet Soviet leader Mikhail Gorbachev. His adventure was widely reported in the West, where most people saw it as a harmless stunt. But the Soviets were not amused. They sentenced Rust to four years in a labor colony for unlawful entry into the Soviet Union, violation of Soviet air space, and "malicious hooliganism."

ANIMALS

The toucan's fabulous beak is actually a useful tool: These tropical birds use their beaks to pick and slice fruit. Rival toucans even duel with their beaks, like practiced swordsmen. And the toucan's beak is just one of the many re-markable animal noses that are designed to perform dozens of different jobs.

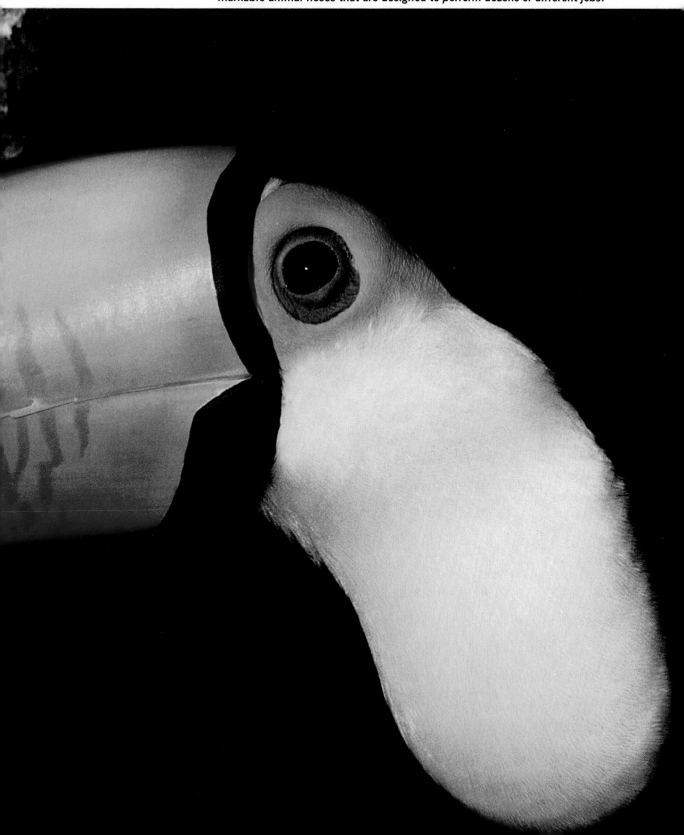

PARROTS: PERSONALITY PLUS

Parrots are the clowns of the bird world, a three-ring circus all in themselves. In the wild, they fly through the air in noisy flocks and clamber about like acrobats in the trees. In captivity, they are prized for their beauty and cleverness—including, sometimes, the ability to mimic human speech.

The parrots that are most familiar are the brightly colored birds often seen in pet stores. They range from common parakeets to exotic macaws and cockatoos. But these birds are just a few of the hundreds of different kinds of parrots that live in the wild. Many are rare, and some are in danger of dying out. Their popularity with people has increased their problems, since they are often captured and sold as pets.

PARROTS IN THE WILD

Parrots are found in warm regions all over the world, but they are most common in Central and South America, South Asia, the South Pacific, and Australia and New Zealand. Europe is the only continent with no native parrots, although fossil records show that parrots once lived there. One American type, the Carolina parakeet, once ranged as far north as Virginia and Ohio. But this bird is now extinct.

Parrots vary greatly in size—some are smaller than sparrows and some are as much as 3 feet (1 meter) long. Many are strikingly colored, although a few are dull green or even black. But all parrots share certain traits, the most distinctive of which is a powerful, sharply hooked beak. Some parrots can easily crack nuts with their beaks. And

This page: left—masked lovebirds; right—scarlet macaw. Opposite page: top left—African gray parrot; top right—rainbow lorikeets; bottom—pink cockatoo.

nearly all use their beaks as an aid in climbing, pulling themselves up tree trunks with this "third foot."

Parrots also have unusual feet. Most birds have three toes pointing forward and one toe pointing back, but parrots have two toes pointing in each direction. Their feet act like pincers, which also helps them climb. And unlike other birds, some parrots can use their feet like hands to hold food. But the odd toe configuration makes them wobble comically when they walk on the ground.

Some people believe that parrots are among the most intelligent birds. They are also highly sociable, gathering in pairs and flocks to roost and feed each day. They're noisy when they gather—their raucous calls fill the air and can be heard miles away.

While the flock is feeding, one parrot will often serve as a lookout, alerting the others with a scream if a predator approaches. Most parrots are vegetarians, eating fruits, nuts, seeds, flowers, grasses, and other plants. Many also eat insects. Parrots have fleshy tongues and appear to have a good sense of taste; they often test food before eating it.

Most parrots prefer to build their nests in cavities, such as a hole in a tree trunk. A few use burrows in the ground, and some Austra-

Despite differences in their looks, all parrots share certain traits. They are, for instance, highly sociable birds. And they have unusual feet. Most birds have three toes pointing forward and one pointing back. But parrots have two toes pointing in each direction.

lian types dig nesting holes in termite mounds. Many kinds of parrots mate for life. They may breed once or twice a year, and both parents help care for the newly hatched chicks.

KINDS OF PARROTS

There are more than 300 different species (types) of parrots, and all belong to the family *Psittacidae*. Scientists have divided them into eight groups, or subfamilies:

• The **owl parrot** is in a group by itself. This bird is extremely rare—in fact, it's close to extinction. The owl parrot is unique

in two ways: It's nocturnal (active at night), and it can't fly. Owl parrots are native to New Zealand. As the name suggests, their bristlelike feathers around the beak make them look more like owls than parrots.

• Another rare species, the **vulturine parrot**, takes after a different bird. With a ruff of feathers around its neck, this crow-sized parrot looks like a vulture.

• Like the owl parrot, the **kea** and its close relative the **kaka** live in New Zealand. These are large, aggressive birds with sharp beaks. The kea is unusual among parrots because it occasionally attacks sheep. But its usual diet is composed of insects and roots.

• The **lories** and **lorikeets** of Australia and the South Pacific include nearly 60 different species. They are small birds with brilliantly colored plumage, and they are among the most beautiful of all the parrots. They have relatively slender bills and use their tongues, which are rough and furry, to feed on the nectar of flowers.

• **Hanging parrots** are small birds with an unusual habit: They sleep hanging head down, like bats, from the branches of trees. (Although sleeping upside down is rare, some other parrot species like to hang head down to bathe.) Hanging parrots are native to Southeast Asia, and there are some ten species.

• The **pygmy parrots** of New Guinea live up to their name—some are no bigger than a man's thumb. The half dozen species have short, stiff tails that they use to brace themselves as they inch up and down tree trunks.

• **Cockatoos** are big birds, with large heads topped by crests of feathers. These birds can expand their crests like fans, for a spectacular display. There are sixteen different species, some white with pink or yellow crests and a few completely black. Found in Australia, New Guinea, and elsewhere in South Asia, cockatoos sometimes gather in flocks of thousands and can cause considerable damage to crops.

• **True parrots** are the largest group, with some two hundred different species found around the world. The most familiar are probably the **Amazon parrots**, square-tailed green birds that are often marked with yellow, red, or blue. True parrots also include the flashy **macaws**, long-tailed birds in hues that range from scarlet to brilliant greens, yellows, and blues. Macaws, which are found in Central and South America, are the largest parrots. And the great blue hyacinth macaw of Brazil is the largest macaw.

Parakeets are also part of the true parrot group. The most familiar parakeets belong to two Australian groups, the ground parakeets and the grass parakeets. Ground parakeets never roost in trees; they even build their nests on the ground. One of the grass parakeets, the **budgerigar**, is the familiar parakeet seen in pet stores.

Lovebirds, native to Africa, are still another kind of true parrot. These small birds earned their name from their habit of mating for life and spending much of their time cuddling up to each other. But it's likely that the birds are just preening each other, not showing true affection.

PARROTS AND PEOPLE

People have been fascinated by parrots for thousands of years, and these birds were among the earliest domesticated animals. They were brought from Asia to Europe in the time of Alexander the Great. The ancient Romans kept parrots as pets, although parrots also showed up as entrées at Roman banquets. Tame parrots were kept by Indians in South and Central America, too.

The birds' cleverness and bright colors account for some of their popularity with people. But what fascinates people most about parrots is probably their ability to mimic human speech. The African gray parrot is famous for its ability to ''talk.'' Many other types, including Amazon parrots and even parakeets, have also been taught to repeat words and phrases. But it's highly unlikely that parrots have any understanding of what they say—to them, the words are just sounds. Teaching a parrot to speak requires great patience because the words must be repeated over and over again.

Parakeets and lovebirds make fine pets, but larger parrots can be difficult ones. While many are docile, they can be noisy, unpredictable, and sometimes destructive. They can't be kept in small cages—they need room to stretch their wings. Like many other birds, parrots also carry psittacosis, a disease that can be transmitted to humans, and other diseases that can spread to poultry. For that reason, every bird imported to the United States and Canada must be inspected and held in quarantine.

Despite these difficulties, large parrots remain popular as pets. And that popularity has created other problems. Many species are becoming rare in their natural habitats. This is partly because many are captured and sold as pets, but even more because the tropical forests where they live are being destroyed as civilization advances.

Some types of parrots are bred for sale as pets. But other types are rare, and they sell for thousands of dollars in pet stores. A hyacinth macaw or a palm cockatoo, for example, can cost as much as $6,000. It may not be possible to obtain a rare parrot at all, since many countries limit or forbid the capture and export of these birds.

Still, the demand for parrots is so great that some people smuggle captured birds. The smuggled birds are often mistreated, and many die. Others may be carrying disease. For these reasons, wildlife experts say that people shouldn't buy rare parrots or keep them as pets. These clever, colorful birds should be allowed to live free in the wild.

Parrots can easily crack nuts with their powerful hooked beaks. And some use their feet like hands to hold food.

ANIMALS IN THE NEWS

In February, 1987, a German shepherd won top honors at the prestigious Westminster Kennel Club dog show for the first time ever. The winning dog was Champion Covy Tucker Hill's Manhattan, or Hatter for short. A popular breed, the German shepherd was developed from old breeds of herding and farm dogs in Germany. Today these dogs often serve as guard dogs, guide dogs for the blind, and family pets.

For the past few years, scientists at zoos in San Diego and Los Angeles have been capturing California condors and trying to breed them in captivity in order to prevent the giant vulture species from dying out. In April, 1987, the last California condor known to be living in the wild was captured. A male, he joined 26 other condors at the two zoos—the last members of this ancient species.

1987 was the Year of the Panda! In late April two giant pandas, Ling-Ling and Yong-Yong (*above, munching on an apple*), were flown from China to New York City for a six-month visit at the Bronx Zoo. From there, they made a temporary home at Busch Gardens, in Florida. In September two other pandas, Yuan-Yuan and Basi, visited the San Diego Zoo, in California. Fewer than 700 of these rare animals remain in the wild. And their numbers are declining as people move into their habitats and as their main food, bamboo, grows scarcer. One wildlife group declared a "panda emergency" and called for increased efforts to save the giant pandas. Meanwhile, hopes that more giant pandas would be bred in captivity were dashed in June, when a panda born at the National Zoo in Washington, D.C., died at the age of four days. (The parents, Hsing-Hsing and Ling-Ling, were given to the zoo by China in 1972.) Pandas have been bred successfully at zoos in China, Mexico, Japan, and Spain, but never in the United States.

The dusky seaside sparrow became extinct in 1987 when Orange Band, a male and the last of these tiny birds, died in June. Dusky sparrows lived only along a short stretch of Florida's eastern coast, and they became increasingly rare as people moved into the area. The last female died in 1980. Orange Band was one of several dusky sparrows that had been captured and mated with birds of a nearly identical species, Scott's seaside sparrow. The hybrid offspring are about $\frac{7}{8}$ dusky.

Three young pilot whales got a new lease on life thanks to some help from humans. The whales were among 60 of their species that beached themselves on Cape Cod, in Massachusetts, late in 1986. (Scientists aren't sure why the whales, which travel in herds, occasionally do this.) Most of the whales died, but three were taken to the New England Aquarium in Boston and nursed back to health. Then, in June, 1987, they were released into the Atlantic ocean—the first time that whales have been rescued, rehabilitated, and returned to the sea. (Below, one whale is loaded aboard a ship for its trip to freedom.) Each carried a radio transmitter, so that scientists could track their travels.

Animal lovers in Hambleden, England, scored a first in 1987: the world's first toad tunnel. The tunnel was built under a busy highway that thousands of toads cross during their mating season in early spring. Before it was built, many toads were killed each year by cars and trucks—even though volunteers carried others across by the bucketful. The tunnel's first season was a success. Toads poured through it at the rate of up to 530 a night. Now more tunnels are being considered for sites in Britain and other countries, to provide safe routes for toads, salamanders, and other small creatures.

Move over, dog—in 1987, the cat became the most popular pet in the United States for the first time. A market research study found that there were almost 5 million more cats than dogs in the country. Why are people turning to cats? Some researchers pointed to changes in the way people live. People are staying single longer, and in many families both spouses work. That means that they have less time to care for a pet. Cats require less exercise and attention than dogs, and unlike dogs they don't mind being left alone for long periods of time.

DINOSAUR DAYS

For 165 million years, dinosaurs ruled the Earth. The ground trembled under the tread of these giant beasts. Then, 65 million years ago, they died out, leaving only fossilized remains as clues to their existence. But that hasn't kept dinosaurs from being a hot topic.

People have long been fascinated by these huge creatures and the riddles they pose. What sort of animals were they? How did they behave when they roamed the Earth? What, exactly, did they look like? And above all, what caused them to die out?

In recent years, paleontologists (scientists who study the fossils of Earth's early creatures) have made startling new discoveries. Their finds have given rise to new theories about dinosaurs and new answers to the questions about them.

WARM-BLOODED, WARM-HEARTED?

The first scientists to piece together the fossilized bones of dinosaurs found that the creatures looked like giant lizards. (In fact, the name "dinosaur" comes from Greek words meaning "terrible lizard.") Thus they assumed that, like present-day lizards and other reptiles, dinosaurs were cold-blooded. The body temperatures of cold-blooded animals fluctuate with the temperature of the air. Warm-blooded animals such as birds and mammals maintain a constant body temperature regardless of the outside air.

Because cold-blooded animals are generally slow-moving, scientists assumed that dinosaurs were sluggish and clumsy. That assumption led to some theories about why they vanished: Perhaps the slow-moving dinosaurs simply couldn't compete with faster-moving mammals and so died out. Or perhaps the Earth's temperature changed and became too cold for them.

Now new studies of dinosaur fossils—including fossilized tracks—show that many dinosaurs weren't slow-moving at all. Many

Based on new discoveries about dinosaurs, scientists now think that the extinct creatures were sleek and active, stood upright on their hind legs and carried their tails in the air, cared for their young, and may even have been brightly colored.

were sleek and agile. Some, it appears, could zip along as fast as 30 miles (48 kilometers) an hour. Many dinosaurs also seem to have stood upright on their hind legs, rather than hugging the ground as modern reptiles do. That meant that their circulatory systems had to have a high enough blood pressure to pump blood up to their heads—a trait of warm-blooded animals.

Dinosaurs seem to have had other warm-blooded traits. Most reptiles don't pay attention to their young. But recently, scientists have found nesting sites that suggest that some dinosaurs cared for their offspring much as birds do.

As an example, the scientists point to duck-billed dinosaurs called *Maiasaurs* (the name means "good mother lizard"). *Maiasaurs* lived in the lowlands of what is now Montana some 80 million years ago. But fossils show that they migrated to higher ground to build nests, lay eggs, and raise their young. The nests were grouped in colonies, like those of many birds. And the parent dinosaurs seem to have brought food—berries and grasses—to the hatchlings for several months, until they were large enough to leave the nests and find their own food.

Many dinosaurs also seem to have traveled in vast herds, with older dinosaurs protecting the young ones. And unlike cold-blooded creatures, young dinosaurs grew fast. Newborn *Maiasaurs* were about a foot (30 centimeters) long at birth and grew as much as 10 feet (3 meters) in their first year of life. A rapid growth rate requires a rapid metabolism—yet another trait of warm-blooded animals. ("Metabolism" refers to all the chemical changes that take place in a plant or animal to keep it alive.)

These and other traits suggest that at least some dinosaurs were warm-blooded. Some scientists even think that certain dinosaurs may have been the ancestors of modern birds. Their theory is supported by fossils of dinosaurs with birdlike bone structures.

MORE DINOSAUR NEWS

Scientists have made other new discoveries about dinosaurs. For example, most people think of dinosaurs as enormous—and many were. The largest dinosaur found so far—dubbed Ultrasaurus and a member of the genus *Brachiosaurus*—was about 60 feet (18 meters) tall and weighed about 80 tons. But in 1986, scientists in Nova Scotia, Canada, found footprints of a dinosaur that was no bigger than a sparrow.

More than 50 new kinds of dinosaurs have been found since 1970. Among the finds was one of the oldest dinosaur skeletons on record, discovered in Arizona in 1985. Nicknamed Dinosaur Gertie, this creature was about the size of an ostrich and lived 225 million years ago.

Dinosaur bones have now been found in all regions of the world, from the Arctic to Antarctica. This supports the theory that the continents were connected in the days of the dinosaurs and later broke apart and moved to their present locations. For example, North America was once linked to Asia, and scientists think herds of dinosaurs migrated between China and Canada.

There are also new ideas about what dinosaurs looked like. Some scientists think that dinosaurs may have been brightly colored, as birds and lizards are today. Rather than dragging their tails on the ground, they may have carried them in the air and used them for balance.

A few years ago, scientists learned that skeletons of *Brontosaurus* had been fitted with the wrong heads—these huge planteating creatures had longer, more tapered heads than had been supposed. Now researchers have given a new look to another familiar dinosaur, *Stegosaurus*. For years, this creature was portrayed with a double row of armor plates sticking up from its back. But a study of *Stegosaurus* fossils has shown that there was only one row of armor plates. Some scientists think the animal could move the plates up and down with its back muscles and may have used them to protect itself from attack or to absorb heat from the sun.

Another study has laid to rest a controversy over whether humans and dinosaurs could have lived at the same time. Most scientists have long believed that the last dinosaurs died out more than 60 million years before the first ancestors of humans appeared. But fossils along the Paluxy River in Texas seemed to show human tracks mingled with dinosaur tracks.

Finally, in 1986, scientists were able to explain the confusing evidence. Most of the tracks in the riverbed were made by dinosaurs that walked on their three toes, as dinosaurs usually did. The ones that looked like human tracks were made by dinosaurs that placed their feet full on the ground. The faint toe marks had been overlooked.

WHY DID DINOSAURS DIE OUT?

The new information about dinosaurs has given rise to new theories about how and why they died out. Scientists no longer blame some defect in dinosaurs themselves, such as the inability to move quickly or maintain their body temperatures. Instead, the evidence points to a worldwide catastrophe: At the time that dinosaurs became extinct, some 70 percent of the world's plant and animal species also died out.

What could have caused such drastic changes? One theory is that the climate turned colder, killing off many plant species. Since many animals depend on plants for food, they died too. Another theory is that changes in Earth's magnetic field allowed increased amounts of deadly radiation from space to reach Earth. Or perhaps the atmosphere changed—in 1987, scientists tested air trapped in samples of amber that were 80 million years old and found it was vastly richer in oxygen than present-day air.

One popular theory blames a freak event:

For many years it was believed that *Stegosaurus* had a double row of armor plates sticking up from its back *(left)*. But fossils have shown that the dinosaur had only one row of armor plates *(above)*.

DELIGHTED WITH DINOSAURS

In 1987 dinosaurs were bigger than ever—not in size, but in popularity. Dinosaurs were hot, especially with kids. Museums dusted off their dinosaur bones and staged special exhibits. Several hosted a touring show of dinosaur art. And dinosaur toys were among the top sellers of the year. All the major toy companies brought out at least one dinosaur item to satisfy the demand. There were dinosaur dolls, model dinosaur skeletons, dinosaur coloring books, and dinosaur clocks. Dinosaurs appeared in games and puzzles and on T-shirts. There were even dinosaur-shaped pasta pieces—called, of course, Spaghettisaurus. And there were dinosaur books, including *Maia: A Dinosaur Grows Up,* a children's book that told the story of a young duck-billed dinosaur.

Why the sudden boom in dinosaurs? New discoveries and theories about the giant creatures probably had something to do with it; dinosaurs were in the news. But as with other fads of recent years, no one was sure how this wave of popularity had evolved—or when it would become extinct.

the crash of a huge asteroid on Earth. According to this theory, the asteroid would have caused earthquakes and tidal waves. It also would have thrown up enough dust to fill the atmosphere for years, blocking the light of the sun. Without sunlight, first plants and then animals would have died. But some living things—such as plants that produced seeds that would lie dormant until the light returned and animals that could hibernate—would have survived.

Scientists who accept this theory point to high concentrations of an element called iridium in sediments that were laid down 65 million years ago. Iridium is rare on the Earth's surface but more common in asteroids. Some scientists note that iridium is present in the Earth's core and could have been thrown up in volcanic eruptions. But the same layers of sediment that contain iridium also contain fractured quartz crystals. The fractures are evidence of a sudden, powerful impact—such as might have been caused by an asteroid.

If a giant asteroid collided with Earth 65 million years ago, it would have left a vast crater. Yet no such crater produced that long ago has been found. Scientists who support the asteroid theory think the crater may have originally been on the ocean floor and was wiped out as the continents shifted over millions of years. In 1987 a discovery was made that lent support to this theory. On the ocean floor off Nova Scotia, scientists found the remains of a huge crater formed by the impact of a comet or asteroid. The crater was thought to be about 50 million years old. The scientists hoped that by studying it, they would learn more about the effects of asteroid collisions.

But the asteroid theory isn't accepted by all scientists, and many questions remain. For example, some fossil evidence suggests that dinosaurs were already on the decline by the time the catastrophic event—whatever it was—took place. Many of the other species that died out around that time also seem to have disappeared gradually. It may be that, if the asteroid crash took place, it was just one of many events in a complex series of changes that brought the days of the dinosaurs to a close.

OLYMPIC EQUINES

Thousands of athletes will come together in Seoul, South Korea, for the 1988 Summer Olympic Games. Among them will be a group different from all the rest—the horses that will compete in the Olympic equestrian events.

The equestrian events are among the most exciting at the Games, combining skill, danger, strength, and beauty. And they're the only events in which human performance alone doesn't decide the outcome. Winning an equestrian event requires perfect teamwork between horse and rider—and each must be a superb athlete.

THE EQUESTRIAN EVENTS

There are three equestrian events at the Olympic Games: show jumping, dressage, and the three-day event. **Show jumping** is one of the most popular events because it combines thrills with pageantry. In this event, the horses must negotiate a course of fences up to 5 feet (1.6 meters) high and 7 feet (2.1 meters) wide. The jumps are often intricate and colorful constructions, surrounded by masses of bright flowers.

The goal is to complete the course within a time limit while knocking down as few fence rails as possible. Faults, or penalty points, are given for each knockdown and also for refusals, when the horse balks in front of a fence or runs around it. If several horses finish the course with the same number of faults, they go again. The winner is the horse that finishes the course with the fewest faults and the fastest time.

Show jumping involves much more than simply galloping up to a fence and popping over it. Riders plan exactly how to ride the course and count strides between fences, urging the horses on or slowing them to meet the next fence correctly. The jump itself depends on the horse's strength and skill, but the rider must stay perfectly balanced to allow the animal to clear the fence.

If show jumping provides thrills, **dressage** provides something else: elegance. The name of this sport comes from the French word *dresser,* which means "to train, straighten, or adjust." Dressage developed as a way of training cavalry horses—horses that would be calm and perfectly obedient in combat. Today it is a way to produce balance, suppleness, and responsiveness in horses.

The event takes place in a rectangular

Show jumping: a combination of thrills and pageantry.

Dressage: elegance and a high level of training.

The three-day event: a grueling competition combining show jumping, dressage, speed, and endurance.

arena. At certain points, the horse must perform various maneuvers. The movements required in the Olympics are quite difficult. They include the half-pass (moving diagonally), the passage (a very slow, collected trot), the piaffe (trotting in place), and the pirouette (turning in place). Judges award one to ten points for each of the movements, and the winner is the high-scoring horse. It's not enough to simply perform the required maneuvers—the horse must stay balanced and relaxed and be completely responsive to the rider's signals.

The **three-day event** is the severest test of horses and riders: It combines dressage and show jumping with tests of the horse's speed and endurance. As its name implies, this event is spread over three days.

On the first day, the horses perform a dressage test—not as difficult as the test for the dressage event, but hard enough to show that they've reached a high level of training. The speed and endurance work comes on the second day. This grueling test has four phases: two phases of riding at slow gaits, over roads and tracks totaling up to 12 miles (20 kilometers); a steeplechase course, in which the horses gallop at high speed over a dozen fences; and, finally, a hilly cross-country course up to 5 miles (8 kilometers) long, with up to 32 obstacles.

On the cross-country course, the horses must gallop over water and all sorts of objects—bridges, walkways, walls, logs in strange configurations, and even replicas of boats, picnic tables, and small buildings. Unlike the show jumping obstacles, the obstacles here are solid and fixed—a horse and rider that hit one can fall and be injured. And when they finish this difficult course, there's more ahead: show jumping on the third and final day of the event.

THE TEAMS

Because the equestrian events require a range of skills, countries that take part field three teams—one each in jumping, dressage, and three-day. In the past, the United States, Canada, and the countries of Western Europe—especially Britain and West Germany—have sent strong equestrian teams to the Olympic Games.

Medals are awarded for both individual and team competition in each event. In 1984, the United States won the team and individual gold medals in show jumping and the team gold in the three-day event. West Germany won the team and individual gold medals in dressage, and New Zealand won the individual three-day gold.

Whoever wins in 1988, the horses will share one distinction: They'll be the only four-legged athletes at the Games.

ELAINE PASCOE
Author, *The Horse Owner's Preventive Maintenance Handbook*

Animal noses do more than just sniff. When friendly elephants meet, for example, they twist their trunks together in an affectionate greeting—one of the many uses of an elephant's talented nose.

WHO NOSE?

Animal noses come in hundreds of different sizes and shapes, from a pig's stubby snout to an elephant's huge trunk. But animal noses aren't just for sniffing. They're designed to perform a wide variety of jobs.

Noses serve as hands, arms, tools, and weapons. They're used to dig, probe, spear, cut, tear, drill, crack, spray, strain, snorkel, and net. Some animals fight with their noses. Some rely on their noses to greet friends, warn enemies, spank youngsters, capture prey, or find their way home in the dark.

SUPER SNIFFERS. The human nose can distinguish thousands of different odors. That's good, but lots of animals can do better. Mammals like dogs, cats, pigs, and rats are much more sensitive to odors than we are. Smells guide these animals to their mates, warn them of their enemies, and help them find food.

A dog's cool, moist nose may not seem large, but it's crammed with smell-sensitive tissue. Inside the nose, this tissue is arranged in many wrinkles and folds. Stretched out flat, it would be 40 times the size of the smell-sensitive tissue in a human nose.

A dog can sense odors that escape us. And it can analyze a complex mixture of many odors and concentrate on one of them. Sniffing through the woods, a hunting dog will pick up the scent of a rabbit that may have hopped by an hour earlier. The dog can tell which way the rabbit was going, then follow the scent.

The champion sniffers among dogs are St. Bernards and bloodhounds. A St. Bernard can smell the victim of an avalanche under 20 feet (6 meters) of snow. A bloodhound can pick up the scent of a person from half a mile away. It can find a missing person by sniffing an article of clothing and then following the scent. Its sad-looking face helps its nose to do a good job—the bloodhound's droopy ears stir up scents from the ground, and its wrinkled skin traps those scents.

Compared to a dog, an anteater has a

highly specialized nose: Its nose is meant to sniff out termites and ants. In South America, the giant anteater shuffles along with its long snout close to the ground. When it sniffs an ant or termite mound, it scratches and digs with its claws, tearing away huge chunks of earth. Then the anteater's long sticky tongue flicks into the inside of the mound and laps up hundreds of insects and their eggs.

Another extra-long nose belongs to the little elephant shrew, which has a trunk like an elephant and long hind legs like a kangaroo, but is no bigger than a rat. The elephant shrew twitches and turns its trunklike nose as it sniffs for insects on the forest floor.

Like many mammals, fish also have a powerful sense of smell. Since they breathe with their gills, they use the nostrils on their snouts strictly for smelling.

A shark has one of the keenest noses of any animal. It can sniff one ounce of fish blood in a million ounces of sea water. It can pick up this scent from more than a quarter-mile away. And once it smells blood, it swims to the source like a guided missile.

Salmon use their noses as amazingly accurate direction finders. When they return from their ocean migrations, they locate their home stream from among hundreds of others by nosing in on its special smell.

ELEPHANTS' TRUNKS. No nose is more useful than an elephant's talented trunk. And no nose is bigger. The trunk of a full-grown elephant can be up to six feet (2 meters) long!

Since it's shaped like a rubber hose, a trunk can bend in almost any direction. When testing for smells, the trunk weaves through the air like a cobra and bends toward the source of every interesting odor. An elephant can check for the smell of food, water, friends, or enemies without even moving its head.

The nostrils at the tip of the trunk can pick up the scent of water 3 miles (5 kilometers) away. They can sniff a person several miles downwind. By smelling a bush or tree, an elephant can tell instantly if the leaves or fruit are good to eat.

Along with its two nostrils, an elephant also has one or two small fleshy "fingers" at the tip of its trunk. The African elephant has two of these fingerlike projections, the Indian elephant only one. With them, an elephant can reach down to pull grass, or reach up to pluck leaves or fruit. The "fingers" are so sensitive and their touch is so delicate that they can pick up an object as dainty as a peanut and carry it to the elephant's mouth.

While the tip of the trunk is sensitive, the trunk itself has plenty of muscle power. Reaching high into a tree, an elephant can

An anteater has a highly specialized nose—it sniffs out termites and ants from the ground.

The little elephant shrew has kangaroo legs and an elephant nose. Its trunklike snout is a good insect-sniffer.

rip off a big leafy branch and bring it down to earth. Its trunk has more than 40,000 muscles and is powerful enough to lift a ton of logs.

When an elephant visits a water hole, it draws the water into its trunk, which holds about a gallon and a half. Then it puts the trunk deep into its mouth and squirts the water down its throat. It takes 20 or 30 squirts to satisfy an elephant-sized thirst.

On hot days, elephants use their trunks to spray cooling water across their ears and backs. They're good swimmers, and in deep water they may hold their trunks above the surface and use them as snorkels. After a swim, an elephant likes to roll in the mud and finish its grooming session with a nice dust bath. It sucks up sand or dirt with its trunk and blows it over its body to help keep biting insects away.

An elephant also "talks" through its trunk, using it to scream with rage or squeal with pleasure. Male elephants, or bulls, test each other's strength by locking trunks in a giant-sized tug-of-war. Mother elephants ca-

ress their babies with a soft touch of their trunks. They punish them with a swift, hard whack. When a herd is on the move, the baby follows along by gripping its mother's tail with its trunk. And when friendly elephants meet, they twist their trunks together in an affectionate elephant greeting.

It takes several months for a baby elephant to learn how to use its trunk properly. Since a full-sized trunk is a fairly heavy burden, an elephant may carry its trunk by resting it across its tusks.

As you might suspect, a sleeping elephant snores loudly through its trunk. And when an elephant sneezes, watch out!

BEAKS AND BILLS. A bird's nose is where its mouth is. Its beak or bill is actually a combination of nostrils and lips. Beaks are made of hardened epidermis, or skin, attached to the bird's jaws.

The beak is important to a bird because it serves as both a hand and a tool. Birds use their beaks to find, catch, kill, and eat their food. Simply by looking at a beak, you can often tell what kind of food the bird likes to eat.

Among birds of prey, the beak is a sharp-edged meat hook. An owl or hawk uses its hooked beak to tear a freshly killed mouse or rabbit into convenient bite-sized pieces.

Seed-eating birds like sparrows or cardinals have short, fat, nutcracker beaks that are strong enough to crush a cherry pit. And a woodpecker has a pointed chisel of a beak that's made for drilling holes in tree trunks. The woodpecker then laps up grubs and insects with a long, barbed, sticky tongue.

Some beaks are designed for probing, poking, or pulling. A curlew uses its long curved beak to pull crabs out of deep mud and crickets out of tall grass. A hummingbird pokes its slim beak into flowers, then flicks out its long tongue and sips up the sweet nectar. And an oystercatcher jabs its pointed beak into partly open oyster shells, paralyzing the oyster before it can snap shut.

The spoonbill's beak resembles a long serving spoon. When feeding, the bird moves its slightly open beak from side to side in wide arcs, sifting the shallow waters for small fish, insects, and other food. The spoonbill also uses its beak to make loud clapping noises when it returns to the nest and greets its mate.

A spoonbill's beak resembles a long serving spoon, and it's used to sift for food in shallow waters.

The drooping nose of a proboscis monkey may grow so long that the animal must push it aside in order to eat.

The long hooked beak of a pelican, with its big flabby pouch, makes an excellent fishing net. White pelicans often fish in groups. They form a semicircle offshore and beat the water with their wings, driving fish into the shallows, then scooping them up with a dipnet motion of their gaping pouches.

Before swallowing a fish, a pelican raises its beak to drain water out of the pouch. That's the moment when a bold seagull may swoop down to snatch the fish from the pelican's pouch.

It's true that a pelican's beak holds more than its "bellican"—a white pelican has a pouch capacity of three gallons, and a stomach capacity of only half that much.

The spectacular, brightly colored beak of the South American toucan is useful too. Notice the saw-tooth edges of the beak. They're designed to slice and dice fruits, insects, lizards, and small snakes in the woodlands where the toucan lives.

With a giant beak like that, a toucan can reach for fruit that might be hard to get otherwise. This bird will often pick a small fruit, toss it into the air, then catch it with its open beak. Toucans also like to duel with their beaks. Two rival birds will knock beaks together like a couple of practiced swordsmen.

The African three-horned chameleon uses the pointed horn at the tip of its snout as a weapon against enemies.

In some toucans, the beak is as long and bulky as the rest of the body, giving the bird a rather top-heavy appearance. Luckily, the beak is honeycombed with air pockets and is almost as light as foam rubber. If it were much heavier, the big-beaked toucan would fall on its nose.

NOSES THAT SOUND OFF. A proboscis monkey is born with a cute turned-up nose. But as the monkey grows up, its nose grows down-ward. By the time a monkey is fully grown, its nose may hang down over its mouth. It may be so long that the monkey has to push it aside to eat. That's why these animals are called proboscis monkeys. "Proboscis" means "long snout."

These monkeys live along rivers and swamps on the island of Borneo in Southeast Asia. And they use their drooping noses to magnify their calls and cries. When a male

The "horns" jutting up from the tip of a rhinoceros viper's snout help to camouflage the reptile in its environment.

honks to call his mate or to warn a rival away from his territory, his long nose fills with sound and acts as an echo chamber. The nose makes the sound of the call louder.

The male elephant seal also has a noisy proboscis. During the mating season, he uses his trunklike nose to make long trumpeting sounds, warning rival males to stay away.

Bats use their noses in a form of sonar. As they fly through the night, they blow great bursts of supersonic sound through their nostrils. The sounds bounce back from any object in the bat's path, and its sensitive ears pick up the echoes.

These echoes keep the bat from flying into obstacles and help it find food. With its nose as a navigational guide, a bat can fly through a dense forest in total darkness without touching a tree. Listening to echoes, it can nose in on a flying insect up to 15 feet (4.5 meters) away.

NOSES TO HIDE BEHIND. The spatulate-nosed tree frog has a nose shaped like a flat spoon, or spatula. When the weather is hot and dry, the frog finds a hole in some rocks and crawls inside. Then it plugs up the entrance with its flat nose. Protected from the sun and wind, the frog can keep its body cool and moist.

The rhinoceros viper has "horns" that jut up from the tip of its snout. This 4-foot (1-meter) long poisonous African snake lives among thorny, spiky plants. As it lies in ambush, waiting to strike out at passing prey, its horny snout helps it blend into the background.

DANGEROUS NOSES. The African three-horned chameleon uses its nose as a weapon. It has a pointed horn at the tip of its snout, with two other horns just above it. It can mount a three-pronged attack when it defends its territory from rivals, charging head-long with its nose.

Among certain kinds of tropical termites, the soldier termites have heads shaped like squirt guns, with snouts like nozzles. When ants or other enemies invade the termites' nest, these soldiers rush forward and squirt a sticky substance from their snouts, trapping the ants or driving them away.

A BORING NOSE. The female snout beetle, or acorn weevil, uses her long tubelike snout to prepare a home for the next generation. With her snout, she bores a hole into an acorn.

With 22 fleshy feelers circling its nostrils, the star-nosed mole wins the prize for the strangest-looking nose!

Then she turns around and drops an egg down the hole. When the egg hatches, the young larva lives safely inside the acorn shell until it has eaten up all the meat.

A STAR AMONG NOSES. The prize for the strangest-looking nose of all goes to the star-nosed mole. This animal has 22 fleshy feelers forming a ring around its nostrils. The two top feelers are held rigidly forward. The rest wiggle constantly as the mole searches for worms and insects to eat.

Moles live in dark underground burrows. The star-nosed mole is nearly blind. It finds its way and its food with the twitching feelers that fringe its nostrils.

While its nose may look odd, it really works. A star-nosed mole finds and eats half its weight in insects and grubs every day.

RUSSELL FREEDMAN
Author, *Animal Superstars*

COLOR THEM WHITE

A snow white peacock? A pink and white koala? Outside a toy store, you wouldn't expect to see such animals. But they exist. They are albinos—animals that, by a quirk of inheritance, are snowy white instead of the usual colors of their kind.

The normal colors of animals are produced by pigment cells in the skin, fur or feathers, and eyes. Pigments are substances that produce color. One animal differs from another in color depending on the amount and kind of pigment these cells contain.

Albinos are animals that can't produce any pigments. True albinos have pure white coats or feathers and pink eyes. The pinkish eye coloring doesn't come from pigment—the color comes from blood in small vessels near the surface of the eye.

An animal may also be partly albino: Color is lacking in just some parts of the body or the animal is extremely pale, but not pure white, all over. Not all white animals are albinos, however. White animals such as polar bears have pigment in their skin and eyes.

Koala

Whitetail deer

Peacock

An albino is an animal that's white when it shouldn't be—it's normally meant to be another color.

Why do some animals lack color? Sometimes illness or stress will make normally colored fur or feathers turn white. But true albinism is an inherited trait. That is, it is passed on from parents to offspring by the genes inside cells. The genes tell the pigment cells which and how much color to produce.

The genes work in pairs, so an animal can inherit the gene for albinism and still be normally colored—as long as it has another gene for color. But suppose this animal mates with an animal that is also carrying the gene for albinism. If one of their offspring inherits genes for albinism from each parent, it will be white.

Albinism is more common among some animals than others, but it can occur in any species. Besides the animals shown here, it has been found in catfish, lobsters, trout, frogs, turtles, giraffes, rhinoceroses, porcu-

Gorilla

Hedgehog

California king snake

pines, squirrels, robins, parrots, and many other animals—including people. In fact, even plants can be albinos. But albino plants won't live past the sprouting stage if they lack the green pigment known as chlorophyll. Chlorophyll helps the plant make food, and without it the plant can't live.

Albino animals have troubles of their own. Their white or pale color makes them easy for predators to spot. In addition, their eyes are sensitive to light because they contain no pigment to act as a sunshade. They often have poor vision and may not see a predator in time to escape.

The fact that albinos face such high risks means that they are quite rare in the wild. But in captivity, people protect them. People have long been fascinated by albino animals. In earlier times, the Indians believed that albino deer and buffalo were sacred and shouldn't be hunted. With their pale beauty, albinos are truly rare and special creatures.

Iguana

Chinstrap penguin

The diverse marine world hidden beneath the waters of Monterey Bay is re-created at the largest aquarium in the United States—Monterey Bay Aquarium.

A FISH-EYE VIEW

Hidden beneath the waters of Monterey Bay, off the coast of California, is a canyon as large and deep as the Grand Canyon. Called the Monterey Canyon, this underwater chasm runs 60 miles (97 kilometers) out to sea. At its deepest point, it's 2 miles (3 kilometers) deep—too deep for sunlight to penetrate.

Monterey Bay and the canyon beneath it teem with life. The depths, the shallower waters, and the coast of the bay create many different habitats, or places for plants and animals to live. There are deep granite reefs, broad plains of sand, and huge underwater forests of seaweed. Along the coast are rocky tidepools, marshes, and sandy beaches.

To a casual visitor, much of this rich and diverse life is a secret, invisible beneath the surface of the bay. But visitors can see all of it—even creatures from the canyon's depths—by visiting Monterey Bay Aquarium.

The aquarium, which is perched on the shore of Monterey Bay, opened in 1984 and was built at the site of a former fish cannery.

It's the largest aquarium in the United States, and it's unusual in another way: While most aquariums display marine life from all over the world, the Monterey Bay Aquarium has only plants and animals from local waters. More than 80 living exhibits re-create the habitats of the bay, providing a fish-eye view of its marine life.

MONTEREY BAY

In the bay's deepest waters, cold granite reefs push up from the seafloor. Here, where there is no sunlight, plants cannot live. But there are many animals. Sponges cling to the rocks, along with bright, flowerlike anemones that use their feathery tentacles to catch food particles. Clouds of striped rockfish float by. Spotted fish called sculpins use their front fins to scuttle across the bottom. The spots and stripes of these fish blend into the rocky background and help them hide from predators—this deep world is a dangerous one. Fierce wolf-eels and lingcod lurk in caves and crevices, waiting for unsuspecting prey to wander near.

Closer to shore, shale reefs have formed on the rising seafloor. Formed over millions of years by sediment deposits, these reefs are now honeycombed with tunnels. The tunnels are created by clams and mussels that dig into the soft rock by tapping their shells against it. Some holes contain working clams. Other holes have been abandoned and are safe homes for worms and small fish like the fringehead.

Near the coast, forests of giant kelp are anchored to rocks that are 30 feet (9 meters) deep. The world's fastest-growing plant, giant kelp can grow 10 inches (25 centimeters) a day and reach heights as tall as 100 feet (30 meters). The flat, leafy blades of this seaweed float near the surface, creating a canopy that filters the sunlight much as treetops filter sunlight in a forest on land. Living among the plants are hundreds of different

Flowerlike anemones, colorful sea slugs, and odd sarcastic fringeheads: The aquarium offers visitors a fisheye view of the bay's many underwater creatures.

kinds of fish and other marine animals—including golden señoritas, turban snails, sea cucumbers, and kelp crabs. Farther down, seaweed ''shrubs'' and algae ''turf'' create hiding places for still other sea creatures that live in the kelp forest.

Much of the seafloor itself is a flat, sandy plain. Also rich with life, it's home to anemones, worms, crabs, and sand dollars. Skates, dappled to match the seafloor, glide across the bottom. Brittlestars bury most of their bodies in the sand.

Above and beyond these habitats is the open sea, where whales, porpoises, and

The aquarium's most spectacular exhibit is an enormous three-story-tall tank that contains an entire kelp forest.

streamlined ocean fish streak by in pursuit of food. Near the surface, the sea is a nourishing soup, filled with millions of tiny, floating plants and animals called plankton. Some of the larger ocean creatures eat the plankton. Others, including sleek, fearsome sharks, hunt and eat one another.

At certain times of the year, marine animals move from one part of the bay to another. Squid, for example, spend most of the year in the open sea. But during breeding season, they gather in shallower waters to mate and lay eggs. Whales and fish—and fishermen—catch many squid at this time. But the open sea is replenished with new squid when the millions of eggs hatch.

Close to shore is yet another habitat, but one made by people. This is the wharf, where barnacles and mussels cluster on wood pilings. Shipworms bore into the wood. And fringeheads, octopus, and other sea creatures make homes in the old cans, cast-off shoes, and other debris that people have tossed into the water.

At the Monterey Bay Aquarium, five of these habitats have been re-created in a huge, hourglass-shaped tank. Walking past this 90-foot (27-meter) exhibit, visitors move from the deep reefs past the sandy seafloor, the shale reefs, and the wharf. Sharks, bat rays, and other open-sea fish cruise back and forth along the length of the tank. Huge acrylic windows offer views of each habitat and the life it contains.

Nearby exhibits highlight certain aspects of bay life. One contains dozens of sand dollars; another, octopus, squid, and their relative the chambered nautilus. The Marine Mammals Gallery features life-size models of whales, dolphins, and porpoises.

But the most spectacular exhibit is an enormous tank that towers three stories tall. Inside is an entire kelp forest, complete with animal life. Special pumps create the water motion the kelp requires, and the tank is open to the sunlight above.

WHERE LAND MEETS BAY

The shore of Monterey Bay is rocky in parts and flat, sandy beach in others. This area, between the high-tide line and the low-tide line, is a difficult one in which to live. For a while, all is covered with water. Then the tide goes out, and plants and animals are exposed to the air and bright sun. In some places, waves crash on the shore, dropping tons of water onto the creatures that live there.

At low tide, the rocky shore seems empty of life. But when the water returns, things change. Mussels attached to the rocks open their shells. Anemones and barnacles spread their tentacles. Small crabs come out from their hiding places. Octopus, eels, and fish arrive, on the prowl for prey.

Tidal pools are rocky formations that catch and hold water when the tide goes out. Because they are seldom dry, they are rich with marine life. Starfish live here, feeding on mussels and clams. So do sea urchins, hermit crabs, and small fish. Like the sea creatures of deeper waters, many of these animals are camouflaged to blend with the rocks around them—and escape predators.

Along the sandy beaches, crabs, clams, and other small animals live buried in the sand at the water's edge. Sandpipers, avocets, and shorebirds scurry about, hunting for them. Behind the beaches are dunes where the birds lay their eggs and raise their young. And beyond the dunes are salt marshes and mudflats, fed by tidal channels and coastal streams.

Many animals live in the sheltered waters of the marshes. Clams dig into the mud, and pipefish move slowly through the half-submerged grasses. Long-legged herons and egrets live in the marshes year-round, at times joined briefly by migrating birds.

The aquarium brings these shoreline habitats up close with several exhibits. One is a walk-through aviary inhabited by shoreline birds. Another shows the life of the salt marshes, and a third the life of coastal streams.

The life of the rocky coast is shown in several exhibits, including a "touch pool" where visitors can pet starfish and other coastal creatures. A wave-crash exhibit shows the force of rushing water at the shore. And outside the aquarium, a great tidal pool has been created and filled with all the diverse life-forms these pools contain.

This tidal pool opens directly into Monterey Bay itself—which is perhaps the greatest exhibit of all. To those who have visited the aquarium, the bay's secrets are hidden no more.

PLAYFUL SEA OTTERS

Among Monterey Bay's most delightful residents are mammals that are at home both on the shore and in the sea. Sleek harbor seals glide in close to the shore, looking for fish. Farther out, sea lions sun themselves on rocky islands, barking when boats pass. And sea otters romp and tumble over the rocks or sleep, wrapped in blankets of kelp, floating in the shallow water close to shore.

Sea otters are the smallest ocean mammals. When they aren't napping, the playful animals are in constant motion—diving, turning somersaults, grooming their thick fur coats, and above all eating. A sea otter eats enough clams, squid, fish, and shrimp to equal 25 percent of its body weight each day.

Sea otters live inside Monterey Bay Aquarium in a special tank with two viewing levels: one at the surface, and one for underwater otter watching. The otters in the tank were rescued as pups after being separated from their mothers by storms. Monterey Bay is the only aquarium that has succeeded in raising otter pups rescued from the wild. The next step: learning how to prepare these otters to return to the open bay.

SCIENCE

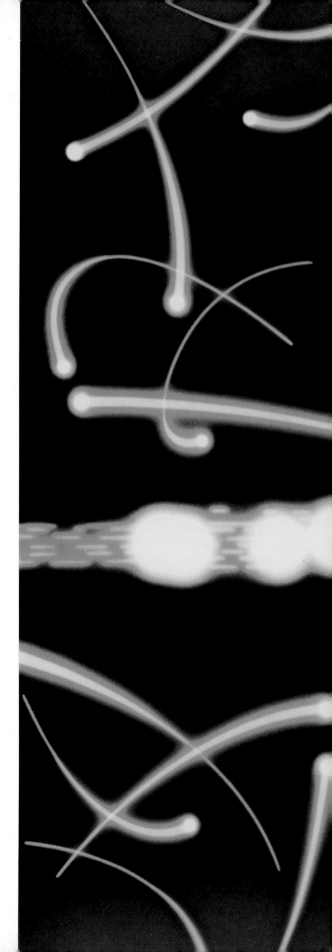

Electricity shoots through a super-conductor in this artist's drawing. Normally, the electrons that carry electric current meet resistance as they travel through a wire—they bump into atoms and into each other, losing energy as they do. But when electricity travels through a superconductor, the electrons encounter no resistance, and virtually no energy is lost. In 1987, scientists announced breakthroughs in research into these amazing materials.

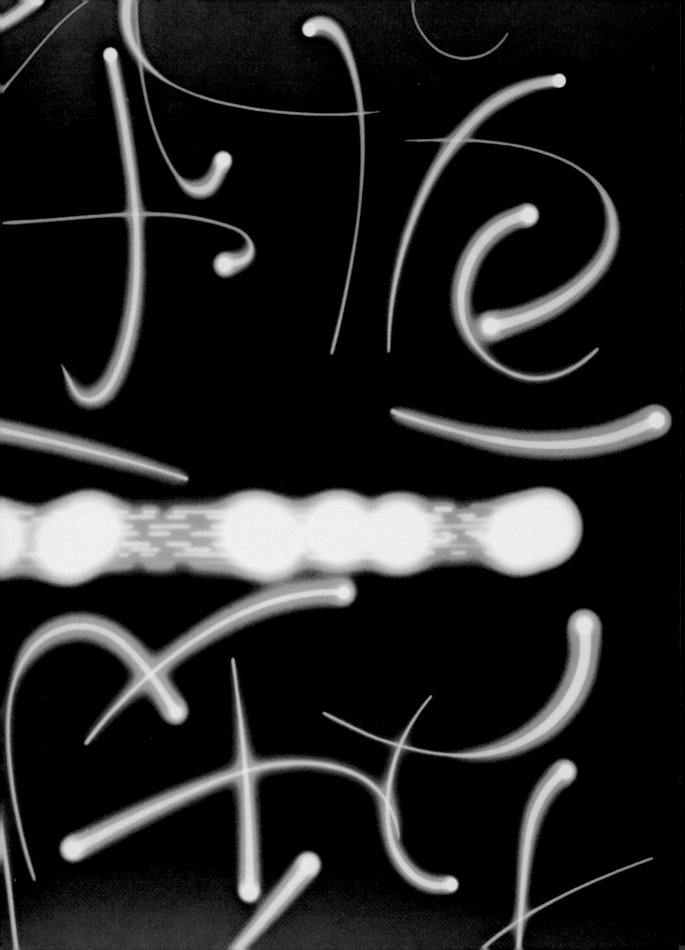

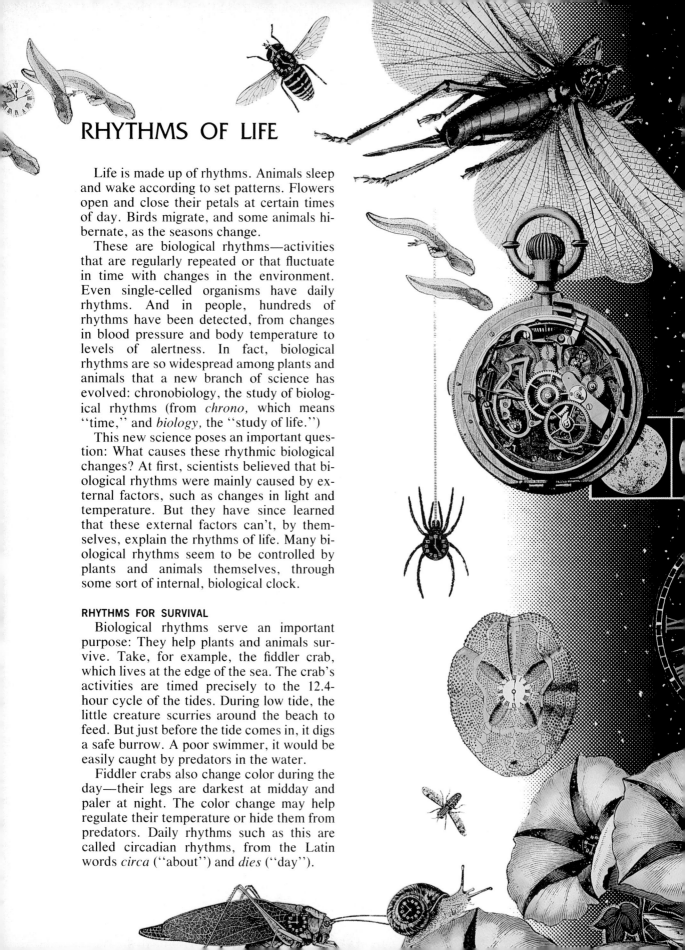

RHYTHMS OF LIFE

Life is made up of rhythms. Animals sleep and wake according to set patterns. Flowers open and close their petals at certain times of day. Birds migrate, and some animals hibernate, as the seasons change.

These are biological rhythms—activities that are regularly repeated or that fluctuate in time with changes in the environment. Even single-celled organisms have daily rhythms. And in people, hundreds of rhythms have been detected, from changes in blood pressure and body temperature to levels of alertness. In fact, biological rhythms are so widespread among plants and animals that a new branch of science has evolved: chronobiology, the study of biological rhythms (from *chrono,* which means "time," and *biology,* the "study of life.")

This new science poses an important question: What causes these rhythmic biological changes? At first, scientists believed that biological rhythms were mainly caused by external factors, such as changes in light and temperature. But they have since learned that these external factors can't, by themselves, explain the rhythms of life. Many biological rhythms seem to be controlled by plants and animals themselves, through some sort of internal, biological clock.

RHYTHMS FOR SURVIVAL

Biological rhythms serve an important purpose: They help plants and animals survive. Take, for example, the fiddler crab, which lives at the edge of the sea. The crab's activities are timed precisely to the 12.4-hour cycle of the tides. During low tide, the little creature scurries around the beach to feed. But just before the tide comes in, it digs a safe burrow. A poor swimmer, it would be easily caught by predators in the water.

Fiddler crabs also change color during the day—their legs are darkest at midday and paler at night. The color change may help regulate their temperature or hide them from predators. Daily rhythms such as this are called circadian rhythms, from the Latin words *circa* ("about") and *dies* ("day").

Many plants have circadian rhythms. Flowers open at certain times to attract certain pollinators—bees, birds, and butterflies during the day; moths and bats at night. The leaves of many plants curl or droop in "sleep" at night and perk up at dawn to catch sunlight, which the plants use to make food. Circadian rhythms may also regulate nectar production and the flow of sap.

Annual rhythms, too, aid survival. The breeding cycles of birds and many animals seem to be keyed to changes in the seasons —newborn animals have a better chance of surviving if they're born in warm months. Bears, hamsters, ground squirrels, and other animals that hibernate save energy during winter, when temperatures are cold and food is scarce. They're active in the warm summer months, when food is plentiful. Many birds fly south for the winter and head north for spring.

These and many other biological rhythms seem to be linked to outside factors. Light is one such factor—as the Earth rotates on its axis, day changes to night and night to day. Temperature is another external factor. As the Earth revolves around the sun each year, annual changes in temperature occur in most parts of the world. Ocean tides are still another external force—and fluctuations in the tides seem linked to rhythms shown not only by fiddler crabs but by many sea creatures. Are these external factors the cause of biological rhythms?

INTERNAL OR EXTERNAL?

In fact, the question of what causes biological rhythms is far more complex. The first clue came in 1729, when the French astronomer Jean Jacques d'Ortous de Mairan conducted an experiment with a mimosa plant. This type of plant, like many others, opens its leaves each morning and closes them at night. De Mairan put his mimosa in a cellar where no outside light penetrated. And he found that the leaves followed the same schedule—with no clues to the time of day.

Later scientists confirmed De Mairan's discovery. And they found that many biological rhythms are maintained when external factors such as changes in light and temperature are eliminated. Fiddler crabs, for example, keep up their cycles of changes in color and activity even when they're kept in constant light or darkness, in a laboratory that's far from the tides. And like the fiddler crabs, hibernating animals keep to their cycles in the lab, without being cued by the changes in temperature and length of day that mark the change in seasons.

Scientists who kept migrating birds in cages under artificial light found that this rhythm, too, was maintained without external cues. As winter approached, the birds grew restless and perched on the south sides of the cages. In spring, they preferred northern perches. How did they know which way to go? Scientists think birds are able to sense the Earth's magnetic field. But that doesn't answer a second question: How did the birds know *when* it was time to migrate?

Experiments such as these convinced many scientists that internal clocks play a major role in governing biological rhythms. But some scientists believed that there might be still other external factors that the experiments couldn't account for—factors such as changes in the magnetic field or in atmospheric radiation.

To rule out those factors, scientists conducted an experiment in space. They sent aloft glass tubes of a fungus that produces spores at set intervals. In most of the tubes, the rhythm of spore production continued even when the spacecraft was beyond the range of the Earth's atmosphere and magnetic field. That was strong evidence that at least some biological rhythms are set by internal clocks.

How do these internal clocks operate? One theory is that animals have a "time center"—the pineal gland and a tiny section of the brain called the suprachiasmatic nucleus have been proposed. But fiddler crabs, plants, one-celled organisms, and many other living things that show biological rhythms don't have these organs. It may be that the rhythms are controlled by individual cells—that every living cell has a tiny clock.

External factors do play a part in biological rhythms. Most scientists now agree that internal clocks work best when combined with cues from the environment. When plants and animals are kept in the laboratory, their clocks often start to run fast or slow— a cycle of 25 or 23 hours, for example, instead of 24. In nature, changes in light and temperature act to reset the clocks and keep them running on time. And some rhythms are more affected by external factors than others. While some flowers seem to run on internal clocks, others won't open unless external conditions are right.

But the theory of internal clocks explains some biological rhythms that seem to be unrelated to the environment, including rhythms that run over periods much longer than a year. Most species of bamboo, for example, bloom every 15 years. One species blooms every 120 years—and all members of the species bloom at the same time, no matter where in the world they're planted.

Where people are concerned, the various theories about biological rhythms have given rise to a lot of speculation. A few years ago, biorhythm charts became quite popular. They were supposed to show a person's best times of day for various activities. But many researchers think that such charts aren't accurate or helpful.

Still, biological rhythms may affect many aspects of life, from how easily you wake up in the morning to how well your body uses medicine to fight disease. In the future, research may unlock the door to these and other secrets of natural rhythms.

FLORAL CLOCKS

Some flowers open and close their petals with such regularity that you can almost set your watch by them. In fact, flowers might *become* your watch —if you plant a clock garden.

The idea of a garden that keeps time isn't new. In the 1700's, the Swedish botanist Carolus Linnaeus noticed that certain flowers opened and closed at set times, regardless of the weather. He used his observations to develop a floral clock, choosing for each daylight hour a plant that would open or close its blooms at that time. A person could tell the time simply by glancing at the garden to see which flowers were open.

Similar floral clocks were popular in Victorian gardens of the late 1800's. The plants were usually set out in a way that mimicked a clock face—in a ring or in a solid circle divided into pie-shaped wedges for the hours.

Flower clocks aren't as precise as mechanical clocks and watches. The exact opening and closing times of the blooms can vary with the weather and the location of the garden. But a floral clock is a fun and unusual addition to any garden. By adding night-blooming plants, you can even extend the time-keeping hours past daylight. Here are some plants that you might include, with their approximate opening and closing times:

MORNING
4:00—Common chicory opens
5:00—Tawny daylily, morning glory, blue flax open
6:00—Sundrop, waterlily open
8:00—Mouse-ear hawkweed, portulaca (moss rose) open

9:00—Lesser celandine opens
11:00—Star of Bethlehem opens

AFTERNOON
12:00—Passionflower opens; morning glory closes
1:00—Mouse-ear hawkweed closes
2:00—Blue flax closes
3:00—Prickly pear cactus opens
4:00—Portulaca closes
5:00—American starflower opens

EVENING
6:00—Evening primrose, catchfly open
7:00—Iceland poppy closes
8:00—Tawny daylily closes
10:00—Moonflower opens
12:00—Night-blooming cactus opens

SUPERCONDUCTIVITY: GOING WITH THE FLOW

It's a Monday morning in the year 2038—time to go to work. You get up and push your bed out of the way, watching as it floats across the floor to its daytime storage spot in the corner of your room. Then, after a quick breakfast, you hop into your electric car and drive to the train station. There you catch a high-speed train that whisks you to the city at 300 miles (483 kilometers) an hour. You have just enough time on the way to finish up some calculations on your computer, which you always carry in your pocket. When you reach the city, you join the throngs of other people who are floating down the sidewalk to their offices.

Floating furniture . . . floating people . . . electric cars . . . computers that fit in your pocket . . . trains that travel 300 miles an hour? It all sounds far-fetched. But these are just a few of the developments that may result from advances in superconductors, materials that are able to transmit electricity in a greatly improved way. In 1987, scientists announced major breakthroughs in research into these unusual materials.

REMARKABLE MATERIALS

Superconductors are remarkable because they do away with the phenomenon of electrical resistance. When electricity travels through a wire, the current is carried by a flow of electrons. Normally, as they travel down the wire, the electrons meet with resistance—they bump into atoms and into each other. In the process, they lose energy, which is given off in the form of heat. Sometimes electrical resistance is useful. Colliding electrons produce the light in lightbulbs and the heat in your electric iron. But much of the time, resistance wastes electricity.

In superconductors, electricity flows without resistance—the electrons don't collide, and virtually no energy is lost. Because of this and other properties they possess, superconductors have great potential for science, industry, and everyday life.

Superconductivity was discovered in 1911, by Heike Onnes, a Dutch scientist. He found that when metal was cooled to absolute zero ($-459°F$, or $-273°C$), resistance disappeared. If scientists have known about superconductivity for more than 75 years, why hasn't it been put to use? One reason is that the property disappeared at higher temperatures. To produce superconductivity, scientists had to keep their materials chilled with expensive liquid helium. This meant that superconductivity found few uses outside the lab.

But in the past few years, scientists have found materials that become superconductors at higher temperatures. In 1987, superconductivity was reported at temperatures as high as $-283°F$ ($-175°C$). Because they don't have to be as cold as earlier superconductors, these new materials can be cooled with liquid nitrogen, which is as cheap as milk and is already widely used in industry. Now researchers are racing to see who will be the first to produce superconductivity at room temperature.

SUPER-USES

The new superconductors still present some problems. They are ceramics made of a group of chemical elements known as rare earths (such as lanthanum and yttrium) and metals. Like other ceramics, they are brittle, which makes them impractical for power lines and many other uses. But scientists are working on flexible versions, and they have thought of dozens of practical uses for them.

If superconductors could be used to transmit electricity over long distance, people could save billions of dollars in power now lost through resistance. Electricity could even be stored—something that's now impossible—by sending it round and round through superconducting rings.

Smaller, faster computers could be built with superconductors. The heat created by electrical resistance puts limits on how small present computers can be. If designers try to pack too many circuits too tightly into the computer, the heat damages the components. But with superconductors, heat would no longer be a problem. Some researchers think all the essential components of a computer could be squeezed into a box smaller than a pocket radio. And without resistance, computers could make their calculations faster than ever.

Other superconductor uses stem from the magnetic properties of electricity. Electrical current produces a magnetic field, and electrical coils are now used to make powerful magnets. But resistance limits the strength of these magnets. With superconductors, the magnets could be far stronger—and smaller.

Superconducting magnetic coils have already been used in medicine, in nuclear magnetic resonance imaging machines. These machines produce images of the inside of the body that are far more detailed than X rays. But they are extremely expensive, and only a few have been built. The new superconductors might make them more common.

Superconducting magnets could also be used to make more powerful electric motors —powerful enough to run a car. Unlike present electric motors, they would hardly ever need recharging. And scientists think that superconductors could be used to create immensely powerful magnetic fields that would help produce nuclear fusion. Nuclear fusion might in turn provide a cheap, safe, and virtually unlimited supply of energy.

Still other uses might arise from a strange, almost magical trait of superconductors: A superconductor will repel any external magnetic field—any magnetic field that the superconductor itself hasn't produced. Thus, if a magnet is placed over a superconductor, the magnet will float above it. The magnetic field acts like an invisible cushion, keeping the two materials apart.

This strange phenomenon, called levitation, might have many uses. For example, trains could ride on superconducting magnetic fields instead of on wheels. Because they would never touch the tracks, there would be no friction, and they could zoom along at unheard-of speeds. A prototype maglev (for magnetic levitation) train has already been built in Japan. It travels silently at speeds up to 300 miles an hour.

Levitation could also be used to reduce friction—and with it wear and tear—in all sorts of machinery. It could be used to make floating furniture, which would be guided by wires in the floor and raised or lowered by turning a dial. It might even be possible to build a new sort of people mover, in which people would float along magnetized tracks in individual cars—or even on foot, by means of special superconducting shoes.

The idea of people floating down a sidewalk is still farfetched. But if superconductors can be perfected, who knows what could result. As one researcher has put it, "It could almost be like the discovery of electricity."

A magnetic cube floats mysteriously above a new superconducting material, which is bathed in liquid nitrogen to keep it cold. Because superconductors repel any external magnetic field, they produce an almost magical phenomenon called levitation.

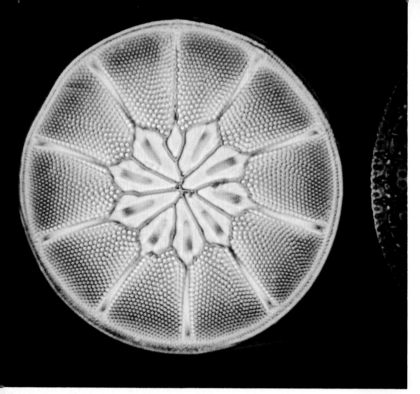

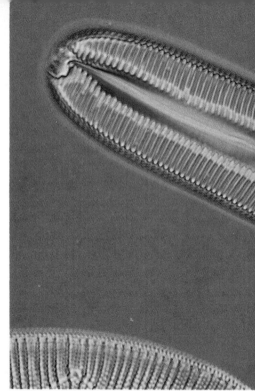

DIATOMS—
GLASSY BEAUTIES

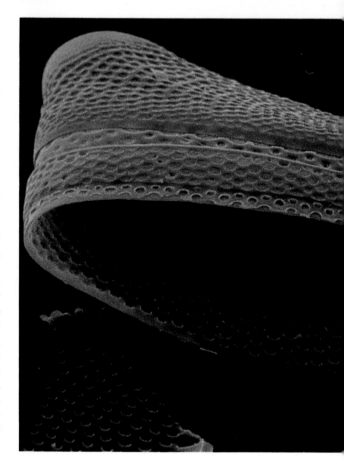

If you've ever looked along the shore of a pond or beneath an ocean pier, you may have seen brown slime coating the rocks and pilings. Did you know that the slime was made up of beautiful living things like those pictured here?

These are diatoms, microscopic one-celled plants that live by the billions in water and damp places. Some are free-floating, and some hang together in chains. Diatoms are at the heart of the ocean food chain—they're eaten by small sea animals, which are in turn eaten by larger fish.

Diatoms are unusual plants. Their most intriguing features are their cell walls, or shells. Diatoms are plants in glass houses—their cell walls are made of silica, the same material used in glass. The shell comes in two halves that fit together like the top and bottom of a pillbox. There are more than 10,000 kinds of diatoms, but each one has a uniquely constructed shell. Because diatom shells are nearly colorless, photographers use colored lights and other tricks to capture their glassy beauty.

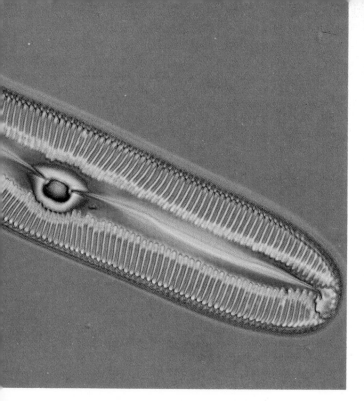
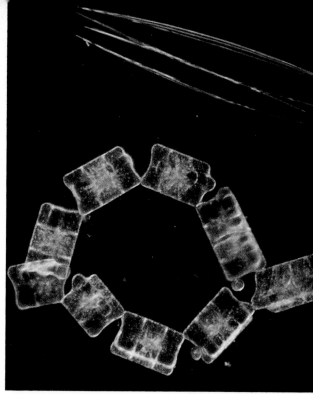
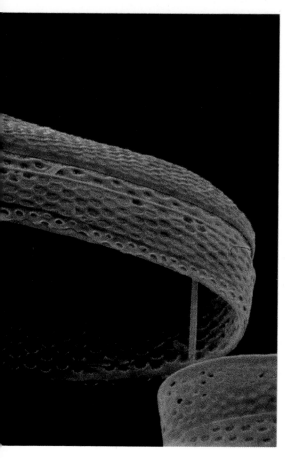
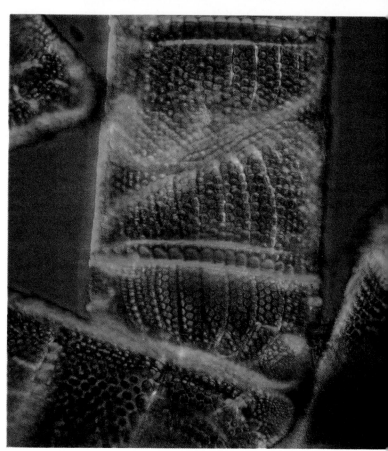

WETLAND WILDERNESSES

Tall marsh grasses bend in a soft breeze, revealing patches of glimmering water at their roots. An egret wades delicately through the grass, while a flock of ducks soars overhead. Nearby a muskrat paddles down a channel, only its head visible above the water. The air is filled with the song of birds and the hum of countless insects.

This peaceful scene is taking place in a wetland. A wetland is an area where the soil is saturated with water, and water is the main factor in determining the kinds of soil and plant and animal life that are found there. There are wetlands all over the world. They form inland, in shallow lakes and ponds that fill with silt and in areas where the land is depressed into bowls that trap water; and along the seacoast, when the ocean water recedes.

People have long considered wetlands to be waste areas because they are unsuitable for building or farming. For that reason, people have often drained them, filled them in, and destroyed them. Now, however, people have begun to appreciate the true value of these rich and varied areas, and they are working to protect them.

Wetlands of various kinds provide homes for a rich variety of plant and animal life. They are also important to surrounding areas. In heavy rains they help control floods by holding back water. In times of drought, they act as water reserves. Some wetlands act as water filters, trapping pollutants from rivers and streams and allowing them to be cleaned out.

Wetlands include marshes like the one described above, as well as bogs and swamps. The lines between these types of wetlands aren't clearly drawn, and many people use the terms interchangeably. But there are distinct differences between the types.

MARSHES

Marshes are generally described as open, watery areas with tall grasslike plants. There are two basic types: inland, freshwater marshes, which form when shallow lakes and ponds begin to fill in with silt; and tidal, or saltwater, marshes, which form along coastal areas.

The specific plants and animals living in marshes vary depending on where the marsh is located. In North America, cattails, sedges, waterlilies, and various pondweeds grow in the freshwater marshes. Freshwater marshes are also home to intriguing insect-eating plants. These include pitcher plants, which drown insects in tube-shaped leaves half-filled with water; sundews, which catch insects on leaves covered with sticky projections; and bladderworts, water plants that capture underwater insects in tiny, balloon-shaped "bladders," or sacs. The plants have no lack of prey—dragonflies, midges, mosquitoes, and many other insects abound in the marsh.

Freshwater marshes are also rich in other animal life. Clams, crayfish, and many kinds of fish live in the water. Frogs, salamanders, turtles, lizards, and snakes hop, crawl, and slither through the grass. Ducks and geese make their homes in the marsh and often raise their young there. So do blackbirds, wading birds such as herons and egrets, and predators such as hawks and owls. Muskrats, beavers, raccoons, rabbits, rats, foxes, mink, deer—and even, in some areas, bears—visit or live in marshes.

In the tidal marshes, the plants are limited to those that can tolerate the brackish, salty water. They include cord grass and various kinds of rushes. Besides the usual marsh birds and animals, there are oysters, crabs, shrimp, snails, and gulls and other seabirds. Tidal marshes are hatcheries for many kinds of fish—experts say that 80 to 90 percent of the fish sold worldwide depend on these shallow coastal waters at some point in their lives. And in North America, tidal marshes along both coasts and freshwater marshes in the center of the continent provide feeding grounds for millions of migrating birds each year.

Some marshlands are seasonal—they form in rainy seasons and dry up at other times of the year. The prairie potholes of North Dakota are an example. These ponds and marshes developed in depressions made by glaciers thousands of years ago. Some hold water all year, but others are so small that they dry up in summer. The following

A marsh is an open, watery area with tall grasslike plants. Bitterns, raccoons, and sundews (insect-eating plants with sticky leaves) are just some of the many living things that enjoy this type of wetland.

spring, however, they fill with rain and melted snow and come back to life. Snails, insect larvae, and freshwater shrimp hatch in the pools, and millions of ducks, geese, and other birds arrive to nest. By some estimates, the pothole region produces half to two thirds of the ducks in North America. But because the potholes are located in rich farming country, they are rapidly being filled in and converted to farmland.

BOGS

Bogs are generally found in northern regions, where glaciers once carved out depressions in the land. Water collects in these areas, and plants take root. But these areas are usually poorly drained and thus receive little oxygen. As the plants die, the poor drainage and lack of oxygen slow the decaying process. Some of the partly decayed plant matter floats to the surface of the water, and a mat of moss and plant stems begins to grow on top of it. The moss usually associated with bogs is sphagnum moss, which is very spongy. This floating mat of living and dead vegetation gets thicker and thicker. The mat may eventually become thick enough to support a person, but it will "quake" as the person walks.

As the water becomes choked with vegetation, some of the decaying plant material begins to accumulate on the bottom in the form of peat. The layers of peat at the bottom and the cushiony mat of plant matter on the surface are the features that separate bogs from marshes and swamps.

Both the sphagnum moss and the peat make the bog highly acidic, and this limits the kinds of plant that can live there. But plants that like an acid environment—including cranberry, sedges, heaths, reeds, the insect-eating plants, and many wildflowers—grow well in bogs. Like marshes, bogs are generally open wetlands. But some have shrubs and trees, including black spruce and white pine. Bogs also have fewer animals than marshes, although insects are just as plentiful. Warblers and other birds live in bogs, along with frogs and small mammals such as mice, voles, and lemmings.

Peat bogs hold fascinating secrets. Because of the acidity, little that falls into them decays. Human and animal remains dating back 5,000 years or more, as well as many ancient artifacts, have been found in bogs and have given researchers many clues to the past. But peat bogs serve another purpose as well. Cut into bricks and dried, peat is an excellent fuel. It has long been used in Ireland and other areas that have extensive peat bogs, and today it is even used to run some electrical power plants.

SWAMPS

Swamps differ from other wetlands chiefly because of the trees and shrubs that grow in them. They represent a later stage in the development of wetlands: The ground has filled in and dried out enough to support some species of trees. But the ground is still poorly drained and wet, with channels of dark, slow-moving water. Some trees, such as the bald cypress, grow right out of the water. Others prefer higher ground and grow on islands, or hummocks, that have been pushed up out of the swamp.

Shaded by moss-covered trees, a swamp can be a dark, spooky place. In fact, one of the largest swamps in the United States, located in North Carolina and Virginia, is called the Dismal Swamp. But swamps teem with life. Many of the same plants and animals that live in bogs and marshes also live in swamps. The huge Okefenokee Swamp, in Georgia and Florida, supports more than 200 different kinds of birds, along with 32 species of amphibians and 48 kinds of reptiles. Many of these species are rare and live only in wetland areas. Some swamps in the southern United States are home to the alligator.

There are three main kinds of swamps. In shallow-water swamps, the ground stays moist all year. Willows, alders, buttonbushes, and other trees and shrubs grow, along with ferns, vines, and many wildflowers. Shallow-water swamps may cover large tracts of land, but many are just pockets of damp ground in the middle of the forest.

Deep-water swamps form along rivers and are flooded at certain seasons. Oaks, cypresses, elms, and other tall trees—draped with hanging vines and Spanish moss—create dense shade. The bottomland hardwood forests of the lower Mississippi River Valley

A bog has a layer of peat at the bottom and a cushiony mat of plant matter, usually sphagnum moss, on the surface. A bog's acidity limits the kinds of plants and animals that live there. But frogs and many kinds of wildflowers (such as these lady's slipper orchids) find it a welcoming environment.

A swamp is a kind of wetland in which the ground has been filled in and dried out enough to support some species of trees. When the trees are covered with moss, the swamp can look dark and spooky. But swamps teem with life, and alligators and egrets are among the animals that call them home.

are typical of this kind of swamp. When they are flooded in winter, they provide breeding grounds for many waterfowl, including about a fourth of the mallard ducks in the United States.

Deep-water and shallow-water swamps are both freshwater swamps. In tropical areas, saltwater swamps sometimes develop along the seacoast. Mangrove trees grow from the water, and the swamps provide homes for pelicans and many sea creatures.

THREATENED WETLANDS

All over the world, wetlands are disappearing at an alarming rate. The United States once had some 250 million acres of wetlands. Now there are less than 100 million, and they are disappearing at a rate of more than 400,000 acres a year. Wetlands are drained for housing developments, shopping malls, and farmland; dredged to make channels for ships; and damaged by polluted water.

In the last few years, however, people have become more aware of the importance of wetlands. Besides providing flood control and water reserves, wetlands are important to the food chain because they provide breeding grounds for so many animals. And because many wetland plants and animals are rare and can live only in their water habitat, destruction of wetlands threatens many species with extinction.

In many areas, laws now protect wetlands and make it more difficult for developers and others to fill them in. Some wetland areas have been set aside as parks or nature preserves. But many of the remaining wetlands are still in danger, and so are the plants and animals that live in them.

One of the largest and richest wetlands in the United States is the Everglades, a two-million-acre expanse of swamp and other wetland areas in southern Florida. Part of the area is protected as a national park, but most is not. The story of the Everglades illustrates what can happen when people alter the delicate balance of a wetland.

The Everglades was created ages ago by drainage from Lake Okeechobee—water flows slowly in a 50-mile-wide sheet from the lake through the swamp to Florida Bay.

Until this century, the Everglades was a wetland paradise. Fish, frogs, turtles, and alligators abounded in the water. Storks, egrets, flamingos, and herons waded about, and countless waterfowl lived there. Raccoons, deer, and other animals—including the Florida panther—made their homes in the glades. Florida Bay, where fresh water from the swamp mixed with salt water from the sea, provided an ideal spawning ground for shrimp, fish, and other sea creatures.

Then, around the turn of the century, Florida began to grow. Developers began to drain the Everglades to create farmland and housing sites. They built dams and levees to control the flow of water, and canals to bring drinking water to the state's growing cities. Slowly at first, and then more quickly, the Everglades began to dry up.

By the mid-1960's, the damage was extensive. Plants and animals began to die out, and brushfires swept through areas that were once marshy. Florida Bay, no longer receiving an influx of fresh water from the swamp, became so salty that the young sea creatures that spawned there couldn't live. Salt levels began to rise in the swamp itself. And people realized that even more was at stake. Most of Florida's water supply comes from a huge underground aquifer that is constantly refilled by water that seeps down from the Everglades. With the swampland vanishing, the aquifer could dry up as well.

At first, the government tried to correct the problem by releasing vast quantities of water into the swamp at set intervals. But that only created more problems—floods alternated with dry spells, and more animals died. Now a new plan has been developed, in which water is released on a schedule that follows the pattern of actual rainfall. Some of the canal and dike work is being undone in an effort to restore the swamp, and the state plans to buy and preserve about 300,000 acres of Everglades land.

Many Everglades animals are still in danger. Only 30 Florida panthers are thought to remain, and more are killed on highways than are born each year. But it's hoped that as the swamp returns to normal, the animals will return, and the Everglades will again be the wetlands paradise it once was.

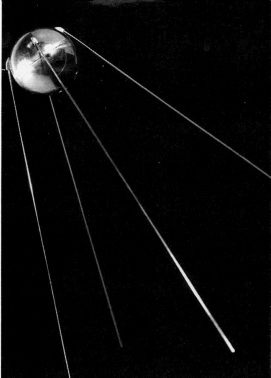

Thirty years ago saw the beginning of the Space Age with the launching of Sputnik I (*above*) into Earth orbit. Thirty years from now, after unmanned and manned missions to Mars (*left*), we may be colonizing that distant planet.

SPACE BRIEFS

"The Space Age Is Here!" This headline announced the launching of the first satellite to be sent into space. The date was October 4, 1957. The satellite was the Soviet Union's Sputnik I, a small, shiny sphere that was less than 23 inches (58 centimeters) in diameter.

In the thirty years since that historic feat, thousands of other vehicles—satellites, spacecraft, and space stations—have been launched into space. They've circled Earth, carried people to the moon, visited other planets, and performed many scientific experiments. For the future, space scientists are planning even more exciting missions.

Many space scientists believe that Mars is the next logical planet for people to visit. It has an earthlike terrain of mountains and valleys, and it may be the only planet in our solar system where people could survive.

As the Soviet Union celebrated the 30th anniversary of the launching of Sputnik in 1987, their space officials called on American and European scientists to join them in their mission to land people on Mars. Their program calls for a series of unmanned missions to begin in 1992, and manned missions to begin early in the next century.

THE U.S. SPACE PROGRAM

For many years, the U.S. space program was the source of much pride for Americans. But on January 28, 1986, the space shuttle *Challenger* exploded, killing the seven astronauts aboard. It was the worst disaster in U.S. space history. All further shuttle flights were postponed indefinitely so that scientists and engineers could find out the cause of the accident and make changes in the design of the shuttle and its booster rockets. The United States experienced still more problems when a series of unmanned rocket launches were unsuccessful.

It appeared that America's floundering space program had put the Soviets, with their many successful and ambitious missions, far ahead in the space race. In fact, a panel headed by former astronaut Sally Ride reported that the United States "has clearly lost leadership" to the Soviet Union in the exploration of Mars and in the use of space stations.

During 1987, however, the United States did make some gains. The shuttle was redesigned and given improved landing brakes, better engines, and a special escape mechanism. Astronauts once again began to train for shuttle flights, and a five-man crew was chosen for the next flight—scheduled for June, 1988. President Ronald Reagan approved $2.1 billion to build a replacement for the *Challenger*. And in October and November, Titan rockets were sent into orbit with secret military satellites—the first successful U.S. launchings of major payloads in two years.

THE SOVIET SPACE PROGRAM

The Soviet Union was the only nation to have people in space during 1987. On February 6, Yuri Romanenko and Aleksandr Laveikin were launched aboard a Soyuz spacecraft. Three days later they linked up with Mir, a sophisticated orbiting space station with six docking ports, launched in 1986.

In March, an unmanned research module called Kvant was launched to dock with Mir. But two attempts by ground control to link the vehicles failed. On April 12, Romanenko and Laveikin donned special space suits and went outside Mir to investigate the problem. They discovered an object inside Kvant's docking unit, removed it, and then supervised while ground control again activated Kvant's automatic docking systems. This time the maneuver was successful, and Kvant became the first experimental module to link with Mir.

In July, another Soyuz spacecraft docked with Mir. Aboard were two Soviet cosmonauts, Aleksandr Viktorenko and Aleksandr Aleksandrov, and Syria's first man in space, Mohammed Faris. Aleksandrov remained on Mir with Romanenko. Laveikin, who developed a heart problem, returned to Earth aboard the Soyuz with Viktorenko and Faris. By September 30, Romanenko had spent more than 237 days in orbit, passing the endurance record in space set by three other Soviet cosmonauts in 1984.

A monkey named Yerosha (meaning "troublemaker") was sent aloft by the Soviets and lived up to its name—it freed one of its paws and played with anything it could touch.

Also in September, in a project not involving the space station, the Soviets launched some nonhuman "cosmonauts." Two monkeys, some rats, insects, fish, and other organisms were sent aloft as part of an international experiment on weightlessness. Once in space, one of the monkeys lived up to its name: Yerosha, which means "troublemaker" in Russian, freed its left paw and began to play with the control panel in the sealed chamber—and anything else it could reach. The Soviets said that Yerosha hadn't caused any damage, but when the craft returned to Earth, it landed thousands of miles off course.

Within the next few years, the Soviets plan to launch their own space shuttle. In May, 1987, they performed the first test launch of Energia, an extremely powerful rocket capable of lifting four times the weight of the shuttle. Energia would also be able to launch larger space stations and major planetary missions.

The Canada-France-Hawaii Telescope on Mauna Kea, a volcano in Hawaii. Because turbulence of the Earth's atmosphere blurs a telescope's images, major observatories are placed on high mountains, where the air is thin.

EYES ON THE SKIES

Look for the stars; you'll say there are none
Look up a second time, and, one by one,
You mark them twinkling out with silvery light,
And wonder how they could elude the sight!

When the poet William Wordsworth wrote those lines in 1834, he could have had no idea how many stars were in fact hidden from his eyes. People have been gazing at the stars as long as . . . well, as long as there have been people. Yet in all those years, astronomers saw only a fraction of what the night sky contains.

Now exciting advances in the tools people use to study the stars are opening new windows on the sky—and changing our view of the universe. Ever more sensitive instruments are gathering not just starlight but radio waves, X rays, gamma rays, and more from deep space. With the information they obtain, astronomers hope not only to find new stars but to learn their secrets—how they form, develop, and die. Eventually, they hope to learn the secrets of the universe itself.

CAPTURING STARLIGHT

The first telescopes were made at the beginning of the 1600's. They were simple tubes that magnified the light of stars with a series of lenses. With such a telescope, Galileo discovered the craters on the moon, the rings of Saturn, and some of Jupiter's moons.

These refracting telescopes, as they are called, had a drawback: The larger their lenses, the more their images became blurred and distorted. That meant there was a limit to how large a refracting telescope could be, and how much it could magnify. In 1668, Sir Isaac Newton overcame the problem with a new kind of telescope that used a concave mirror rather than a lens to focus and magnify light. Reflecting telescopes like Newton's didn't distort images the way refracting telescopes did, and so they could be made far larger.

By the middle of the 20th century, huge reflecting telescopes were being built—the 200-inch (5-meter) Hale Telescope on Mount Palomar in California, and the 236-inch (6-meter) Bolshoi Alt-azimuth Telescope in the Soviet Union. But that seemed to be the limit. Besides magnifying the stars, mirrors over 200 inches in diameter also magnified the turbulence of the Earth's atmosphere, which blurred their images.

Astronomers have tried to solve the problem of air turbulence by placing their telescopes on high mountains, where the air is thin. For example, major observatories are located on Mauna Kea, a volcano in Hawaii, and at Las Campanas in the Chilean Andes.

Today, astronomers have another way to solve the turbulence problem: by placing telescopes *beyond* the Earth's atmosphere, in space. Small telescopes have already been placed on satellites; the information they receive is transmitted back to Earth and analyzed by computers. Plans for several large space telescopes have been delayed, but astronomers hope such a telescope will be orbited in the near future. There are even long-range plans to place observatories on the moon.

Several new projects are also under way on the ground. One is the Keck Telescope, which is to be placed on the top of Mauna Kea. Its huge 394-inch (10-meter) mirror will be made of 36 six-sided segments, each of which will be aligned by computers 100 times a second. The telescope's designers say it will be powerful enough to capture the light of a single candle from a distance as far as the moon. An even larger telescope, with a mirror made of 72 separate segments, is planned for the famous Las Campanas observatory in Chile.

Another proposed telescope, nicknamed the "two-shooter," would combine images from two giant 315-inch (8-meter) mirrors, in much the way binoculars combine images from two lenses. And designers in Europe and the United States are working on plans for telescopes with four 315-inch mirrors. These mirrors could be trained on separate objects, or they could be combined to give more than three times the power of a 200-inch telescope.

Scientists are also experimenting with new ways of making giant mirrors. Traditionally, these mirrors are made from blocks of glass that are painstakingly ground down to the proper curve. The process takes years. In one new method, however, the glass is formed in the proper curve while it's still hot—by spinning the oven in which it is cast. The faster the oven spins, the deeper the curve that's formed.

Astronomers have also turned their attention to refining the images their telescopes receive. In the newest telescopes, images are received by electronic detectors, which transmit their images to a computer screen. Because the detectors are far more sensitive to light than the human eye or a photographic plate, they reveal much more. Astronomers can see farther into space, detecting dim, distant stars that were previously unknown.

CAPTURING THE INVISIBLE

Stars and other objects in space radiate energy, but only a small portion of that energy is produced as visible light. The rest is invisible—infrared and ultraviolet light, X rays, gamma rays, and radio waves. Astronomers are developing better ways of capturing these clues to the stars' secrets as well.

Radio telescopes use huge, saucer-shaped antennas to capture radio waves from distant objects in space. These radio waves pass freely through clouds of dust in space and through the clouds in the Earth's atmosphere. The wider a radio telescope is, the more detail it can detect. Today the most powerful radio telescope, in New Mexico, has 27 antennas. But scientists have started to link such telescopes together to get even more detail. One new project will consist of ten radio telescopes built at different sites across the United States and then linked together to act as one.

Sensitive radio telescopes can locate and map distant galaxies and measure the distances to them. They have discovered pulsars—the remains of old stars that exploded

and now send radio signals sweeping across space as they spin. And by detecting materials that are the ingredients of life on Earth, radio telescopes may one day give astronomers clues to the presence of life elsewhere in the universe.

Infrared light can also penetrate stellar dust. New telescopes and cameras that can capture and record it are revealing newborn stars that were hidden dust clouds and old, dying stars that give off only dim light. Because warm air currents can disturb infrared images, this equipment is usually housed in specially cooled, tightly insulated mountaintop observatories.

The hottest objects in space radiate most of their energy as ultraviolet light. And most of this light is screened out by the Earth's atmosphere. But with satellite detectors placed in orbit above the atmosphere, astronomers can detect it. Such satellites were used to study Halley's comet on its visit to Earth in 1985–86.

Like ultraviolet light, X rays and gamma rays are screened out by the atmosphere. But from satellites, astronomers have detected X-ray emissions from strange and fascinating objects in outer space. One is a pair of stars, one orbiting the other, that are invisible but send out blasts of radiation in the form of X rays. Since X rays are given off only in bursts of enormous energy, they may give clues to the formation and death of stars. Bursts of gamma rays have also been detected, and scientists aren't sure where they originate. One theory is that they come from neutron stars, the dense, collapsed cores of stars that have exploded.

Visible and invisible, all the information gathered by these new tools of astronomy is producing a revised picture of space. If you could count all the stars you can see in the night sky, you might come up with about 4,000. But scientists now estimate that there are 400 *billion* stars in our galaxy, the Milky Way, alone—and that there may be as many as 10 billion other galaxies beyond it.

With these billions of stars are quasars, pulsars, clouds of interstellar dust, and objects that remain mysterious. It seems that although people have been studying the sky for thousands of years, they are just beginning to see it.

Proposed telescopes: Above, the "two shooter" would combine images from two giant mirrors in much the same way that binoculars combine images from two lenses. Below, this telescope's four giant mirrors could combine light to give three times the power of a 200-inch telescope.

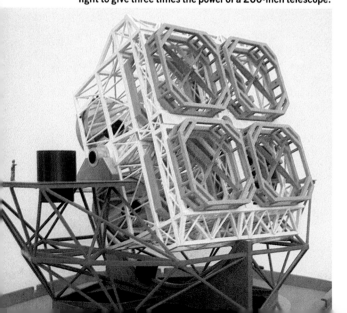

Supernova 1987A (the starlike glow above) gave a rare look at an exploding star.

A STAR EXPLODES

In 1987, astronomers trained their telescopes on one of the most exciting stellar events in memory. It was a supernova—an exploding star—that suddenly appeared in the night sky in February. The supernova, named 1987A, was discovered by Ian Shelton, a Canadian astronomer working at the Las Campanas Observatory in Chile. It was about 160,000 light years from Earth, making it the closest and most easily studied supernova since the year 1604. (A light year is the distance that light travels in a year—nearly 6 trillion miles, or 10 trillion kilometers. Supernova 1987A thus formed 160,000 years ago, and its light was just now reaching Earth.)

A supernova is caused by the collapse of a very massive star. There are two ways in which this can happen. In a Type I supernova, the star pulls matter from a nearby star until it becomes so huge that it collapses. In a Type II supernova, the core of the star cools and, without the core's intense heat, its outer layers of gas collapse. (Scientists weren't immediately sure which type 1987A was.) In either case, the result of the collapse is a huge explosion that sends shock waves and an expanding shell of glowing gas hurtling out into space.

Astronomers turned all their most sophisticated equipment on the explosion, gathering reams of data in the weeks it was visible. Besides revealing secrets about the death of stars, they hoped that the supernova would shed light on other mysteries. For example, one theory holds that the shock waves from supernovas and the material they throw off help form new stars and planets.

The scientists quickly discovered that 1987A didn't behave the way supernovas were supposed to behave. The explosion was caused by a middle-aged star—not an old star, as most supernovas are. Instead of growing bright and then quickly fading, it brightened, leveled off, and then brightened again before gradually growing dimmer. And when astronomers studied images of the supernova, they saw a second glowing spot beside it. "Once again," said one astronomer, "nature has been more imaginative than the astronomers."

Supernova 1987A could be seen without a telescope, and it looked like a moderately bright star. Supernovas that bright occur only four times in each thousand years. But astronomers—both professional and amateur—often detect less brilliant explosions. In fact, an amateur astronomer in Australia, using a homemade telescope, has discovered fifteen supernovas since 1981. So when you gaze at the stars, keep your eyes peeled for something new.

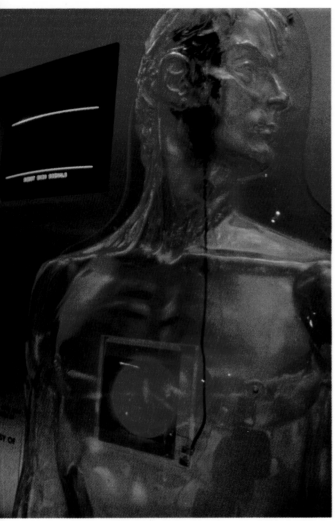

This robot said, "Hey! Cut it out!" when visitors at the exhibit touched its pressure-sensitive "skin."

ROBOTS AND BEYOND

Robots and other "intelligent machines" can perform amazing feats. They play chess, draw pictures, help assemble cars, "speak," "hear," and "see." A typical industrial robotics system takes a minute and a half to complete a task that takes a human worker 30 to 40 minutes. Moreover, the system does the job with 98 percent accuracy, compared to 65 percent accuracy for the worker.

But are robots really as intelligent as people? Well, no robot is clever enough to tie a pair of shoelaces. Most of those that "speak" and "hear" use fewer words than the average 3-year-old child. Those that "see" have limited vision—one robot, specially equipped with two video-camera eyes, took more than an hour to cross a room while avoiding obstacles in its path.

Despite their limitations, however, robots are getting better all the time. Artificial intelligence—the art of making machines that perform tasks requiring intelligence—is an exciting field, one where new developments are occurring all the time. In 1987, this field became the subject of a special exhibit, "Robots and Beyond: The Age of Intelligent Machines." The exhibit opened at the Museum of Science in Boston and was scheduled to travel to seven other U.S. cities before closing in 1989.

The exhibit focused on four areas of artificial intelligence: robot senses (the ability to see, feel, and hear); robots in the workplace; expert systems (computers that act as experts in a given subject); and robots of the future.

Robot Senses. Vision remains one of the most difficult problems in artificial intelligence, and machines that can see as well as people have yet to be developed. But already existing are scanners that can read printed material and bar codes on the packages in supermarkets. The exhibit featured a machine that could read text aloud, in a computer synthesized voice, and one that could recognize simple objects like combs and keys.

Another demonstration showed how machines can be programmed to recognize objects using motion cues. Visitors walking up to one display could watch themselves on a video screen—but when they stopped moving, they disappeared. A companion display took the opposite tack: As long as visitors stood still, they could see themselves. When they moved, the image was scrambled.

Robots can also respond to the human voice. Such robots are used in some factories, and the exhibit had a device that allowed visitors to play a game by talking to a computer. Most robots that can "hear" have a vocabulary of just 100 to 1,000 words, but a few of the newest systems can recognize as many as 20,000 words. But recognizing words—written or spoken—isn't the same as understanding language or using it to form sentences that make sense. Computers and robots require extensive programming to understand even the simplest statements.

Another display at the exhibit demonstrated the sense of touch. Visitors who touched a patch of "skin" on this robot heard responses that ranged from "Oooh, I can feel that" to "Hey! Cut it out!" The "skin" was really piezoelectric film that changed pressure into electrical impulses.

Workers and Experts. Robots have made their greatest gains in the workplace, where they are taking over many monotonous and dangerous factory jobs. The exhibit offered insight into how robot workers do their jobs. One display showed how robot "muscles" are precisely controlled by computers and special motors. Others showed robots at work on an assembly line. And visitors could use a computer keyboard to control tiny robots working in a factory made of plastic building blocks.

Expert systems are computer programs that solve problems usually left to such experts as doctors, lawyers, geologists, and engineers. One such program, for example, takes information about land regions and forecasts what valuable minerals might be found there. Expert systems are stocked with information from living experts—not just facts, but hunches and rules of thumb that the real experts follow.

Several displays at the exhibit showed how expert systems work. One was a computerized game of three-dimensional tic-tac-toe. This machine had seven "experts" on tap, one for every aspect of the game. For example, one part of the program looked only for winning moves, and one looked for defensive moves. And another part of the program weighed the recommendations and decided among them.

Into the Future. Scientists estimate that, to be as intelligent as the human brain, a computer would have to be as big as the state of Texas and 100 stories tall. But machines are already making inroads into activities once considered for people only. The exhibit had a machine that could compose music in any style and one that could draw—not just mechanical drawings, but works of art. That raised a question: Were these machines creative, or were the true artists the people who programmed them?

The exhibit also showed how robots may help people in the future. Hero 2000—a mobile computer with sensors, a voice, and an arm—was on display. This robot is designed to be a home helper, and the day may come when every home has a similar device.

It was a robot, of course, that best summed up the exhibit. Jorel, a machine that mimicked human voice and movement, greeted visitors by announcing, "Humans, you are witnessing the beginning of a great new era."

Omnibot, a home robot of today, will most probably be replaced with more sophisticated "helpers" in the future.

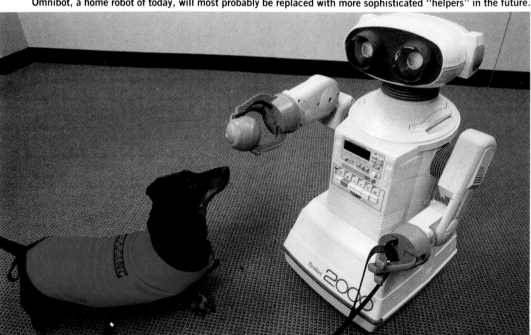

121

PLANT PUZZLES

- How can a plant reproduce if its seeds never fall to the ground?
- What do you get if you cross a firefly with a tobacco plant?
- Can a plant talk, or at least send out messages?
- What plant produces the world's largest flower?

These questions may sound as if they come from a trivia game or a book of silly riddles. But in fact, scientific researchers have turned up fascinating—and surprising—answers to all these plant puzzles.

ROADBLOCKS TO REPRODUCTION

Flowering plants reproduce through pollination, usually with the help of insects. As insects fly from blossom to blossom to drink the sweet nectar produced by the flowers, they carry a few grains of pollen from the stamens of one bloom to the pistil (ovary) of the next. There, the pollen fertilizes eggs, which develop into seeds and fall to the ground. In time, the seeds grow into new plants.

This reproduction process is difficult for a beautiful South African shrub called *Gar-*

Only certain animals can help the lovely *Gardenia thunbergia* reproduce. This is because the flower's nectar is hard to reach in the long, thin tubes where it is produced; and the plant's seeds are contained in hard-shelled fruits that don't break open.

denia thunbergia. The first roadblock that the plant faces has to do with pollination. Unlike the flowers of cultivated gardenias, the flower of *thunbergia* is a long, thin tube topped by a ring of white petals. Nectar is produced at the base of the tube—well out of reach of most insects. But help comes from a long-tongued nocturnal moth. Some species of hawkmoths (sometimes called sphinx moths) have tongues up to 5½ inches (14 centimeters) long! It's easy for them to reach the nectar, and they carry pollen from shrub to shrub on their nighttime feeding rounds. (The moth's tongue, or proboscis, rolls into a neat coil when the insect isn't feeding.)

Gardenia thunbergia must get past yet another roadblock to reproduction. After the shrub has been pollinated, the seeds develop inside oval-shaped fruits, about 3 to 4 inches (7 to 10 centimeters) long. But the fruits have hard wooden shells that don't break open, and they never fall from the branches.

If the seeds never fall to the ground, how does the plant reproduce? Again, animals come to the rescue. The fruits are a favorite snack for several species of antelope and Cape buffalo. The animals chew open the woody shells and eat the seeds. Then, scientists think, the seeds pass through the animals' digestive tracts and are deposited on the ground. This unusual method of scattering seeds seems to be very successful—the *Gardenia thunbergia* is found throughout the high grasslands of southern and eastern Africa.

GROWING AND GLOWING

If you cross a firefly with a tobacco plant, you don't get a self-lighting cigarette. You get a tobacco plant that glows in the dark.

Scientists at the University of California at San Diego produced such plants in an experiment in genetic engineering. In genetic engineering, scientists alter genetic material or transplant genes from one cell to another. The field holds great potential in many areas, from farming to medicine.

The California scientists wanted to learn more about how genes work. All cells contain all the genes needed for all body functions. Cells perform different functions because only some of the genes are "switched on." Thus, in a plant, genes order

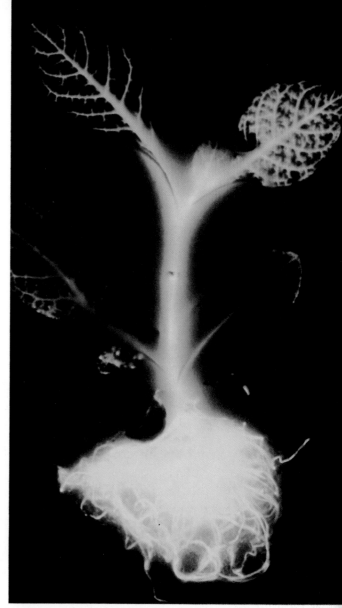

The light-producing gene from a cell of a firefly was transferred into the cells of a tobacco plant. The result: a tobacco plant that glows in the dark!

some cells to form leaves; others, stems; and still others, roots. But how—and when—are the genes that direct the cells turned on and off?

Most genes perform their jobs unseen, making it hard for scientists to study them. An exception is the gene that allows fireflies to produce light. Basically, the gene tells firefly cells to produce luciferase, an enzyme. When luciferase combines with oxygen and other chemicals in the cells, the firefly lights up.

The scientists reasoned that the luciferase gene was an ideal subject for genetic engineering because the light would make it easy to see whether the gene was working after a transplant. Using special chemicals, they "snipped" the gene from firefly cells and inserted it into the genetic material of a bacterium that infects plants. The bacterium containing the firefly gene was used to infect tobacco plant cells, which were then grown into full-fledged plants.

The last step in the experiment was to irrigate the plants with a solution containing the other chemicals found in a firefly's cells that are needed to produce the firefly's light. The result was a glowing tobacco plant. (The faint glow can be seen only in a dark room, and it is recorded with special photographic techniques.) The scientists now want to link the firefly gene to specific plant genes—such as those that order cells to form leaves. Thus they hope to be able to *see* how and when plant genes are turned on.

AN ALARM PLANT

Can a plant talk? Of course not. But a plant may be able to tell you something all the same. For example, researchers have found a plant that can sound an alarm—against air pollution.

The plant is *Tradescantia,* a hybrid form of the spiderwort, which is often found in the wild. *Tradescantia* looks quite ordinary: It has long, grassy leaves; waxy, knobby stems; and tiny bluish-lavender flowers. But in polluted air, the plant does something quite extraordinary—it changes color.

Tradescantia is a cross between a pink-flowering spiderwort and a blue-flowering spiderwort. The blue color is dominant, so in clean air the flowers are blue. But certain pollutants can alter the genes that determine flower color. If the plant is exposed to these pollutants just before it blooms, tiny hairs in the stamens (the pollen-bearing structures at the center of the flower) change from blue to pink.

The plant has great promise as a way of detecting harmful substances in the air. It's said to be sensitive to low-level radiation, pesticides, fungicides, and other harmful chemicals, as well as to ordinary industrial air pollution. And since no single plant species can be expected to react to all possible

The *tradescantia* is a hybrid form of the spiderwort, and its flowers are usually blue. But if the plant is exposed to certain pollutants before it blooms, the flowers turn pink.

Rafflesia arnoldii, a plant that grows in Indonesia, produces the largest flowers in the world. Not only are the flowers huge and exotic, they also have a distinctive smell—like rotten meat.

forms of pollution, scientists are testing other plants to see if they have similar talents. Among those being studied are corn, barley, and a variety of mustard plant. One day, it may be possible to monitor the quality of the air simply by looking at your garden.

THE WORLD'S LARGEST FLOWER

What plant produces the largest flower in the world? The answer to that trivia question is *Rafflesia arnoldii*, a plant that grows in the rain forests of Sumatra and Borneo, in Indonesia. But there's nothing trivial about the flowers—they can measure more than 3 feet (1 meter) across and weigh about 15 pounds (7 kilograms).

Rafflesia arnoldii was named for two British explorers, Sir Thomas Stamford Raffles and Dr. Joseph Arnold, who spotted it in southwestern Sumatra in 1818. Indonesians call it *bunga patma,* or lotus flower. It's quite rare. And as its rain-forest habitat is gradually destroyed by advancing civilization, it's becoming rarer still.

The plant is something of a mystery. It has no proper roots and no leaves to provide nourishment. Instead, it grows out of the roots or stems of certain tropical vines. Just how the tiny seeds take hold and start to grow is a bit of a puzzle in itself. But after about a year of growth inside the host plant, a bud about 2 inches (5 centimeters) wide bursts through the surface. The bud continues to grow for nine months before it opens completely to reveal its full splendor.

The flower is not only huge—it's exotic, with heavy reddish-brown petals marked by pale patches. It emits a distinctive scent that some people have compared to the odor of rotten meat. The scent has given rise to some other common names for the plant: corpse flower and stinking corpse lily. It also draws flies, which are the plant's chief pollinators. Some *Rafflesia* flowers are males and produce only pollen; others are females and produce only eggs. The flies must carry the pollen from one to the other.

Although it takes months to develop, the *Rafflesia* flower blooms for just four days and then dies. But if the plant is a female, it produces a fruit filled with thousands of seeds. The fruit ripens in about seven months, and the mysterious cycle of this exotic plant begins again.

CD-ROM: SHARING INFORMATION A NEW WAY

Your teacher has assigned a report on penguins. How do you get the information you need? You could go to the library and spend a few hours searching through the card catalog and the indexes of various encyclopedias. Or, perhaps, you could sit down at your computer, tap a few keys, and within seconds have the information you need right on your computer screen.

The technology that makes this quick research possible is called CD-ROM. The letters "CD" stand for *compact disc*—this system uses the same shiny plastic discs that have revolutionized the recording industry. But instead of Bach or the Beatles, CD-ROM discs contain text and drawings. The letters "ROM" stand for *read-only memory*. That means that the information on CD-ROM discs can be "read" but not erased. Nor can you record your own data on the disc.

CD-ROM is one of the most exciting new technologies to come along in years. And the possibilities it holds for the future are even more intriguing.

HOW IT WORKS

CD-ROM is the result of a marriage between the compact disc and the personal computer. To use it, you need a special disc player connected to a computer. You also need retrieval software, which tells the computer how to find specific information on the compact disc and how to display it on the computer screen.

The information on the compact disc is in code. This code is etched onto the surface of the disc in the form of microscopic pits. When you put the disc in your CD-ROM player, a laser "reads" the pattern of pits, translates it into the code, and sends the information to the computer. And the computer translates the code into words and pictures and displays them on the screen.

CD-ROM's biggest advantage can be summed up in a single word: convenience. One compact disc just 4.72 inches (12 centimeters) in diameter can store about 100 million words—the equivalent of about 150,000 printed pages. That's a lot of information. For example, the entire text of the *Academic American Encyclopedia*—a 20-volume set—is available on CD-ROM. And it takes up only about a fifth of a disc!

Finding, or retrieving, the information is a snap. To use a CD-ROM encyclopedia for your report on penguins, for example, you just type the word "penguin" on your computer. In seconds, a list of every article containing the word "penguin" appears on the computer screen. You can then look at the article title list and choose the article you want to read. After you have read the article, you might wish to print it out or save it to a floppy disc; both are easy to do.

These advantages have made CD-ROM useful for all sorts of research—in businesses and labs as well as in homes and libraries. Instead of paging through huge catalogs, manufacturers can use CD-ROM to find the equipment they need instantly. One company has stored a list of 370,000 poisons and their antidotes on a compact disc that is being used by hospitals. When the name of a poison is typed into the computer, the correct antidote appears on the screen. The system will even calculate the correct dosage, based on the weight of the victim.

FOR THE FUTURE

These uses are only the beginning. New systems are being developed that will make compact discs even more exciting. The discs of the future will contain much more than text and computer graphics. They'll combine all kinds of material—sound, still photographs, even motion pictures.

In one system being developed, no computer is needed—you enter your instructions right into a special CD player that is connected to a television. (The CD player has a computer built into it.) Because this system will be simple to use, its developers hope it will become a popular form of home entertainment. They plan to combine sound and pictures to produce game and educational discs. For example, one disc being planned is a sort of time machine. A user picks a year and sees a map, headlines, and audio-visual presentations that show what the world was like in that year.

Another new system, using a regular computer, would bring full-motion video to compact discs. Until recently, this wasn't practical because the information that was required to display motion pictures took up too much space on the disc—so much space that an entire CD-ROM disc could store only about 30 seconds of full-motion video. But researchers have found a way to compress that information so that it takes up only a fraction of the space. In this way, a disc can store a full hour of motion video. When the disc is played, the information is fed through special computer circuits that restore full sound and picture qualities.

In the future, these circuits may be used for discs that combine motion pictures with still pictures, text, and sound. And users won't simply watch as the discs are played.

By entering instructions into the machine, they will actually control the presentations.

Some experimental discs have already been made. One is an educational adventure that takes you on a "walk" through an ancient Mayan site. At any point, you can stop, turn, retrace your steps, or switch to text about the Mayans. Another disc lets you simulate a jet flight over the English countryside. A third allows you to design a living room, choosing furniture, paint, and wallpaper from a "catalog" of photographs that can be displayed on the screen. You can even view the room from different angles.

This exciting technology is just in its early stages. It will get bigger and better, opening up whole new ways of sharing information.

JENNY TESAR
Designer, Computer Programs

SECRETS
OF SNOWFLAKES

If you've ever caught a snowflake on your mitten or your sleeve and stopped to look closely at it, you know how beautiful these delicate ice crystals are. Captured under a microscope, snowflakes reveal the full range of their beauty. Each is a crystal clear, intricate, six-pointed star, and each is different from the next.

Snowflakes are full of secrets. What causes them to form in six-sided shapes? What's responsible for their patterned beauty? Why do no two snowflakes look exactly the same? Scientists have puzzled over these questions for years. Now, with the help of computers and mathematical models, they've begun to find answers.

The birth of a snowflake begins after water evaporates from the surface of the earth and rises as much as 6 miles (10 kilometers) into the atmosphere. There, where temperatures are colder, the water vapor condenses into tiny droplets and forms clouds.

What happens next depends on the temperature. Below -40°F (-40°C), the droplets freeze instantly into ice crystals. At temperatures that are warmer but still below freezing, the droplets need a "seed"—a particle, such as a speck of dust—to freeze around. When a suitable particle comes along, the water droplets evaporate and recondense on the particle's surface. The specific structure and electrical charge of a water molecule cause all ice crystals to have a hexagonal (six-sided) shape.

Now the ice crystal begins to grow into a snowflake. Its final intricate design is determined by the changes in temperature and moisture the crystal encounters as it swirls around in the cloud and begins to fall to earth. As it descends, it picks up more water droplets. Most of the moisture condenses on the six corners of the hexagon because they stick out farthest. The corners begin to grow into long arms, or dendrites, each with a pattern of branches.

When the snowflake meets a change in temperature or moisture, its pattern of growth changes. No two snowflakes take exactly the same path to earth, so each encounters slightly different conditions. Thus each snowflake is slightly different from the next. But within each snowflake, all the dendrites encounter the same conditions at the same times, and they grow in almost exactly the same way. This is what makes the snowflake appear so symmetrical.

Scientists have learned much about the general ways in which different conditions affect the growth of snowflakes. They have long known, for example, that at temperatures above 5°F (-15°C), the water droplets tend to form needle-like crystals rather than flat, lacy stars. Extreme cold tends to produce dendrites with sharper tips.

Now, with the help of computers, some scientists are starting to unravel the complex physical forces that determine *precisely* how snowflakes form. One computer program can take information on temperature, humidity, and other factors and produce a picture of the snowflake that would form in those conditions. But the calculations are so complex that it takes the machine eight hours.

Tiny changes in weather conditions can produce almost infinite variations in the shape of snowflakes. But mathematicians say it may not be true that no two snowflakes are ever exactly the same. There may be 18 million snowflakes in a cubic foot of snow, and snow has been falling for a couple of billion years. It's likely that, at some point, at least one snowflake formed that was just like one that had formed before. But it's still unlikely that you'll ever see two identical flakes at the same time.

Sometimes weather conditions make it impossible even to distinguish individual flakes. In warmer air, the crystals link together to form clumps of snow, sometimes up to an inch across. Such a clump may contain several thousand snowflakes.

And when snowflakes of any size reach the ground, they change their shape. Even if the crystals don't melt, evaporation and condensation reshape them into tiny smooth-sided granules within a very short time. The beautiful patterns disappear, taking the snowflakes' secrets with them.

FEARFUL PHOBIAS

Darkness. Bridges. Flying in airplanes. Thunder and lightning. Riding in elevators. Snakes. Spiders. A visit to the dentist.

You may consider these things unpleasant, or you may think nothing of them at all. You may think some of them—an airplane trip or a window-rattling thunderstorm—are fun and exciting. On the other hand, you may turn pale and start to shake at the mere thought of one of these objects or situations. For some people, they're sources of deep, overwhelming fear.

These are people who suffer from phobias,

or irrational fears. People may develop phobias toward almost anything—even objects, situations, and activities that other people consider pleasant. A person may be terribly afraid of cats or dogs, for example. People have even been reported to panic at the sight of such everyday objects as eyeglasses and three-legged stools.

These fears may sound silly to people who don't share them. But to people who have them, phobias are no joke. Phobias can disrupt people's lives, causing them to drive miles out of their way to avoid crossing a bridge, to give up a vacation to avoid getting on an airplane, or even to stay home all the time.

Phobias are far from rare. Many people have them—an estimated thirteen million in the United States alone. Psychologists who have studied these fears aren't sure what causes them. But they have learned one thing: Most phobias can be cured.

FEARS OF ALL KINDS

The term "phobia" comes from the Greek and Latin words for fear. Dozens of specific phobias have been given Greek and Latin names, too. Claustrophobia, for example, is the fear of being trapped or confined. The name comes from the Latin word *claustrum*, meaning "confined place."

Psychologists divide phobias into five major groups. A **simple phobia** is a fear of a specific object or situation. Fear of heights is a common example of a simple phobia. Other simple phobias include fear of elevators, tunnels, driving, flying, crossing water, swimming, darkness, crowds, strangers, and drafts.

Social phobias are fears of public embarrassment. A person with a social phobia may panic at the thought of speaking before a group, for instance. The fears of eating in public and of signing one's name in front of others are also examples of social phobias.

Some people suffer from **animal phobias**— fear of dogs, cats, birds, or other animals. Fear of snakes is common, and so is the fear of spiders and certain insects, even moths and other innocent-looking bugs. There are also **injury phobias,** in which the person panics at the sight of blood or the thought of injury. People who suffer from injury phobias are often terrified by the thought of a visit to the doctor or the dentist.

Agoraphobia is the most complex form of phobia. This is the fear of being in open spaces or away from a safe person or place. A person with agoraphobia may start to panic anytime he or she is in an open, public place, like a shopping mall. People with severe agoraphobia may be terrified to leave their homes at all or to be left alone for even a few minutes.

People who suffer from phobias don't simply shy away when they're confronted with the objects and situations they fear. They experience what psychologists call a panic reaction. They may shake or sweat and feel dizzy. Their hearts race, they feel short of breath, and they may feel as if they were choking or smothering. Worst of all, they're overwhelmed by fears that they'll do something uncontrollable, faint, or even die. A person who is afraid of driving across bridges, for example, may think, "What if I lose control of the car?" A person who is afraid of heights may think, "What if I faint —and fall?"

Most people who have phobias realize that their fears don't make sense. But the panic reaction is so unpleasant that they go out of their way to avoid the situations that produce it. They may even start to panic at the thought of having the reaction. Then they develop phobophobia—the fear of fear itself.

FINDING CAUSES AND CURES

Psychologists who have studied phobias say that the people who suffer from them are perfectly normal in all other ways. They are good family members, good workers, and good friends. Often, they're warm, sensitive, and imaginative people. Why, then, do the phobias develop?

Many researchers believe that most animal phobias stem from frightening experiences in childhood. Events that older children and adults take in stride—an insect bite, a barking dog, a scratching cat—can make a big impression on a small child. This theory is supported by the fact that animal phobias often begin in childhood, while other phobias usually emerge between the ages of 15 and 30.

The other phobias are more difficult to explain. Frightening experiences may play a part, but heredity and upbringing have also been blamed. Stress may also be a factor. Many phobias seem to begin or worsen when people experience some stressful event, such as the death of a loved one or a move to a new city.

WHAT'S EVERYONE SO AFRAID OF?

Acrophobia—fear of heights

Agoraphobia—fear of open spaces or being away from a safe place or person

Ailurophobia—fear of cats

Amaxophobia—fear of vehicles or driving

Aquaphobia—fear of water or swimming

Astraphobia (or **tonitophobia**)—fear of thunder and lightning

Aviophobia—fear of flying

Blennophobia—fear of slime

Cathisophobia—fear of sitting down

Claustrophobia—fear of confinement

Cynophobia—fear of dogs

Entomophobia—fear of insects

Gephyrophobia—fear of crossing a bridge or large body of water

Murophobia—fear of mice

Nyctophobia—fear of darkness

Ochlophobia—fear of crowds

Ophidiophobia—fear of snakes

Panophobia—fear of everything

Phobophobia—fear of fears

Selenophobia—fear of the moon

Tropophobia—fear of moving

Xenophobia—fear of strangers

Zoophobia—fear of animals in general

UNLUCKY THIRTEEN

The year 1987 was a dreadful one for people who suffer from triskaidekaphobia—fear of the number thirteen. The thirteenth day of the month fell on a Friday three times, in February, March, and November. And as triskaidekaphobes know, that's an especially unlucky combination.

More a superstition than a true, panic-inducing phobia, triskaidekaphobia has a long history. The idea that thirteen is an unlucky number reaches back to ancient Greece and to Biblical times. In the Middle Ages, witches were thought to gather in covens of thirteen members. Some people still believe that it's unlucky to travel on the thirteenth day of the month or to have thirteen people at dinner. In Paris, a triskaidekaphobe can even hire a fourteenth guest at the dinner table.

Combining thirteen with Friday makes matters even worse. Friday has long been considered an unlucky day—right through the 1800's, executions were held on that day, which was called Hangman's Day.

Every year has at least one Friday the Thirteenth. No year has more than three, so 1987 had the maximum. But, fortunately for triskaidekaphobes, this won't happen again until 1998.

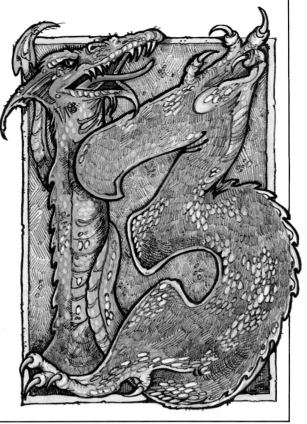

Regardless of their cause, phobias create more than inconvenience for the people who suffer from them. They can also disrupt family life. And they can affect business—by some estimates, the fear of flying costs the airline industry as much as $1.5 billion a year.

But as research has led to better understanding of phobias in recent years, new methods of treatment have been developed. In the United States, there are now more than 50 clinics and hundreds of specialists who treat phobias. They are able to cure the problem 70 to 80 percent of the time. There are also special programs for specific phobias. Some airlines, for example, sponsor programs for people who are afraid to fly.

Several different techniques, including psychotherapy and the short-term use of drugs that can block panic attacks, are used. One popular treatment technique is called exposure therapy. In this technique, a group of people who suffer from the same phobia meet with a therapist and learn how to deal with their fear. They also learn ways to reduce panic and stay in control, such as counting backward by threes from 100 or reciting a poem or the words of a song. Deep breathing and other relaxation techniques are also taught.

Then they begin to confront the real situation. People who are afraid to fly, for example, may just sit in a parked airliner and practice relaxation techniques. The exposure is gradually increased until, finally, they're able to take long airplane trips without fear. A person who's afraid to drive across bridges may start with dozens of trips across short spans and gradually work up to longer, higher bridges.

Most of the time, people in these programs find that they can control their fears and end the panic attacks—and resume normal, happy lives.

MAKE & DO

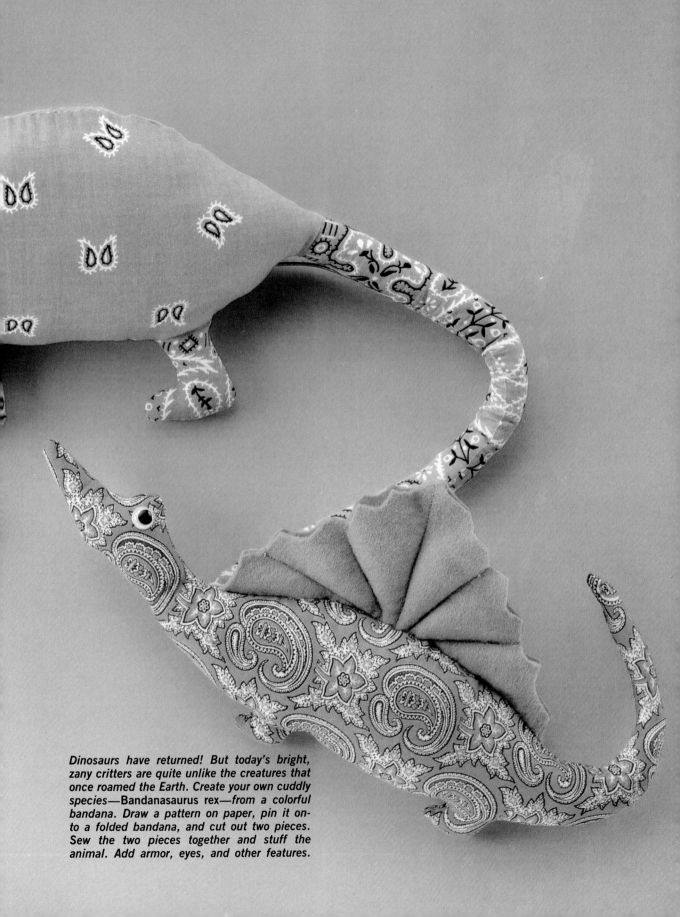

Dinosaurs have returned! But today's bright, zany critters are quite unlike the creatures that once roamed the Earth. Create your own cuddly species—Bandanasaurus rex—from a colorful bandana. Draw a pattern on paper, pin it onto a folded bandana, and cut out two pieces. Sew the two pieces together and stuff the animal. Add armor, eyes, and other features.

COUNTRY WOOD

Spring flowers, folk dolls, calico cats—capture the charm of the country with these delightful craft projects. Each uses ready-made wood cutouts that are available in craft stores, and you can buy hundreds of different kinds. They can be used to make clothes and key racks, wall plaques, table centerpieces, tree ornaments, even jewelry. It's a wonderful way to use your imagination and have a lot of fun at the same time.

Whichever project you decide on, certain basic supplies are needed: fine sandpaper, acrylic paints, paintbrushes, polyurethane or clear acrylic spray, and glue. If you're making an object that's meant to be hung on a wall, you'll need a sawtooth hanger and small nails with which to attach the hanger to the back of the object.

And no matter what the project, certain basic steps should be followed: First, sand each piece of wood until there are no rough edges. Then paint the pieces. After they dry, give them a second coat of paint. Sometimes you may decide to stain an object rather than paint it. This works well for baskets, boxes, plaques, and other background pieces onto which you'll glue the wood cutouts. Stained items don't need a second coat unless you want to give them a deeper color. Last, cover the painted or stained surfaces with several coats of polyurethane or acrylic spray. Let the pieces dry in-between coats. (Take care not to use polyurethane or acrylic on surfaces that will be glued together. These coatings tend to diminish glue's holding power.)

Now let's see how the objects shown here are made. The wood tulips pictured on the opposite page are placed in a mushroom basket that can be gotten at a supermarket. But any type of basket, box, or other container can be used. Paint the flowers and container in colors that will match the decor of the room in which the object will be placed. Glue thick layers of foamboard to the inside bottom of the container. Then embed the flower stems in the foamboard and secure them in place with glue. A layer of fine wood shavings called excelsior is used to cover the foamboard. Excelsior is a widely used packing material. It's also available in craft stores.

You can keep your room tidy with a peg rack like the one shown below. Paint the peg rack a bright color. If you wish, paint the pegs a different color than the background wood. Decide which wood cutouts you'd like to attach to the top of the rack— children, animals, a row of houses, a black silhouetted horse and

carriage. With a pencil, lightly draw designs on the cutouts (they can also be painted solid colors). When you paint the designs, make sure to let each color dry before you border it with a second color. When the paint is completely dry, glue the cutouts to the rack and use the polyurethane or acrylic spray.

For a whimsical touch, wrap a string of hearts around one of the pegs. Each of the hearts shown here actually consists of two wood cutouts—a large heart painted red and a small one painted pink. The small heart is glued to the center of the large heart. The string is glued to the backs of both large hearts.

A plaque holding a gaggle of geese or two smiling cats will steal your heart—or the heart of anyone you might give it to. Many different backgrounds can be used: fence designs (such as the ones shown here), squares, ovals, circles. Paint or stain the background. Then paint your country critters and a big red heart. Center these on the plaque and glue them in place. Cover with polyurethane or acrylic.

Basket lids are another popular background for country crafts.

These are available in craft stores, but sometimes you can get them from supermarkets. They can be decorated in many different ways, using not only wood cutouts but also pinecones, dried flowers, colorful bows, and stuffed calico animals.

The basket lid shown here holds half a straw basket, made by cutting a lightweight basket in half. The half basket is attached to the stained lid by using glue from a hot glue gun. Bright green satin ribbons are woven through openings in the basket and held in place with glue. A matching bow is glued to the front. The basket is filled with white foam packing "peanuts." Excelsior or sphagnum moss can also be used. Three brightly painted tulips are set into the basket.

Basket lids can be edged with curved messages such as "Welcome," "Season's Greetings," or "I love country!" You can buy individual letters to create your message, or you can buy curved messages all ready for painting.

Try your hand at these fun crafts. You'll be delighted with the charm of country wood!

SEASONS OF SPICE

In spring, many trees are covered with pink blossoms. As the blossoms die, green leaves open, covering the trees through the warm days of summer. The leaves turn to shades of yellow and red in autumn, then fall to the ground. In winter, the trees' brown branches are exposed to view.

Using dried herbs and spices, you can make a wall hanging that re-creates this passing of the four seasons. Use sesame seeds or onion flakes for the blossoms of spring (you can give them a pink tone with watercolors or a felt-tip marker). For the leaves of summer, use a bright green herb such as parsley or chives. Crushed red pepper can represent autumn's colorful foliage. Cloves form the branches of winter. Pieces of cinnamon stick make the tree trunks.

Begin by deciding on the size and shape of the hanging. You may want to make a vertical arrangement, such as the one shown here. But horizontal and square arrangements are attractive too.

Next choose the background. Fabrics such as burlap and felt work well for vertical wallhangings. Wood or heavy cardboard can be used for arrangements of any shape. Heavy cardboard set inside a picture frame is a good choice for a square arrangement.

If the wallhanging is made of burlap, pull out a few of the vertical threads on both sides to create frayed edges. Then turn under the top and bottom edges and glue them in place.

On scrap paper, draw a model tree, cut it out and make three copies. Place these on the background to be certain that they can be evenly arranged on the material. Lightly trace around them.

Use white glue to attach the herbs and spices to the background. After the glue has dried, you might add a second and even a third layer to some of the treetops. This will increase the three-dimensional look. You can also add "grass" around the bases of the trunks, using tarragon or rosemary. Color the spring treetop after all the layers have been added and the glue has completely dried. Be gentle, or the "blossoms" will fall off!

Find a special spot in your home where you can display the four spicy seasons.

A SHADOWY CELEBRATION

Every year since 1887, a special event has taken place in the town of Punxsutawney, Pennsylvania. It's an event that is eagerly awaited both by people who love winter and by people who can't wait for the coming of spring. And in 1987 this famous ''happening'' celebrated its 100th birthday.

To discover the name of the event, you need a pencil and a sheet of lined paper. Carefully follow the directions given below. Hint: It will be easier if you rewrite the complete word(s) at each step.

The solution is on page 381.

1. Print the word PUNXSUTAWNEY.

2. Place an O in front of every U.

3. Find the third letter from the right. Replace it with a D.

4. Remove the first vowel from the right.

5. Place an R after the first consonant from the left.

6. Find the letter that comes before Y in the alphabet. Replace it with two G's.

7. Place an H between the U–T combination.

8. Remove the first and ninth consonants from the left.

9. Find the letter that comes first in the alphabet. Move it between the D–Y combination.

10. Put a space between the third and fourth letters from the right.

11. Place the third consonant of the alphabet between the two G's.

12. Remove all S's and T's.

13. Reverse the order of the last four letters of the first word.

14. Remove the third vowel from the left.

15. Find the fifth letter from the left. Move it to the beginning of the first word.

If you visit Punxsutawney on February 2, there's not ''a shadow'' of a doubt that you'll find out if it's going to be a long winter or an early spring.

BUTTERFLY BEAUTIES

Here are colorful cloth insects that will brighten up your life. Attach magnets and they decorate a refrigerator. Attach glue and place them on a gift for a friend. Attach bobby pins and wear them in your hair.

To make one of these butterflies, you will need scraps of two different fabrics and two fuzzy pipe cleaners. If your fabrics are thin, they may be stiffened with spray starch. Use

the patterns shown here for the wings—if you want to make a larger butterfly, simply enlarge the patterns.

The wings of each butterfly are made of eight pieces of fabric, grouped into four pairs. The top piece of fabric in each pair is the same shape but slightly smaller than the bottom piece. All the top pieces should be made from one fabric, and all the bottom pieces from the second fabric.

Take your first fabric and cut two pieces following pattern 1 and two pieces following pattern 3. Then take your second fabric and cut two pieces following pattern 2 and two

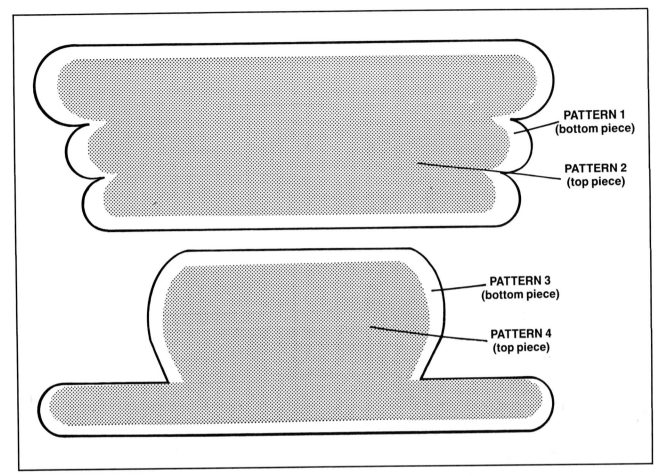

PATTERN 1
(bottom piece)

PATTERN 2
(top piece)

PATTERN 3
(bottom piece)

PATTERN 4
(top piece)

pieces following pattern 4. Now put the pairs together—center each pattern 2 piece on a pattern 1 piece, and each pattern 4 piece on a pattern 3 piece.

Find the center of each pair and accordian pleat the fabric from top to bottom. Arrange the four pleated pairs one above the other, slightly overlapping each pair. The wings from patterns 1 and 2 should be on top, and those from patterns 3 and 4 on the bottom.

Now take one of the pipe cleaners and fold it in half. Place it around all the wings at the center, and twist it closed at the top of the wings. The excess length becomes antennae, which can be curled or decorated with pompoms. Take the other pipe cleaner and twist it around a pencil; then attach it over the first pipe cleaner and tuck the ends in back.

STAMP COLLECTING

A wide variety of stamps were issued around the world in 1987, on subjects that ranged from lacemaking to help for the homeless. Meanwhile, stamp collecting continued to be a popular hobby, and stamp auctions showed a strong market for rare and unusual issues.

U.S. STAMPS

Several issues celebrated the 200th anniversary of the signing of the U.S. Constitution. One, a 22-cent stamp showing a section of the Constitution's preamble with a hand holding a quill pen, was released on September 17 (the official anniversary) in Philadelphia, where the document had been signed. Another issue was a booklet pane of five 22-cent stamps that together showed the full text of the preamble. Other 22-cent stamps honored Delaware, Pennsylvania, and New Jersey, the first three states to ratify the Constitution.

Another 1987 event was honored on a 22-cent stamp: the 150th anniversary of Michigan statehood. This stamp showed a white pine (the state tree) silhouetted against a Lake Huron sunset. The Pan American Games, which are held every four years, were also marked with a postal issue. The stamp for the 1987 games, held in Indianapolis, Indiana, showed stylized runners in a race.

One of the most spectacular issues of the year was a sheet of 50 stamps showing animals native to North America. Animals from all 50 states were included. Another special issue was part of the American Folk Art series: a group of four stamps showing different forms of lacework, displayed in white against blue backgrounds. And a special booklet held panes of stamps for special occasions, with messages such as "Get Well!" and "Keep in Touch!"

The 1987 addition to the "Love" stamp series depicted a decorative heart in pastel shades. And several stamps were added to the U.S. coil-stamp series on transportation. They included stamps showing an antique tractor, a canal boat from the 1880's, a 1911 Marmon "Wasp" racecar (winner of the first

Indianapolis 500 race), and a 1920's tow truck. A booklet pane of five stamps showed antique locomotives.

Famous Americans whose portraits appeared on stamps included Julia Ward Howe, the 19th-century social reformer who wrote the words to "The Battle Hymn of the Republic"; Mary Lyon, founder of Mount Holyoke College; author William Faulkner; the Sioux chieftain Red Cloud; and Jean Baptiste Pointe Du Sable, the first black settler of Chicago. The Italian-born operatic tenor Enrico Caruso, who won lasting fame in the early 1900's, appeared on a 22-cent stamp costumed for a role in *Rigoletto*.

STAMPS AROUND THE WORLD

Several notable omnibus issues (stamps from many countries on a single theme) appeared in 1987. Seven countries released more than 50 different stamps marking the 100th anniversary of the birth of the modern painter Marc Chagall. Each stamp showed a different work by the artist, who was born in Russia, worked for most of his life in Paris, and died in 1985.

The 1987 Europa stamps, issued by the member countries of the European Conference of Postal and Telecommunications Administrations, took modern architecture as their theme. Among them were a West German stamp showing Mies van der Rohe's design for the German pavilion at a 1928–29 international exhibition in Barcelona, Spain, a British stamp showing the Pompidou Center in Paris, and a Belgian stamp showing the church of Louvain La Neuve.

Toronto, Canada, hosted Capex '87, an international stamp show, in June, and a number of countries issued stamps for the event. Sierra Leone incorporated Disney cartoon characters in their release, showing Mickey Mouse, Dumbo, and Goofy visiting Canadian landmarks. Canada's stamps for the show showed early Canadian post offices. Other 1987 Canadian issues included a set honoring early explorers and one showing antique household tools—a butter stamper, a linen chest, an iron kettle, and a hand-drawn cart. A special stamp marked the 75th

**1987 STAMPS
FROM AROUND
THE WORLD**

POLSKA 2.50 ZŁ
H.MATUSZEWSKA   PWPW-68

**A TOPICAL
COLLECTION OF
FAIRY TALE AND FABLE
STAMPS**

POLSKA 20 GR
H.MATUSZEWSKA   PWPW-68

대한민국 우표
REPUBLIC OF KOREA
7

대한민국 우표
REPUBLIC OF KOREA
20

5 DDR   10 DDR
RUMPELSTILZCHEN   RUMPELSTILZCHEN

20 DDR   25 DDR
RUMPELSTILZCHEN   RUMPELSTILZCHEN

1959   20
MAGYAR POSTA
LÁBOR ÉVA

LE PETIT CHAPERON ROUGE   MONACO 1,00
1628-1978 CONTES DE PERRAULT

LE PETIT POUCET   MONACO 1,70
CONTES DE PERRAULT 1628-1978

MONACO 1,90
1628-1978 CONTES DE PERRAULT
RIQUET A LA HOUPPE   R.LAMBERT

БЪЛГАРИЯ 13 СТ
РАН БОГОЛЕК·НЕЗНАЕН ЮНАК·

БЪЛГАРИЯ 20 СТ
Х.К.АНДЕРСЕН·ОГНИВОТО·

НР БЪЛГАРИЯ 2 СТ   НАРОДНИ ПРИКАЗКИ
·ДЯДОВАТА РЪКАВИЧКА·

Le Lièvre et la Tortue 1,00 +0,25   Le Rat de ville et le Rat des champs 1,20 +0,30
FRANCE   FRANCE
POSTES 1978   POSTES

대한민국 우표
해와 달 이야기
10
REPUBLIC OF KOREA

anniversary of the Gray Cup, the top honor in Canadian football. The many roles of engineering, especially in high technology, were honored in another stamp. And four stamps looked forward to the 1988 Calgary Winter Olympics, with scenes of speed skaters, bobsledders, a ski jumper, and a cross-country skier.

Sports were a popular topic for stamps in other countries as well. Four West German stamps honored sailing, judo, Nordic skiing, and gymnastics, with part of the funds from sales of the stamps going to promote sports. An Egyptian stamp celebrated soccer, and a stamp from Suriname marked the Pan Am Games.

Transportation was another popular subject. Finland produced a souvenir sheet showing antique trains that once carried the mails, with a map of their routes also appearing on the sheet. Ireland showed tramcars from the late 1800's and early 1900's on a group of four stamps. Canada showed old steamships on two stamps but took a more modern theme on a third, a stamp that marked the 50th anniversary of Air Canada by showing the airline's global route.

Several countries also honored the achievements of women with stamps. Ireland's issue showed a woman surveyor, while West Germany depicted two famous women: Clara Schumann, one of the most important pianists of the 1800's, and Christine Teusch, who in 1947 became the first female cabinet minister in that country.

A set of stamps from Britain showed unusual aspects of British plant life in reproductions of photographs. The stamps highlighted the color and detail of four plants —globe thistle, blanket flower, autumn crocus, and echeveria—by setting them against dark backgrounds. Another set of four British stamps marked the 300th anniversary of the publication of Sir Isaac Newton's *Mathematical Principles of Natural Philosophy,* which included the scientist's work on the law of gravity.

One of the year's more unusual issues came from the Caribbean country of Antigua and Barbuda. It featured portraits of famous entertainers, including three popular singers (Judy Garland, Elvis Presley, and John Lennon) and five movie stars (Orson Welles, John Wayne, Grace Kelly, Rock Hudson, and Marilyn Monroe). Another interesting issue came from Ireland, which released two ''Love'' stamps for 1987. One chose a postal theme and showed a postman spreading messages of affection. The other stamp showed brightly colored flowers and a butterfly. On a less lighthearted note, the Soviet Union honored one of its founders, Ilyich Ulyanov Lenin, with five stamps showing different versions of his portrait.

The 40th anniversary of UNICEF, the United Nations Children's Fund, was marked in a set of five stamps from Kenya that took special note of the organization's efforts to save children's lives through improved health care. And as it does each year, the United Nations itself issued stamps on a number of different subjects. Marking 1987 as the International Year of Shelter for the Homeless, the U.N. released a set of stamps showing people at work building and improving housing. Another U.N. set took note of the international group's efforts to combat drug abuse. And three commemoratives honored Trygve Lie, the Norwegian statesman who was the first Secretary General of the United Nations (1946–53).

A TOPICAL COLLECTION

Literature has always been a popular subject for stamps. Especially appealing are stamps that depict fairy tales and fables. These stamps would make an excellent topical collection—a collection built around a single theme.

Many countries have issued stamps showing stories known to their children and, sometimes, to children all over the world. *Little Red Riding Hood, Rumpelstiltskin, Hansel and Gretel,* and *Sleeping Beauty* are just a few of the famous fairy tales that have been illustrated on stamps. Fables, such as the well-known stories of *The Tortoise and the Hare* and *The Grasshopper and the Ant,* can also be found. So can folktales from countries around the world. These stamps can do more than form an attractive collection—they can help bring some of your favorite stories to life.

CHARLESS HAHN
Stamp Editor
Chicago Sun-Times

A SEEDY PICTURE

You don't need paints to create a painting. Instead, use beans to express your artistic talents. A walk through a supermarket will show you that dried beans come in a wide variety of colors: red kidney beans, brown lentils, green and yellow split peas, speckled pintos, and much more. There is great variety in shape and size, too, which will give your bean "painting" interesting textures.

Begin by getting an appropriate piece of wood, perhaps a piece of lumber or even a kitchen cutting board. Sketch your picture onto the wood. You can also use a picture from a book or magazine and trace it onto the wood. Decide which beans have the best colors, shapes, and sizes for your design, and arrange them on the picture. Then glue the beans to the wood using white glue. When the glue has dried, cover the picture with several coats of polyurethane to preserve the beans.

Enclose your bean picture in a natural or painted wood frame. Or create the frame shown above—a border of rope and several rows of dark beans.

A WORLDLY FEAST

You and your friends are going to put together the most delicious meal ever. In fact, you're going to travel all over the world in search of the tastiest foods.

Complete the following clues to learn where you'll do your shopping. (You may want to use maps in your encyclopedia to help you.)

You'll get tacos in a city on Puget Sound.	TACO _ _
Buy barbecued ribs in the capital of Suriname.	_ _ _ _ _ _ RIB _
Get baked beans in a sea east of Central America.	_ _ _ _ _ BEAN
Buy ham in a port city in Ontario . . .	HAM _ _ _ _ _
. . . or in the largest city in Alabama.	_ _ _ _ _ _ _ HAM
Buckets of peas await your arrival atop a famous Colorado mountain.	_ _ _ _ _ PEA _
For corn on the cob, head for Indian islands in the Bay of Bengal.	_ _ COB _ _
Chefs along this Pennsylvania river are preparing baked chicken legs.	_ _ LEG _ _ _ _
You'll get smoked eel in a city in West Virginia.	_ _ EEL _ _ _
The ingredients for liver pâté will be bought in the Beatles' hometown in England.	LIVER _ _ _ _
Then head halfway around the world to buy pears at a naval base in Hawaii.	PEAR _ _ _ _ _ _
Sticky buns hot out of the oven are at a popular summer resort on the coast of Maine.	_ _ _ _ _ BUN _ _ _ _ _
Finally, pick up jam for the buns on a tropical island in the Caribbean.	JAM _ _ _ _

ANSWERS: Tacoma, Paramaribo, Caribbean, Hamilton, Birmingham, Pikes Peak, Nicobar, Allegheny, Wheeling, Liverpool, Pearl Harbor, Kennebunkport, Jamaica.

E FOR EXCELLENCE

Surnames beginning with the letter E aren't as plentiful as those beginning with many other letters of the alphabet. Nevertheless, a quick look through an encyclopedia or a biographical dictionary shows that many outstanding people have E surnames. Amelia Earhart, the famous aviator, is an example. So are the 22 other people listed below (in the left column). Match each person to his or her accomplishment (in the right column).

1.	Eakins, Thomas	a.	Invented the first simple, reliable camera
2.	Eames, Charles	b.	Civil rights leader
3.	Earhart, Amelia	c.	French engineer
4.	Eastman, George	d.	Basketball player nicknamed Doctor J
5.	Eastwood, Clint	e.	Dutch scholar during the Renaissance
6.	Edison, Thomas Alva	f.	Furniture designer
7.	Eiffel, Alexandre	g.	34th president of the United States
8.	Einstein, Albert	h.	Tennis player
9.	Eisenhower, Dwight D.	i.	Movie star and mayor of Carmel, California
10.	Eliot, T. S.	j.	Surrealist painter and sculptor
11.	Ellington, Duke	k.	Dramatist of ancient Greece
12.	Ellison, Ralph	l.	Mathematician of ancient Greece
13.	Emerson, Ralph Waldo	m.	First woman pilot to cross the Atlantic
14.	Erasmus, Desiderius	n.	Scientist known for theory of relativity
15.	Ericson, Leif	o.	Viking explorer of North America
16.	Ernst, Max	p.	Author of *The Waste Land*
17.	Ervin, Sam	q.	Novelist better known as George Eliot
18.	Erving, Julius	r.	American realist artist of the 1800's
19.	Euclid	s.	Author of *Invisible Man*
20.	Euripides	t.	Invented the first phonograph
21.	Evans, Mary Ann	u.	Jazz musician and composer
22.	Evers, Medgar	v.	U.S. Senator who headed Watergate investigation
23.	Evert, Chris	w.	Wrote the poem "The Concord Hymn"

ANSWERS: 1.r; 2.f; 3.m; 4.a; 5.i; 6.t; 7.c; 8.n; 9.g; 10.p; 11.u; 12.s; 13.w; 14.e; 15.o; 16.j; 17.v; 18.d; 19.l; 20.k; 21.q; 22.b; 23.h.

Next, go on a hunt. The last names of all 23 people are hidden in this search-a-word puzzle. Try to find them. Cover the puzzle with a sheet of tracing paper. Read forward, backward, up, down, and diagonally. Then draw a neat line through each name as you find it. One name has been shaded in for you.

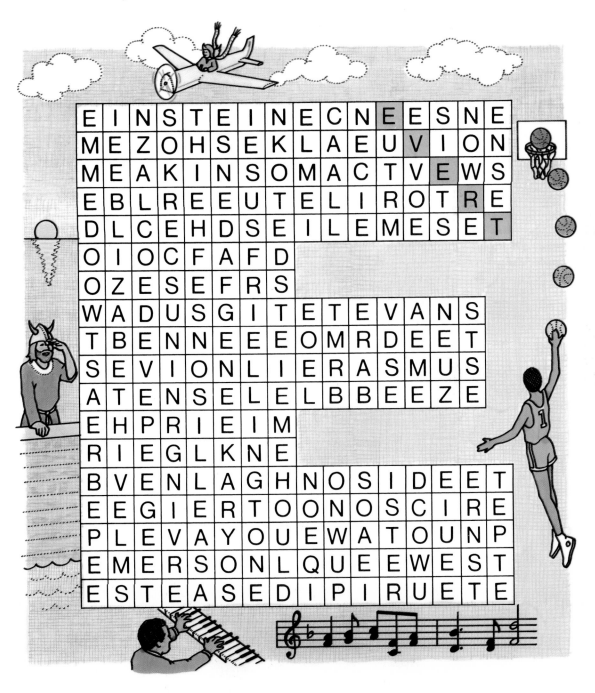

```
E I N S T E I N E C N E E S N E
M E Z O H S E K L A E U V I O N
M E A K I N S O M A C T V E W S
E B L R E E U T E L I R O T R E
D L C E H D S E I L E M E S E T
O I O C F A F D
O Z E S E F R S
W A D U S G I T E T E V A N S
T B E N N E E E O M R D E E T
S E V I O N L I E R A S M U S
A T E N S E L E L B B E E Z E
E H P R I E I M
R I E G L K N E
B V E N L A G H N O S I D E E T
E E G I E R T O O N O S C I R E
P L E V A Y O U E W A T O U N P
E M E R S O N L Q U E E W E S T
E S T E A S E D I P I R U E T E
```

POPULAR CRAFTS

Fabrics are among the most popular materials for crafts—and no wonder! They're easy to work with, everyone has them or can find them, and they come in an almost endless variety of colors, patterns, and textures. There are calicos and ginghams for country kitchens, satins and laces for feminine bedrooms, denims and corduroys for sturdy cushions, plaids and paisleys for scarves—decide what you'd like to make and you'll be able to find the appropriate fabric.

The success of any project often depends on advance planning. Before you begin, decide not only what you want to make but how you plan to use it. For example, if you want to make a pillow cover, decide where you'll use it. If you plan to use it outdoors, you'll want to make it from terry cloth or some other fabric that washes easily. Or you might use vinyl, which can be wiped clean. Save satins and other delicate fabrics for indoor pillows. And if the item is to be a gift, choose fabrics that your friend or relative will enjoy.

Here are some fabric crafts that you might have fun making.

SOCK ANIMALS

With a sock and a little imagination, you can create an adorable stuffed animal. Tiny baby socks can be turned into bunny rabbits, tweedy knee socks can become monkeys, and with colorful tube socks you can make such fantasy animals as pink elephants and purple cows.

Why not start with Moo-na Lisa! This purple cow is made from a lavender sport tube sock. You'll need matching felt for the ears, a white pom-pom, white yarn, black yarn, a cowbell, and narrow satin ribbon.

Lay the sock flat and cut it into four parts. The toe area of the sock will be shaped into the cow's head. The next section—almost half the length of the sock—will be the cow's body. The third piece will be about 1½ inches (3.8 centimeters) long for the horns. Finally, the ribbed cuff will be cut to make the four legs.

Stuff each part of the animal with polyester. Then shape it, and sew it closed. Attach a braided white tail and a white pom-pom udder to the body. On the head, stitch the eyes, nostrils, and mouth. Then attach eye-

Moo-na Lisa, an adorable stuffed purple cow, was made from a tube sock, felt, and yarn.

lashes, horns, floppy felt ears, and a fore-head tuft of white yarn. Sew the head and legs to the body. Tie the cowbell around the neck with the ribbon.

Don't forget Moo-na Lisa's red-feathered friend. The little bird is made from a red pom-pom, scraps of red and yellow felt, and a pair of wiggle eyes. A spot of glue will keep the bird from falling off the cow's back.

HANGING HOOPS

An embroidery hoop is a wooden or plas-tic circular band that actually consists of two hoops—one inside the other. Its purpose is to hold a piece of fabric taut while you em-broider a design on the fabric. But people have found that embroidery hoops can also be used much like picture frames, to hold fabric "pictures."

All sorts of hoop pictures are possible. You might create a rural scene from pieces of felt . . . or a floral arrangement with var-ious calico prints . . . or a black-hatted witch and a sequined orange pumpkin for Halloween . . . or a stuffed doll, such as the one shown here.

Begin by stretching your background fab-ric between the two parts of an embroidery hoop. The fabric should be flat and unwrin-kled. Then glue your design onto the fabric.

For trim, glue lace and calico ruffles around the back of the hoop. Tie a ribbon bow and glue it to the front of the ruffles, underneath the picture. Finally, back the hoop with a circle of felt and add a hanger.

THE ART OF APPLIQUÉ

Appliqué is a process by which small pieces of fabric are attached, or appliquéd, to a larger background fabric. Usually, the pieces are sewn on, either by hand or with a sewing machine. You can also glue them on. Many beautiful items can be created: deco-rative sweatshirts, aprons, banners, wall hangings, pillows, and tote bags such as the one pictured on the following page.

When making an appliquéd item, the back-ground fabric must be firm enough to support the fabrics attached to it. It's also important to use closely woven fabrics for the appli-quéd pieces, because they are less likely to fray when you cut them.

The tote itself is shaped like a paper bag. The front and back rectangular panels are

An embroidery hoop decorated with calico ruffles and lace makes a charming "frame" for a fabric picture.

connected by narrow strips of fabric along the sides and bottom. Handles are attached to the top of the front and back.

For the appliqués, begin by making a drawing of your design on paper. Outline each section that's to be cut from different fabric. Then trace the outlines of the sections onto another piece of paper, and cut them out to use as your patterns.

This tote uses solid-color fabrics for a stained-glass effect. Each piece is edged with black binding to give a dramatic look.

Use the patterns to cut out the flower pieces from scraps of fabric. Pin them in place on the front panel of the tote. Next, pin the black strips in place. When all the pieces are positioned, sew them down.

To give the finished tote extra body, you can line it with the same or a contrasting fabric.

PILLOWS WITH POCKETS

Pillows come in many sizes and shapes. They can be used in every room of your

The dramatic stained-glass effect on this appliquéd tote bag makes the carryall eye-catching as well as useful.

angular, or some other standard shape, nothing says they *have* to be. You can make pillows in the shape of hearts, mice, dinosaurs, bananas . . . whatever you want!

With a little imagination you can even turn a basic pillow into a cuddly animal that will hold your favorite bedtime story.

The cat and dog pillows shown here are made like the cover of a book. The front and back are both stuffed pillows. The front is decorated with ears, eyes, and other features of an animal's face. The two parts are connected by a narrow, unstuffed "spine." This lets you fold the pillows together.

Now comes the surprise: The back has a pocket sewn on that is large enough to hold a book.

HIGH-TECH QUILTS

Millions of people enjoy quilting—it's one of the most popular of all crafts. Quilts are

A pillow surprise: These cuddly pet pillows have hidden pockets in the back that can hold your favorite books.

home—singly, in pairs, or in large groupings. And by making your own pillows, you get exactly what you want to fit any decor.

You can make a pillow simply by sewing together two pieces of fabric of the same size and stuffing foam or some other filling inside. Almost any kind of fabric can be used. And there are many different kinds of stuffing— foam forms, polyester fiber, kapok, down. Some people even stuff pillows with fabric scraps and old socks and stockings.

Pillows can be edged with ruffles, fringe, or lace. You can buy or make your own piping. You can put tassels at the corners of a square pillow or a big cloth-covered button in the center of a round pillow. And although most pillows are square, round, oblong, tri-

This colorful robot was sewn to the top layer of a bed quilt—ideal for snuggling under on a cold winter night.

usually used on beds, perfect for snuggling under on cold winter nights. People also make quilted jackets, vests, and tote bags, and even hang quilts from walls, like paintings and other pieces of art.

Any quilted item consists of three layers. The top layer is decorative. It may have an appliquéd or stitched design. Or it may consist of a pattern made from many small pieces of fabric sewn together. The bottom, or backing, of the quilt is usually a single sheet of fabric. In between these two layers is a layer of padding.

Quilting involves stitching the layers together so that the padding is held firmly in place between the two outer layers. Some people hand-stitch their quilts; others use sewing machines. It isn't difficult, but it takes time, particularly if you make a large quilt or one with an intricate design.

Many quilts use traditional patterns passed down from generation to generation. But you can break with tradition and make a quilt with an appliquéd robot. The top layer of this quilt uses three main fabrics—a star-patterned background, a red window shade, and a blue border.

Sometimes small pieces are appliquéd onto larger pieces, which are then appliquéd to the quilt top. The robot is made from scraps of several different materials. The eyes, nose, and mouth are sewn onto the face, and the words "Good Night" are embroidered on his TV monitor. Then the larger pieces are appliquéd to the top layer. This robot may be a high-tech friend, but the quilt guarantees a high-touch response!

NANCY TOSH
Editor
Crafts 'n Things magazine

COIN COLLECTING

Commemorative coins drew the attention of collectors in 1987, as did new and continuing series of gold bullion coins. Coin collectors had many opportunities open to them as they decided which of the new issues they most wanted to acquire.

U.S. COINS

One of the highlights of U.S. coinage for 1987 was the striking of commemorative coins honoring the bicentennial of the sign-

U.S. silver dollar honoring the 200th anniversary of the Constitution

ing of the Constitution. The U.S. Mint produced two different designs reflecting this theme: a $5 gold piece and a silver dollar. Both coins incorporated a quill pen in the design and carried the dates 1787 and 1987.

Also significant for U.S. collectors was the fact that 1987-dated half dollars weren't produced for circulation. The only way to obtain these half dollars was to purchase a special collector set from the U.S. Mint. Finding a 1987 Kennedy half dollar in your change from the grocery store will thus be just about impossible.

The Kennedy half dollar was issued both in uncirculated sets, which contain coins that are like those struck for circulation but are untouched, and in proof sets. The mint produces proof coins from specially prepared dies that give the coins much sharper detail and a cameo effect—the raised portions of the coins are frosted in appearance, and the background is reflective, like a mirror. Only collectors have an interest in these proof coins, which carry an "S" mint mark for the San Francisco branch of the U.S. Mint. And

because of the special care taken in preparing them, they cost more than the coins you carry in your pocket.

The U.S. bullion coins, called American Eagles, also saw continued production. Bullion coins are designed to be sold as units of precious metal—gold and silver—and so their price is tied to the price of the metal they contain rather than to their official denominations. The value of proof and commemorative coins, on the other hand, is tied to their inherent beauty and resulting desirability, as well as to their scarcity.

As in 1986, investors purchased hundreds of thousands of the Eagles. But late in 1987, the U.S. Mint also struck proof versions of the coins and introduced a new type. In addition to proof versions of the silver Eagle and the gold 1-ounce Eagle, the mint struck and sold to collectors a gold half-ounce Eagle.

Collectors also looked forward to commemoratives honoring the 1988 Olympic Games. Congress has authorized these coins, and their issue would mark the first time that U.S. coins would commemorate events taking place in other countries (South Korea and Canada are hosting the Games).

Olympic commemoratives: Canada's $20 silver coin showing figure skating (*above*) and South Korea's 5,000-won silver coin showing their tiger mascot (*below*)

WORLD COINS

The 1988 Summer Olympic Games will be held in Seoul, South Korea, and to mark the event the South Korean government is issuing a series of 24 coins, some in 1987 and the remainder in 1988. The coins not only honor the Games but also highlight South Korean history, cultural activities, and popular children's games. When completed, the set will include eight gold and sixteen silver coins. The subjects portrayed in the designs released in 1987 ranged from running and diving to volleyball and archery. One, the 5,000-won denomination, carried the tiger mascot of the 1988 Summer Games.

Canada, the other host country, issued four coins honoring the 1988 Winter Games, to be held in Calgary, Alberta. The coins showed figure skating, curling, ski jumping, and bobsledding. The 1987 coins marked the completion of a ten-coin series made of silver and released several at a time since 1985. Late in the year, Canada also released a $100 gold Olympic commemorative.

Canadians also began using a new dollar coin in 1987, with a reverse design depicting a loon swimming in a lake. The loon design replaced the *voyageur* ("fur trader") theme that had been used on Canadian dollars since

Gold bullion coins: Australia's Nuggets (*above*) and one of China's popular Panda coins (*below*)

Canada's new 11-sided, gold-toned dollar coin

1935. Similar in size to the Canadian quarter dollar, the new coin incorporates features designed to avoid confusion between the two. For one, the loon dollar isn't round but rather 11-sided. It's also gold-toned as opposed to silver colored. The new dollar coins, nicknamed "Loonies," are intended to replace Canada's paper dollar bills by the end of 1989.

As in the United States, mints around the world continued to strike bullion coins in precious metals. Britain joined these nations with the introduction of the gold Britannia. Australia stepped up production of its own gold coins, called Nuggets. And Pandas, the gold coins produced by China and named for the animal they feature, increased their popularity in 1987. In addition to the 1/20-ounce through 1-ounce sizes (which range in size from smaller than a dime to about the size of a half dollar), the Chinese released a limited number of huge 12-ounce Pandas (also called Grand Pandas) during the year.

Finally, the possibility of international coinage inched closer to reality with the introduction of Belgium's ECU coin. (ECU stands for European Currency Unit.) The coin contained approximately half an ounce of gold and had a value pegged to that of several European currencies—the West German mark, the French franc, the British pound, and others. Belgian authorities said that the striking of the coin was largely symbolic, however—a standard unit of currency for all the nations of Europe remains for the future.

EARL A. SHOEMAKER
Numismatic News

157

COOKIE CUTTER CARDS

The next time you need a greeting card, make your own. It's a personal and fun way to tell people that you think they're extra special.

One way to make greeting cards is by using cookie cutters. Cutters are available in many different designs, which can be used singly or in groups.

Make the card itself from colorful construction paper. First, fold the paper in half so that it opens like a greeting card. Then position the cookie cutter on the underside of the card's front page and trace around the cutter. Cut along the lines, leaving a hole in

158

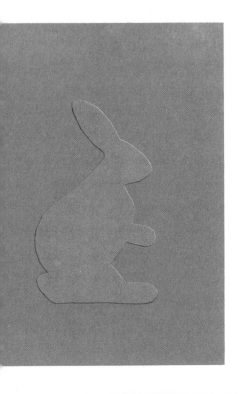

the card. Back this hole with construction paper of another color—or with patterned wrapping paper or fabric.

To give the inside of the card a neat appearance, cut out a piece of construction paper that's almost as large as the front of the card. Glue this over the complete underside, thus covering the material used for the design.

You may want to draw borders and other decorations on the front of the card. Use a felt-tip marker to give a dinosaur an eye, or bits of construction paper to jazz up a gingerbread man.

Now write your message on the inside of the card—"Happy Birthday," "Thanks!" or just simply "Hi, friend."

MANY FRIENDS COOKING

BERRY SHAKE, from Finland

Red lingonberries, yellow cloudberries, blueberries, deep red raspberries—colorful and delicate berries of all kinds are grown and eaten in Finland. Fresh berries are mixed into desserts or drinks like this berry shake. Use strawberries for your first shake. Then create a berry shake of your own.

INGREDIENTS

- 10 fresh strawberries *or* 6 tablespoons frozen, sliced strawberries in syrup (thawed)
- 2 cups cold milk
- 1½ teaspoons sugar or honey

EQUIPMENT

paring knife
measuring cups
mixing bowl
measuring spoons
eggbeater
2 glasses

HOW TO MAKE

1. Wash the strawberries (if fresh) and cut the stems.

2. Cut the strawberries into small pieces. (If you're using frozen strawberries, drain the syrup into a small bowl and save it for step 4.)

3. Pour the milk into the mixing bowl. Add the strawberries.

4. If you're using fresh strawberries, add the sugar or honey. If you're using frozen strawberries, add 3 tablespoons of the strawberry syrup instead of sugar.

5. Beat with the eggbeater for one minute.

6. Pour the drink into the glasses.

   This recipe serves 2 people.

GROUNDNUT SOUP, from Nigeria

In Nigeria when it's time for *chop,* it's time for food—that's what *chop* means. One food that grows easily in this tropical country is the groundnut—or peanut, as we call it. Protein-rich groundnuts are eaten in many ways: raw, roasted, boiled, pressed into cooking oil, and ground into butter. They're put into spicy stews, as well as into simple soups like this one. If you like the taste of peanuts, you'll like this groundnut soup.

INGREDIENTS

- 1 large tomato
- 1 large potato
- 1 medium onion
- 2 cups water
- 1 beef bouillon cube
- ½ teaspoon salt
- 1 cup shelled unsalted, roasted peanuts *or* ½ cup peanut butter, crunchy or smooth
- ½ cup milk
- 2 tablespoons rice

EQUIPMENT

vegetable peeler
paring knife
large saucepan and cover
measuring cups
measuring spoons
chopper
medium bowl
mixing spoon

HOW TO MAKE

1. Peel the potato and the onion.
2. Dice the potato, onion, and tomato into very small pieces.
3. Put the diced vegetables into the saucepan. Add the water, the bouillon cube, and the salt. Cover.
4. Boil gently for 30 minutes.
5. Chop the peanuts. Put them in the bowl and combine them with the milk. (If you are using peanut butter, mix it with the milk until it is smooth.)
6. Add the peanut mixture and the rice to the potato, tomato, onion, and water, and mix well.
7. Lower the heat and simmer for 30 minutes or more.
8. Pour into soup bowls and serve.

This recipe serves 6 people.

SPORTS

Jackie Joyner-Kersee (yellow shoes) hit full stride on the 1987 track and field circuit. At the Pan Am Games in August, she tied the world record in the women's long jump with a leap of 24 feet, 5½ inches. The following month, at the World Track and Field Championships in Rome, Italy, she won two gold medals: in the seven-event heptathlon competition (including the 100-meter hurdles, below) and in the long jump.

The United States regained the prestigious America's Cup from Australia in a four-race sweep.

THE AMERICA'S CUP RACE

In 1851 the schooner *America* won a yacht race around England's Isle of Wight, and skipper John Cox Stevens carried home an ornate silver cup. The trophy was turned over to the New York Yacht Club, which declared it an international challenge cup. The trophy—and the challenge races—became known as the America's Cup.

Over a period of 132 years, U.S. yachtsmen successfully defended the America's Cup against 24 foreign challenges, and the trophy remained firmly in the hands of the New York Yacht Club. But in September,

1983, the U.S. winning streak came to a stunning halt. In the waters off Newport, Rhode Island, a sleek challenger called *Australia II* swept past the American defender, *Liberty*, in four out of seven races. The America's Cup was removed from its case at the New York Yacht Club and carried away by the jubilant Australians.

In early 1987, off the coast of Fremantle, Western Australia, the America's Cup went up for grabs once again. The Australians wanted desperately to keep the trophy. The Americans wanted just as desperately to win it back. Teams from a number of other countries—including New Zealand, Canada, and France—also took aim at the prize. The outcome was a victory for the Americans, who prevailed after a hard-fought contest.

SETTING SAIL

The yachts that compete in the America's Cup are of the 12-meter class, a designation that refers not to the boat's length but to a formula based on length, width, sail area, and other factors. Every three or four years, the country in possession of the Cup defends its claim against the top challenger. The final competition is preceded by several months of qualifying rounds. Yachts from the host country compete in a series of races to determine which one will defend the Cup. Meanwhile, the other countries hold a round-robin elimination to determine the final challenger. In October, 1986, a total of thirteen yachts set sail in quest of the America's Cup. Each entry represented years of intensive preparation and millions of dollars in investment.

In the Australian camp, six yachts vied for the right to defend the Cup. Among the entries was a group headed by Alan Bond, whose *Australia II* had won the Cup in 1983. To the surprise of many, however, Bond's new yacht, *Australia IV,* was defeated in the qualifying round by a speedy entry called *Kookaburra III.* (A kookaburra is a large Australian bird with a loud cry.) The aluminum boat represented the Royal Perth Yacht Club, and it was skippered by 28-year-old Iain Murray.

Among the international challengers, *New Zealand* appeared to be the most formidable entry. In reaching the finals of the qualifying round, *New Zealand* compiled a record of 37 victories and only 1 defeat. Opposing *New Zealand* for the right to challenge *Kookaburra III* was an American entry, *Stars & Stripes,* of the San Diego Yacht Club. At the helm of *Stars & Stripes* was Dennis Conner, the skipper who had lost the America's Cup in 1983. Again to the surprise of many, *Stars & Stripes* defeated *New Zealand* in four out of five races. The United States had earned a chance to win back the Cup.

THE RACE IS ON

The course in America's Cup competition is 24.3 miles long, with a total of eight legs.

Prior to the final match series, *Stars & Stripes* was considered the faster yacht, but *Kookaburra III* was considered more maneuverable. The Americans were expected to have an advantage in strong winds, where the premium is on speed. (The sea winds off the coast of Western Australia were known to be generally strong and shifting.) The Aussies were expected to have an advantage in lighter winds, where the premium is on fast tacking (turning).

The first race in the best-of-seven series, held on January 31, proved the experts wrong. Sea winds were mostly light, but Conner and his ten-man crew maneuvered *Stars & Stripes* with clockwork precision. The challengers cruised home with a victory margin of 1 minute, 41 seconds.

The following day, the winds picked up, *Kookaburra III* squeaked out an early lead, but *Stars & Stripes* rushed back quickly. The Americans built steadily on their margin and crossed the finish line 1 minute, 10 seconds ahead of the Aussies. The challengers led 2–0 but refused to be overconfident.

With weather forecasters calling for light and variable breezes, the Australians were anxious to get the third race under way. *Kookaburra III* managed another early lead, but *Stars & Stripes* jumped back with some brilliant tactics and skillful maneuvering. Then the breeze freshened, and the Americans sped away to a 1 minute, 46 second victory. Still they refused to count their chickens. After all, *Liberty* had led 3–1 in 1983 and lost the Cup.

After a one-day layoff, the series resumed on February 4. If there had been any doubts as to which was the faster yacht, the answer came once and for all in the fourth race. *Kookaburra III* employed aggressive tactics from the outset, but *Stars & Stripes* sailed a flawless race and led every step of the way. The Americans won by a whopping 1 minute, 59 seconds, completing a 4–0 sweep of the 1987 challenge series.

And so, just as in 1851, the ornate silver trophy was carried off to the United States. Even as it went on display at the San Diego Yacht Club, however, potential challengers from around the world were planning for the next America's Cup series, in 1990 or 1991.

JEFFREY H. HACKER
Editor, *The Olympic Story*

CAPTAIN AMERICA

Dennis Conner had a score to settle. In 1983, when his yacht *Liberty* suffered defeat at the hands of *Australia II* in the America's Cup final, Conner became known as the first U.S. skipper to lose yacht racing's most coveted prize. For the next three years, the California native was consumed by a single ambition—to win back the historic trophy.

"Almost as soon as I lost the Cup in '83," he said, "I began figuring ways to get it back."

In February, 1987, at the helm of a speedy new yacht called *Stars & Stripes,* the 44-year-old skipper finally settled his score. By defeating *Kookaburra III* in four straight races off the coast of Western Australia, Dennis Conner became the first U.S. yachtsman to *regain* the America's Cup.

The son of an engineer, Conner grew up in San Diego, California. He hung around boating marinas the way some kids hang around pool halls and basketball courts. The San Diego Yacht Club finally accepted him as a junior member, and he began learning the finer points of sailing. Curiously, one thing Conner never did learn was how to swim. Even today, as the world's most famous sailor, he's afraid of falling in the water!

Conner still lives in San Diego, where he owns a drapery manufacturing business. He also still hangs around the San Diego Yacht Club; in fact, *Stars & Stripes* represented his old club in the 1987 Cup challenge. Perhaps one thing that has changed for Conner is his feeling toward the sport. "I don't like to sail," he now says. "I like to compete."

Prior to 1987, Conner had competed in three America's Cup finals. In 1974 he helped win the trophy as the starting helmsman on *Courageous.* Under skipper Ted Hood, *Courageous* defeated challenger *Australia,* 4–0, in the best-of-seven competition. In 1980, as the skipper of *Freedom,* Conner successfully defended the Cup by defeating *Australia,* 4–1. And then came the disaster of 1983. At the helm of *Liberty,* Conner took a 3–1 lead over *Australia II* but then lost the last three races. The America's Cup went "Down Under," and Dennis Conner set about getting it back. He raised money (about $16 million) for the 1987 challenge, hired engineers to design a new yacht, and began training a crew.

Even after settling his score and winning back the trophy, Conner was hardly ready to go sailing off into the sunset. His competitive instincts had him looking toward the next Cup defense . . . and the one after that. "I wonder how many skippers have won the America's Cup four times," he said moments after his 1987 triumph.

BASEBALL

The Minnesota Twins won baseball's championship in 1987, and their entire season, from opening day to their final victory over the St. Louis Cardinals in the seventh game of the World Series, proved the truth of the saying, "There's no place like home."

Home for the Twins is the Hubert H. Humphrey Metrodome in Minneapolis, an indoor stadium, where the team compiled a fine 56–25 record during the regular season. On the road, the Twins posted a dismal 29–52 mark. Their overall record, however, 85–77, was enough to win the American League Western Division title by two games over Kansas City.

Entering the playoffs, the Eastern Division champion Detroit Tigers had a 98–64 record, four top starting pitchers, and a group of sluggers who had slammed 225 home runs, the most in the majors.

The Twins leaned heavily on two starting pitchers, lefty Frank Viola (17–10) and right-handed veteran Bert Blyleven (15–12). Minnesota's hitters, no weaklings themselves, had poked 209 homers. But the Twins had another weapon—their home, the Dome, where the playoffs' first two games would be contested.

In Game 1, Twins third baseman Gary Gaetti homered twice, but the Tigers rallied to take a one-run lead into the bottom of the 8th inning. Undaunted, the Twins scored four times to win, 8–5.

Bert Blyleven faced Tiger ace Jack Morris in Game 2. The Twins' starter emerged the victor; the score was 6–3. Game 3, played in Detroit, was a seesaw battle. It was finally decided when Tiger right fielder Pat Sheridan hit a two-run homer in the bottom of the 8th, and Detroit won, 7–6.

The left arm of Frank Viola was a key weapon in the Minnesota Twins' drive for the championship of major league baseball. Viola was named MVP of the World Series for his victories in Games 1 and 7.

Andre Dawson of the Chicago Cubs earned National League MVP honors with 49 home runs and 137 RBI's.

Not even waiting to get back to Minnesota, the Twins took Games 4 and 5 by scores of 5–3 and 9–5, wrapping up their first pennant since 1965.

Over in the National League, the Cardinals won the Eastern Division title by three games over the New York Mets. In the West, the San Francisco Giants won by a comfortable six-game margin.

Leading 3 games to 2 in the playoffs, the Giants were on the verge of winning their first pennant in 25 years. But in the last two games, Cardinal pitchers blanked the Giants by scores of 1–0 and 6–0. The Cards moved into their third World Series in six years.

For the first time since the Series began in 1903, each game was won by the home team. Game 1 was a rout. Frank Viola pitched the Twins to a 10–1 victory, and left fielder Dan Gladden cracked a grand slam home run. Game 2 was little different, except for the score, 8–4. Bert Blyleven pitched seven strong innings for the victory.

But just as during the regular season, the Twins were a bust as the visiting team. In St. Louis, they could manage only five runs in three games. The Cards won Game 3, 3–1, behind John Tudor. In Game 4, the score was 7–2, as Viola took the loss. And Game 5 ended with the Cards up, 4–2.

Back home for Game 6, the Twins erupted once again. They pounded out fifteen hits, including a grand slam by Kent Hrbek. The final score was 11–5.

During the regular season, Jack Clark and Terry Pendleton had combined for half the Cardinals' home runs. But Clark was injured and sat out the entire Series; Pendleton was hobbled and couldn't play at full steam. Finally, the Cards' lack of power did them in —that and Frank Viola. In Game 7, Viola was masterful, winning 4–2. The Twins were the world champs, and Viola was the Series' Most Valuable Player (MVP).

During the regular season, Boston Red Sox ace Roger Clemens missed spring training but went on to win 20 games and earn his second consecutive American League Cy Young Award. In the National League, Philadelphia Phillie reliever Steve Bedrosian got the Cy Young Award for his 40 saves. The American League MVP was outfielder George Bell of the Toronto Blue Jays, who blasted 47 home runs and knocked in 134 runs. In the National League, Chicago Cub Andre Dawson won the MVP title for his 49 homers and 137 runs batted in. Rookie-of-the-year awards went to the Oakland A's Mark McGwire, who set a first-year record of 49 home runs, and San Diego Padres catcher Benito Santiago, who also established a rookie record by hitting safely in 34 straight games.

1987 WORLD SERIES RESULTS

		R	H	E	Winning/Losing Pitcher
1	St. Louis	1	5	1	Joe Magrane
	Minnesota	10	11	0	Frank Viola
2	St. Louis	4	9	0	Danny Cox
	Minnesota	8	10	0	Bert Blyleven
3	Minnesota	1	5	1	Juan Berenguer
	St. Louis	3	9	1	John Tudor
4	Minnesota	2	7	1	Frank Viola
	St. Louis	7	10	1	Bob Forsch
5	Minnesota	2	6	1	Bert Blyleven
	St. Louis	4	10	0	Danny Cox
6	St. Louis	5	11	2	John Tudor
	Minnesota	11	15	0	Dan Schatzeder
7	St. Louis	2	6	1	Danny Cox
	Minnesota	4	10	0	Frank Viola

Visiting team listed first, home team second

MAJOR LEAGUE BASEBALL FINAL STANDINGS

AMERICAN LEAGUE

Eastern Division

	W	L	Pct.	GB
Detroit	98	64	.605	—
Toronto	96	66	.593	2
Milwaukee	91	71	.562	7
New York	89	73	.549	9
Boston	78	84	.481	20
Baltimore	67	95	.414	31
Cleveland	61	101	.377	37

Western Division

	W	L	Pct.	GB
*Minnesota	85	77	.525	—
Kansas City	83	79	.512	2
Oakland	81	81	.500	4
Seattle	78	84	.481	7
Chicago	77	85	.475	8
California	75	87	.463	10
Texas	75	87	.463	10

NATIONAL LEAGUE

Eastern Division

	W	L	Pct.	GB
*St. Louis	95	67	.586	—
New York	92	70	.568	3
Montreal	91	71	.562	4
Philadelphia	80	82	.494	15
Pittsburgh	80	82	.494	15
Chicago	76	85	.472	18½

Western Division

	W	L	Pct.	GB
San Francisco	90	72	.556	—
Cincinnati	84	78	.519	6
Houston	76	86	.469	14
Los Angeles	73	89	.451	17
Atlanta	69	92	.429	20½
San Diego	65	97	.401	25

* pennant winners

MAJOR LEAGUE LEADERS

AMERICAN LEAGUE

Batting
(top 10 qualifiers)

	AB	H	Avg.
Boggs, Boston	551	200	.363
Molitor, Milwaukee	465	164	.353
Trammell, Detroit	597	205	.343
Puckett, Minnesota	623	207	.332
Mattingly, New York	569	186	.327
Seitzer, Kansas City	641	207	.323
Fernandez, Toronto	578	186	.322
Franco, Cleveland	495	158	.319
Sheets, Baltimore	469	148	.316
Yount, Milwaukee	635	198	.312

Home Runs

	HR
McGwire, Oakland	49
Bell, Toronto	47
Evans, Detroit	34
Evans, Boston	34
Hrbek, Minnesota	34
Joyner, California	34
Tartabull, Kansas City	34

Pitching
(top qualifiers, based on number of wins)

	W	L	ERA
Clemens, Boston	20	9	2.97
Stewart, Oakland	20	13	3.68
Langston, Seattle	19	13	3.84
Higuera, Milwaukee	18	10	3.85
Saberhagen, Kansas City	18	10	3.36
Morris, Detroit	18	11	3.38
Hough, Texas	18	13	3.79

NATIONAL LEAGUE

Batting
(top 10 qualifiers)

	AB	H	Avg.
Gwynn, San Diego	589	218	.370
Guerrero, Los Angeles	545	184	.338
Raines, Montreal	530	175	.330
James, Atlanta	495	154	.311
Clark, San Francisco	529	163	.308
Galarraga, Montreal	551	168	.305
Smith, St. Louis	600	182	.303
Thompson, Philadelphia	527	159	.302
Bonilla, Pittsburgh	467	140	.300
Santiago, San Diego	546	164	.300

Home Runs

	HR
Dawson, Chicago	49
Murphy, Atlanta	44
Strawberry, New York	39
Davis, Cincinnati	37
Johnson, New York	36

Pitching
(top qualifiers, based on number of wins)

	W	L	ERA
Sutcliffe, Chicago	18	10	3.68
Rawley, Philadelphia	17	11	4.39
Scott, Houston	16	13	3.23
Hershiser, Los Angeles	16	16	3.06
Gooden, New York	15	7	3.21
Welch, Los Angeles	15	9	3.22
Smith, Atlanta	15	10	4.09

SOUTHPAW SENSATION

Jim Abbott is a lefty pitching star for the University of Michigan, one of the nation's top twenty teams in 1987. As a 19-year-old sophomore, the 6-foot, 3-inch fireballer compiled a record of 10–3, with an earned run average of 2.44. Major league scouts came out in droves to see him pitch. "Very impressive," reported one. "He has all the tools to pitch in the majors," said another. After the season, Abbott was chosen to com- pete on the U.S. team in the Pan American Games. Against Nicaragua, the promising southpaw hurled an 18–0 shutout.

Jim Abbott has one hand.

Born with a single ill-formed finger at the base of his right wrist, Abbott learned a glove-switching technique that allows him to pitch and field with his one good hand. As he winds up for a pitch, the inside of his glove is balanced on his right nub. Then, after releasing the ball, he slips his left hand inside the glove. On a fielding play, he catches the ball, presses the glove against his body under his right arm, pulls out his hand, and makes the throw.

"When my father came up with this idea," said the amazing southpaw, "it was just to play catch in the backyard." Now Abbott does the switch so fast that some spectators don't even notice. Batters who try to take advantage of his handicap by bunting find out very quickly just how well he plays his position.

Abbott hardly considers himself handicapped. "It's not that big a factor in my life," he says matter-of-factly. Growing up in Flint, Michigan, he ignored his parents' initial urgings to stick with soccer. It was baseball he loved—and football and basketball, too. In high school, he was the regular punter on the football team. In one state playoff game, he also threw three touchdown passes. On the basketball court, Abbott led the school intramural league in scoring.

But it is on the baseball diamond that Abbott's athletic ability has stood out most. As a high school senior, he averaged two strikeouts per inning and only two hits per game. He also batted .427, with seven home runs. After graduation, a major league team offered him $50,000 to sign a contract. But Abbott turned down the money to attend the University of Michigan. As a freshman, he compiled a record of 6–2. During one stretch in his sophomore year, he hurled 35 straight innings without giving up an earned run.

Even if Jim Abbott dismisses his handicap, anyone who has seen him pitch marvels at his skill. His coaches and fellow players admire him even more for his attitude. At the Pan Am Games in August, Abbott was given the honor of carrying the American flag in the opening-ceremony parade. It was a highlight in what may be a long career in sports.

LITTLE LEAGUE BASEBALL

The 1987 Little League World Series was highlighted by the most one-sided championship game in the 40-year history of the event. Before an international television audience and a crowd of 35,000 in Williamsport, Pennsylvania, the team from Hua Lian in Taiwan defeated the squad from Irvine, California, 21–1, to capture the title. The Hua Lian victory marked the 17th time in 21 years that a team from the Far East had won the series. It was also the 12th championship in 14 appearances for a Taiwanese team.

Hua Lian blew open the final contest with five runs in the first inning, nine runs in the second inning, and seven runs in the third. The hero was left fielder Pang Yu-Long, who hit a grand slam in the second and a two-run homer in the third. Lin Yi-Hung and Wang Chi-Kwou each added a two-run homer in the third-inning outburst. Hua Lian's 21 runs were the most ever in a series final.

The Taiwanese pitcher, Lin, went the distance in the six-inning contest, allowing six hits while striking out nine batters and walking two. Irvine scored its only run of the game in the top of the third inning, when center fielder Geoff Ebdon stole home.

Irvine's starting pitcher, Aron Garcia, who had allowed only one run in his previous 60 innings, had instant control problems. In two and two-thirds innings, he had four wild pitches in addition to giving up thirteen hits and six walks. Ryan O'Toole finished up with two and one-third innings of scoreless relief.

Hua Lian had arrived in Williamsport with a 13–0 record in Far East regional competition. In the eight-team final tournament, the Taiwanese youngsters advanced with a 7–0 quarterfinal victory over Dharhan, Saudi Arabia, and a 4–0 semifinal win over Moca, Dominican Republic. The latter game was scoreless after six innings, halted by darkness after seven innings, and completed the following day in the eighth inning.

Irvine took a 16–0 mark to Williamsport and earned a place in the championship game with an 11–0 victory over Dover, New Hampshire, in the quarterfinals (featuring a no-hitter by Garcia) and an 8–1 triumph over Chesterfield, Indiana, in the semifinals.

Little Leaguers from Hua Lian, Taiwan, won the 1987 World Series, defeating the team from Irvine, California, 21–1.

BASKETBALL

A guard called Magic and a legendary 40-year-old center led the Los Angeles Lakers to the National Basketball Association (NBA) championship in 1987. Magic—Earvin Johnson—piloted the Lakers' relentless fast break, and scored and passed and rebounded and stole the ball from opposing players. The center—7-foot, 2-inch Kareem Abdul-Jabbar, the leading scorer in NBA history—played with the verve of a youngster half his age. With Magic, Kareem, and a strong supporting cast, the Lakers dominated the playoffs. In the finals, they overmatched the defending-champion Boston Celtics, winning 4 games to 2.

Before the season started, coach Pat Riley had challenged the Laker players to have the finest year of their careers. The team responded with the league's best regular-season record, 65–17. They then won eleven of twelve playoff games prior to the finals, rolling past Denver, Golden State, and Seattle in impressive fashion.

Games 1 and 2 of the finals were played on the Lakers' home court, where they rarely lose. True to form, they trounced the Celtics by scores of 126–113 and 141–122. In the first game, forward James Worthy led the Lakers with 33 points. In the second game, Michael Cooper set an NBA championship record with six 3-point field goals. Cooper totaled 21 points, Byron Scott had 24, Worthy and Abdul-Jabbar had 23, and Magic Johnson chipped in with 22. The Lakers were in high gear, and the Celtics were badly shaken.

But the next three games were scheduled for Boston Garden, and the Celtics, too, rarely lose at home. In Game 3, Boston's star forward Larry Bird scored 30 points, sparking his team to a 109–103 victory.

Game 4 was a classic playoff battle with a thrilling finish. With twelve seconds to play, Bird hit a 3-pointer that gave Boston the lead. But with two seconds remaining, Magic's running hook shot put the Lakers ahead, 107–106. A final attempt by Bird bounced off the rim as the buzzer sounded.

The Celtics regrouped to win Game 5, by 123–108. But the scene now shifted back to

Earvin "Magic" Johnson of the Los Angeles Lakers had a banner year, winning MVP honors for the NBA regular season and playoffs. His brilliant performance in the playoff finals sparked a Laker triumph over Boston.

NBA FINAL STANDINGS

EASTERN CONFERENCE

Atlantic Division

	W	L	Pct.
Boston	59	23	.720
Philadelphia	45	37	.549
Washington	42	40	.512
New Jersey	24	58	.293
New York	24	58	.293

Central Division

	W	L	Pct.
Atlanta	57	25	.695
Detroit	52	30	.634
Milwaukee	50	32	.610
Indiana	41	41	.500
Chicago	40	42	.488
Cleveland	31	51	.378

WESTERN CONFERENCE

Midwest Division

	W	L	Pct.
Dallas	55	27	.671
Utah	44	38	.537
Houston	42	40	.512
Denver	37	45	.451
Sacramento	29	53	.354
San Antonio	28	54	.341

Pacific Division

	W	L	Pct.
L.A. Lakers	65	17	.793
Portland	49	33	.598
Golden State	42	40	.512
Seattle	39	43	.476
Phoenix	36	46	.439
L.A. Clippers	12	70	.146

NBA Championship: Los Angeles Lakers

COLLEGE BASKETBALL

Conference	Winner
Atlantic Coast	North Carolina (regular season) North Carolina State (tournament)
Big East	Georgetown
Big Eight	Missouri
Big Ten	Indiana, Purdue (tied)
Ivy League	Pennsylvania
Metro	Louisville (regular season) Memphis State (tournament)
Missouri Valley	Tulsa (regular season) Wichita State (tournament)
Pacific Ten	UCLA
Southeastern	Alabama
Southwest	Texas Christian (regular season) Texas A&M (tournament)
Western Athletic	Texas–El Paso (regular season) Wyoming (tournament)

NCAA: Indiana

NIT: Southern Mississippi

Los Angeles, and the Lakers were ready to clinch the championship in front of their home crowd.

Behind 56–51 after a weak first half, the Lakers erupted in the third period, outscoring the Celtics 30–12. The fourth period was a celebration for Abdul-Jabbar, who scored 14 of his game-high 32 points. Magic added 16 points, 19 assists, and 8 rebounds. The final score was 106–93, and the Lakers were champs for the fourth time in eight years.

Magic was named the most valuable player (MVP) of the playoffs. He also won MVP honors for regular-season play.

In addition to Magic, Abdul-Jabbar, and Bird, some brilliant stars shone during the 1986–87 season. The electrifying Michael Jordan of the Chicago Bulls led the NBA in scoring, averaging 37.1 points per game. Charles Barkley, the powerful young forward of the Philadelphia 76ers, topped the league in rebounding with 14.6 per game.

And an era ended in the NBA as Philadelphia's fabulous "Dr. J"—Julius Erving—retired from the game. He will be remembered for his acrobatic moves, his competitive spirit, and his classy personality.

College Play. The Indiana University Hoosiers won the National Collegiate Athletic Association (NCAA) men's championship, defeating the Syracuse University Orangemen in the tournament final, 74–73. Guard Keith Smart threw in 12 of Indiana's last 15 points, including a jump shot from the left side with five seconds remaining that iced the game. Smart, who was voted the game's outstanding player, finished with 21 points.

Indiana had reached the championship game with a 97–93 victory over Nevada–Las Vegas in the semifinals. Syracuse had ousted Providence in the other semifinal, 77–63.

Indiana's triumph gave Hoosier coach Bob Knight his third national title. He joined Adolph Rupp (Kentucky) and John Wooden (UCLA) as the only coaches to win more than two NCAA championships.

The Lady Volunteers of the University of Tennessee won the NCAA women's championship, topping Louisiana Tech in the final, 67–44. Tonya Edwards, Bridgette Gordon, and Sheila Frost each scored 13 points for Tennessee. Edwards, a freshman, was named the tournament's MVP.

FOOTBALL

Football in 1987 began with a giant cele-bration—that is, a New York Giant celebra-tion. A strike threatened to ruin the 1987 regular season, but didn't. A long-time power in Canadian football exulted in yet an-other Grey Cup victory. And a young man from a university rich in football tradition won the Heisman Trophy.

THE NFL PLAYOFFS AND SUPER BOWL XXI

In 1986–87, the New York Giants enjoyed one of the finest seasons in their long Na-tional Football League history. They com-piled a 14–2 regular-season record to lead the National Conference's Eastern Division. They then thrashed their first two playoff op-ponents and went on to win Super Bowl XXI convincingly.

Only one other team had a regular-season record as good as that of the Giants: the Chi-cago Bears, defending Super Bowl champs, who led the National Conference's Central Division. The other National Conference playoff teams were the Western Division champion San Francisco 49ers and the two wild-card teams, the Los Angeles Rams and the Washington Redskins.

In the wild-card game, the Redskins knocked out the Rams, 19–7, and a week later they upset the Bears, 27–13. The Giants, meanwhile, were routing San Fran-cisco, 49–3, as New York running back Joe Morris gained 159 yards.

In the National Conference title game, the Giants defeated the Redskins for the third time in the 1986–87 season. The score, 17–0, testified to the Giants' excellent defense, led by linebacker Lawrence Taylor, who was named the NFL's most valuable player.

In the American Conference, the New En-gland Patriots led the Eastern Division, the Cleveland Browns topped the Central Divi-sion, and the Denver Broncos took the West-ern Division title. The two wild-card teams were the New York Jets and the Kansas City Chiefs.

The Jets eliminated the Chiefs in the wild-card game, 35–15. A week later, they had Cleveland on the ropes, but the Browns made up a 10-point deficit in the fourth quar-ter and eventually won, 23–20, in double overtime. Cleveland's Bernie Kosar set a playoff record by passing for 489 yards.

Another fine quarterback, Denver's John Elway, sparked his Bronco teammates to a 22–17 victory over New England in their first playoff game. The following week, against Cleveland in the American Confer-ence championship game, Elway engineered a 98-yard fourth-quarter drive to tie the score. Denver won in overtime, 23–20, and they were off to the Super Bowl to face the Giants.

NFL owners hired "replacements" during a three-week players' strike, but few fans attended the games.

Super Bowl XXI was played in the Rose Bowl in Pasadena, California, on January 25, 1987. As good as John Elway was, he was only the second-best quarterback on that day: The game was a showcase for veteran Giant signal-caller Phil Simms. His team was behind 10–9 at the intermission, but Simms ignited a Giant eruption in the second half. New York won, 39–20. For the game, Simms completed 22 of 25 passes, including three for touchdowns. He was named the Super Bowl's most valuable player. New York fans rejoiced at their team's first NFL championship in 31 years.

THE 1987 NFL REGULAR SEASON

A player strike interrupted the 1987 regular season. One week's games were canceled, and three weeks' games were contested by teams consisting mostly of "replacement players." Then the strike ended, and the regular players returned; each team finally played fifteen games, one less than normal.

Despite the shortened season, San Francisco's Jerry Rice set a record by catching 22 touchdown passes. And L.A. Raider Bo Jackson, a rookie running back, became only one of a few athletes in history to compete in two professional sports: He also played baseball for the Kansas City Royals.

In the National Conference, the division titlists were the Washington Redskins, the Chicago Bears, and the San Francisco 49ers; the wild-card teams were the New Orleans Saints and the Minnesota Vikings.

The American Conference division champs were the Cleveland Browns, the Indianapolis Colts, and the Denver Broncos. The wild-card teams were the Seattle Seahawks and the Houston Oilers.

THE CANADIAN FOOTBALL LEAGUE

For five straight years, from 1978 to 1982, the Edmonton Eskimos won the Grey Cup, representing the championship of the Canadian Football League. After a four-year dry spell, the Eskimos won again in 1987, nipping the Toronto Argonauts in the Grey Cup game by the score of 38–36. The November contest, played in Vancouver, British Columbia, featured a 115-yard touchdown run by the Eskimos' Henry Williams on a return of a missed Toronto field goal attempt. Es-

L.A. Raider Bo Jackson, who also plays professional baseball, emerged as a top running back in 1987.

kimo quarterback Damon Allen completed 15 of 20 passes for 255 yards and was named the game's most valuable offensive player. But it took a 49-yard field goal by Jerry Kauric in the last minute to give Edmonton the victory.

COLLEGE FOOTBALL

The University of Miami and the University of Oklahoma both finished the regular season with 11–0 records, but Miami was ranked first in the country after defeating Oklahoma in the Orange Bowl. In the final rankings, Oklahoma was number three. Florida State, 10–1 during the regular season, was ranked second after its victory over Nebraska, also 10–1, in the Fiesta Bowl. Syracuse (11–0) tied Auburn (9–1–1) in the Sugar Bowl; Michigan State (8–2–1) topped Southern California (8–3) in the Rose Bowl; and Texas A&M (9–2) whipped Notre Dame (8–3) in the Cotton Bowl.

Notre Dame has a legendary football tradition, and Tim Brown continued the tradition in winning the Heisman Trophy. An outstanding pass receiver, he was also a superb punt and kickoff returner.

Notre Dame receiver Tim Brown won the 1987 Heisman Trophy as the best college player.

1987 NFL FINAL STANDINGS

AMERICAN CONFERENCE

Eastern Division

	W	L	T	Pct.	PF	PA
Indianapolis	9	6	0	.600	300	238
Miami	8	7	0	.533	362	335
New England	8	7	0	.533	320	293
Buffalo	7	8	0	.467	270	305
N.Y. Jets	6	9	0	.400	334	360

Central Division

	W	L	T	Pct.	PF	PA
Cleveland	10	5	0	.667	390	239
Houston	9	6	0	.600	345	349
Pittsburgh	8	7	0	.533	285	299
Cincinnati	4	11	0	.267	285	360

Western Division

	W	L	T	Pct.	PF	PA
Denver	10	4	1	.700	379	288
Seattle	9	6	0	.600	371	314
San Diego	8	7	0	.533	253	317
L.A. Raiders	5	10	0	.333	301	289
Kansas City	4	11	0	.267	273	388

NATIONAL CONFERENCE

Eastern Division

	W	L	T	Pct.	PF	PA
Washington	11	4	0	.733	379	285
Dallas	7	8	0	.467	340	348
Philadelphia	7	8	0	.467	362	368
St. Louis	7	8	0	.467	337	380
N.Y. Giants	6	9	0	.400	280	312

Central Division

	W	L	T	Pct.	PF	PA
Chicago	11	4	0	.733	356	282
Minnesota	8	7	0	.533	336	335
Green Bay	5	9	1	.367	255	300
Tampa Bay	4	11	0	.267	286	360
Detroit	4	11	0	.267	269	384

Western Division

	W	L	T	Pct.	PF	PA
San Francisco	13	2	0	.867	459	253
New Orleans	12	3	0	.800	422	283
L.A. Rams	6	9	0	.400	317	361
Atlanta	3	12	0	.200	205	436

COLLEGE FOOTBALL

Conference	Winner
Atlantic Coast	Clemson
Big Eight	Oklahoma
Big Ten	Michigan State
Pacific Coast	San Jose State
Pacific Ten	Southern California, UCLA (tied)
Southeastern	Auburn
Southwest	Texas A&M
Western Athletic	Wyoming

Cotton Bowl: Texas A&M 35, Notre Dame 10
Fiesta Bowl: Florida State 31, Nebraska 28
Orange Bowl: Miami 20, Oklahoma 14
Rose Bowl: Michigan State 20, Southern California 17
Sugar Bowl: Auburn 16, Syracuse 16

Heisman Trophy: Tim Brown, Notre Dame

In 1987, Laura Davies won the U.S. Women's Open, and Larry Mize won the Masters tournament.

GOLF

PROFESSIONAL		AMATEUR	
	Individual		**Individual**
Masters	Larry Mize	**U.S. Amateur**	Billy Mayfair
U.S. Open	Scott Simpson	**U.S. Women's Amateur**	Kay Cockerill
Canadian Open	Curtis Strange	**British Amateur**	Paul Mayo
British Open	Nick Faldo	**British Ladies Amateur**	Janet Collingham
PGA	Larry Nelson	**Canadian Amateur**	Brent Franklin
World Series of Golf	Curtis Strange	**Canadian Ladies Amateur**	Tracy Kerdyk
U.S. Women's Open	Laura Davies		
Ladies PGA	Jane Geddes		**Team**
		Walker Cup	United States
	Team		
World Cup	Wales		
Ryder Cup	Europe		

HOCKEY

As the 1986–87 National Hockey League (NHL) season got under way, the Edmonton Oilers had something to prove. They had a reputation to restore. They had memories to forget. Led by center Wayne Gretzky, aptly nicknamed the "Great One," the talented Oilers had won the Stanley Cup in 1984 and 1985, and there was talk of a dynasty. In 1986, however, the Blue and Orange were eliminated from the playoffs in a major upset by the Calgary Flames. The players, the coaches, and the fans were stunned. From that moment on, they looked to 1986–87 as a season of redemption.

And the Oilers rose to the occasion. They finished the regular season with the best record in the NHL (50–24–6, 106 points) and also led the league in scoring (372 goals). In the playoffs, they rolled to the final round with apparent ease and then defeated the tenacious Philadelphia Flyers in a memorable seven-game series. When all was said and done, the flashy Edmontonians had won their third Stanley Cup in four years.

For the 26-year-old Gretzky, the 1986–87 season added another chapter to an already remarkable career. For the eighth year in a row, he won the Hart Trophy as the league's most valuable player. For the seventh year in a row, he won the Ross Trophy as the NHL's top scorer. His point total of 183 was 75 more than that of the runner-up, linemate Jari Kurri (108). Mario Lemieux of Pittsburgh and Mark Messier, also of Edmonton, tied for third in the scoring race with 107. Gretzky's 62 goals during the regular season also led the league. Later, he broke the all-time playoff scoring record of 176 points, held by Jean Beliveau.

In their quest for the Stanley Cup, Coach Glen Sather's Oilers skated past the Los Angeles Kings (4 games to 1) in the first playoff round. Gaining momentum, the well-oiled Edmonton machine then swept the Winnipeg Jets in four straight for the Smythe Division title. In the Campbell Conference finals against the Detroit Red Wings, the Oilers lost Game 1 but then won four straight.

In the Wales Conference, meanwhile, the rough-and-tumble Philadelphia Flyers won their first two playoff rounds against the New York Rangers (4 games to 2) and the New York Islanders (4 games to 3). The Isles had advanced with one of the most dramatic victories in NHL playoff history, a 3–2 win over the Washington Capitals in the *fourth*

Wayne Gretzky (*left*) broke the all-time playoff scoring record and led Edmonton to its third Stanley Cup. Playoff MVP honors, however, went to Philadelphia goalie Ron Hextall (*right*) for his strong defensive play.

NHL FINAL STANDINGS

WALES CONFERENCE

Adams Division

	W	L	T	Pts.
Hartford	43	30	7	93
Montreal	41	29	10	92
Boston	39	34	7	85
Quebec	31	39	10	72
Buffalo	28	44	8	64

Patrick Division

	W	L	T	Pts.
Philadelphia	46	26	8	100
Washington	38	32	10	86
N.Y. Islanders	35	33	12	82
N.Y. Rangers	34	38	8	76
Pittsburgh	30	38	12	72
New Jersey	29	45	6	64

CAMPBELL CONFERENCE

Norris Division

	W	L	T	Pts.
St. Louis	32	33	15	79
Detroit	34	36	10	78
Chicago	29	37	14	72
Toronto	32	42	6	70
Minnesota	30	40	10	70

Smythe Division

	W	L	T	Pts.
Edmonton	50	24	6	106
Calgary	46	31	3	95
Winnipeg	40	32	8	88
Los Angeles	31	41	8	70
Vancouver	29	43	8	66

Stanley Cup: Edmonton Oilers

OUTSTANDING PLAYERS

Hart Trophy (most valuable player)	Wayne Gretzky, Edmonton
Ross Trophy (scorer)	Wayne Gretzky, Edmonton
Vezina Trophy (goalie)	Ron Hextall, Philadelphia
Norris Trophy (defenseman)	Ray Bourque, Boston
Selke Trophy (defensive forward)	Dave Poulin, Philadelphia
Calder Trophy (rookie)	Luc Robitaille, Los Angeles
Lady Byng Trophy (sportsmanship)	Joe Mullen, Calgary
Conn Smythe Trophy (Stanley Cup play)	Ron Hextall, Philadelphia

overtime of Game 7. In the Wales Conference finals, the Flyers faced the defending Stanley Cup champion Montreal Canadiens, who had advanced by beating the Boston Bruins (4 games to 0) and the archrival Quebec Nordiques (4 games to 3). The Flyer-Canadien series was a hard-fought battle that will be remembered for a bench-clearing brawl before the opening whistle of Game 6. The Flyers won that contest, 4–3, and the chance to take on Edmonton in the finals.

The championship series began in Edmonton, where the home team skated to a 4–2 triumph. Gretzky set the pace with one goal and one assist. In Game 2, also at Edmonton, the Oilers sent the game into overtime on a late goal by Glenn Anderson. They won, 3–2, on a tally by Jari Kurri.

In Philadelphia for Game 3, Edmonton shot to a 3–0 lead and seemed in full command of the series, but the injury-plagued Flyers rallied for a 5–3 win. Game 4, also in Philadelphia, marked another great performance by Gretzky, who had three assists in a 4–1 Oiler triumph.

Edmonton thus had a 3–1 series lead and an apparent lock on the Stanley Cup. But now it was the Flyers who played as if they had something to prove. Back in Edmonton for Game 5, the Flyers rallied from a 3–1 deficit and won the contest, 4–3. In Game 6 the Philadelphians treated their hometown fans to another come-from-behind victory. After trailing 2–0, they scored three straight goals to send the series to a seventh game.

It was as if the Oilers suddenly remembered their calling. On home ice in Game 7, they fell behind 1–0 after two minutes and then moved into high gear. The defense shut down Philadelphia the rest of the way, and the offense proved splendid. Messier tied the score later in the first period. Kurri, on a pass from Gretzky, put the Oilers ahead late in the second period. And with less than three minutes left to play, Anderson scored the clinching goal. The Oilers won, 3–1, and the defeat of 1986 became a thing of the past.

Canada Cup. In the six-nation Canada Cup tournament, the host country emerged victorious by defeating the Soviet Union in the three-game final series. All three games ended in a score of 6–5.

In 1987, Swiss skier Maria Walliser (*above*) placed first in two events at the world alpine championships and then went on to win the World Cup. And Brian Orser of Canada (*right*) captured the world men's figure-skating title.

ICE SKATING

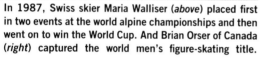

FIGURE SKATING

World Championships

Men	Brian Orser, Canada
Women	Katarina Witt, E. Germany
Pairs	Ekaterina Gordeyeva/Sergei Grinkov, U.S.S.R.
Dance	Natalya Bestemianova/Andrei Bukin, U.S.S.R.

United States Championships

Men	Brian Boitano
Women	Jill Trenary
Pairs	Jill Watson/Peter Oppegard
Dance	Suzanne Semanick/Scott Gregory

SPEED SKATING

World Championships

Men	Nikolai Gulyaev, U.S.S.R.
Women	Karin Kania, E. Germany

SKIING

WORLD CUP CHAMPIONSHIPS

Men	Pirmin Zurbriggen, Switzerland
Women	Maria Walliser, Switzerland

WORLD ALPINE CHAMPIONSHIPS

Men

Downhill	Peter Mueller, Switzerland
Slalom	Frank Woerndl, W. Germany
Giant Slalom	Pirmin Zurbriggen, Switzerland
Super Giant Slalom	Pirmin Zurbriggen
Combined	Marc Girardelli, Luxembourg

Women

Downhill	Maria Walliser, Switzerland
Slalom	Erika Hess, Switzerland
Giant Slalom	Vreni Schneider, Switzerland
Super Giant Slalom	Maria Walliser
Combined	Erika Hess

SWIMMING

WORLD SWIMMING RECORDS SET IN 1987

EVENT	HOLDER	TIME
	Men	
50-meter freestyle	Tom Jager, U.S.	22.32
200-meter individual medley	Tamas Darnyi, Hungary	2:00.56
400-meter individual medley	Tamas Darnyi, Hungary	4:15.42
800-meter freestyle relay	West Germany	7:13.10
	Women	
800-meter freestyle	Anke Moehring, E. Germany	8:19.53
1,500-meter freestyle	Janet Evans, U.S.	16:00.73
100-meter breaststroke	Silke Hoerner, E. Germany	1:07.91
800-meter freestyle relay	East Germany	7:55.47

Two U.S. swimmers set world records in 1987. Janet Evans (*left*) established the mark in the 1,500-meter freestyle. Tom Jager (*below*) set the standard in the 50-meter freestyle.

Steffi Graf, 18, the year's top woman player.

TENNIS

The world rankings in professional tennis were hotly contested in 1987, as some of the game's top veterans were challenged by up-and-coming young stars. Ivan Lendl, the 27-year-old Czechoslovakian native, retained his position as the number-one men's player —but not without a fight. On the women's side, Martina Navratilova was knocked out of the top spot by 18-year-old Steffi Graf of West Germany—but just barely.

Lendl captured the men's singles titles in two Grand Slam tournaments—the French Open and the U.S. Open—but the prestigious Wimbledon championship continued to elude him. In previous years, the American John McEnroe and the West German teenager Boris Becker had barred the door. This time it was Pat Cash, a 22-year-old Australian, who defeated Lendl in the Wimbledon final, 7–6, 6–2, 7–5.

Lendl was in top form at the U.S. Open, winning for the third year in a row. But it wasn't without remarkable resistance from Sweden's Mats Wilander. The final match took a record 4 hours, 47 minutes, with Lendl emerging victorious, 6–7, 6–0, 7–6, 6–4. Lendl also defeated Wilander in the French Open finals, 7–5, 6–2, 3–6, 7–6.

For young Steffi Graf, 1987 was a year of spectacular success. In June, when she was still only 17, Graf won the first Grand Slam event of her short career. Her victory over 30-year-old Navratilova in the finals of the French Open (6–4, 4–6, 8–6)—along with her numerous other tournament triumphs throughout the year—established her as the top player on the women's circuit.

Graf's losses, however, came at the hands of Navratilova in the finals of the most important events of the year—Wimbledon (7–5, 6–3) and the U.S. Open (7–6, 6–1). The triumph at Wimbledon was Navratilova's sixth straight (a record) and eighth overall (tying the record). The U.S. Open victory was her fourth in five years.

TOURNAMENT TENNIS

	Australian Open	French Open	Wimbledon	U.S. Open
Men's Singles	Stefan Edberg, Sweden	Ivan Lendl, Czechoslovakia	Pat Cash, Australia	Ivan Lendl, Czechoslovakia
Women's Singles	Hana Mandlikova, Czechoslovakia	Steffi Graf, West Germany	Martina Navratilova, U.S.	Martina Navratilova, U.S.
Men's Doubles	Stefan Edberg, Sweden/ Anders Jarryd, Sweden	Anders Jarryd, Sweden/ Robert Seguso, U.S.	Ken Flach, U.S./ Robert Seguso, U.S.	Stefan Edberg, Sweden/ Anders Jarryd, Sweden
Women's Doubles	Martina Navratilova, U.S./ Pam Shriver, U.S.	Martina Navratilova, U.S./ Pam Shriver, U.S.	Claudia Kohde-Kilsch, West Germany/ Helena Sukova, Czechoslovakia	Martina Navratilova, U.S./ Pam Shriver, U.S.

Davis Cup Winner: Sweden

TRACK AND FIELD

WORLD TRACK AND FIELD RECORDS SET IN 1987

EVENT	HOLDER	TIME, DISTANCE, OR POINTS
	Men	
100-meter run	Ben Johnson, Canada	0:09.83
2,000-meter run	Said Aouita, Morocco	4:50.81
2-mile run	Said Aouita, Morocco	8:13.45
5,000-meter run	Said Aouita, Morocco	12:58.39
High jump	Patrik Sjoberg, Sweden	7'11¼"
Pole vault	Sergei Bubka, U.S.S.R.	19'9¼"
Shot put	Alessandro Andrei, Italy	75'2"
	Women	
2-mile walk	Giulianna Salce, Italy	13:59.93
5-kilometer walk	Yan Hong, China	21:20.20
10-kilometer walk	Xu Yongjiu, China	44:26.50
100-meter hurdles	Ginka Zagorcheva, Bulgaria	0:12.25
High jump	Stefka Kostadinova, Bulgaria	6'10¼"
Triple jump	Li Huirong, China	46'¾"
Shot put	Natalya Lisovskaya, U.S.S.R.	74'3"
Javelin throw	Petra Felke, E. Germany	258'10"

The outstanding track performance of the year—and perhaps of the decade—was turned in by Ben Johnson of Canada (#145). At the World Track and Field Championships in Rome, Italy, Johnson shattered the world record in the 100 meters with an amazing time of 9.83 seconds.

Colorful ceremonies opened the 10th Pan Am Games, in Indianapolis. Wilma Rudolph, a native of the city and 1960 Olympic track and field champ, lights the torch.

THE 1987 PAN AMERICAN GAMES

There were representatives from the United States and Nicaragua, from Canada and Cuba, from Mexico and El Salvador and Brazil and Argentina. All together, 38 countries from North, South, and Central America took part. Was it a regional peace conference? Or a meeting to discuss the international debt problem?

No. It was the 10th Pan American Games, held at Indianapolis, Indiana, in August, 1987. It was the largest multisports event of the year, setting the stage for the 1988 Olympics. It was fifteen days of running, jumping, throwing, swimming, and shooting—a total of 34 sports in all.

The Pan Am Games are open to all nations in the Western Hemisphere. They are held every four years, each time hosted by a different city. The 1987 event marked the first time in 28 years that the Games were held in the United States. (Chicago played host in 1959.) Indianapolis, a city that boasts some of the most modern and extensive sports facilities in the country, staged one of the most memorable Pan Am Games in the history of the event. A record 4,350 athletes paraded in the colorful opening ceremonies, held at the famous Indianapolis Motor Speedway. The next two weeks saw stirring performances and exciting competition in almost every arena and on almost every field. And there were some surprising results.

The Competition. Pan Am competition is traditionally dominated by three countries—the United States, Cuba, and Canada. In that respect, the 1987 Games were hardly out of the ordinary. When all was said and done, the United States had won a record 369 medals (168 gold, 118 silver, and 83 bronze). Cuba finished second with 175 (75 gold, 52 silver, and 48 bronze). Canada was a close third with 162 (30 gold, 57 silver, and 75 bronze).

By no means, however, did all the glory go to the three athletic superpowers. The United States, for example, suffered defeats in the two major sports it *invented*—baseball and basketball. The Big Three certainly had their share of stars, but there were gold medalists from countries as small as Costa Rica, Jamaica, and Suriname. In fact, of the 38 countries represented at the Games, 27 won medals.

The biggest upset came in men's basketball. The United States hadn't lost a game in Pan Am competition since 1971. Going into the finals against Brazil, the Americans had won 34 games in a row, most by huge margins. But to the disbelief of 16,400 fans at Market Square Arena, the Brazilians captured the gold with a 120–115 come-from-behind victory. More than half their points were scored by two players, Oscar Schmidt (46 points) and Marcel Souza (31 points).

Another stunning performance was turned in by a 16-year-old swimmer from Costa Rica named Silvia Poll. Although the United States won 27 of the 32 swimming events, Poll was the obvious star of the pool. The 6-foot, 2-inch freestyle and backstroke sensation won 3 golds, 3 silvers, and 2 bronzes.

In addition to swimming, U.S. athletes excelled in track and field, gymnastics, and several of the team sports. The highlight of the track and field competition came in the women's long jump, when Jackie Joyner-Kersee leaped 24 feet, 5½ inches to tie the world record. In gymnastics, U.S. women won the team competition and finished 1-2-3 in the all-around competition. On the men's side, the United States also earned the team title; and top performer Scott Johnson won four golds, including the all-around title.

Other outstanding performers from the United States included diver Greg Louganis (the Olympic champion), who won both the platform and springboard competitions for a record third straight time; 13-year-old archer Denise Parker; 17-year-old softball pitcher Michele Granger; and two members of the baseball team—switch-hitting second baseman Ty Griffin and the amazing one-handed lefty pitcher Jim Abbott, who carried the U.S. flag in the opening ceremonies.

The baseball tournament itself was one of the most exciting events of the Games. The United States managed to upset the powerful Cuban squad (which hadn't lost since 1967) in an early round, but the Cubans rebounded for an impressive 13–9 victory in the gold-medal rematch. Cuba also excelled in boxing (taking 10 of the 12 gold medals); weightlifting (with 9 different entries winning golds); wrestling (including 7 golds in Greco-Roman); and a variety of other sports.

Canada was the most improved team in Pan Am competition. Its 162 medals in all (30 gold) compared with only 109 (18 gold) four years earlier. The Canadians excelled in such sports as rowing, shooting, and the equestrian events.

The 1987 Pan Am Games weren't without problems and controversies. Early on there was confusion when the athletes' village ran out of space. Later, six athletes were disqualified for drug use. And there were several minor outbreaks of political violence.

All in all, though, it was the competition and the city of Indianapolis that commanded center stage. At the closing ceremonies, held in the 65,000-seat Hoosier Dome, the torch of the 10th Pan American Games was extinguished, the U.S. flag was lowered, and the flag of Cuba—host of the 1991 Games—was raised.

The United States won a record 369 medals at the Games. The stars included gymnast Scott Johnson, who won four golds, and 13-year-old archer Denise Parker.

Ever watched a sporting event and thought, "Hey, that's as easy as falling off a log"? Well, at the World Lumberjack Championships in Hayward, Wisconsin, one competitor found out it was true! Throughout 1987, amateur athletes everywhere experienced the joy of victory and the disappointment of defeat.

SPORTS BRIEFS

Professional football players went on strike. Major league baseball players argued about corked bats and scuffed balls. And, as they do every year, top athletes in every sport battled it out for world championships and zillion-dollar paychecks. But what about everybody else? What about the ordinary people who are just out for some friendly competition and an occasional thrill? Well, the amateurs didn't always make big headlines in 1987, but there were plenty of things to cheer about, plenty of things to marvel at, and plenty of ways that ordinary people were just having fun.

THE "OTHER" NATIONAL PASTIME

If you ask a group of Americans the national pastime, most will probably answer baseball. Many will say football. But if you head over to the nearest schoolyard on a summer evening or on a Sunday afternoon,

chances are you'll find another game in progress: softball. The fact is, softball is the most popular team sport in the United States, at least when it comes to playing. Some 40 million Americans play the game every year—young and old, men and women, bosses and employees, teachers and students.

The year 1987 was a special one for the sport, as the game marked its 100th anniversary. To commemorate the centennial, softball marathons, celebrity tournaments, and other special events were held around the country. The Amateur Softball Association sponsored a marathon torch run from Chicago, Illinois—the game's birthplace—to Oklahoma City—the site of the National Softball Hall of Fame. Events there included the official opening of a new $2 million Hall of Fame Stadium.

The Abner Doubleday of softball was a young reporter named George Hancock. The date was Thanksgiving Day, 1887. The place was the Farragut Boat House in Chicago. Hancock and a group of friends had gathered in the Boat House gymnasium to hear the score of the Harvard-Yale football game. When they heard that Yale had won, one of the Yale rooters picked up a boxing glove and tossed it gleefully at one of the Harvard men. The Harvard man grabbed a broomstick and playfully swatted the glove away.

That gave Hancock an idea: indoor baseball! He tied the boxing glove into a ball, unscrewed the broom handle, and chalked off bases on the floor of the gymnasium. Teams were chosen, and a century of softball was under way.

Hancock's new sport quickly caught on as a version of baseball that could be played indoors during the winter months. That's why a softball diamond is smaller than a baseball diamond. (The bases are 60 feet apart in softball, 90 feet apart in baseball.) At various times in its history, the game has been called "kitten ball," "army ball," "mush ball," and "indoor-outdoor." The name "softball" became official in 1933.

As millions of players can tell you, a softball today isn't really soft at all. It's bigger than a baseball but almost as hard. And the game is played in different ways in different leagues: men's and women's fast- and slow-pitch, church slow, industrial slow, girls' and boys' fast and slow, and others.

All together, there are about 200,000 organized softball teams in the United States today—not to mention many more in other countries throughout the world. After 100 years, George Hancock's brainstorm has become an *international* pastime.

THE HOTTEST THING ON SNOW

A more recent idea in weekend recreation has become popular on snow-covered mountainsides rather than on sun-drenched dirt fields. And clearly it takes more courage than a casual game of softball. The sport is called "snowboarding," and it was the hottest new craze at ski resorts everywhere during the winter of 1987.

What is snowboarding? The simplest answer is a mixture of surfing, skateboarding, and skiing. Another answer is a sport that you shouldn't try unless you have very good balance—or don't mind the taste of snow.

The snowboard itself is a cross between a surfboard and a ski. It's about 5 feet long and 10 inches wide and is made of laminated wood or fiberglass. The board has fixed bindings that strap around any heavy boot. No poles are used.

Softball, the most popular team sport in the United States, marked its 100th anniversary in 1987. Softball marathons, celebrity tournaments, and other special events were held around the country.

Snowboarding—a combination of surfing, skateboarding, and skiing —was the hottest new craze at ski resorts during the winter of 1987.

The sport of snowboarding is only about five years old, but it has grown increasingly popular each winter. By 1987, there were believed to be about 100,000 enthusiasts in the United States alone. A few U.S. ski areas have banned snowboarding, but more than 100 around the country allow and even encourage the sport. One of them, Stratton Mountain in Vermont, held an international competition in March, 1987. More than 200 snowboarders, from as far away as Australia and Japan, showed up for the event. Not bad for a sport that was just getting off the ground.

NOT JUST HOT AIR

Richard Branson of Britain and Per Lindstrand of Sweden aren't highly paid professional athletes, but neither can they be described as "ordinary" people. In July, 1987, the two thrill-seekers set out on a journey that no one had ever completed: a flight across the Atlantic in a hot-air balloon.

The 3,400-mile adventure began in the early morning of July 2, on the coast of Maine. Branson and Lindstrand climbed inside a pressurized capsule that hung from their huge black balloon, the *Virgin Atlantic Flyer*. As tall as a 21-story building, it was believed to be the largest hot-air balloon ever made.

Within a few hours of takeoff, Branson and Lindstrand had reached an unexpected speed of more than 140 miles per hour and an altitude of nearly 28,000 feet. "It has been the most spectacular and magnificent flight," reported Branson by radio. Only ten hours into the journey, the men broke the all-time distance record for a flight in a hot-air balloon—907 miles.

The flight went smoothly until the balloon crossed the coast of Ireland the next afternoon. Descending rapidly, it scraped the ground in Northern Ireland. Then it began to climb, but only for a short while. With the landing target in Scotland literally in sight, the balloon fell into the Irish Sea. Fortunately, Branson and Lindstrand were able to leap from their capsule as it hit the water. Royal Navy rescue teams hauled the two men to safety.

Should Branson and Lindstrand have been credited with the first transatlantic crossing in a hot-air balloon? The International Aeronautical Foundation wasn't sure. More sympathetic followers said, "Close enough!"

THE SPECIAL OLYMPICS

No sportsman or sportswoman in 1987—not the winners of the Super Bowl, not snowboard daredevils, not transatlantic balloonists—could have had a greater thrill than the athletes and spectators at the Seventh International Summer Special Olympics in South Bend, Indiana. The 4,717 mentally retarded athletes who participated in the nine-day event hailed from 70 countries and ranged in age from 8 to 81. They represented more than one million athletes involved in Special Olympics programs throughout the world.

Conceived by Eunice Kennedy Shriver, now the organization's chairwoman, the Special Olympics have been held every four years since the 1960's. Although they have the trappings of the Olympic Games—a torch, a parade, medals for the winners—the Special Olympics have very different goals. They are a promotional event to get more services for the mentally retarded. They are an international showcase to generate greater public interest and understanding of mental retardation. And, perhaps most of all, they are an opportunity for the participants to join together in friendly competition, to test their limits, and to celebrate *themselves.*

The Special Olympics isn't about who is faster or stronger. The winners are awarded medals, but every competitor gets a hug at the finish line, a special ribbon, and a place on the victory stand. The important things are effort and hope and just taking part. The spirit is summed up in the Special Olympics Oath: "Let me win, but if I cannot win, let me be brave in the attempt."

BRIEF BRIEFS

The *Eagle,* an 88-pound experimental plane designed by engineers at the Massachusetts Institute of Technology, broke the world record for human-powered flight in January, 1987. At Edwards Air Force Base, California, 26-year-old medical student Glenn Tremml pedaled the plane on a 37.2-mile flight . . .

Stephen Roche became the first Irishman ever to win the prestigious Tour de France bicycle race . . .

Edwin Moses, who had won a record 122 straight 400-meter hurdles races dating back to August, 1977, finally lost in June, 1987. He was defeated in Madrid, Spain, by Danny Harris . . .

Amateur athletes throughout the world were training hard for the 1988 Olympic Games. The city of Calgary in western Canada finished preparations for the XV Winter Olympic Games, scheduled for February 13 through 28. Seoul, South Korea, neared completion of facilities for the XXIV Summer Games, to be held September 17 through October 2.

Heidi and Howdy—mascots of the 1988 Winter Olympic Games, to be held in Calgary, Canada, in February.

LIVING HISTORY

Americans marked a momentous event in 1987: the 200th anniversary of the U.S. Constitution. Below, the framers of the document meet to sign it in Independence Hall, Philadelphia. Among them are George Washington (standing, right), Benjamin Franklin (seated, center), and James Madison (right of Franklin).

A SALUTE TO THE CONSTITUTION

Through the summer of 1787, a group of men met in Philadelphia's Independence Hall. Their goal was to hammer out a new form of government for the fledgling United States, which had won its independence from Britain just six years before. The job wasn't an easy one—the heat of the delegates' debates was matched only by the sweltering summer weather outside the high-ceilinged room where they gathered. But in the end, they succeeded.

They produced a document that established the framework of the country, truly joining the states together into a nation for the first time. The document—four sheets of parchment, hand-written with a feather quill—was the Constitution of the United States. At the time, the Constitution was something of an experiment. It was filled with compromises, and few of the delegates agreed with all its provisions. George Washington himself said that he didn't expect it to last more than twenty years. But the Constitution survived, and it shaped the nation.

In 1987, people in the United States celebrated the Constitution's 200th anniversary with ceremonies, events, and renewed interest in the document itself. Philadelphia, naturally, was the site of some of the most important events. The city staged exhibits, parades, concerts, various shows and re-enactments, and even a mock constitutional convention for high school students. Other communities and states also planned events.

One goal of the bicentennial events was to increase public knowledge of the Constitution. Polls showed that many people were ignorant of some of its basic provisions. (Only four of every ten people polled, for example, knew that the first ten amendments make up the Bill of Rights.) So as part of the celebration, millions of copies of the document were distributed. And there was fresh interest in what some people have called a miracle—the story of how the group of men in Philadelphia overcame their differences to draw up the Constitution.

A NATION IN TROUBLE

The Constitutional Convention was called because the United States was in trouble. Since independence, the thirteen original states had been governed under the Articles of Confederation. Under this constitution, each state was practically a separate power, bound into a loose association with the others. The U.S. government consisted of a weak Congress that had very little power.

As a result, the states had begun to squabble among themselves. They argued over territory and levied taxes on trade that crossed state lines. Each state also issued its own currency, and some were printing quantities of paper money that quickly became worthless. Congress had no power to stop these acts. Moreover, Congress couldn't levy direct taxes—it could only ask for assessments from the states, based on the states' own estimates of what they could afford to pay. The new government was therefore practically broke—it even owed money to soldiers who had fought in the Revolutionary War.

In 1786, a brief but violent uprising of farmers in Massachusetts (Shays' Rebellion) created grave new worries about the country's future. There were also threats along the borders: Spain had closed the lower Mississippi River to American ships, choking off trade. Britain, violating an agreement made at the end of the Revolutionary War, was refusing to give up forts in the Northwest Territory, thus blocking American expansion to the west.

If the United States was to survive and thrive, it seemed clear that a stronger central government would be needed. Some people even suggested a monarchy. But those who had fought to win freedom from Britain weren't ready to give up their democratic ideals. Instead, Congress called for a convention to amend and strengthen the Articles of Confederation.

THE CONVENTION

The 55 delegates who assembled in Philadelphia in the summer of 1787 represented twelve of the thirteen states. (Rhode Island refused to attend.) They included some of the most important and influential people in the country—lawyers, judges, landowners. Nearly all had held public office at some time. Washington came, although he was reluctant to leave his farm. Also on hand was Benjamin Franklin, 81 and so troubled by gout that he had to be carried about the city in a sedan chair. But most of the other delegates were relatively young—shy, soft-spoken James Madison, for example, was 36; the brilliant Alexander Hamilton, 32. A few major figures were missing. Thomas Jefferson was in Paris, as minister to France. And Patrick Henry refused to attend, saying that he "smelt a rat."

On May 25—a gray and rainy Friday—the convention opened. Washington was named presiding officer, and a few ground rules were adopted. One was that no vote would be final until the convention had a completed document before it; until then, the delegates could change their minds on any provision.

Another rule was that the proceedings would take place in absolute secrecy. Jefferson wrote from Paris that he was "sorry they began their deliberations by so abominable a precedent as that of tying up the tongues of their members." But Madison and other delegates believed that secrecy would allow the delegates to speak their minds freely at the convention. He later wrote that "no Constitution would ever have been adopted by the convention if the debates had been made public." His notes on the proceedings, which were published after his death, provide a detailed account of the convention.

In fact, Madison's ideas set the tone for the debates. His Virginia Plan, presented at the outset, called for a "national government, with a supreme legislative, executive and judiciary." That idea went much farther than amending the Articles of Confederation —it was a call to throw the old constitution out the window and begin all over again.

Most of the delegates agreed that strong measures were necessary. But what form should the new government take? Madison's plan called for a strong bicameral (two-house) legislature and a weaker executive. Representatives in the legislature would be elected by proportional representation—that is, more seats for the more populous states. But delegates from the small states objected strongly. William Paterson of New Jersey, for example, said he would never consent to the plan because his state "would be swallowed up."

There was also debate on how the representatives should be elected. Some delegates viewed the "people" as uneducated, and they were against direct elections (by popular vote). "The evils we experience flow from the excess of democracy," said Elbridge Gerry of Massachusetts. But others believed that the support of the people was essential for the new government.

The convention nearly foundered on these issues. But in the end, the delegates agreed on a compromise that was proposed by Roger Sherman of Connecticut. It called for a House of Representatives with proportional representation, elected by popular vote, and a Senate in which all states would have equal representation. Senators were to be chosen by the state legislatures (the system was later changed to direct elections).

The legislature wasn't the only issue that provoked argument. It took the delegates 60 votes to decide how the President should be picked, how much power he should have, how long his term should be, and whether he could be impeached. Everyone knew that Washington, the most respected and best-known person in the country, would most likely be the first President. But, as Benjamin Franklin put it, "The first man put at the helm will be a good one. Nobody knows what sort may come afterwards."

200 YEARS AGO . . .

While the framers of the Constitution debated, daily life went on outside Independence Hall. Here are some items that were in use in 1787: Instead of a purse, a woman used a lady's pocket. It tied around the waist and was worn under her dress . . . This baby's bottle is made of pewter. Most families had seven to ten babies, but many didn't live to adulthood . . . Ice skates like this one, with its elegant curled toe, tied on with leather straps and required strong ankles . . . Chamber pots took the place of indoor plumbing and came in all shapes, even a porcelain cat. Corn husks and newsprint were used as toilet paper.

The convention also divided sharply on the subject of slavery. Some delegates wanted the Constitution to outlaw slavery; others wanted a clause that would sanction it. Again, a compromise was reached: Congress would be forbidden from outlawing slavery until 1808.

Not all the delegates stayed through the long debates. Many came and went as personal business allowed. Some, including Alexander Hamilton, despaired of ever seeing the convention finish its work and left altogether. (Hamilton later returned.) Those who stayed in Philadelphia generally met six days a week. They struggled with constitutional questions—and the heat—from 10 A.M. to 3 or 4 P.M., when they adjourned for hearty dinners at the City Tavern, the Black Horse, the George, and other popular inns.

When the delegates had finally reached agreement on the Constitution's provisions, the final wording was entrusted to Gouverneur Morris of Pennsylvania. He wrote the famous preamble that begins "We the People . . ." And on September 12, 1787, the finished Constitution was presented to the delegates.

Even then, there were disagreements. Some felt the document was too vague. George Mason of Virginia called for a bill of rights. Madison wanted provisions for a national university. But most of the delegates wanted to finish and go home. On September 17, all but three signed the document. Franklin summed up the feelings of many when he told Washington, "I consent, sir, to this Constitution because I expect no better."

A FLEXIBLE CONSTITUTION

The new Constitution still faced major hurdles: approval by Congress and nine of the thirteen states. The public debates it produced were, if possible, even more heated than the secret discussions of the convention. But by June 21, 1788, the Constitution had been ratified (approved) by the required nine. Two key states, Virginia and New York, gave their approval soon after.

Within two years, the Constitution was widely accepted and respected. It had also begun to change—the first ten amendments, making up the Bill of Rights, were adopted in 1789. Over the following years, sixteen other amendments were adopted. They outlawed slavery, gave women the right to vote, lowered the voting age to 18, and made other alterations. The government created by the

Constitution changed in some ways, too. For example, both the executive and judicial branches gradually grew stronger than was originally envisioned.

But the basic provisions of the Constitution remained, and they proved flexible enough to serve as the supreme law of the land for 200 years. Today there are many calls for changes, even for a second constitutional convention. Some people want to add specific provisions, such as an amendment requiring a balanced federal budget. Others feel the system of government needs changing. They argue that the three-branch system, set up to provide checks and balances in power, now produces stalemates—so that nothing gets done.

But the calls for change worry other people, who fear that too much tinkering with the Constitution may destroy the democratic system of government that has worked well in the United States. The Constitution, they argue, is a delicate instrument. The fact that it has survived so long and worked so well is proof that the delegates of 1787 were far more successful than they ever could have imagined.

Red, white, and blue balloons form a giant flag in front of Independence Hall, in celebration of the bicentennial.

We the People

INTERPRETING THE CONSTITUTION

The U.S. Constitution provides a general plan of government. Many of its clauses are broadly phrased, and they can be interpreted in more than one way. Moreover, the Constitution today must be adapted to developments—from television news to computer record-keeping—that could never have been foreseen in 1787. Thus disputes often arise over what the Constitution truly means.

The final say in such matters belongs to the U.S. Supreme Court. The Constitution established the Supreme Court as "the judicial power of the United States." But the Court's role in interpreting the Constitution wasn't fully spelled out in the document. Thus, "Equal Justice Under Law"—the saying engraved on the Supreme Court building in Washington, D.C.—hasn't always been an easy principle to apply.

The Supreme Court's role was more firmly established in the first years after the Constitution was adopted. In the famous case *Marbury* versus *Madison* (1803), the first chief justice, John Marshall, ruled that the Court has the power to decide if an existing law violates the Constitution. Using this power, called judicial review, the Court has since overturned more than 100 acts of Congress, as well as executive actions and many state laws.

The Court is made up of nine justices (one chief and eight associates), who are chosen by the President with the approval of the Senate. They make constitutional rulings only when actual cases are presented to them. Most cases are appeals to overturn rulings that were made by lower courts. Usually, the Court selects just 150 to 180 of the 5,000 cases submitted each year.

In each of the cases, the justices hear the arguments on both sides of the dispute. They study the records of the case, the Constitution, and any relevant laws and precedents (similar cases that have been previously decided). Then they meet to dis-

cuss the case. When the outcome has been decided, one of the justices writes the majority opinion. (Justices who disagree with the ruling, or agree with it on other grounds, may write separate opinions.)

Supreme Court rulings on constitutional matters are final—short of amending the Constitution itself, there is no way to overturn them. But occasionally the Court overrules itself. For example, in 1896, in *Plessy* versus *Ferguson,* the Court ruled that segregation between blacks and whites didn't violate the Constitution. In 1954, in *Brown* versus *Board of Education of Topeka,* it found that segregation was unconstitutional.

The example shows that Supreme Court interpretations change with the times. And because justices are appointed by whatever President is in power when an opening comes up, the interpretations may also change with the political mood of the country. But because an appointment to the Court is an appointment for life, openings are few, and change is slow.

Some observers feel that in recent years the Court has moved from broad, liberal interpretations to narrower, more conservative rulings. This trend was much in the news in 1987, when Associate Justice Lewis F. Powell, Jr., resigned. President Ronald Reagan nominated Robert H. Bork, a judge and legal scholar known for his strong conservative views, to take his place. The Senate, however, didn't confirm the appointment, because a number of senators feared his vote would tip the balance of the Court and cause it to overturn many of its past rulings.

Whether conservative or liberal, however, Supreme Court rulings must in the end be based on the Constitution. Following are two famous Supreme Court cases. Before you read how the Court ruled in each case, take a few minutes to decide

Equal Justice Under Law

how you would rule. If you're in doubt, refer to the Constitution—especially the Bill of Rights—for help in deciding.

IN RE GAULT (1967)

This case involves issues of the Fifth, Sixth, and Fourteenth amendments, which protect the rights of people accused of crimes.

The Facts. Gerald Gault, 15, was arrested for making obscene phone calls and was brought before a judge in an Arizona juvenile court. He wasn't given a chance to have a lawyer, and the judge didn't explain exactly what he was charged with. His accuser (who had received the phone calls) didn't appear in court to say what he had done wrong. But Gault had previously been arrested for purse-snatching. Based on his two arrests, a police officer told the court that he was a delinquent. He was sentenced to a state reform school, where he could be held until age 21.

A retired lawyer stepped in and appealed the decision on Gault's behalf. It eventually reached the Supreme Court.

The Arguments. Gault's lawyer argued that he had been denied "due process"—that is, his case hadn't been decided in the legal way. Under the Sixth Amendment, a person accused of a crime is entitled to have a lawyer, to hear the charges against him, and to confront his or her accusers.

Lawyers for the State of Arizona argued that juvenile courts are different from adult courts. To help young people straighten out, they said, judges must be free to decide what is best, in much the same way that parents decide what is best for their children.

How would you decide?

The Ruling. The Supreme Court ruled 7–2 in Gault's favor. It said that juveniles, just like adults, have a right to have lawyers, hear the charges against them, and question their accusers. This case became a landmark in juvenile justice.

NEW YORK TIMES V. UNITED STATES (1971)

This case, known as the Pentagon Papers case, concerns issues of the First Amendment, which protects freedom of speech, press, and religion.

The Facts. In 1971, *The New York Times* obtained a copy of a secret government study that detailed the development of U.S. policy in Vietnam. (The report, known as the Pentagon Papers, covered the years 1945–68.) When the newspaper began to run a series of articles based on the study, the federal government went to a district court and got a temporary order blocking further publication. The court that imposed the order later lifted it, but an appeals court re-imposed it. The *Times* appealed to the Supreme Court. (A second newspaper, the *Washington Post,* had also run articles on the study and had run into similar problems. The Court heard both cases together.)

The Arguments. Lawyers for the newspapers argued that the ban on publication amounted to censorship—that is, the government was deciding what could and could not be printed. Government control of the press is forbidden by the First Amendment. If the ban stood, it would mark the first time that a court had ordered a newspaper not to print something.

Lawyers for the government argued that the United States would be damaged if the information in the report was made public. They said that publication would create a serious threat to national security and might even affect the lives of U.S. soldiers who were then fighting in Vietnam.

Who was right?

The Ruling. The Supreme Court ruled 6–3 in favor of the newspapers. It said that the government had failed to show good reason for overriding the First Amendment. Several justices wrote opinions saying that the publication of information couldn't be blocked unless it would do grave and immediate harm, such as costing lives. The government hadn't proved that such a danger existed.

THE
DREADFUL DRAGON

Long, long ago, an old story tells, the people of a city in North Africa lived in terror of a menace outside their gates—an evil dragon. Each day the dragon appeared, demanding food. At first the people gave it sheep, but it soon demanded men and then young maidens.

To satisfy the dragon's horrid appetite, the king of the city ordered that all the young maidens draw lots each day to see who would be sacrificed. The lot finally fell to the king's own daughter. Sick at heart, he watched her walk through the city gates to face the waiting dragon.

Suddenly a strange knight appeared. Raising his sword, he spurred his horse at the dragon and battled it until the evil beast fell to the ground. Then he cut off its head.

The knight was George of Lydda, and the story is the famous tale of St. George and the dragon. In some versions, he marries the princess; in others, he rides off to do more good deeds. But St. George is only one of many heroes who have fought dragons through the pages of myth and legend.

Dragons appear in stories from nearly every part of the world. Some, like the dragon in the St. George tale, are evil. Others, especially in Chinese myths, are powerful but kind, even helpful. Stories of dragons are among the oldest in the world—some reach back nearly 4,000 years.

MYTHICAL MONSTERS

The stories agree on what a dragon is in general terms: a huge, scaly, lizardlike creature that can spit fire. But they differ on the specifics of dragon appearance.

Many dragons had batlike wings and could fly. Some had horns, sharp spines along their backs, and barbs on the ends of their tails. All had sharp fangs. Most dragons had legs and claws —two legs or four legs, like the legs of eagles or lions. But some were more like snakes: legless, wingless, or both.

Some dragons were said to live in wells or in deep forest pools. Other dragons were thought to live in swamps, rivers, and lakes; underground, in caves; or on high, inaccessible mountains. Dragons were believed to share a common love for jewels and other treasure. But while European dragons were heartless predators with insatiable appetites for human flesh, Chinese dragons were said to be content with an occasional bird.

The reason dragons varied so much is simple: They appear in many stories, but there is no evidence that they ever appeared on Earth. They are mythical creatures, so they take any form that the imagination gives them.

Some people have suggested that dragons represent a distant memory of dinosaurs. But dinosaurs died out long before humans appeared on Earth. Most dragons are something like certain living creatures—crocodiles, for example, or large lizards. On the island of Komodo in the Malay Archipelago, lizards called Komodo dragons grow up to 10 feet (3 meters) long. It's possible that the first dragon stories sprang up after people saw startling creatures like these.

The absence of real dragons hasn't prevented people from claiming to see them and even producing "specimens." Reports of dragon sightings were common in Europe through the 1600's, and preserved "dragon babies"—usually stitched together from lizard skins and bat wings—were sold. A few dragon sightings have even been reported in this century. But most people today accept the fact that dragons lived only in legend.

EARLY DRAGONS

Monsters of many kinds figured in the tales told by early peoples, especially in stories of the world's creation. Often it's unclear what these monsters were supposed to look like, but some are thought to have been dragons.

Another ancient tale arose in Babylonia, about 1800 B.C. It tells that at the dawn of the universe, the forces of evil and chaos were led by the dragonlike goddess Tiamat. The Babylonian sun god, Marduk, defeated her by using the wind as his ally. When the dragon opened her gaping jaws to devour him, he drove the wind into her mouth so that she couldn't close it. Then he shot an arrow down her throat to her heart (a dragon-slaying method used by many later heroes) and killed her.

The ancient Egyptians told of a huge serpent, Apophis, who was the enemy of their sun god, Re. Each night the sun god disappeared into the underworld to fight this monster. Each morning, having won the battle, he reappeared.

Our word "dragon" comes from the Greek word *drakon,* which was used to refer to any type of snake. Many Greek tales tell of heroes who defeated dragonlike monsters. The god Apollo, for example, slew the serpent monster Python. These tales are similar to stories about dragons that became popular in Europe during the Middle Ages. Like the later tales, they show the forces of good (represented by the hero) triumphing over evil (represented by the dragon).

DRAGONS OF EUROPE

The evil dragons of medieval Europe were always causing trouble. If a well went bad, the reason was doubtless that a dragon was living in it. If fire broke out in the middle of the night, dragons flying overhead had caused it with their fiery breath. Even when dragons didn't cause calamity, they were connected with it. Sightings of dragons were often reported just before catastrophic events such as invasions or outbreaks of plague. Dragons were pictured at the edges of early maps, marking the beginnings of dangerous, unknown lands.

Europeans believed there were several distinct types of dragons. The wyvern, for example, was a fierce, flying dragon that carried the plague. The amphiptère was a legless dragon that lived in Egypt and Arabia and guarded the trees that produced frankincense resin. The lindworm had no wings and was said to live in Central Asia, where Marco Polo claimed to have seen several. The guivre lacked legs as well as wings and was said to live in forests and wells. Most fantastic of all was the vouivre, a dragon that lived in the French Alps and was covered head to claw with jewels.

Besides these types, there were many famous individual dragons. One of the best known in Norse mythology is Fafnir, who began life as a giant. Fafnir killed his father to gain a hoard of gold and a magic ring that could make more gold. Then he changed into a dragon to guard his treasure better.

Fafnir ravaged the countryside until the hero Siegfried came along. Siegfried, like many other dragon-slayers, used brains as well as brawn to defeat his scaly foe. He dug a pit along a path the dragon used and waited in it. When the dragon came down the path and passed over him, he drove his sword into the monster's unprotected underside.

If the number of tales are any indication, Britain must once have fairly crawled with dragons. Among them was the Laidly Worm of Northumberland—a princess who was changed into a dragon by her wicked stepmother. Her brother returned from overseas, changed her back with a kiss, and turned the stepmother into a toad.

Another story tells how the heir of Lambton Hall went fishing one day and caught an odd-looking, fanged worm. Unthinkingly, he tossed it into a well on his way home. Years later the creature emerged from the dank well as a full-grown dragon and set about terrorizing the countryside. The young lord killed it with a clever plan: He wore spiked armor, so that when the dragon wrapped its coils around him it wounded itself.

Russians who listened to fireside tales knew that it was unwise to strike a bargain with a dragon. According to one tale, Gorynych, a dragon with several heads and even more tails, lived near Kiev. He was defeated in battle by Dobrynja Nikitich, who let him live on the condition that he stop destroying the countryside and carrying off young maidens. That, however, was what European dragons did best—so it wasn't long before Gorynych swooped down on Kiev and snatched a princess. Dobrynja galloped in pursuit to the dragon's lair, where he freed the princess and dispatched the monster once and for all.

CHINESE DRAGONS

The Chinese believed that dragons were powerful, magical, and friendly beings—not evil monsters to be slain. Dragons were honored and feared because their powers over the forces of nature were so great. By simply flying up into the sky, they could bring gentle rains to make crops grow. Chinese farmers would beat gongs to frighten the dragons into the air when they needed rain. But when dragons were angry, they caused floods, windstorms, and destruction.

Many Chinese scholars separated dragons into four types, each with its own job. The T'ien-lung, or Celestial Dragon, supported the palaces of the gods in heaven. The Shen-lung, or Spirit Dragon, governed wind and weather. It was said to be a lazy dragon that always tried to hide from work. The Ti-lung was the Dragon of the Earth, with power over rivers and streams. Every river was said to have its own dragon lord, who lived in a palace beneath the water. The fourth type was the Fu ts'ang-lung, or Dragon of Hidden Treasure, who guarded all the precious minerals underground.

Other writers classified dragons according to differences in their appearance. For example, the Imperial Dragon had five claws and was a symbol reserved for the emperor. Some dragons were thought to look like, and be related to, fish or horses. Nine dragons with different traits were believed to protect objects ranging from bells and swords to gates, bridges, and rooftops. Some tales told that dragons could assume human form and even shrink themselves to the size of mice.

Still other writers divided dragons by color. Blue dragons, for example, were considered omens of spring. Red and black dragons fought in the clouds and produced storms. Yellow dragons were the most honored, symbols of intelligence and virtue. But some people said that dragons could change color if they chose.

The Chinese believed that dragons hatched from huge, jewel-like eggs. These eggs lay near riverbanks for as long as 1,000 years before the young, snakelike creatures emerged. Newborn dragons immediately began to grow, taking 3,000 years to reach their final form. Along the way, they passed through various stages, sprouting scales, shaggy manes, claws, horns, and wings.

Parts of a dragon's body were thought to have strong medicinal powers. Chinese apothecaries sold powders that were said to be ground dragon's bone (for fevers and paralysis) or teeth (for madness and headache). Dragon blood was said to turn to amber when it touched the ground.

The Chinese believed that most important of all was a dragon's pearl, which it kept in its mouth or in the folds of skin under its

jaw. The pearl was said by some to symbolize wisdom and by others to stand for the sun, the moon, or life itself. But by all accounts, the pearl possessed great magic.

One Chinese story tells of a poor boy who finds a dragon's pearl lying in a field. He takes it back to the house where he lives with his widowed mother and puts it in the empty rice jar. In the morning, the jar is full. The boy and his mother find that the pearl will provide them not only with rice but with all the food they need, as well as silk and money. They keep it secret, and their wealth grows.

Soon the other people in the village grow jealous, and the headman goes to the boy's house to investigate. The boy hides the pearl by putting it into his mouth. But he swallows it by mistake—and is changed into a fire-breathing dragon.

In Chinese culture today, the dragon remains an important symbol, associated with prosperity and good luck. But few people would expect to find a dragon's pearl. If dragons ever existed, the days when they roamed the world are gone.

Basil Rathbone strikes a familiar pose in one of his sixteen film portrayals of the great Sherlock Holmes.

SHERLOCK HOLMES— STILL ALIVE AT 100

"Mr. Holmes thanks you for your letter. At the moment he is in retirement in Sussex, keeping bees."

Every week, dozens of letters addressed to "Mr. Sherlock Holmes" are mailed to "221B Baker Street in London, the fictional residence of the world's greatest detective. In the building where 221 would have stood, the occupants send out gracious replies, informing correspondents that the celebrated sleuth has retired to his favorite hobby.

Tall and lean, dressed in a deerstalker hat and Inverness cape, smoking a pipe, and peering through a magnifying glass, Sherlock Holmes is one of the most familiar figures in all of literature. Certainly no other fictional character has been mistaken more often for a real person. In 1987, 100 years after his liter-

ary debut, Holmes was still being celebrated by hero-worshippers around the world.

The character of Sherlock Holmes—with his faithful friend, Dr. Watson—was the creation of the British writer Sir Arthur Conan Doyle. The brilliant private detective was introduced in a short novel, *A Study in Scarlet,* published in 1887. Before retiring to Sussex, Holmes appeared in a total of four novels and fifty-six short stories. Over the decades, millions of readers—in 57 different languages—have followed Holmes' adventures and delighted in his ability to solve the most baffling mysteries.

CONAN DOYLE—AUTHOR AND ADVENTURER

Sir Arthur Conan Doyle, creator of the master detective, was born on May 22, 1859, in Edinburgh, Scotland. As a young boy he loved to read adventure tales, and he wrote stories of his own. After studying at Jesuit schools in England and Austria, he entered the University of Edinburgh and received a bachelor of medicine degree in 1881.

Graduation from medical school brought adventure for Conan Doyle. First he spent seven months as ship's surgeon on a whaler bound for the Arctic. Then, upon his return, he signed up for a voyage to West Africa. His experiences on those journeys had a major influence on the rest of his life—and on his writings.

In 1882, after returning from Africa, Conan Doyle set up a medical practice in Southsea, England. Patients were scarce, however, and so the young doctor took to writing. He managed to sell a few adventure stories, but they earned him very little money.

The year 1885 marked a turning point in Conan Doyle's life. That summer he was awarded his doctor of medicine degree from the University of Edinburgh. A few weeks later he was married to Louise Hawkins. And it is believed to be the year in which he conceived the character that would become one of the most popular in all of literature.

INTRODUCING SHERLOCK HOLMES

How was Sherlock Holmes "born"? Where did the idea come from?

Having decided to write a detective novel, Conan Doyle began to think about a main character. His mind drifted back to medical school, and he remembered a professor named Dr. Joseph Bell. Bell was a tall, thin man with a prominent nose and sharp, penetrating gray eyes. A professor of surgery, Bell constantly urged his students to develop their powers of observation. Gather facts carefully, he taught, then examine them closely and put them together to form logical conclusions. It was precisely these skills—keen scientific observation and brilliant deductive reasoning—that Conan Doyle gave to his detective.

When Conan Doyle began writing *A Study in Scarlet,* he named his sleuth "Sherrinford Holmes" (after the American author Oliver Wendell Holmes). For the good Dr. Watson, he originally thought of "Ormond Sacker." One wonders how successful the stories would have been if he had kept those names.

Like most of the other Sherlock Holmes stories, *A Study in Scarlet* is told in the words of Dr. Watson. It is in this book that Watson meets the great detective for the first time:

"Dr. Watson, Mr. Sherlock Holmes," said Stamford, introducing us.

"How are you?" he said cordially, grip-ping my hand with a strength for which I should hardly have given him credit. "You have been in Afghanistan, I perceive."

"How on earth did you know that?" I asked in astonishment.

Intriguing as the character of Sherlock Holmes was, Conan Doyle's creation wasn't an immediate success. A number of publishers rejected *A Study in Scarlet* before it finally appeared in 1887 in a British magazine called *Beeton's Christmas Annual.* But even then it didn't catch on, and Conan Doyle thought of giving up his character.

A break came in 1888, when an American publisher asked Conan Doyle to do another Sherlock Holmes novel. It was this second story, *The Sign of Four,* that launched Holmes and Watson to international fame. A few years later, Conan Doyle left medicine to write full-time.

THE LEGEND GROWS

The first Holmes short story, "A Scandal in Bohemia," was published in the *Strand Magazine* in July, 1891. Many others followed. With each adventure the great detective won new admirers, and Conan Doyle

The Sir Arthur Conan Doyle Foundation re-created the sitting room of Holmes and Watson at 221B Baker Street. It's an exact replica, reproducing the details as described in the original stories.

A STUDY IN SCARLET

An American named Enoch J. Drebber is found dead in an empty house at 3 Lauriston Gardens, London. There is no evidence as to how the man met his death, and the two Scotland Yard detectives assigned to the case, Lestrade and Gregson, are baffled. For help, they call on Sherlock Holmes.

The case is called *A Study in Scarlet,* the first of 60 mysteries to which the great Sherlock Holmes applies his remarkable powers of observation and deduction. As ever, the story is told by Holmes' loyal companion, Dr. John H. Watson.

The investigation begins upon Holmes' arrival at 3 Lauriston Gardens. After examining the grounds in front of the house, the keen-eyed sleuth moves inside to the dining room—the scene of the apparent crime . . .

Sherlock Holmes approached the body, and, kneeling down, examined it intently. "You are sure that there is no wound?" he asked, pointing to numerous splashes of blood which lay all round.

"Positive!" cried both detectives.

"Then, of course, this blood belongs to a second individual—presumably the murderer, if murder has been committed. . . ."

As he spoke, his nimble fingers were flying here, there, and everywhere, feeling, pressing, unbuttoning, examining, while his eyes wore the same far-away expression which I have already remarked upon. So swiftly was the examination made, that one would hardly have guessed the minuteness with which it was conducted. Finally, he sniffed the dead man's lips, and then glanced at the soles of his patent leather boots.

As Holmes ponders the case and discusses the evidence with Gregson, Detective Lestrade makes an eerie discovery. On the wall in a dark corner of the room, a single word has been scrawled in blood: "Rache." Detective Lestrade is triumphant. "You mark my words," he declares, "when this case comes to be cleared up, you will find that a woman named Rachel has something to do with it."

Holmes isn't so sure . . .

He whipped a tape measure and a large round magnifying glass from his pocket. With these two implements he trotted noiselessly about the room, sometimes stopping, occasionally kneeling, and once lying flat upon his face. So engrossed was he with his occupation that he appeared to have forgotten our presence, for he chattered away to himself under his breath the whole time, keeping up a running fire of exclamations, groans, whistles, and little cries suggestive of encouragement and of hope. As I watched him I was irresistibly reminded of a pure-blooded, well-trained foxhound as it dashes backwards and forwards through the covert, whining in its eagerness, until it comes across the lost scent. For twenty minutes or more he continued his researches, measuring with the most exact care the distance between marks which were entirely invisible to me, and occasionally applying his tape to the walls in an equally incomprehensible manner. In one place he gathered up very carefully a little pile of grey dust from the floor, and packed it away in an envelope. Finally he examined with his glass the word upon the wall, going over every letter of it with the most minute exactness. This done, he appeared to be satisfied, for he replaced his tape and his glass in his pocket.

"They say that genius is an infinite capacity for taking pains," he remarked with a smile. "It's a very bad definition, but it does apply to detective work. . . ."

"I'll tell you one thing which may help you in the case," he continued. "There has been murder done, and the murderer was a man. He was more than six feet high, was in the prime of life, had small feet for his height, wore coarse, square-toed boots and smoked a Trichinopoly cigar. He came here with his victim in a four-wheeled cab, which was drawn by a horse with three old shoes and one new one on his off fore-leg. In all probability the murderer had a florid face, and the finger-nails of his right hand were remarkably long. These are only a few indications, but they may assist you."

Lestrade and Gregson glanced at each other with an incredulous smile.

"If this man was murdered, how was it done?" asked the former.

"Poison," said Sherlock Holmes curtly, and strode off. "One other thing, Lestrade," he added, turning round at the door: " 'Rache' is the German word for 'revenge'; so don't lose your time looking for Miss Rachel."

With which parting shot he walked away, leaving the two rivals open-mouthed behind him.

earned greater fame and fortune. But by 1893, after two dozen stories, Conan Doyle grew tired of his character. He decided to kill him off. In a story called "The Final Problem," Holmes and his archenemy, Professor Moriarty, fall to their deaths over the Reichenbach Falls in Switzerland. Conan Doyle was overwhelmed with letters pleading with him to bring Holmes back to life. "Let's Keep Holmes Alive" clubs were started in several U.S. cities. Magazines offered huge sums of money for new stories.

Conan Doyle, meanwhile, had many other interests to pursue. He had a daughter, Mary Louise, and a son, Kingsley. (Later there would be three more children by a second marriage.) He was a lover of sports and outdoor life. He was active in British politics. He wrote "serious" historical novels. And in 1900, eager to witness the Boer War, he sailed for South Africa, where he ran a field hospital for British troops. His book about that conflict, *The Great Boer War* (1900), is still a standard historical reference. In 1902, Conan Doyle was knighted for his support of the British war effort. He became *Sir* Arthur Conan Doyle.

HOLMES LIVES!

All the while, pressure had continued to build for the return of Sherlock Holmes. Finally, Conan Doyle heeded the call. In 1902, after an eight-year absence, Holmes made his reappearance in a new novel, *The Hound of the Baskervilles*. In a later story it was revealed that Holmes had survived the plunge into the Reichenbach Falls.

Over the decades, it has become clear that the great detective will never die again—at least not in the minds and hearts of his readers. Sir Arthur Conan Doyle spent the last ten years of his life writing and lecturing about spiritualism, the belief that spirits of the dead can communicate with the living. He died on July 7, 1930. As for Holmes, the future held permanent retirement in Sussex, keeping bees.

The legend of Sherlock Holmes has lived on in movies, plays, television and radio shows, and other adaptations of his sleuthing adventures. There has been a Broadway musical and even a ballet. The 60 original stories have never been out of print, and a

Holmes studies an important clue in *A Study in Scarlet*— the master detective's first adventure. What does "Rache" mean? Elementary! It's German for "revenge."

number of biographies—both of Conan Doyle and of Holmes himself—have been written. And then there are hundreds of literary societies and other special groups throughout the world devoted to Sherlock Holmes. The most famous is called the Baker Street Irregulars, named after the street urchins who gathered information for the great detective.

The 100th anniversary of *A Study in Scarlet* was marked by countless special events and commemorations. Meanwhile, as ever, the mail continued to pour into 221B Baker Street.

JEFFREY H. HACKER
Author, *Carl Sandburg*

207

HOORAY FOR HOLLYWOOD!

Hollywood: It's as much an idea as a place. It's Tinseltown, all glitter and no substance. It's the Dream Factory, spinning out fantasies that offer brief escape from the drabness of everyday life. It's the motion picture capital of the world, and few places have taken so strong a grip on so many imaginations. In 1987, the "place"—the city of Hollywood—celebrated the 100th anniversary of its founding in suitably brash style, with parties, parades, and other special events.

Hollywood's heyday belongs to the first half of this century. Much of the city's glitter has become tarnished in recent years, and few films are actually made there today. But some people believe that Hollywood—the city whose name has come to stand for all the glamour, past and present, of motion pictures—has begun to enjoy a revival. And the story of how the city and the motion picture industry grew up together is a part of American history.

A CITY IS BORN

A hundred years ago, Hollywood was just a tract of undeveloped land in Los Angeles County, California. A developer from Kansas, Harvey Wilcox, bought it and divided it into lots for resale in 1887. His wife named the subdivision Hollywood after the summer home of a friend—no holly trees grew on the land. To some, even the story of the name symbolizes the trait Hollywood has been most criticized for: artificiality.

Hollywood's early settlers were Midwesterners who outlawed theaters along with saloons. But in the early 1900's, the town began to change. The basic techniques of motion picture photography had been invented by Thomas Edison and others in the late 1800's, and by the turn of the century motion pictures were becoming popular entertainment. Most movies were made in New York City. But filmmakers soon began to move to the West Coast, seeking a better climate, cheap land and labor, and a variety of natural scenery.

In 1911, the Nestor Company built the first movie studio in Hollywood. Other filmmakers followed suit, among them D. W. Griffith and Thomas Ince. Jesse L. Lasky and Cecil B. De Mille made Hollywood's first feature-length film, *The Squaw Man,* a western. Films such as Griffith's *The Birth of a Nation* (1915), which chronicled the Civil War and Reconstruction eras, showed that movies could be epic productions. By 1920, filmmaking was one of the largest industries in the United States, and four out of five films were made in Hollywood.

The 1920's saw the film industry come to full flower. The major studios—Paramount, Fox, Metro-Goldwyn-Mayer, and others—had stables of stars under contract and shot their films on elaborate sets constructed on their enormous back lots. They ground out new feature films nearly every week and distributed them to their own theaters around the country.

Up to the mid-1920's, movies were silent. In theaters, a piano player would accompany a film. But then sound films were invented, and by the end of the decade "talkies" were shown everywhere. The Hollywood studios teetered on the edge of bankruptcy in the Great Depression of the 1930's, but the industry kept going: People went to the movies to forget their troubles. And in the mid-1930's, movies got a new boost from the use of color photography.

The films Hollywood produced were reflections of their times and of the dreams people held. In historical epics such as *Gone With the Wind* (1939), they re-created the past. In fantasies and fairy tales like *The Thief of Bagdad* (1924), they created times that never were. In wartime, Hollywood films promoted patriotism. In the hard times of the Great Depression, they glorified the

struggles of ordinary people in films like *The Grapes of Wrath* (1940)—and showed how high-rollers and criminals lived in countless gangster films. In Westerns, comedies, and dramas of all kinds, they always entertained.

Each new film was met by eager fans. And as the film industry grew, so did Hollywood's glamorous image. The city of Los Angeles grew up around it, but Hollywood remained separate—and special.

THE HOLLYWOOD STARS

From the earliest days of Hollywood through its heyday in the 1930's and 1940's, it was the leading actors and actresses who captured the public's attention—both on screen and in their not-so-private lives. Fans kept up with the latest news of the stars by reading *Photoplay* and other movie magazines. And there was plenty to keep up with

In 1887, Harvey Wilcox, a developer from Kansas, bought a piece of land in Los Angeles and divided it into lots for resale. His wife named the subdivision Hollywood after the summer home of a friend. Shown below is the first subdivision tract map for Hollywood—which in time became the motion picture capital of the world.

—Hollywood quickly developed a reputation for fast living, excess, and scandal.

The studios were quick to realize that famous actors and actresses drew people to the movies. They scoured the world for talent, and they created the star system. Stars were "discovered" and promoted—sometimes with new names, capped teeth, dyed hair, and other changes. But the greatest movie stars had a natural on-screen appeal that couldn't be created.

Among the great stars of silent films were comedians such as Charlie Chaplin, who came to Hollywood from Britain and was best known for his "Little Tramp" character. Like Chaplin, most of the early stars played stock characters on screen. Canadian-born Mary Pickford, for example, usually appeared as a spunky small-town girl and became known as "America's Sweetheart."

Clara Bow was the "It" girl, the embodiment of the 1920's flapper. Douglas Fairbanks played swashbuckling adventurers, and Rudolph Valentino played smoldering Latin lovers. When Valentino died unexpectedly at the age of 31, thousands mourned his death.

Many stars of the silent era didn't make the transition to talkies—their voices weren't as appealing as their looks. Among those who did make the switch was Greta Garbo, the glamorous Swedish leading lady who brought a sense of mystery to the screen. And new stars came to Hollywood with the era of sound films. Will Rogers drew audiences with his homespun cowboy humor. Clark Gable's rough-edged appeal made him a top leading man of the 1930's, along with Cary Grant, Jimmy Stewart, and Gary Cooper. Joan Crawford, Carole Lombard,

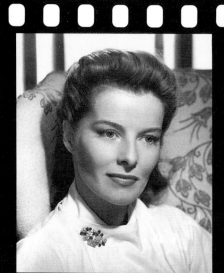

Bette Davis—there was no lack of leading ladies either. But perhaps the biggest star of the 1930's was a child: Shirley Temple.

In each decade new Hollywood stars emerged—among them Humphrey Bogart, Gregory Peck, Spencer Tracy, and Katharine Hepburn in the 1940's; James Dean, John Wayne, Marilyn Monroe, and Audrey Hepburn in the 1950's; Elizabeth Taylor, Doris Day, Rock Hudson, and Paul Newman in the 1960's. In most cases, their careers continued for many years.

The studios paid their stars fabulous salaries and guarded their images, sometimes even choosing the clothes they wore off-screen. Hollywood stars set fashion trends in clothing, hairstyles, and makeup. Their footprints and handprints were immortalized in wet cement on the sidewalk outside Grauman's (now Mann's) Chinese Theater. Peo-

ple gossiped about their marriages (and divorces) and sighed over their luxurious Hollywood homes. And young people everywhere dreamed of becoming glamorous movie stars. Many went to Hollywood, in the hope of being ''discovered'' or of just catching a glimpse of their favorites outside the Brown Derby restaurant and other haunts of the stars.

BEHIND THE SCENES

As important as the stars were, however, they never could have appeared on screen without the efforts of many other people. Making a film, now as in Hollywood's early days, is a team effort, involving everyone from directors and producers down to wardrobe and lighting assistants.

The process begins with a script put together by one or more screenwriters. Pro-

ducers figure out a budget for the film, and actors and actresses are cast for the main roles. Then set designers and costume designers go to work. If the film is to be shot on location—that is, away from the studio—production teams go out looking for suitable filming sites.

But often exotic locations are re-created at the studio, using constructed sets, painted backdrops, and other tricks. A shot of a ship at sea, for example, might be set up using a model boat in a tank of water. In the 1923 epic *The Ten Commandments,* the parting of the Red Sea was simulated with blocks of quivering gelatin. Today such special effects are created with computers and other high-tech tools. They have become increasingly important and sophisticated in the science fiction films of recent years.

Once the sets and costumes are ready, filming can begin. Filming may take weeks or months, and scenes are shot in the most convenient order—not in the order in which they'll appear in the film. Each day, the director reviews the day's shots, or rushes, and selects the best ones.

When the shooting is over, the reels of film are edited. Scenes are put in the correct order, and the movie is trimmed to an appropriate length. A background musical score is added, along with background sounds like train whistles and engines. Finally, the film is ready for distribution.

In Hollywood's heyday, the opening of a major new film was a celebrity event. Fans, photographers, and reporters lined up outside premiere theaters in Hollywood or New York to watch the stars, decked out in evening dress, arrive in limousines to view the film. Today such grand openings are still held, but they seldom attract so much attention. That's just one of the changes that have come to Hollywood in recent times.

END OF AN ERA

The seeds of Hollywood's decline were planted in the late 1940's. Rising labor costs and strikes increased the studios' expenses. They were charged with violating antitrust laws and ordered to sell off their theaters to independent operators. Then television arrived on the scene, and sales of movie tickets fell. People could stay home and be entertained in their living rooms. New film techniques—wide-screen CinemaScope and 3-D movies—and ever more spectacular films failed to win the customers back.

These events brought many changes to the movie industry. Producers found that it was often more economical to make films abroad, where labor costs were lower. Even so, the studios became more cautious and cost conscious about their films. Many studios were taken over by large business conglomerates and branched out into television and recording. Today the film studios mainly finance and distribute films made by independent producers, rather than producing their own. The average film now costs about $14 million to produce.

Only one major studio, Paramount, is still located in Hollywood, and many back lots have been converted to office space. As the studios left, so did the stars, moving on to posh homes in Beverly Hills and the Los Angeles suburbs. Stores and other businesses closed, street crime increased, and the once-glamorous Hollywood streets took on a tawdry air.

In recent years the movie industry has faced a new challenge: the home video, which makes movies available to anyone who has a video player. But the industry has also seen a revival. New directors and producers have scored successes with films directed toward younger audiences. And new stars have appeared.

Most people agree that the film stars of today are different from those of the 1940's. Few command the degree of public attention that the earlier stars received. Nor are they eager to be typecast—they're more interested in showing their versatility as actors by playing a variety of roles. Most are more independent and less closely tied to the studios, and some are producers and directors in their own right. But their new faces have helped revitalize the movie industry.

With the revival of the film industry has come the beginning of a revival of Hollywood. People have begun to restore some of the city's famous buildings. Some filmmakers have returned, and groups such as the Screen Actors Guild have been persuaded to keep their headquarters in town. As Hollywood marked its 100th anniversary, it had good reason to celebrate its future as well as its past.

HOLLYWOOD: LEGEND AND REALITY

As Hollywood celebrated its 100th birthday, a special exhibit called "Hollywood: Legend and Reality" was midway through a two-year tour of six U.S. cities. The exhibit, organized by the Smithsonian Institution, explored the development of the motion picture industry and its impact on American culture.

On display were many items that recalled Holly-wood's golden era and gave glimpses behind the scenes of some famous films. Among them were props, such as the piano that was the centerpiece of Rick's Café in the film *Casablanca* (upper left), and costume sketches, such as Cecil Beaton's sketch for the costume Audrey Hepburn wore as the cockney flower seller in *My Fair Lady* (upper right). Also in the exhibit were a neon theater sign (lower left), from the days when major studios owned their own chains of movie theaters, and a matte painting (lower right) used in the filming of *The Wizard of Oz*. The painting allowed filmmakers to create the illusion of the Emerald City without actually building a set.

RAT AND MOUSE—THAT MEANS HOUSE

TOM: How's your bricks and mortar?
WILL: Her plates hurt. She needs new how-
   d'ye dos.
TOM: I had to get how-d'ye dos for my one
   and t'other. I don't know where the
   bees will come from.
WILL: Have you had your Tommy Tucker?
TOM: Just a clothes peg and some stand at
   ease.

Who are these men? And what are they
saying?

These men are cockneys from London,
England. According to tradition, a cockney
is anyone born within the sound of Bow bells
—the bells of St. Mary-Le-Bow, a historic
London church. Today, the word cockney is
usually applied to natives of the East End of
London and to their unusual English accent.
(Eliza Doolittle, the heroine of the movie *My
Fair Lady,* had a cockney accent.)

Cockneys are also well known for their
use of "rhyming slang," in which a rhyming

word or phrase is substituted for the word
actually meant. For example, "bricks and
mortar" is a substitute for *daughter.*

Rhyming slang is said to have begun in the
early 1800's. At that time, Britain was a
major trading country, and its merchants
were eager to ship their wares to distant
lands. But London didn't have enough
docks. Groups of poor, tough cockney men
were hired to build docks, along with railway
tracks and wide roads to accommodate carts
laden with goods. It was hard, often brutal
work.

To add some humor to their lives, the men
took the names of well-to-do people—especially those who got into trouble—and substituted them for commonly used words. For
instance, "cash" became "Sir Harold
Nash," after an embezzler.

The use of rhyming slang also became
popular as a way to take revenge on the
toffs, or members of the upper class. Toffs

generally were the only people in London who received an education. Many toffs looked down on poor people, calling them "the great unwashed." They used words that the cockneys and other uneducated people couldn't understand. As a way of mocking the toffs' educated language, the cockneys developed a language the toffs couldn't understand.

At first, this simply involved rhyming substitutions, such as "Rosy Lee" for *tea*, "How-d'ye dos" for *shoes*, and "turtle doves" for *gloves*. But before long, many of the substitutions were shortened. For example, the rhyme for *feet* was "plates of meat," which became "plates." *Eyes* were "mince pies," which became "minces." *Money* was "bees and honey," which became "bees."

Using this information, let's translate Tom and Will's conversation:

TOM: How's your daughter?
WILL: Her feet hurt. She needs new shoes.
TOM: I had to get shoes for my brother. I don't know where the money will come from.
WILL: Have you had your supper?
TOM: Just an egg and some cheese.

There are hundreds of words ("dicky birds") in a cockney rhyming slang dictionary. New words are always being added. For example, when Gregory Peck and Errol Flynn became well known, cockneys began saying such things as "I have a pain in my Gregory!" or "He hit me on the Errol!"

People who have a King Lear for dicky birds find listening to cockney rhyming slang fun. But translating isn't always easy. You have to use your down the drains. And sometimes you need a bit of Donald Duck!

HEADING FOR THE LOLLIPOP

Here's a brief dictionary of cockney rhyming slang, followed by a story for you to translate. Of course, you can also make up your own stories—and your own rhyming slang, too.

almond rocks—socks	frog and toad—road	one and t'other—brother
ball of chalk—walk	gates of Rome—home	plates of meat (plates)—feet
bees and honey (bees)—money	Gertie Gitanas—bananas	rat and mouse—house
bird lime—time	Gregory Peck—neck	rhubarb pill—hill
Bo Peep—sleep	how-d'ye dos—shoes	Rosy Lee—tea
bricks and mortar—daughter	Jack's alive—five	rub-a-dub—club
clothes peg—egg	Joanna—piano	Scotch pegs (Scotches)—legs
currant bun—sun	Joe Blake—steak	skein of thread—bed
daisy roots (daisies)—boots	Khyber Pass (Khyber)—glass	stand at ease—cheese
ding dong—song	King Lear—ear	Tommy Tucker—supper
Donald Duck—luck	lollipop—shop	trouble and strife (trouble)—wife
down the drains—brains	loop the loop—soup	turtle doves—gloves
Errol Flynn—chin	mince pies (minces)—eyes	

Will and Tom were headed for the lollipop. The currant bun was shining brightly. Will wanted some almond rocks. Tom was looking for new daisies.

"I don't have much bird lime," said Will. "My one and t'other will be at the rat and mouse soon. He's having his Tommy Tucker with us."

"What's the trouble making?" asked Tom.

"Loop the loop. And Gertie Gitanas for dessert," replied Will.

"I'm having Joe Blake," said Tom. "Then I'm off to the skein of thread. I need some Bo Peep. I didn't get home til Jack's alive this morning. I can barely move my Scotches."

After they left the lollipop, the men took a ball of chalk down the frog and toad to their rub-a-dub, where they had a Khyber of Rosy Lee. They joined some friends around the Joanna for a few ding dongs. Then Will said good-bye and went up the rhubarb pill to his gates of Rome.

ONCE UPON A FLOWER

Tulips in a garden, goldenrod by the side of the road—who would think that these common flowers are bits of living history and legend? But every flower has a story to tell. Some of the flowers that are best loved today have been favorites since early times. And over the years, they've become surrounded with lore—some fact, some fancy, but all fascinating.

BACHELOR'S BUTTON

The bright blue cornflowers that are called bachelor's buttons figure in many legends, some of them very old. The ancient Greeks recounted how Chiron, the centaur, cured an arrow wound by covering it with these flowers. Right through the 1800's, bachelor's buttons were used in some medicines. And some people believed that burning them would drive away snakes.

The flower's odd name is thought to have come from a practice that developed in Scotland long ago. There, a young man who was unsure of his girlfriend's affections would pick a cornflower and put it in his pocket. If it survived unwilted for a day, all was well, and the two were sure to be married.

CARNATION

The showy florists' carnations we're familiar with are a modern creation. For most of its history, the carnation was a smaller, simpler flower, more like its close cousin the pink. Both these flowers belong to the genus *Dianthus,* and the genus name reflects their ancient history. It was bestowed by the Greeks in the fourth century B.C., and it means "flower of Zeus."

The ancient Romans loved carnations for their spicy fragrance as well as for their

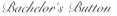
Bachelor's Button

Carnation

Chrysanthemum

beauty. One story tells that the armies of Julius Caesar spread carnations through Europe as far as Britain—by accidentally carrying the seeds in the mud on their boots. It's more likely, however, that carnations spread at a later date and by more usual means.

However they arrived in Britain, carnations became favorites with British gardeners in the Middle Ages. They were called by another name—gillyflower, which means clove flower—because the scent and flavor of carnations mimicked that of cloves, at that time a rare and valued spice. Carnations were often used as flavoring in beer, ale, and wine.

The origin of the name "carnation" is unclear. The name may come from the Latin word *carne* ("flesh"), for the pink color of early carnations. Then again, the English poet Edmund Spenser called the flower "coronation," and some people think that may have been the origin of the name.

CHRYSANTHEMUM

The name "chrysanthemum" comes from two Greek words meaning "golden flower." Some chrysanthemums are golden-colored, but among the 150 different types of this flower there are many colors and sizes. One characteristic they share, however, is that each flower has many, many petals.

Chrysanthemums have long been honored in Asia, where they are said to symbolize long life, purity, and perfection. In Japan, the Order of the Chrysanthemum is the highest honor that can be awarded to a person. And a Chinese legend tells how the first chrysanthemum came to be.

According to the tale, a young girl named Golden Flower was soon to be married to her sweetheart. But she was plagued by one worry: How long would her marriage last? One day she spotted an elf sleeping under a bush. Knowing that an elf must answer truthfully the first question put to him by a mortal, she woke him up and asked how many years she would be married.

"As many years as the flower you choose has petals," replied the elf, who was annoyed that he had been caught napping. Then he vanished.

The girl set out to find a flower with as many petals as possible. But try as she might, the best she could find was a flower with seventeen petals—not nearly enough, to her mind. Finally, she had an idea. She took the flower and, plucking a hairpin from her hair, slit each petal again and again, until the flower had dozens and dozens of petals.

Golden Flower and her sweetheart were married and lived a long and happy life together. They planted the flower, and all its descendants were many-petaled, too.

FORGET-ME-NOT

The tiny blue forget-me-nots that bloom by streams and ponds have a rich history. There are also many legends surrounding their name. One of the best-known stories tells of a German knight who walked along the bank of a river with his beloved. Spotting the pretty blue flowers of the plant, he climbed down the riverbank to pick them but fell into the swift-flowing stream. As the water swept him away, he managed to toss the flowers to the lady, crying out, "Forget me not!"

However the forget-me-not got its common name, its scientific name is based on the way its leaves look. The name is *Myosotis,* which comes from Greek words that mean "mouse's ear."

Forget-me-nots became an important symbol in English history in the late 1300's, when the nobleman Henry of Lancaster chose them as one of his emblems. Henry fell into disfavor with King Richard II, who exiled him in 1398 and then confiscated his estates. But a year later, Henry and his supporters invaded England and took control of the throne. As King Henry IV, Henry of Lancaster continued to use forget-me-nots as an emblem. They appeared in embroidery on his clothes and on enameled metal collars worn by his supporters.

GOLDENROD

This common roadside wildflower—often considered a weed when it takes hold in the garden—figures in many old superstitions. Some people believe that if goldenrod springs up near a house where people haven't planted it, good fortune is sure to come to the people who live there. Others say that treasure is buried where goldenrod blooms.

Some people have used the stalks of goldenrod plants as divining rods to search for precious minerals or water below the ground. A person walks slowly over the ground, holding out the stalk. When the stalk tips down, according to this belief, it's time to start digging.

Goldenrod is one of the many plants that were once used to make medicines for everything from chest pains to ulcers. On the other

Goldenrod

Forget-Me-Not

218

Iris

Marigold

hand, the most commonly held belief about goldenrod in times past was that it caused an illness: hay fever. It's easy to see why people believed this—every year when the goldenrod bloomed, people who suffered from allergies to pollen would start to sniffle and sneeze. But today we know that goldenrod was falsely accused. Another common plant, ragweed, blooms at the same time that goldenrod does. Its flowers are so inconspicuous that no one notices them—but its pollen is often to blame for hay fever.

IRIS

There are many varieties of this flower, from tall bearded irises to the smaller water irises, which are also called flags. Irises are among the oldest garden flowers—records show they were grown in ancient Egypt and ancient Greece, where they were used to decorate tombs. In Greek mythology, Iris was the goddess of the rainbow.

Iris flowers were also the basis of the fleur-de-lis, the symbol of French kings. Their association with the French throne is said to have begun in the 400's, when Clovis was king of the Franks. According to legend, a hostile force invaded Frankish territory and pressed Clovis' army to the banks of the Rhine River. The king thought he was trapped—until he saw a stand of yellow flags growing in the water. That told him that the river was shallow enough to ford. He was able to escape his enemies, circle around, and defeat them.

In celebration, Clovis redesigned his banner to show three yellow flags, symbolizing faith, wisdom, and bravery. Hundreds of years later, when the French King Louis VII organized the Second Crusade, he chose the same emblem and covered his banners with stylized irises. Thus the design became known as the fleur (flower) de Louis—or, over time, fleur-de-lis.

MARIGOLD

''Marigold'' is a name that's been given to many different flowers. The ones we're most familiar with today are the marsh marigold, a yellow wildflower that blooms near streams and bogs in early spring; the pot marigold, a garden flower that is also called

219

Violet

Narcissus

the calendula; and the French and African marigolds—both of which actually originated in Mexico.

"Calendula" comes from *kalends,* the Roman term for the first day of the month. The flowers of the calendula were supposed to open on that day every month of the year. The English named the calendula "pot marigold" because they once used its petals as seasoning in soups and stews. The petals were even dried and stored in barrels for use in winter. Early colonists took seeds of the plant to North America, and it was blooming in colonial gardens by the mid-1600's.

The flowers we call French and African marigolds were already firmly established in the New World by then. Spanish explorers found the French marigold growing wild in Mexico, while the African marigold was cultivated by the Aztecs. It's thought that the Aztecs honored their dead with gifts of marigolds, because this flower has been called *flor del muerto* in Mexico.

The Spanish took both types back to Spain. The plants quickly spread—the wild type to France, and the cultivated type to North Africa. Later, other Europeans "discovered" these flowers growing in their new habitats and named them for those places.

NARCISSUS

Narcissus are delicately scented flowers that bloom in the spring. The blossoms are white or yellow, with six petals surrounding a trumpet-shaped tube. Daffodils and jonquils are considered kinds of narcissus.

The narcissus is another ancient flower—it was used in funeral wreaths in ancient Egypt more than 3,500 years ago. The Romans believed that its sweet fragrance could put people to sleep, and it has long been used in perfume.

There are also many myths about the origin of this flower. The best known is the Greek tale of the boy named Narcissus. One day, while he was out hunting in the forest, Narcissus leaned over a pool to take a drink and was captivated by the reflection of his own handsome face—in fact, he fell in love with his image and couldn't bear to stop looking at it. He died right there at the side of the pool, and the gods turned him into a narcissus flower. Today people who are too concerned with themselves are sometimes said to be narcissistic.

TULIP

This popular garden flower is wrapped in Turkish history. By the mid-1500's, Turkish sultans had conquered North Africa, the Middle East, and large parts of eastern and southern Europe. Ferdinand I, the ruler of Austria, sent an ambassador to the Turkish court in 1554 to arrange peace terms. The ambassador succeeded in winning peace— and he was also delighted by the Turkish gardens that he saw. Growing there were brilliant red and yellow flowers that looked like the turbans, or *tulibands,* worn by Turkish men. The ambassador called the flowers *tulipans* and took some back to Vienna, to be planted in the royal gardens.

Tulips spread and, over time, became the rage in European gardens, especially the gardens of Holland. At first the bulbs were cheap, so everyone could afford to plant them. Then, in the 1600's, a strange thing happened. Some of the bulbs began to produce flowers with streaks and combinations of colors. Because these bulbs were so rare, people were willing to pay huge amounts of money for them.

The changes in the flowers were caused by a virus spread by insects. But growers tried all sorts of formulas to make tulip bulbs change and produce new types of flowers, including soaking the seeds in ink. For a few years, "tulipomania" gripped Holland, and fortunes were made and lost by speculating in tulip bulbs. Today, the tulip's many different sizes, shapes, and color combinations are achieved mostly through hybridization.

VIOLET

Violets are woodland plants that have become favorites in shady gardens. The way the small purple flowers peek out from under the broad leaves has led people to use words like "shy" and "modest" to describe them.

According to legend, violets were created by the Greek god Zeus. It's told that Zeus fell in love with a woman named Io—and his wife, Hera, became enraged. He was forced to change Io into a pure white heifer to protect her from Hera's wrath. Saddened by his act, he decided to give Io a special diet. He waved his hand, and violets sprang up.

The Greeks believed that a wreath of violets, worn around the head, would bring pleasant dreams. Later, in Germany, violets were thought to bring good luck and were used to decorate cradles. In France during the time of Napoleon, violets also became an important symbol. Napoleon was sometimes called Corporal Violette, and his supporters wore violets to show their loyalty.

Thus the shy violet, like so many other flowers, has fascinating tales to tell.

Tulip

AMELIA EARHART: THE MYSTERY LINGERS ON

In the early days of aviation, it took a strong heart and a true sense of adventure to take off into the skies. Flying wasn't considered a woman's sport—women were supposed to stay safely at home. Yet one of the most daring fliers of the 1920's and 1930's was a woman: Amelia Earhart. She was the first woman to fly solo across the Atlantic Ocean, and she set many other records.

But Earhart's career was tragically short. In 1937, while attempting a round-the-world flight, she disappeared over the Pacific Ocean. No trace of the pilot, her navigator, or their plane was ever found. In 1987, fifty years after the incident, Amelia Earhart's disappearance remained a mystery.

A SENSE OF ADVENTURE

The daughter of a railroad attorney, Amelia Earhart was born in Atchison, Kansas, on July 24, 1898. As she grew into a tall, freckled, smiling girl, her sense of adventure was already evident. She wore bloomers, could shoot a .22-caliber rifle, and played football. She also developed an interest in science. She left college in her senior year to work as a nurse in Toronto during World War I, and she later briefly studied medicine.

But medicine wasn't to be her life's work. In 1920, while living with her parents in California, she visited an air show and was fascinated by what she saw. She immediately decided she would learn to fly, and she began to work to earn money for lessons. By 1922, she had her first airplane, and she soon set a new women's altitude record by flying to 14,000 feet (4,200 meters).

Earhart's flying career went on hold for a few years when her family suffered financial problems. She moved to Boston and found a job as a social worker, but she continued to fly in her spare time. Then, in 1928, came an offer: A group that was sponsoring a transatlantic flight asked her to go along as the first woman to make the trip. The idea was as dangerous as it was exciting. Charles Lindbergh had made the first solo crossing the year before, but nineteen other people had died attempting the trip that year. With her sense of adventure, however, Earhart needed only moments to decide—the answer, of course, was yes.

In June, Amelia Earhart, Wilmer Stultz, and Lou Gordon made the 2,500-mile (4,025-kilometer) flight, from Newfoundland to Wales. Although she was named commander of the *Friendship,* the men actually flew the plane. Still, the crossing was hailed as a great achievement, and Earhart became a celebrity. She wrote a book about the trip and married her publisher, George Putnam, in 1931.

Despite her fame, Earhart wasn't satisfied. "I was just baggage, like a sack of potatoes," she said of her historic voyage. She continued to fly, and she set a new autogiro altitude record of 18,415 feet (5,615 meters) in 1931. (An autogiro was an early helicopter.) But she knew she would have to repeat the Atlantic crossing at the controls of her plane. And she did so in May, 1932, piloting her single-engine craft from Newfoundland to Ireland to become the first woman to fly across the Atlantic alone.

Awards and honors showered down on her. She was wined and dined by heads of state, and the press followed her everywhere. But she didn't rest on her laurels. Later in 1932, she flew from California to New Jersey to set a new women's transcontinental speed record—and then broke her own record the next year. In 1935, she made the first solo flight from Hawaii to the U.S. mainland, crossing 2,400 miles (3,860 kilometers) of the Pacific Ocean. She told her friends that she did it for fun.

AROUND THE WORLD

By 1937, Earhart was ready to attempt her greatest challenge: a flight around the world. Her first try, on an east-west route along the Equator, ended in Hawaii when the plane was damaged on takeoff. She set off on her second attempt on June 1, just a couple of months before her 39th birthday. She and her navigator, Fred Noonan, took off from Miami and headed east. Flying in stages, they crossed Africa, India, and Southeast Asia.

On July 2, Earhart and Noonan left New Guinea for the most difficult part of the trip, a long stretch over the Pacific to Howland Island. Somewhere over that stretch, radio contact with their plane was lost.

The U.S. Navy mounted an exhaustive, sixteen-day search of the area. But nothing was found—Earhart had simply vanished. It was assumed that the plane had gone down in the ocean. But in the years that followed, rumors and theories about the disappearance kept cropping up. Some people claimed that Earhart and Noonan had been captured by Japanese soldiers and had died in captivity. There was even a story that they had been on a secret spying mission for the United States. Other people contended that the famous woman aviator was still alive, living on some Pacific isle.

None of these stories has been proved—or disproved. Although it's most likely that Earhart's plane simply went down in the ocean, the actual events may never be known. Still, Earhart's true legacy isn't the mystery she left behind but the example she set. She showed that women, through courage and commitment, could accomplish anything. Fifty years later, her daring feats are still inspiring.

Amelia Earhart and her navigator, Fred Noonan, discuss the flight plan for their trip around the world. That flight ended in the disappearance of both plane and crew—and led to a mystery that lingers on even today.

YOUTH

Clocking in at work is becoming part of life for more and more teenagers. In 1987, teens were working at all sorts of jobs after school and on weekends. But parents and teachers worried about the effects of the trend.

TV TURN-ON

It's a scene played out in homes everywhere, day after day: You come home from school and flick on the television. Then your mother or father walks in and says, "Why are you wasting your time with that junk?"

The quality of television programs, especially programs for children, is something that's constantly debated. In recent years, however, a few children's programs have broken out of the standard mold. Some, taking their cue from public television's long-popular "Sesame Street," seek to combine entertainment with education. They include "Square One TV," "3-2-1 Contact," and "Owl/TV." Another show, "Faerie Tale Theatre," brings top actors, directors, and writers to productions that are designed especially for kids.

MAKING MATH FUN

"Square One TV" made its debut on public television in 1987. It was developed for 8- to 12-year-olds by Children's Television Workshop, the group that created "Sesame Street" to entertain younger children while teaching the basics of reading. And what "Sesame Street" does for reading, "Square One" tries to do for math.

The idea of the show is to use bright, jazzy entertainment to conquer "math phobia"—the dread of the subject that makes many students avoid it. Unlike classroom instruction, the show doesn't concentrate on teaching children specific mathematical methods. Instead, it tries to show that math can be both useful and fun.

"Square One" does this through fast-paced skits and songs. Take the subject of combinatorics—an intimidating name for the mathematical principles that govern the ways in which different objects or numbers can be combined. The show makes this subject fun and understandable with a skit in which the **Battle of the Bulge Caterers** figure the possibilities of combining ham, turkey, and American, Swiss, and provolone cheese in sandwiches.

Mathman, an animated segment that echoes the video game Pac-Man, uses dot-gobbling characters to introduce the properties of numbers, such as which numbers are multiples of three. Ancient Romans show up at a pop-music recording session to introduce Roman numerals. And problems in mathematical logic are presented in riddles.

Many of the skits are send-ups of other television shows. A segment called **Mathnet** is a takeoff on the old detective series "Dragnet." In this version, however, the deadpan detectives solve problems through

"Square One TV" teaches basic math concepts through jazzy skits that often parody other TV shows.

Using a magazine format and weekly themes, "3-2-1 Contact" makes the world of science and technology come alive.

mathematical logic. And a takeoff on "American Bandstand" features characters straight out of "Star Trek" and teaches the basics of averaging.

In the 75 "Square One" shows shown in 1987, seven regular actors played dozens of roles, and guests also appeared. The daily shows were so lively that some critics faulted them for being too entertaining—and not concentrating enough on education. But the show's producers say that entertainment must come first—if no one watches the show, it won't help anyone learn.

FOCUS ON SCIENCE

When "Square One" made its debut, another Children's Television Workshop show was in its fifth season. This was "3-2-1 Contact," a show that aims to make science and technology exciting and understandable to 8- to 12-year-olds.

The show uses a "magazine" format, in which young hosts travel around the world in search of scientific information. Film shot on location and in the studio, documentaries, animation, and music make up each daily episode. Each week's episodes share a common theme, such as space, electricity, light, farms, or flight.

For the 1986–87 season, there were four new themes: signals, oceans, motion, and eating. During **signals week**, American Indians demonstrated hand signals, and shepherds from the Pyrenees Mountains in France showed how they communicate over long distances by whistling. The shows also featured some modern signals: picturephones in use in Biarritz, France, and computer signals that help put out a newspaper.

Oceans week explored such questions as why the oceans are salty, what an oceanographer does, and how to move a whale from one tank to another (by crane). Segments showed the young cast members exploring a sunken Civil War paddle wheeler off the coast of Bermuda and swimming with penguins at Sea World in San Diego, California.

Motion week examined the forces of nature that influence motion—for example, how a snake uses friction to move, and how reducing friction enables a French train to travel at more than 200 miles (320 kilometers) an hour. One cast member demonstrated how levers and pulleys work by using them to lift another cast member. And a veterinarian explained how anatomy affects the ways animals move. Elephants, for example, don't jump—because they're just not built to.

During **eating week**, the show focused on how people and animals obtain, process, and

227

"Owl/TV" is a fast-paced nature and science series that is based on the popular Canadian children's magazine.

use food. Films showed how special zoo diets are prepared and then gave a close-up look at some picky eaters: koalas, zebras, pygmy hippos, and lesser pandas. The show also had archeologists analyzing the diet of people who lived 6,000 years ago in Texas. What did they eat? Lizards, insects, rodents, and flowers!

"3-2-1 Contact" had some other new features for its fifth season. One was a series of short comments by famous scientists, who talked about what had sparked their interest in science when they were youngsters. And for the first time, the show produced some segments jointly with a French television network, for broadcast in both countries. In all, "3-2-1 Contact" has been broadcast in 32 countries.

DISCOVERING NATURE

"Owl/TV," a nature and science discovery series for 7- to 12-year-olds, is the television version of the popular Canadian children's nature magazine *Owl*. The weekly series entered its second season in 1986–87. Produced in Canada, it is also aired by U.S. public broadcasting stations.

Each half-hour show is divided into four segments, linked by fast-paced mini-features and jokes. The segments show young people exploring the world of animals, the environment, and science. They're chosen from seven recurring features that are based on feature departments in the magazine.

The Mighty Mites are three children who shrink (with the help of trick photography) to explore microscopic environments. In some episodes, they've been seen inching their way up leaves and swimming in a fish tank with guppies.

Fooling Around With Science features Dr. Zed, a brilliant (if eccentric-looking) scientist. He guides young visitors through a range of experiments, from turning milk into cheese to splitting light into the colors of the rainbow.

Animals Close Up explores the animal world. Kids go on location to interview zoologists and other experts on animals, and they meet the animals firsthand. One show visited an unusual laboratory in New Mexico —a laboratory where bats are studied.

Tomorrow/Today looks into the future. The show travels to working laboratories where the technologies and products that will influence the future are being developed. One of these features showed how cars of the future are being designed, and another explored the medical uses of snake venom.

You and Your Body features one of the show's most popular stars: Bonapart, a joke-cracking skeleton whose eyes light up when he speaks. He helps viewers unravel such mysteries as the workings of the inner ear and the skin.

Real Kids focuses on young people who are working to improve the environment. The cases featured on the show are real, and they help demonstrate that individuals of any age can improve their world.

The Hoot Club is the final segment of each show. Here, club members work together on a project—anything from making scarecrows to building an inflatable spaceship.

In some of the 1986–87 shows, viewers saw what it was like to travel by dogsled in the Arctic, track hibernating bears, visit Pueblo Indians in New Mexico, and watch a llama being born.

HAPPILY EVER AFTER

"Faerie Tale Theatre" has been broadcast on the cable television network Showtime since 1982. Each show in the series is an hour-long production of a famous fairy tale.

Among the more than two dozen that have been presented are "The Princess and the Pea," "Rumplestiltskin," "Hansel and Gretel," "Sleeping Beauty," "Pinocchio," "Cinderella," and "The Snow Queen."

What makes these presentations truly special is their high level of acting, directing, and production. The show was the brainchild of the actress and producer Shelley Duvall, who called on her contacts to help carry out the idea. Among the well-known performers who have appeared in the series are Joan Collins, Robin Williams, Liza Minnelli, Christopher Reeve, James Earl Jones, and Vanessa Redgrave. Directors have included Francis Ford Coppola and Roger Vadim.

The show enlists top writers in the film industry to rewrite the tales for television, and top designers to develop sets based on the works of such famous artists and illustrators as Maxfield Parrish and N. C. Wyeth. Special video effects add to the settings, creating an underwater world for "The Little Mermaid," for example, and lending a dreamlike quality to "Rip Van Winkle."

All the effort put into the productions has helped make "Faerie Tale Theatre" one of the most praised children's shows on television. The many awards the show has won leave no doubt: Children's television can be good—and good for you, too.

"The Little Mermaid" and other high-quality presentations have made "Faerie Tale Theatre" a hit with kids.

TEENS AT WORK

"Get a Job" was the title of a song that was popular with teenagers in the early days of rock and roll. Probably few teens today have heard it. But in 1987, teenagers seemed to be taking the song's advice to heart as they went to work in record numbers.

Teens were taking part-time jobs in supermarkets, fast-food restaurants, gas stations, clothing shops, and any other sort of business that needed part-time help. These weren't just summer jobs—statistics showed that three-fourths of high school seniors worked during the school year. And about a third worked more than twenty hours a week.

As teenagers went to work, parents and teachers asked some tough questions: Why were so many teens taking part-time jobs? And was combining work and school a good or a harmful experience for young people?

WHY TEENS ARE WORKING

One reason that teenagers were going to work was that in many areas, well-paying part-time jobs were widely available. Teens today are part of the "baby-bust" generation —they were born after the 1960's, when the birthrate dropped sharply in the United States and many other developed countries. But while the number of teens has stayed level or (in some areas) declined, the need for all kinds of products and services has grown. The businesses that provide these products and services need workers. And those that rely on part-time help find that they have fewer and fewer workers to choose from.

In 1987, then, teens in many areas could take their pick of well-paying part-time jobs. Although young part-time workers have traditionally earned close to the minimum wage ($3.35 an hour in the United States, and $4.35 in Canada), some employers offered as much as $5 or $6 an hour—and sometimes more—to attract them.

Jobs weren't equally available in all areas, however. The greatest numbers were found in the suburbs of major cities, especially those that have grown rapidly in recent years. Many fewer jobs were found in the

In 1987, teens went to work in record numbers. They worked in ice-cream parlors, gas stations, clothing shops, and any other business that needed part-time help.

cities themselves, especially those that were experiencing hard economic times. Among black teens in cities, unemployment was especially high, as it has been for many years. But some experts predicted that even that situation would change as more inner-city teens were drawn into the job market.

The teens who took jobs in 1987 had many different goals. One study showed that 30 percent were saving some or all of their earnings for a college education. A few were helping to support their families. Many others were hoping to save enough money to buy their own cars. But a lot of the teenage workers weren't saving much at all—they were spending their money as fast as they earned it on clothes, stereos, and other consumer goods.

HELPFUL OR HARMFUL?

Up to the age of 16, laws sharply limit both the kind and amount of work a young person can do. But after that age, part-time and summer jobs have widely been regarded as good for young people. Going to work, many believe, does more than provide teenagers with pocket money. It teaches them responsibility, and they learn to manage money that they earn themselves. They also learn to manage their time and to handle difficult situations, such as dealing with a difficult boss or an irate customer. These skills can be useful later in life.

But as more teens went to work, some parents and educators began to have second thoughts about the benefits of part-time jobs. They worried that if teens worked too many hours, their schoolwork would begin to suffer. They would spend less time on assignments and, to make life easier, take less demanding courses. In class, they'd be too groggy from hours of work to take an interest in what was presented.

There were other concerns, too. Teenagers who worked had less free time. That prevented them from exploring interests and activities that might lead to fulfilling hobbies and careers. Their jobs rarely related to the careers they hoped to pursue later in life—few planned to spend their lives flipping hamburgers or packing groceries—and they weren't learning skills that would help them in other jobs.

With the high pay being offered by many

Working in a pet store could be both fun and profitable. But adults worried that if teens worked too many hours, they might not have time to keep up their school grades.

employers, many adults also worried that teenagers would learn not to manage money but to waste it. With their parents paying their basic living expenses, many teen workers were free to spend their earnings on whatever struck their fancy. Later, as young adults, they wouldn't be able to spend as freely—but they wouldn't have learned to budget their money and save for the things they wanted.

To lessen these dangers, some experts recommended that teens work no more than 15 or 20 hours a week and that they restrict their jobs to weekends, leaving weekdays free for schoolwork. But with the population of teenagers continuing to shrink, no one expected the trend toward teenage employment to slow. It seemed likely that more and more young people would follow in the footsteps of their older brothers and sisters—and get a job.

SPOTLIGHT ON YOUTH

Four-foot, four-inch **Seth Green** was a little guy with a big career in 1987. The 13-year-old actor had already appeared in commercials, TV shows such as "Saturday Night Live," and five films, including *The Hotel New Hampshire* and *Radio Days*. (In *Radio Days,* he starred as a boy representing Woody Allen, the film's director and narrator.) Seth, who started acting at the age of 6, lives in Philadelphia.

Michele Granger, 17, starred at the 1987 Pan Am Games as pitcher for the U.S. women's softball team. In the first two games at the competition, held in Indianapolis, she pitched a no-hitter (against El Salvador) and a one-hitter (against Belize). That kind of top-notch performance was nothing new for Michele, a high-school senior from Placentia, California: In 1986, she was named Sportswoman of the Year in softball by the U.S. Olympic Committee.

It's fun to feed your pet—but cleaning up afterward isn't so much fun. Six-year-old inventor **Suzanna Goodin** of Hydro, Oklahoma, found a neat solution to that problem: a spoon-shaped, edible pet-food server that can be gobbled up by the pet after it's used. The idea won Suzy top honors for her age group in the 1987 *Weekly Reader* invention contest, one of several such contests for young people.

A virtuoso on the violin at the age of 10, **Stefan Milenkovic** of Zemun, Yugoslavia, is also pretty hot on a skateboard. He's pictured demonstrating his skills on a sidewalk outside Lincoln Center in New York City, where he appeared in a concert of classical works in 1987. That was just one of some 400 concerts that Stefan—who has earned the nickname ''the demon of Zemun''—has given since he began playing the violin at the age of 3.

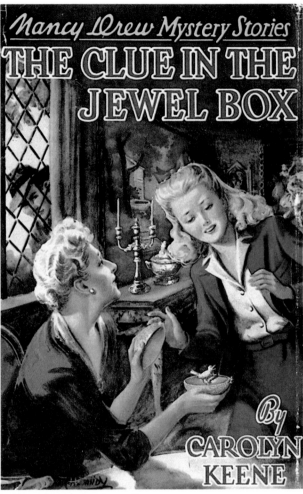

Nancy Drew, the fictional girl detective whose adventures have been enthralling young readers since the 1930's, has been given a modern look—she now wears jeans, goes to rock concerts, and drives a sporty Mustang convertible. This is Nancy as she is portrayed in a new series of mysteries that began to appear late in 1986. Called The Nancy Drew Files, the new series is aimed at 12- to 15-year-olds. (The first book in the series is shown at the left, next to one of the older books.) Like the earlier books, the new ones were written by various authors under the pen name Carolyn Keene. Nancy wasn't the only fictional sleuth to be updated for the 1980's—new versions of the well-known Bobbsey Twins and Hardy Boys mysteries are being brought out, too.

The **Girl Scouts of the United States** celebrated their 75th anniversary in 1987—and no less than Nancy Drew, the Scouts have changed. Founded in 1912, the group is now one of the world's largest organizations for girls. Scouts used to earn badges for camping and housekeeping skills, but today they can earn them for studying business, computers, and aerospace. Special programs address child abuse and other social problems. Fitness may mean an aerobics class. But the group still stresses traditional values and self-confidence—so the anniversary took the motto "Tradition with a Future." It was marked with special events around the country, and the U.S. Postal Service issued a stamp in honor of the group.

A ticket to Broadway is what winners in the annual **Young Playwrights Festival** receive—but it's not an average ticket. Sponsored by the Dramatists Guild, the festival selects a handful of plays submitted by authors around the country, all of them under the age of 19. The winning works are given professional presentations in New York City, some in staged readings and some in full productions. Above is a scene from one of the 1987 plays, *Sparks in the Park,* by 18-year-old Noble Mason Smith of Yakima, Washington. It's about —of all things—a young playwright whose characters come alive. Other 1987 winners were Juliet Garson of New York City; Jonathan Marc Sherman of Livingston, New Jersey; Pamela Mshana of Ontario, California; and Debra Neff of Jamaica Estates, New York.

Louise Chia Chang won first prize in the 1987 Westinghouse Science Talent Search, the oldest and most prestigious U.S. competition for young scientists. Louise, a 17-year-old high-school senior from Westmont, Illinois, conducted research into genes that are active in certain types of cancer cells. (In her display, she represented the proteins in these genes with strings of colored beads.) She plans a career in cancer research after college studies in biology and medicine.

Seventeen-year-old **John Chrisley** was cutting his first album in 1987—and was well on his way to becoming a top blues musician. Little John (as he is called) grew up in Morgan Hill, California, and taught himself to play the harmonica at age 11. He was a natural at it. And by the time he reached senior year in high school, he had already played with such famous musicians as Willie Nelson, B. B. King, and Huey Lewis.

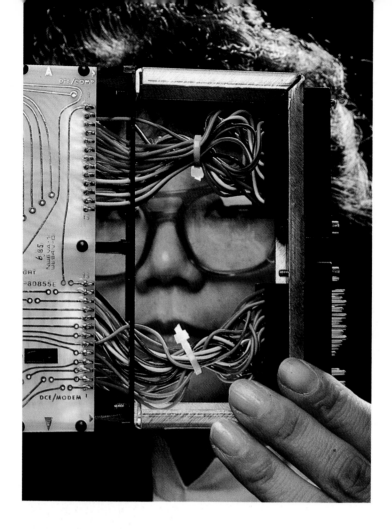

CAREERS IN COMPUTERS

We're living in the Age of Computers. Computers are everywhere—in homes, schools, and every type of workplace. Banks, farms, supermarkets, movie studios, factories, publishers: Name a business, and chances are you'll find people there working with computers. Even junkyards use computers, to keep track of their stocks of parts from wrecked cars!

The rapid spread of computers into all parts of society has led to an equally rapid growth in the number of computer-related jobs. People who can design, program, build, sell, or use computers are in great demand. In fact, the computer industry is the fastest growing industry in the world. It's probable that in coming years, more new jobs will be created in the computer field than in any other area.

What are these jobs? Which of them might be suitable for you? Here is a sampling of the many occupations available in the computer field. Each has its own training and educational requirements—and its own demands and rewards.

CREATING NEW COMPUTERS

Computer engineers design and develop new computers and peripherals—joysticks, printers, disk and tape storage units, modems, and other parts of computer systems.

The main part of a computer—its "brain" —consists of small processing units called chips. A chip contains thousands of tiny, interconnected electrical circuits. Engineers decide how many circuits to put on a chip and how they are to be connected. They design different chips for different types of computers, and they design the printed circuit boards that hold the chips.

Often, many computer engineers are involved in the design of a new computer. Each makes contributions in his or her specialty. For instance, the chips are designed by electrical engineers. The chemical processing needed to produce the circuit boards is handled by chemical engineers. The overall design of the computer is done by mechanical engineers.

Some engineers are encryptologists. They design codes that are built into computers to prevent unauthorized people from using the computers. Many kinds of private information—tax records, health records, school records—are stored in computers. Encryptologists try to ensure that such information is available only to those who have a right to see it. Unauthorized people who try to see the information get static or gibberish on their computer screens.

If you are interested in developing new computers, you need a good background in science and math. Computer engineers usually have college and graduate school degrees in one or more branches of engineering. They continue to study after they begin working, to keep up with the many changes that are taking place in computer technology.

Many kinds of **technicians** assist computer engineers in creating new products. Electrical technicians inspect and test the electronic parts and wiring that go into the computers. Chemical technicians etch the printed circuit boards. Drafters prepare drawings and blueprints that will be used by the people who manufacture the computers.

Technicians usually have attended vocational or technical schools. They may also receive on-the-job training. The amount of education or training they need varies with the type of work they do.

PROGRAMMERS

Programmers write the instructions—called programs, or software—that tell a computer what to do. There are two types of programmers. **Systems programmers** develop software that tells the computer how to operate itself and its peripheral equipment. **Applications programmers** write software that tells the computer what tasks to do.

Many applications programmers specialize in a specific business or kind of software. Scientific programmers develop programs in aerospace, medical, and other technical fields. Game programmers develop game software. Educational programmers develop programs used to teach important skills. One specialty that is expected to grow during the coming decade is robotics programming—writing programs that give robots the instructions they need to perform specific types of work.

Programmers are often part of a development team. For instance, creating an educational program may involve several programmers—each working on a different part of the program—as well as teachers, artists, and even musicians.

Programming requires clear, logical thinking. It also requires patience, because programs must be tested and revised over and over again until they are free of errors.

Some programmers are self-taught and begin working while still in high school.

Computer engineers examine a large drawing of a chip they designed. The drawing shows the layout of the thousands of transistors that make up the integrated circuits on the tiny chip.

Most programmers, however, have college degrees in computer science, engineering, or math.

SYSTEMS ANALYSTS

Pretend that you own a chain of sporting-goods stores and you've decided to computerize your operation. You want the computers to keep track of inventory, handle billing and employee records, and write checks. What kind of computers do you need? What kinds of programs?

A business that uses computers needs someone to plan, organize, and evaluate how the computers can best be used. Such a person is called a **systems analyst**. Systems analysts are problem solvers. They look at a business's needs and develop plans to meet those needs with computers. Sometimes they develop plans for expanding an existing computer system.

After the business managers approve the plan for a computer system, the analysts supervise installation of the equipment. When the system is operating, the analysts evaluate it. If they feel improvements can be made (which often happens as new products come on the market), they design updates.

Some systems analysts work for companies that have large computer systems or want to install such systems. Others work for consulting firms that develop systems under contract. Sometimes systems analysts also design software. Say your sporting-goods business needs a special inventory

GETTING STARTED IN COMPUTERS

There are many ways to begin a career in computers. Discuss the subject with school guidance counselors, and read books about it. Take a part-time job in a local computer store, or become active in a computer club. Write reviews of new computer products for your school newspaper. Teach others how to use a computer. Try designing your own computer programs.

Additional information on computer careers, their educational requirements, and student financial aid can be obtained from professional organizations and from educational institutions that offer computer courses. Here are a few organizations that can supply you with career information:

American Society for Information Science—1424 Sixteenth Street, NW, Washington, D.C. 20036

Institute of Electrical & Electronics Engineers— 345 East 47th Street, New York, NY 10017

Institute of Electrical & Electronics Engineers, Canadian Region Office—7061 Yonge Street, Thornhill, Ont. L3T 2A6

Data Processing Management Association—505 Busse Highway, Park Ridge, IL 60068

Data Processing Management Association of Canada—1501 Carling Avenue, Ottawa, Ont. K1Z 7M1

Association for Computer Art and Design Education —88 Garfield Avenue, Madison, NJ 07940

National Computer Graphics Association—2722 Merrilee Drive, Suite 200, Fairfax, VA 22031

Chips and other computer components are inserted into a circuit board, which is then tested to ensure that all its parts function properly.

program—one very different from anything being sold in computer stores. A systems analyst can create the specifications for this program. These specifications are then given to a programmer, who creates the needed software.

To become a systems analyst, you need a college degree and experience as a programmer. Many systems analysts also have specialized training in the industries in which they work, such as banking or insurance.

COMPUTER OPERATORS

The people who run computers are called **computer operators**. They load the needed programs, which are usually on disks or reels of tape, into the computers. When the programs are finished, the operators remove them and put them away. Then they set up the computers for their next tasks. If printers are attached to the computers, the operators make sure there is paper in the printers.

For example, say you want an inventory report on your sporting goods operation. Then you want a payroll report and printed checks for all your employees. You can tell the computer operator to handle all these tasks for you, one after the other.

At all times, operators watch their computer systems to make certain that everything is functioning correctly. They keep log books in which they indicate what programs were run and what problems occurred. If the computer screen, or monitor, shows that an error has been made, the operators locate the problem. They may try to solve the problem, or they may stop the program until a service technician can fix the system.

If the computer system is small, one operator may run the computer and all the peripheral equipment. Businesses with large computer systems may have dozens or even hundreds of operators. Some will specialize in operating the computers; others, in operating one type of peripheral. In such a business, a **supervising operator**, or **operations manager**, is in charge. This person hires employees, sets their schedules, and helps them solve problems. The supervisor also schedules how the computers will be used and makes sure that the computers are kept in good condition.

Most computer operators attend two-year community colleges or technical schools.

This student uses educational software developed by programmers, computer artists, and other specialists.

After gaining experience and proving themselves on the job, they may become supervising operators.

SERVICE TECHNICIANS

Service technicians are also known as **field engineers** and **service engineers**. They are the people who keep computer systems running smoothly. They install new equipment, maintain it, and make repairs.

Some service technicians work for a specific manufacturer and handle only that manufacturer's computers. Others work for companies that sell computers made by a number of different manufacturers. These technicians must be able to service a variety of equipment.

Like many others in the computer field, technicians are problem solvers. They have to be able to determine what's wrong with a machine and how it can best be fixed. To do this, technicians must understand basic electronics and be able to use oscilloscopes and other types of testing equipment. They must be familiar with the technical manuals and maintenance procedures for the equipment they service.

Some technicians begin working after high school as apprentices to qualified technicians. Most, however, attend vocational or technical schools that offer courses in this field. They continue to take courses after graduation because new computer equipment is always being introduced.

HANDLING INFORMATION

A collection of related information, or data, is called a data base. The telephone directory, a library's card catalog, and a baseball team's records are examples of data bases. Vast data bases can be stored in computer files. To retrieve information from a computerized data base, a data base management system is needed. A data base management system is software that creates the computer files and allows you to manage the data in a useful way. When you want to find a specific piece of information, the computer quickly sorts through the files and finds the information.

Most government agencies and large corporations have data base management systems. The person in charge of the system is called a **data base administrator**. This person helps organize the system and keeps it up to date. The administrator makes certain that there are backup copies of data, in case of emergencies. He or she may also make improvements in the system, to make it easier for people to get the data they need.

Data base administrators need college degrees. They also need experience in programming and systems analysis, as well as an understanding of the business or industry in which they are working.

People who enter the information into data bases are called **data entry operators**. The kind of data they work with depends on where they work—customer orders for a sporting-goods store, patient records for a hospital, information on new paintings for a museum. Data entry operators usually have high school diplomas and good typing skills, and they are well-organized.

Many companies have large collections, or libraries, of computer tapes, disks, programs, instruction books, and other materials related to computers. These organizations may hire **computer librarians** to organize and catalog the materials. The librarian also controls the circulation of the materials, keeping track of who borrows what and making certain that materials aren't borrowed by people who have no right to use them. When materials are returned to

Software programmers develop programs that do many things. For example, a simulation program produced this picture of the magnetic field of Jupiter. The program took numerical data sent to Earth by a space probe and turned the data into a simulation, or representation, of the planet.

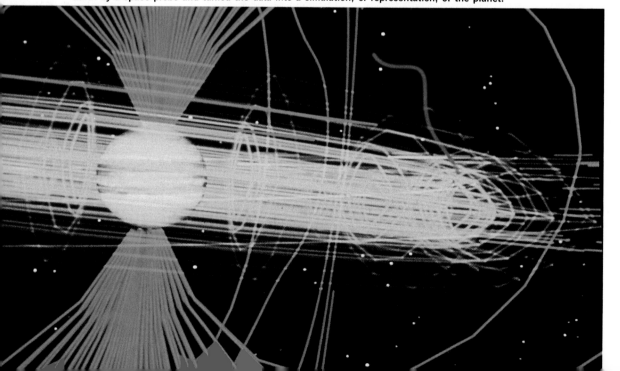

the library, the librarian inspects them for damage and makes any needed repairs. Then the items must be stored in the appropriate place, so they can be easily retrieved when needed again.

Computer librarians usually have degrees in library science and have taken courses in computer science.

COMPUTER ARTISTS

Many traditional fields have expanded as a result of computers. One of the most exciting is computer graphics—using computers to create all sorts of illustrations. **Computer artists** use graphics software to design advertisements, record jackets, book illustrations, television commercials, even movie scenes. Some computer illustrations are so finely "drawn" that they resemble paintings or photographs. **Technical drafters** work in a related field, in which computers are used to create engineering blueprints and similar plans.

Most computer artists have studied at schools of art or design. Like other artists, they have a good sense of color and a talent for drawing. They may also have programming experience and a basic understanding of computer technology. Technical drafters generally have technical school training in drafting, as well as a good grounding in math and an understanding of engineering drawings.

OTHER CAREERS

There are many other careers in the computer field, some requiring more technical knowledge than others. **Technical writers** develop the manuals that tell people how to use computers and software. Besides knowledge of computers, they need strong language skills, so they can present the instructions clearly and logically.

A **sales representative** may work for a manufacturer, selling that company's computers directly to businesses, or for a store, selling computers to the public. Computer salespeople often have college degrees in business or economics, rather than in computer science. They must be able to get along well with people.

Training specialists teach other people how to use computers and programs. Many computer and software manufacturers employ

Computer artists use graphics programs to create a variety of illustrations—everything from television commercials to drawings that look like actual paintings.

training specialists to teach their customers how to get the most out of their machines and programs.

Even if you aren't planning a career in computers, you should become familiar with these machines. Millions of people—doctors, secretaries, insurance agents, chemists—use them in their jobs. Knowing what a computer can do and how to use one can help you along the road to success no matter what career you choose.

JENNY TESAR
Designer, computer programs

243

YOUNG PHOTOGRAPHERS

A photograph can be as striking and as haunting as a great painting or a fine poem. Today's young photographers know that, and they experiment to achieve the best results—with bold black-and-white patterns, hand-tinted colors, and other unusual effects.

The photographs on these pages were all winners in the 1987 Scholastic/Kodak Photo Awards program. The program offers scholarships and awards to junior and senior high school students in the United States. But besides the awards, the young photographers whose work is shown here had the satisfaction of producing beautiful pictures.

Spiral into Web of Light, by Mike Merriman, 16, Columbus, Ohio

Crayons and Spruttle, by Robbie Parker, 15, Miami, Florida

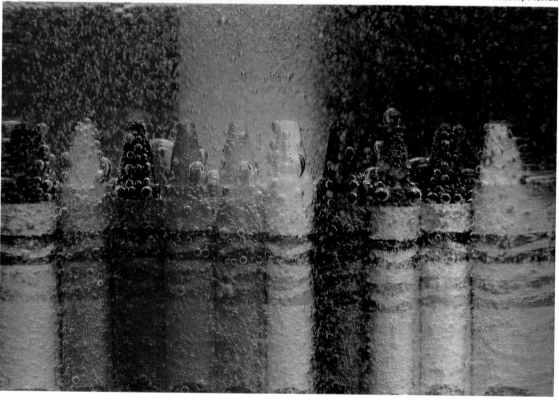

Reflection by Hand, by Jimmy Hirabayashi, 17, Palos Verdes, California

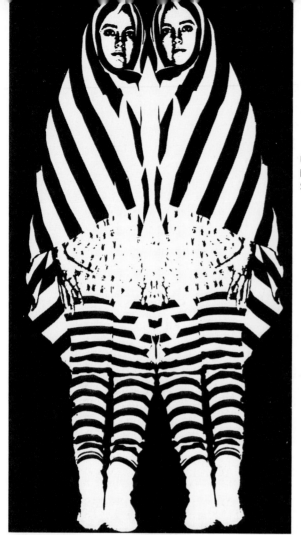

Untitled,
by Dylan Long, 17,
South Bend, Indiana

For Esme,
by Elizabeth Fox, 17,
Winter Garden, Florida

Untitled,
by Bryan Horne, 17,
Burbank, California

Sax,
by Ron Horn, 16,
Tucson, Arizona

247

CREATIVITY

Made of exquisite silks and ivories and richly decorated with paintings, spangles, feathers, and pearls, fans have long been admired for their beauty. Today many are considered works of art and are prized by collectors. This delicate, hand-painted ivory fan was made for a fashionable French woman in the 1800's.

FAN-FARE

Hand-held fans have a practical purpose: On a hot day or in a stuffy room, they create a cooling breeze. But throughout their long history, fans have been far more than useful objects.

Delicate and richly decorated, these accessories have been symbols of rank and aristocracy and "musts" for fashionable women. Special fans have been created to commemorate important events and even to advertise products. And today, when air conditioning has replaced the fan as the most common cooling device, beautiful fans are valued as works of art.

FAN HISTORY

People may have used fans before the dawn of history—the first ones were probably large leaves or palm fronds. They were followed by fans made of ostrich plumes and other feathers. Such fans were used in ceremonies and by royalty in many ancient civilizations. But the Chinese may have been the first to have fans for ordinary use, perhaps as early as 2000 B.C. These fans were carried by both men and women.

Early Chinese fans were handscreens—flat, rigid boards—made of wood, woven rushes, and paper or embroidered fabrics stretched over wooden frames. Handles were formed of ivory, jade, gold, silver, laquered wood, and other materials. These fans came in many shapes, including heart-shaped, moon-shaped, and pear-shaped. The Chinese are also thought to have been the first to paint designs on fans.

In the 600's A.D., the Japanese invented the folding fan, formed of flat sticks riveted together at one end. Folding fans were far less bulky than handscreens, and their popularity quickly spread. Again, all sorts of materials were used. There were even iron-ribbed fans that warriors could carry into battle. This wasn't as silly as it sounds—not only did these battle fans make good weapons, the Japanese commanders also used them to send signals to their troops.

Off the battlefield, Chinese and Japanese court etiquette dictated how fans should be held and used. For example, high-ranking Chinese officials who passed each other on the street were allowed to cover their faces with their fans. That way, they wouldn't have to acknowledge each other and go through elaborate rituals of greeting. Etiquette also decreed that fans should be used only in warm weather, and certain types of fans were reserved for the hottest days. Fans were often presented as gifts, to show esteem and goodwill.

Fans have an ancient history in Western countries, too. Bearers carrying long-handled ostrich-plume fans attended the rulers of ancient Egypt. Feather fans were also used in ancient Greece and Rome, and women of that time often carried handscreens. Our word "fan" comes from the Latin word *vannus,* the name of a flat, fan-like tool used in winnowing grain.

Fans were an important part of Greek and Roman religious rituals, and the early Christian church used them in its ceremonies. In Medieval Europe, court ladies (and sometimes men) carried flag-shaped leather handscreens or cockades—folding fans that opened to a full circle, with end sticks that formed a long handle. Fans made from peacock, ostrich, and parakeet feathers, with jewel-studded handles of ivory and silver, were popular in the 1400's and 1500's.

As European explorers began to roam the world's oceans at about this time, they brought back many strange items. Among them were folding fans from China and Japan. Europeans were quick to adopt this new fashion, first in Italy and then in France and other countries. Although handscreens and cockades remained in use, folding fans soon became the most popular type.

Royalty and the nobility were the primary users of fans at this time. Queen Elizabeth I of England was said to have been especially fond of them. From the early 1600's on, however, the fan more and more became an accessory that no well-dressed, sophisticated woman could do without. European craftsmen turned out thousands of fans each year, and thousands more were imported from China.

By the end of the 1700's, men had stopped carrying fans. But women used fans to shield their faces from the heat of open fireplaces in winter. In summer, fluttering fans cooled them and shooed away insects and unpleasant odors. A fashionable woman needed several fans—everyday fans, fancy-dress fans,

Ivory brisé fan, China, mid-1800's

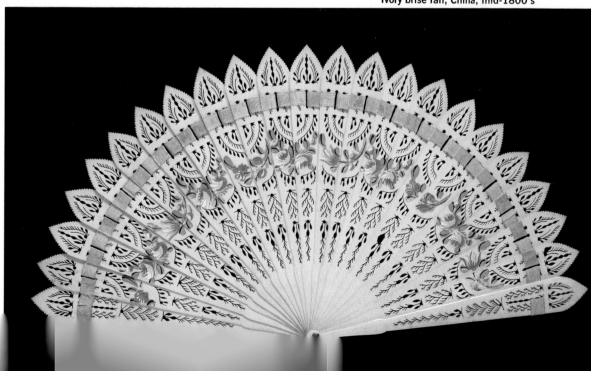

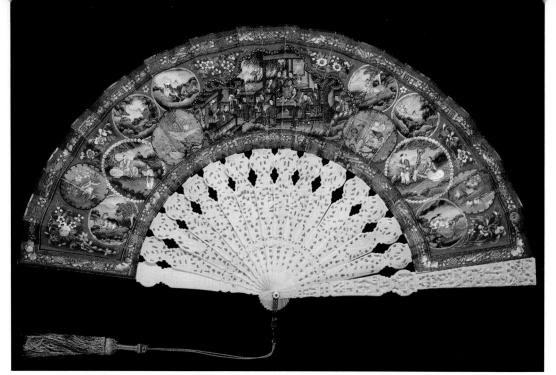

Ivory and silk pleated fan, China, mid-1800's

fans to go with different outfits. And special fans were made for special occasions. Bridal fans—made of ivory, satin, and lace and carrying pictures of Cupid, hearts, and other symbols of love—were given by grooms to their brides. A woman who was in mourning might carry a black or gray fan, with discreet decorations.

A fan was more than a useful accessory—it was a mark of grace and style. Etiquette manuals gave instructions on proper fan use. "Even the most charming and elegant woman, if she cannot manage her fan, appears ridiculous," cautioned one author.

The way a woman held and used her fan even became a method of communication. It was said that in the "language of fans," different motions had meanings. When a

Tortoise shell, silk, and ostrich feather pleated fan, United States, 1920's

woman held her open fan by her left ear, for example, she was saying, "Do not betray our secret." A half-open fan pressed to the lips meant, "You may kiss me." Historians doubt that such set meanings were ever really used. But there is no question that a woman could communicate many things by the way she snapped, fluttered, and carried her fan.

FABULOUS FOLDING FANS

There are two basic types of folding fans, the *brisé* fan and the pleated fan. *Brisé* is the French word for "broken" or "collapsible." This type of fan is formed of wide, flat sticks that fold up between decorative end pieces (called guards). A rivet fastens them together at the base of the fan. At the top, a ribbon links them so that they overlap slightly when

253

Ivory and silk cockade fan, United States, mid-1800's

and pieces of ivory and mica. Modern fans are often made of plastics and other synthetics that mimic these finer materials.

Like other articles of fashion, fans have been subject to fads and whims in East and West alike. The pictures and designs painted on them generally reflected the styles of art popular at the time they were made. Chinese and Japanese fans, for example, were made in many different styles and often carried short messages or poems in delicate calligraphy. The paintings were considered works of art, and the artists signed them. Sometimes the leaves of pleated fans would be removed from their frames and collected in albums.

Like other Chinese and Japanese paintings, these fan paintings often showed birds, flowers, and scenes from nature, delicately rendered in simple brushstrokes. Silk and paper with a gold or silver sheen were popular background materials. Bright red paper with gold designs was used in fans designed for special occasions like birthdays and New Year celebrations. In China, black was a color once reserved for the lower classes, but in the late 1800's black fans with gold and silver decorations became popular even with the aristocracy.

During their heyday in the West, fans likewise had many styles of decoration. Chinese designs were always popular because they suited the folding fan's origin in Asia. Sometimes the sticks and guards of a pleated fan would have a Chinese look, while the leaf bore a Western design. The reason was that, especially in the 1700's, sticks and guards were often imported from China and fitted with leaves when they arrived. Scenes from classical, Biblical, and mythological tales were also very popular in the 1700's, and fans of this time often carried miniature copies of famous paintings.

In the mid-1800's, the Victorians turned from painted scenes to elaborately carved and decorated sticks, painted designs, and exotic materials such as satin, lace, sequins, and feathers. But after new trade links were opened between Japan and the West in the 1860's, Japanese designs enjoyed a wave of popularity. And around the turn of the century, fans reflected the art nouveau style, with swirling, free designs based on peacocks, flowers, and other natural forms.

the fan is open. In a pleated fan, the upper parts of the flat sticks support a semicircular band of paper or other flexible material. This band, called the leaf, is pleated so that it will fold up neatly between the guards when the fan is closed.

Both methods of construction are clever. But the materials and decoration that have been used are what make folding fans truly delightful. Sticks and guards have been made of ivory, bone, mother-of-pearl, horn, tortoiseshell, metal, and wood, including bamboo and fragrant sandalwood. They have been carved, painted, gilded, lacquered, pierced to look like lace, and studded with metal pins, spangles, and gems.

The leaves of pleated fans have been made of parchment, lace, silk, linen, and other fine fabrics, as well as of paper. Like the sticks, the leaves have been pierced, painted with all kinds of scenes and designs, and decorated with spangles, feathers, tiny pearls,

While most fans were designed to look elegant and made use of rich materials, some were designed to deliver a message. For example, after the French Revolution, the French currency collapsed, and people began to carry fans papered with worthless bank notes and IOU's. And from the late 1700's on, printed fans were very popular.

Some printed fans were aids to memory—they carried rules for card games, dance steps, the words and music of songs, historical information, and maps. Church and chapel fans had prayers and psalms. Children's fans—smaller than adults' fans—carried the alphabet.

Other special fans were made to commemorate important events, such as the first balloon flight, in 1783. Travelers brought back souvenir fans that showed scenes of the places they visited. And as time went on, advertisers got into the game. Fans carried messages that plugged everything from hotels to cologne. Because these fans were designed to be given away, they were often cheaply made, with plain wooden (or, later, celluloid) sticks and thin paper leaves. But many had lovely designs.

Some fans were conversation pieces, with riddles or cartoons that poked fun at the society or the politics of the times. Another type of fan that was sure to spark comment was the autograph fan—a plain white fan that could be "decorated" with the signatures of friends and famous people.

Telescope fans became popular in the 1800's. These fans had telescoping sticks that could be shortened, so that the folded fan could be tucked in a small handbag. And at one time or another, many other gimmicks were added to fans.

Trick and puzzle fans were two special types of *brisé* fans. A trick fan looked like any other *brisé* fan—as long as it was opened from left to right. If your friend tried to open it from right to left, it would appear to fall apart, as though the ribbon holding the tops of the sticks had broken. Puzzle fans showed four different pictures: one on each side when opened from right to left, and two more when opened from left to right.

Domino and mask fans had eyeholes, so that the bearer could hide her face and peer out. Lorgnette fans featured a small magnifying glass, usually set in one of the guards.

The French queen Marie Antoinette, who was nearsighted, had one of these fans. And in the late 1800's, all kinds of odd fans were invented—pistol fans, parasol fans, fans made of rubber.

By World War I, however, fans were falling out of fashion in Western countries. Women were becoming more emancipated and didn't need to hide behind their fans. Clothing was more comfortable, and houses could be cooled with electrical fans.

Flashy ostrich-plume fans made a brief comeback in the 1930's, as accessories for evening gowns. But by this time, fans no longer served a useful purpose, and they were gradually set aside. Today the delicate and lovely fans of the past can be seen in museums and private collections, where they stand as reminders of the elegance of the past.

Painted cardboard handscreen, France, late 1800's

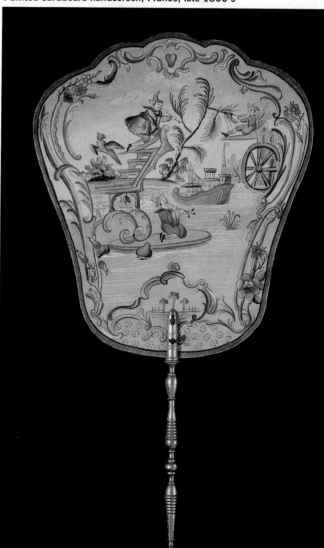

Tom Berenger in *Platoon* (best motion picture).

1987 ACADEMY AWARDS

CATEGORY	WINNER
Motion Picture	*Platoon*
Actor	Paul Newman (*The Color of Money*)
Actress	Marlee Matlin (*Children of a Lesser God*)
Supporting Actor	Michael Caine (*Hannah and Her Sisters*)
Supporting Actress	Dianne Wiest (*Hannah and Her Sisters*)
Director	Oliver Stone (*Platoon*)
Cinematography	Chris Menges (*The Mission*)
Song	''Take My Breath Away'' (*Top Gun*)
Foreign Language Film	*The Assault* (The Netherlands)
Documentary Feature	*Artie Shaw: Time Is All You've Got* and *Down and Out in America* (tied)
Documentary Short	*Women—For America, For the World*

Paul Newman (best actor) in
The Color of Money.

Mia Farrow, Barbara
Hershey, and Dianne Wiest
(best supporting actress)
in *Hannah and Her Sisters*.

A BIRTHDAY PARTY FOR SNOW WHITE

In 1937, the Walt Disney studio released a film that was unlike any that had ever been shown before. The film was *Snow White and the Seven Dwarfs,* and it was the very first feature-length animated cartoon.

At the time, people thought Disney was mad—audiences would never sit through a feature-length cartoon, they predicted. But audiences quickly proved the doubters wrong: *Snow White* became one of the most popular films of all time. In 1987, the Disney studio celebrated *Snow White*'s 50th anniversary with a host of special events, and audiences flocked to see it once again. In the years since its making, the film has come to be regarded as a true classic.

A DARING VENTURE

Snow White is based on a Grimm brothers fairy tale that tells of a princess, Snow White, whose wicked stepmother orders her killed. She takes refuge in the forest with a group of dwarfs, but her stepmother finds her and poisons her. Then a handsome prince appears and kisses her. She awakens, and they live happily ever after.

When Walt Disney decided to make a film based on this tale in 1934, he was met with a chorus of objections. Not only was the idea of a feature-length animated film outlandish, but fantasies were notorious box-office flops. Adults wouldn't want to see a fairy tale, and children—well, their ticket purchases would never cover the estimated $250,000 it would cost to make the film.

Nonetheless, Disney went ahead.

Critical in the early stages was the process of developing the characters. Dozens of Snow Whites were drawn and rejected, and the final design was refined again and again. In the end, the character of Snow White was a breakthrough—the first cartoon figure to seem human. The dwarfs also received careful attention, right down to their names. (The dwarfs in the original fairy tale have no names.) The Disney team considered and rejected dwarf characters with names such as Hotsy and Shifty before settling on the now-famous seven—Sneezy, Sleepy, Dopey, Happy, Bashful, Grumpy, and Doc.

Each character also needed a voice, and dozens of actors were auditioned for these parts. Snow White's voice was provided by Adriana Caselotti. But when the studio couldn't find an appropriate voice for Dopey, it decided to let him remain silent throughout the film.

In all, nine story adapters, two character developers, six directors, seven background painters, ten art directors, and twenty-eight animators worked on the film. (Disney himself did none of the drawing.) Animators took months to produce each scene of the movie, studying films of live actors and pains-

Snow White and the Seven Dwarfs was the first feature-length animated cartoon and one of the most popular films of all time. It celebrated its 50th anniversary in 1987.

takingly drawing each frame for the most lifelike effect. The animated figures were then combined with painted backgrounds.

Music was also an important part of the film, and several composers worked on it. *Snow White* included several songs that became famous—the dwarfs' march, with its "heigh-ho" refrain, Snow White's "Some Day My Prince Will Come" and "Whistle While You Work." But Disney also used background music to help move the story along. Each character had a separate musical theme—romantic themes for Snow White and her prince; an evil, brooding theme for the wicked Queen; and comic themes for the dwarfs.

The final cost of the picture was far more than had been estimated—$1.5 million. Most of the money was borrowed, putting the studio on shaky ground. But if Disney worried about turning a profit on the film, he needn't have. It opened in Hollywood on December 21, 1937, and was an instant hit. *Snow White* earned more than $8 million in its first year, becoming the biggest box-office money-maker of its time.

A CLASSIC IS BORN

Snow White also earned rave reviews from critics. The famous comic Charlie Chaplin called Dopey "one of the greatest comedians of all time." A New York critic wrote, "It is a classic. . . . If you miss it, you'll be missing the 10 best pictures of 1938." Soon *Snow White* was drawing audiences in some 40 countries, with soundtracks in ten languages. The film was *Blanche-Neige et les Sept Nains* in France, and *Schneewittchen und die Sieben Dwerge* in Germany.

In fact, the film never lost its popularity. Disney (and other filmmakers) made many other full-length cartoon features. But whenever *Snow White* was shown again, audiences turned out in huge numbers. By the time the film turned 50, it had earned some $330 million worldwide.

The Disney studio celebrated *Snow White*'s anniversary by declaring 1987 the "Year of Snow White." There were "Snow White" parades at the Disney theme parks —Disneyland in California and Walt Disney World in Florida. Entertainers dressed as Snow White and the dwarfs toured children's hospitals and made special appearances at the New York Stock Exchange, the Smithsonian Institution, and even at the White House Easter Egg Roll. *Snow White* commemorative coins and a special *Snow White* rose were produced. And a brass star bearing Snow White's name was embedded in a Hollywood sidewalk, next to stars with the names of live actors.

Meanwhile, the film itself was released again in 60 countries. Audiences around the world found that on screen, Snow White hardly looked her age—she seemed as fresh and charming as ever. Her prince was just as handsome, the evil Queen just as threatening, and the dwarfs just as lovable as they had been 50 years before.

As part of the birthday celebrations, entertainers dressed as Snow White and the dwarfs made appearances at children's hospitals, the Smithsonian Institution, and the New York Stock Exchange (*shown here*).

SHOPPING BAG ART

Who doesn't have a shopping bag or two folded away in a drawer or on a closet shelf? After you carry your purchases home from the store, a shopping bag has dozens of uses —beach bag, tote bag, picnic carrier, storage container, and more. But you might want to take your bags out of the closet and give them a closer look: Shopping bags are also portable art.

From humble beginnings as brown paper satchels, shopping bags have evolved into colorful, eye-catching graphic presentations. Some mimic the styles of famous artists or reproduce their works. Some feature cartoon characters. Many bags, however, are original creations, making use of the latest trends in design.

Most shopping bags are made of heavy paper, but plastic, cloth, and metallic foil are also used. Some of the most eye-catching bags are put out by department stores, which use specially designed bags to advertise promotions and certain shopping seasons, such as Christmas. But all sorts of shops offer bags—and, generally, the more exclusive the shop, the more elaborate and unusual the bag. Museums, libraries, and even political groups have used shopping bags for promotions. And greeting card stores sell bags to use in place of gift wrap.

As shopping bags have become more fanciful, many people have come to appreciate them for their design qualities and even to collect them. Among the collectors of shopping bag art is the Smithsonian Institution, which recently staged a touring exhibit of hundreds of bags. So hang on to your shopping bags—you may have the start of an art collection in your closet.

THE MUSIC SCENE

Newsweek called them "the rock phenomenon of 1987." Their new album was both a popular success and critically acclaimed for its social conscience. Add a sold-out U.S. and European tour and a *Time* magazine cover story, and you have a band well on its way to superstardom. That band was U2, the Irish rock group that dominated the year's music scene. Their 1987 album *The Joshua Tree* sold more than 2 million copies and produced the best-selling singles "With or Without You" and "I Still Haven't Found What I'm Looking For."

U2's tremendous success, although seemingly sudden, didn't occur overnight. *The Joshua Tree* was the group's sixth album. The five members of U2—lead singer Bono (Paul Hewson), lead guitarist the Edge (David Evans), bass guitarist Adam Clayton, and drummer Larry Mullen, Jr.—formed the band as teenagers in Dublin in 1976. They released their debut album in 1980, but their first major success came with 1984's *The Unforgettable Fire.*

The band has been at the forefront of the new generation of socially concerned rock musicians, beginning with their 1983 song "Sunday Bloody Sunday," about the violence in Northern Ireland. They were among the musicians performing at 1985's Live Aid concert and at the 1986 concerts for the humanitarian organization Amnesty International. On *The Joshua Tree,* U2's combination of driving music and idealistic themes won the hearts and minds of listeners seemingly ready for music with a message.

NEW SOUNDS FROM OLD FRIENDS

The year was a productive one for many established musicians who followed up past successes with ambitious new efforts. Two stars especially—Madonna and Michael Jackson—shone with well-publicized albums, videos, and concert tours. Madonna followed up a starring role in the movie *Who's That Girl* with an international concert tour that cemented her reputation as a dynamic entertainer. Also during the year, Madonna won an MTV music video award for the video of her controversial 1986 song "Papa Don't Preach."

Eager anticipation surrounded the release of Michael Jackson's new album, *Bad.* The LP was his first since 1982's blockbuster *Thriller,* which by 1987 had sold nearly 40 million copies—more than any record in history. Despite mixed reviews from music critics, *Bad,* too, seemed destined to be a

The Irish group U2 dominated the year's music scene. Their 1987 album *The Joshua Tree* sold more than 2 million copies.

best-seller. Its title-song video, directed by noted filmmaker Martin Scorsese, showcased Jackson's impressive dancing abilities. And the album's first single, "I Just Can't Stop Loving You," a duet with Siedah Garrett, soon reached number-one on the charts. In the fall, Jackson launched his first solo world tour in Japan, where his overwhelming popularity caused the Japanese press to label him "Typhoon Michael."

Rock superstar Bruce Springsteen added another facet to his image with a new album, *Tunnel of Love*, released in October. The LP arrived in record stores almost unannounced, with little of the publicity that had trumpeted the release in 1986 of a five-record set of live Springsteen recordings. *Tunnel of Love* was a departure in other ways, as well. Its songs were very different from the rousing rock anthems of Springsteen's 1984 hit album *Born in the U.S.A.* Recorded with little back-up from his E Street Band, the new album offered simple yet powerful songs about the uncertainties of love and romance.

Whitney Houston's second album, *Whitney*, lived up to the promise of her acclaimed 1985 debut album. Following the successful formula of her first LP, *Whitney* showed the singer's versatility with a mix of songs ranging from ballads to dance tunes.

Prince's latest album, *Sign O' the Times*, contained the dance hit "U Got the Look,"

Michael Jackson released *Bad*, his first LP since 1982.

One of the year's hottest new groups was Lisa Lisa and Cult Jam, whose sound was a blend of 1960's-style girl-group vocals and 1980's-style funk.

performed with Sheena Easton. A new double LP by Sting, . . . *Nothing Like the Sun,* appeared late in the year. It dealt with the heroism of women and other serious themes. The Cars released *Door to Door,* their first album of new material in three years. Heart, led by sisters Ann and Nancy Wilson, had a hit single, "Alone," from their album *Bad Animals.* And the most recent effort by Tom Petty and the Heartbreakers was *Let Me Up (I've Had Enough).*

Many music veterans were on the scene in 1987, some after long absences. Former Beatle George Harrison released *Cloud Nine,* his first album in five years. *Coming Around Again* was songstress Carly Simon's latest album. The members of Fleetwood Mac, after pursuing individual careers for five years, regrouped to make *Tango in the Night.* Rolling Stone Mick Jagger released *Primitive Cool,* his second solo album, while David Bowie checked in with *Never Let Me Down.* The smooth and soulful tones of Smokey Robinson could be heard again on his album *One Heartbeat.* And fans of the Grateful Dead (known as "Deadheads") welcomed the release of *In the Dark,* the perennially popular group's first album in seven years.

NEW VOICES

Several promising newcomers were heard from during the year. One of the summer's hottest groups was Lisa Lisa and Cult Jam, whose sound was a catchy blend of 1960's-style girl-group vocals and 1980's-style funk. "Head to Toe," a single from their album *Spanish Fly,* shot to number-one. The group was fronted by Lisa Velez, a 20-year-old whose singing style reminded some listeners of the young Diana Ross.

Crowded House, a three-man group whose members hail from Australia and New Zealand, scored with their debut album. Their song "Don't Dream It's Over" was a top-selling single, and its video won the group an MTV music video award for best new artists. Other young singers whose debut albums produced popular singles included 16-year-old Debbie Gibson ("Only in My Dreams"), Richard Marx ("Don't Mean Nothing"), and Robbie Nevil ("C'est la Vie").

An amazing variety of musical styles was to be found among artists who reached the spotlight in 1987. For example, the English group T'Pau's hit "Heart and Soul" was a danceable pop tune with a synthesized sound, while the Georgia Satellites' "Keep

Your Hands to Yourself'' had the growling guitar licks characteristic of Southern rock and roll. The album *Strong Persuader* and its single ''Smoking Gun'' won widespread recognition for the classic blues technique of singer/guitarist Robert Cray. Singer Suzanne Vega, who springs from a folk-music tradition, expanded her following with her second album, *Solitude Standing,* and its hit single ''Luka.'' And Regina Belle's debut album, *All By Myself,* featured love songs performed in the soulful style of Anita Baker and Sade.

ROCK WITH A CONSCIENCE

The trend toward social activism, pursued most noticeably in 1987 by U2, was also continued by other musicians. Canada's Bryan Adams, who established himself as a teen idol with 1985's multi-platinum album *Reckless,* turned to more serious subjects on his fifth LP, *Into the Fire.* Determined to be appreciated as a mature artist, Adams took on social and political issues like unemployment, war, and the rights of native Americans. Another Canadian, Bruce Cockburn, a highly respected folk artist, recorded ''Stolen Land,'' a song about the struggles of a tribe of Indians in British Columbia to preserve their native lands.

In the United States, John Cougar Mellencamp released a new album of social commentary. Like his previous album *Scarecrow, The Lonesome Jubilee* identified with the overlooked people of America's heartland. Underscoring this, the video for the album's first single, ''Paper in Fire,'' was filmed in a poor black neighborhood of Savannah, Georgia. Mellencamp and his band were praised for broadening their hard-rock style on the album with the use of traditional instruments such as fiddle, hammered dulcimer, and accordion.

In April, a benefit concert for Amnesty International was held in London. Performers included Lou Reed, Peter Gabriel, Dire Straits' Mark Knopfler, and Duran Duran. Musicians in favor of stopping U.S. aid to the Nicaraguan contras held a series of concerts in the latter part of the year. Peter, Paul, and Mary, Judy Collins, Joan Baez, and former Eagle Don Henley were among those participating in the concerts, which took place in Los Angeles, Washington, D.C., and New York City.

MUSIC AND THE MOVIES

Several soundtrack albums made the charts in 1987, including *Who's That Girl, Dirty Dancing,* and *Beverly Hills Cop II.* The

Hard-rock band Bon Jovi's *Slippery When Wet* sold some 8 million copies.

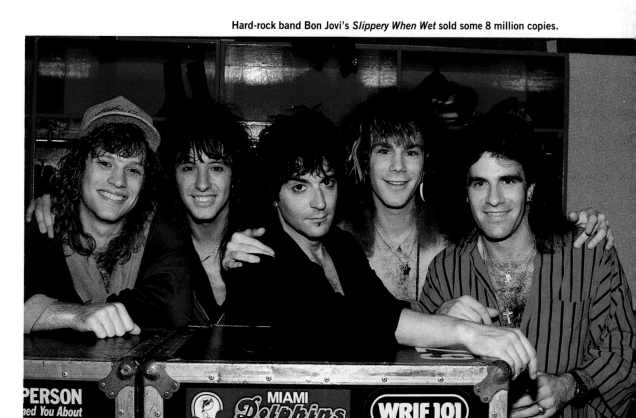

PERSON
ed You About

Sgt. Pepper's Lonely Hearts Club Band, the Beatles' landmark album, celebrated its 20th anniversary in 1987.

last produced a hit song, "Shakedown," for Bob Seger.

A fourth movie that spawned a successful soundtrack was *La Bamba*, which chronicled the life and tragic early death of 1950's rock and roller Ritchie Valens. The title song, the album, and the video all reached number-one on the charts. Valens' music was performed by the California Tex-Mex rock band Los Lobos, whose members, like Valens, have a Mexican-American heritage.

At year's end, rock and roll legend Chuck Berry starred in the film portrait *Chuck Berry: Hail! Hail! Rock 'n' Roll*. Centered around Berry's 60th-birthday concert in St. Louis, the documentary featured appearances by Jerry Lee Lewis, Keith Richards, and Bruce Springsteen. Berry also published his autobiography during the year.

OTHER SOUNDS

The success of *La Bamba* was one sign of an increasing Spanish influence in popular music. Not only did the movie tell the story of a Mexican-American rock star, but its title song, as performed by Los Lobos, was the first Spanish-language song ever to become a number-one hit in the United States.

Further evidence of this trend could be heard on the airwaves as a number of pop singers began to insert Spanish words and phrases into their songs. Two such songs, Madonna's "La Isla Bonita" and "Who's That Girl," became number-one singles. Other artists, including Suzanne Vega, recorded Spanish-language versions of their songs. Spanish lyrics could also be heard on *Agua de Luna*, the latest release by Panamanian salsa star and actor Ruben Blades.

Hard-rock band Bon Jovi's 1986 LP *Slippery When Wet* remained on the charts, selling 8 million copies and generating the popular hits "Livin' on a Prayer," "You Give Love a Bad Name," and "Wanted Dead or Alive." English rocker Billy Idol softened his sound slightly on *Whiplash Smile*, his fourth U.S. release. Albums by two other hard-rock performers, Whitesnake and Sammy Hagar, also made the lists of top-selling LPs.

Heavy-metal performers continued to attract a following, particularly younger music fans. British group Def Leppard had a top-selling album, *Hysteria*, their first release in four years. Also making the charts were *Girls, Girls, Girls* by Mötley Crüe and *Permanent Vacation* by Aerosmith.

Rap also remained popular, as seen by the success of albums by LL Cool J (*Bigger and Deffer*), the Fat Boys (*Crushin'*), and the Beastie Boys (*Licensed to Ill*).

A country music revival continued to gain momentum with the release of follow-up albums by three of country music's newest artists, Randy Travis, George Strait, and Dwight Yoakam. These so-called "new traditionalists" use spare, mostly acoustic arrangements and heartfelt vocal styles reminiscent of such country music greats as Hank Williams and Merle Haggard. Strong female performers also contributed to the resurgence. The Judds, a mother-daughter duo, had a popular third album in *Heart Land*. Singers Dolly Parton, Emmylou Harris, and Linda Ronstadt blended their voices on *Trio*, an album of country songs.

MILESTONES

August 16 was the tenth anniversary of Elvis Presley's death, and fans from around the world gathered in his hometown of Memphis, Tennessee, for a week-long observance. On the eve of the 16th, some 15,000 fans took part in an all-night candlelight procession past Presley's grave on the grounds of Graceland, his mansion. Thou-

1987 GRAMMY AWARDS

Category	Title	Artist/Credit
Record of the Year	"Higher Love"	Steve Winwood, artist
Album of the Year	*Graceland*	Paul Simon, artist
Song of the Year	"That's What Friends Are For"	Burt Bacharach, Carole Bayer Sager, songwriters
New Artist of the Year		Bruce Hornsby and the Range
Pop Vocal Performance—female	*The Broadway Album*	Barbra Streisand, artist
Pop Vocal Performance—male	"Higher Love"	Steve Winwood, artist
Pop Vocal Performance—group	"That's What Friends Are For"	Dionne & Friends, artists
Rock Vocal Performance—female	"Back Where You Started"	Tina Turner, artist
Rock Vocal Performance—male	"Addicted to Love"	Robert Palmer, artist
Rock Vocal Performance—group	"Missionary Man"	Eurythmics, artists
Country Vocal Performance—female	"Whoever's in New England"	Reba McEntire, artist
Country Vocal Performance—male	*Lost in the Fifties Tonight*	Ronnie Milsap, artist
Country Vocal Performance—group	"Grandpa (Tell Me 'bout the Good Old Days)"	The Judds, artists
Rhythm and Blues Vocal Performance—female	*Rapture*	Anita Baker, artist
Rhythm and Blues Vocal Performance—male	"Living in America"	James Brown, artist
Rhythm and Blues Vocal Performance—group	"Kiss"	Prince and the Revolution, artists
Score for a Motion Picture	*Out of Africa*	John Barry, composer
Cast Show Album	*Follies in Concert*	Thomas Z. Shepherd, producer
Music Video	*Brothers in Arms*	Dire Straits, artists
Classical Album	*Horowitz: The Studio Recordings, New York, 1985*	Vladimir Horowitz, artist

sands also attended a three-hour memorial service held the next morning at Memphis State University. RCA Records marked the anniversary with the release of four new collections of Presley's music.

Another musical milestone, the 20th anniversary of the release of the Beatles' landmark album *Sgt. Pepper's Lonely Hearts Club Band*, was reached in June. The 20-year mark was especially noteworthy given the first lines of the album's title song: "It was 20 years ago today, Sgt. Pepper taught the band to play."

The Beach Boys celebrated their 25th year together with a concert in Hawaii broadcast on national television. One of the most popular U.S. bands during the 1960's, the Beach Boys continued to play the California surfer sound through the 1970's and 1980's. In 1987 they contributed their distinctive harmonies on a remake of the Surfaris' "Wipeout" by rap artists the Fat Boys.

ARNOLD SHAW
Author, *A Dictionary of American Pop/Rock* and *Honkers and Shouters*

Steve Winwood's "Higher Love" won the 1987 Grammy Award as best record of the year.

Rue McClanahan (best actress, comedy series) and guest star Frank Aletter in "The Golden Girls" (best comedy series).

1987 EMMY AWARDS

CATEGORY	WINNER
Comedy Series	"The Golden Girls"
Actor—comedy series	Michael J. Fox, "Family Ties"
Actress—comedy series	Rue McClanahan, "The Golden Girls"
Supporting Actor—comedy series	John Larroquette, "Night Court"
Supporting Actress—comedy series	Jackee Harry, "227"
Drama Series	"L.A. Law"
Actor—drama series	Bruce Willis, "Moonlighting"
Actress—drama series	Sharon Gless, "Cagney & Lacey"
Supporting Actor—drama series	John Hillerman, "Magnum, P.I."
Supporting Actress—drama series	Bonnie Bartlett, "St. Elsewhere"
Special—drama	"Promise"
Special—variety, music, or comedy	"The 1987 Tony Awards"

Cybill Shepherd and Bruce Willis (best actor, drama series) in "Moonlighting."

Harry Hamlin and guest star Barbara Bosson in "L.A. Law" (best drama series).

269

FANCIFUL FLOATERS

A flying elephant? Uncle Sam in the sky? Of course. Anything's possible in the adventurous world of ballooning. Always colorful, hot-air balloons now have a new feature: Many are unique and fanciful creations.

Some unusual balloons are designed for special events. The flying elephant, for example, was made for a goodwill tour of Asian

countries (it's shown here over Brunei, a country on the island of Borneo).

Other eye-catching balloons are used as advertising messages. You may recognize Tony the Tiger at right—he's associated with a breakfast cereal. And still other balloons are made simply to stand out in a crowd—such as the face below. Called Miss Chic I. Boom, the balloon is modeled on Carmen Miranda, a well-known singer of the 1940's who wore hats adorned with fake fruit.

Next time you spot a hot-air balloon floating in the sky, take a closer look. It may be someone— or something—you know.

POETRY OF THE PHYSICAL

Where is the line between craft and art? Both words refer to objects that are made by hand. Dictionary definitions say that the word "craft" implies expert workmanship, while "art" suggests creative force. Many people think of craft objects as items that are made to be used, while a work of art embodies a personal statement by the artist.

But in recent years, the line between craft and art has become blurred. This trend was shown clearly by "Craft Today: Poetry of the Physical," an exhibit of modern American crafts that made a two-year tour of the United States. The exhibit opened late in 1986 in New York City, where it inaugurated the new home of the American Craft Museum. Then it traveled to Colorado, California, Wisconsin, Kentucky, and Virginia.

Crafts have a long history in North America. The Indians and the early settlers who arrived from Europe had to make the tools,

The Object as Statement: *Tri-Color Arch*, by Claire Zeisler . . .

. . . and *Shard Rockets*,
by Richard Marquis.

clothing, and other items they needed by hand. They strove to make these items beautiful as well as useful, so that each item would enhance daily life.

In the 1800's, machines took over the making of many everyday items, and mass production became the rule. But crafts enjoyed a revival near the end of the century. People missed the beauty and individuality that had been characteristics of handmade items. And many people discovered that making an object by hand provided great satisfaction.

In the 1900's, crafts became more closely associated with architecture and design. Craft techniques were taught at art schools and universities. And new trends toward individual expression in art began to have an effect on crafts. In the 1960's, crafts re-

The Object Made for Use (this page):
Chest of Drawers, by Wendy Maruyama . . .
and *Lamp*, by Louis Mueller.

The Object as Vessel (opposite page):
Face Goblets, by William Bernstein and Katherine
Bernstein . . . and *Avery Series—Perfume Bottles*,
by Andrew Magdanz and Susan Shapiro.

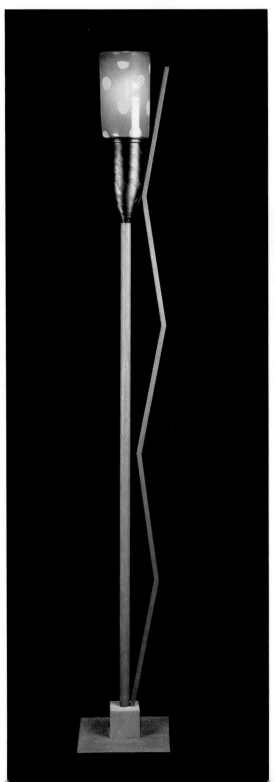

ceived yet another boost. Many people turned away from what they saw as the materialism of society and sought satisfaction through crafts.

The objects in the "Poetry of the Physical" exhibit were all made in the 1980's. Like traditional craft objects, they showed appreciation for beauty and for the nature of the materials used, as well as great skill in working with the materials. They also reflected the personal creativity of the people who made them. But they represented a wide range of styles, materials, and ap-

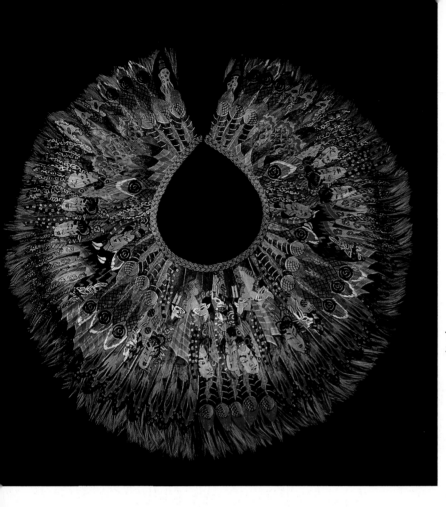

The Object for Personal Adornment:
Shinto Shards, by K. Lee Manuel . . .

proaches. Some were the kinds of items that usually come to mind when people think of crafts—furniture, pottery, jewelry, quilts. Others didn't have clear uses, and they weren't as easy to categorize.

The exhibit separated these objects into four divisions. In **the object as statement** were works that had been created not for specific uses but primarily for their beauty. The objects in this division made unique personal statements. They included wall hangings made of fibers, paper, and other substances, and three-dimensional pieces in a wide range of materials. Many of the works were similar to the constructions and other types of contemporary sculptures shown in art museums. Some were abstract; others seemed to make humorous comments on society.

The division called **the object made for use** focused on items that had been designed for specific functions. These included desks, chairs, and other pieces of furniture, lamps, fireplace tools, mirrors, spoons, and many other implements. But the objects were far from traditional. Some made use of classic designs and materials, such as plastic laminates, along with vivid colors and bold graphics.

Bowls, cups, vases, bottles, and other containers were featured in **the object as vessel.** All the traditional materials used to make such items, including glass, metal, and ceramics, were included. But again, the artists added personal expression to old forms and took the materials in new directions.

Jewelry and clothing were grouped in the division called **the object for personal adornment.** Wearability was an important factor in the design of these items, but many were also meant to be put on display when they weren't being worn. The jewelry included pieces in traditional metals and in newer materials such as plastic. Many of the articles of clothing used fabrics that had been designed and made for them alone, so that the look of the fabric became an important part of the finished item.

The exhibit showed that crafts have taken on a new role in society. People no longer need to make everyday items themselves. But the desire to make beautiful objects by hand is still there, as is the ability to appreciate the beauty, skill, and creativity seen in finely crafted work.

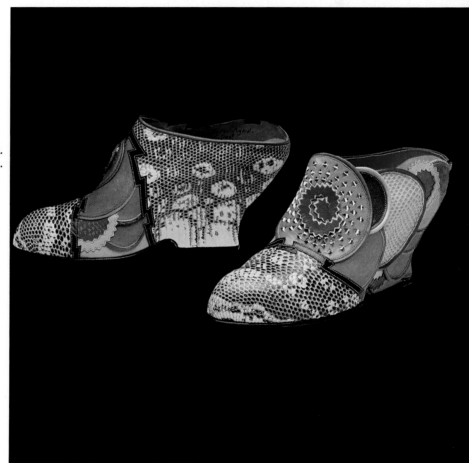

. . . and *Never Say Never Again. Right, Den?,* by Gaza Bowen.

FACES, PLACES, EVENTS

One of the fastest rising stars of 1987 was 21-year-old **Marlee Matlin**, a newcomer to films who became the first deaf performer to win an Academy Award. She won as best actress for her role in *Children of a Lesser God,* in which she played a deaf young woman who overcomes her anger with the help of a sympathetic teacher. Matlin, who grew up near Chicago, had previously appeared in a stage production of the story.

With his too-small suits, crew cut, red bow tie, and cloddy white shoes, **Pee-wee Herman** is—well, a little weird. In 1987 he was also the star of the hottest new kids' TV show, "Pee-wee's Playhouse." Pee-wee (comedian Paul Reubens, 34) poked fun at the adult world as he cavorted around his wildly painted house, which contained such features as an armchair that hugged sitters and a window that announced who was coming up the walk. The show had wide appeal—nearly a third of its viewers were 18 or older.

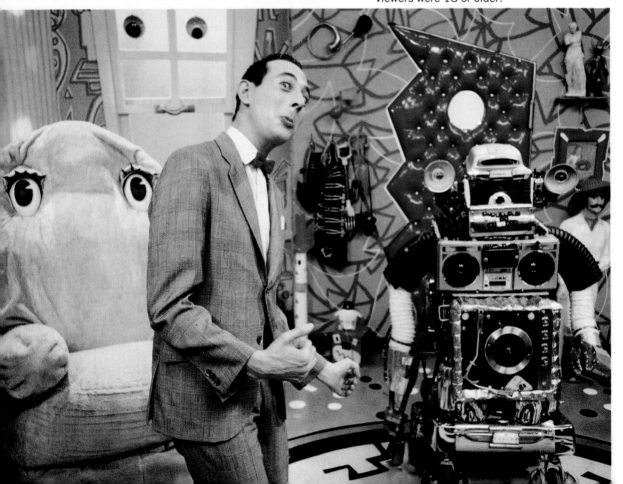

Richard Wilbur, 66, was named poet laureate of the United States in April, 1987. (Robert Penn Warren, who in 1986 had become the first poet to hold the post, stepped down because of poor health.) Wilbur, who lives in Massachusetts, had previously won a Pulitzer Prize for his poems. His duties as poet laureate included delivering lectures and public readings and advising the Library of Congress on poetry.

Looking for a place to get away from it all on your next vacation? You might want to consider the bottom of the sea. **Jules' Undersea Lodge**, anchored on the bottom of a lagoon off Key Largo, Florida, was the most unusual new hotel of 1987. Guests could watch tropical fish swim past their windows as they relaxed in climate-controlled rooms equipped with refrigerators, stereos, and VCR's. Meals were brought down to them in waterproof cases. Room rates ran $300 a person per night, though—and you couldn't open the windows!

Television **game shows** enjoyed phenomenal success in 1987. These shows, in which contestants play a game or solve a puzzle to win such fabulous prizes as new cars, cash, and jewelry, have been around since the early days of television. What accounted for their new burst of popularity wasn't clear. But millions of people were tuning in to shows such as "Wheel of Fortune" and "The $100,000 Pyramid" (*left*). There was even a new game show for kids, "Double Dare" (*below*), on the Nickelodeon cable network. On this show, teams of contestants competed in a trivia quiz, in stunts that often featured mounds of whipped cream and vats of green slime, and in an obstacle course that included a human hamster wheel. Winners could take home up to $240 in cash and as much as $3,900 in prizes, including bicycles, televisions, and trips to such places as Disney World.

Marc Chagall (1887–1985) has long been widely recognized as one of the masters of modern art. Yet his work has been virtually ignored in his native country, the Soviet Union, where the government strictly limits artistic freedom. That changed in 1987, when, to mark the 100th anniversary of the artist's birth, the Soviet Union scheduled its first major exhibition of his paintings. (The decision to hold the exhibition was seen as part of a trend toward more openness in many areas of Soviet society.) Chagall was born in the Russian village of Vitebsk and left the Soviet Union in 1922. Although he spent most of the rest of his life in France and returned to his homeland only once, for a visit, many of his paintings recall his early days there. In paintings such as the one above, people, angels, flowers, and animals float freely over village scenes, creating dreamlike fantasies of Russian village life.

More than a third of artists are women, but U.S. and Canadian museums have traditionally hung mostly works by men. To correct that, the **National Museum of Women in the Arts** opened in Washington, D.C., in April, 1987. Housed in an elegant restored building, the museum was founded by Wilhelmina Cole Holladay (*left*). Its collection includes 500 works by more than 150 women artists.

For 13 years, **Garrison Keillor** treated radio listeners to tales of Lake Wobegon, the fictional Midwestern town "that time forgot and the decades cannot improve." But in 1987, 44-year-old Keillor ended his American Public Radio show, "A Prairie Home Companion," to devote himself to writing. He was already the author of the best-selling novel *Lake Wobegon Days*.

Thirty-three-year-old **Oprah Winfrey**'s nationally syndicated TV talk show zoomed in popularity in 1987. In its first year, the show brought its host two daytime Emmy awards and beat the competition, including the long-established Phil Donahue show, in many areas. Winfrey, who began her career as a TV reporter, first gained national attention when she appeared in the 1986 film *The Color Purple*. Her frank, caring on-the-air manner was credited with her talk show's success.

A hoard of golden treasure and fabulous art objects toured museums in Washington, D.C., Chicago, and New York City in 1987. The exhibit featured objects from the court of **Sultan Süleyman the Magnificent**, who ruled the Ottoman Empire from 1520 to 1566. Süleyman vastly expanded the empire and was also a patron of the arts. Among the objects on display were paintings, fabrics and utensils covered with rich decoration, and a gold- and jewel-encrusted helmet (*right*).

FUN
TO READ

The bathroom becomes a battleground in To Bathe a Boa, a picture story by C. Imbior Kudrna. In rhyming words and humorous illustrations, the book describes the antics of a pet boa that refuses to be scrubbed. Who wins the battle? The picture here tells all.

The Arabian Nights *is among the best-known pieces of Arabic literature in the West. It's a collection of stories within a story—tales told by a princess to save her life.*

The heroine of the stories is Princess Scheherazade. She marries Sultan Shahriyar, who has killed his first wife for being unfaithful. Every night since then, he has married a new wife, and then had her beheaded the next morning. Scheherazade avoids the same fate by entertaining him each night with a story—stopping just before she reaches the end. The following night she finishes the tale and begins a new story. After a thousand and one nights, the Sultan realizes that she is a good and faithful wife.

The true origins of the stories are unclear. Many are thought to be based on old tales told by Indian, Persian, and Arab storytellers. They are believed to have been first written down in Egypt, in the 1400's. In the 1700's, a French translation called A Thousand and One Nights *appeared, and several English translations followed. Along the way new tales were added, and different versions of the older stories were given.*

One of the most famous tales,"Aladdin and the Wonderful Lamp," follows. This was one of the stories that were added to the collection, and its origin is unknown. Like many of the other tales, it has appeared in many different versions.

Aladdin
and the Wonderful Lamp

Long, long ago there lived a tailor named Mustapha. He was so poor that he could barely support his wife and son. Now, his son, whose name was Aladdin, was very lazy and didn't obey his parents, and he played all day in the streets with other lazy boys. His father was so upset with his son that he became ill and died in a few months.

One day, as Aladdin was playing with his friends, a stranger passed by and stopped and stared at Aladdin. This stranger was a magician. Taking Aladdin aside, he said, "Boy, isn't your father Mustapha the tailor?" "Yes," replied the boy. "But he is now dead."

At these words, the magician kissed him and cried, "I am your uncle. I have been in Africa for many years and have now come home." Then he gave the boy some money and said, "Go and tell your mother that I will visit her tomorrow."

As soon as the magician had gone, Aladdin ran to his mother overjoyed. "Mother," he said, "I have met my uncle!" "No, my son," answered his mother, "you have no uncle by your father's side or mine." But the next day, as Aladdin's mother was preparing dinner, the magician entered, his arms filled with meats and various fruits. He greeted Aladdin's mother and told her how upset he was that he hadn't arrived in time to see his brother.

Then he turned to Aladdin and asked him what trade he had

chosen. At this question Aladdin hung down his head, embarrassed, while his mother replied that he was a lazy boy, living on the streets.

"This is not good," said the magician. "If you have no desire to learn a craft, then I will get a shop for you and furnish it with fine merchandise." Aladdin's mother, who hadn't until then believed that the magician was really her husband's brother, now could no longer doubt it. She thanked him for his kindness to her son.

The next day the magician took Aladdin to a merchant who provided the boy with a handsome suit of clothes. Together they went to the richest shops, the largest mosques, and the most well-known inns. The magician then led Aladdin out of the city, and they traveled many miles until they reached a valley between two great mountains.

"We will go no farther," said the magician. "I will now show you some extraordinary things. First, gather up some loose sticks." When Aladdin had done that, the magician set fire to them. At the same time, he muttered several magical words and cast incense upon the flames. Immediately, a great smoke arose and the ground began to shake. Then the ground opened up, revealing a great stone slab with a brass ring in the middle.

Aladdin was so frightened that he started to run away, but the magician caught hold of him and knocked him to the ground. Aladdin stood up, trembling, and with tears in his eyes he asked what he had done to deserve such a punishment. "I have my reasons," answered the magician harshly. "Now my boy," he continued, softening his tone, "under this stone is hidden a treasure that is destined to be yours. And fate decrees that no one but you may lift the stone or enter the cave, but to do so, you must obey my instructions."

Aladdin promised that he would. The magician told him to take hold of the ring and lift the stone, and to say at the same time the names of his father and grandfather. Aladdin followed the instructions and raised the heavy stone with ease. When the stone was pulled up, there appeared a cave with steps leading down.

"Listen, my boy," said the magician, "to what I tell you. Go down the steps and at the bottom you will find an open door. Beyond the door are three great halls. Pass through them without stopping. At the end of the third hall you will find a door that opens out into a garden filled with fine fruit trees. Walk across the garden to a terrace, where you will see a lighted lamp in a niche in the terrace wall. Take down the lamp, pour out the oil, and bring it to me."

The magician then took a ring from his finger and placed it on Aladdin's finger, telling him that it would protect him from all evil. Aladdin went into the cave, descended the steps, and found the three halls just as the magician had described. He passed through, crossed the garden, took down the lamp, poured out the oil, and started to leave with it. But as he came down from the

terrace, he stopped to look around. He saw that all the trees were filled with what seemed to be glass fruits of different colors. Actually, the white fruits were pearls, the transparent were diamonds, the red were rubies, the green were emeralds, the blue were sapphires, and the purple were amethysts. Aladdin didn't realize their worth, but he was so pleased with their beauty that he gathered some of every kind.

Aladdin returned the way he had come and found the magician waiting impatiently for him. Now the magician was planning to take the lamp from Aladdin before the boy got out of the cave and then to push Aladdin down the steps so there would be no witness to what had occurred. But Aladdin refused to give up the lamp until he was out of the cave. This so enraged the magician that he used his magic to move the stone that had covered the cave back into place. And, having lost all hope of getting the wonderful lamp, the magician returned to Africa. Of course, he was not Aladdin's uncle at all. He had just needed the boy to get the magic lamp.

When Aladdin found himself thus buried alive, he sat down on the steps, without any hope of ever again seeing the sun. He remained like this for two days, without eating or drinking. On the third day, clasping his hands in despair, he accidentally rubbed the ring that the magician had forgotten to take back. Immediately an enormous and ferocious looking genie appeared, and said, ''I am the slave of any who may possess the ring. What would you have me do?''

Aladdin answered without hesitation. "Whoever you are, deliver me from this place!" He had no sooner spoken these words than he found himself outside the cave. He quickly made his way home and joyfully greeted his mother. Aladdin related to her all that had happened and showed her the transparent fruits of different colors. The mother, too, was unaware of their value and laid them carelessly aside.

Aladdin slept soundly until the next morning, but upon waking he found that there was no food in the house, nor any money. "Alas, my son," said his mother, "I haven't a bit of bread to give you." "Mother," replied Aladdin, "give me the lamp I brought home with me yesterday. I will go and sell it."

Aladdin's mother brought the lamp, and because it was very dirty, she took some fine sand and water to clean it. But as soon as she began to rub it, a hideous genie appeared before her and said in a voice like thunder, "I am the slave of any who may possess the lamp. What would you have me do?"

Aladdin said, "We are hungry. Bring us something to eat." The genie disappeared and in an instant returned with a silver tray on which were twelve silver dishes containing the most delicious foods. These he placed on a table and disappeared.

Mother and son had enough food for two days. On the third day, Aladdin went to the silver market and sold one of the silver dishes and bought enough food to last for some time. When all the dishes had been sold, Aladdin brought out the lamp again. In this way, he and his mother continued to live for some time. And although they had an incredible treasure in their lamp, they lived quietly and frugally.

Meanwhile, through his friendship with the jewelers, Aladdin learned that the fruits he had gathered in the garden were very valuable and not just brightly colored glass.

One day, a royal order proclaimed that the Princess Badroulboudour, the Sultan's daughter, would be passing through the city. And when Aladdin saw her, he fell immediately in love. When he returned home, he announced to his mother, "I love the Princess more than I can expresss, and I am going to ask the Sultan for her hand in marriage."

Aladdin's mother burst out laughing. "My son," she said, "you must be mad to talk thus!" "I assure you, my mother," replied Aladdin, "that I am not mad, and I expect you to use your persuasion with the Sultan." "I, go to the Sultan?" answered his mother, amazed. "I cannot undertake such an errand. And who are you, my son," she continued, "to think of the Sultan's daughter? Have you forgotten that your father was one of the poorest tailors in the city? Besides, no one ever goes to the Sultan without taking him a fitting present." Aladdin replied, "Wouldn't those jewels that I brought home from the garden make an acceptable present?" And he arranged the brilliant stones in a large porcelain dish.

The next morning, Aladdin's mother took the precious gift and set out for the Sultan's palace. She entered the audience chamber and placed herself before the Sultan, the Grand Vizier, and the great lords of the Court. She saluted the Sultan, and he said to her, "My good woman, what business brings you here?"

Aladdin's mother told him about her son's love for the Princess and his desire to marry her. She ended by presenting the porcelain dish to the Sultan. The Sultan's amazement was inexpressible when he saw so many beautiful and valuable jewels. He turned to his Grand Vizier and said, "Is not such a present worthy of the Princess?"

These words upset the Grand Vizier because he had hoped that the Princess would marry his son. So he whispered to the Sultan, "The present is certainly worthy of the Princess, but I beg you to grant me three months. In that time I hope that my son will have a richer present than Aladdin, who is a complete stranger to his majesty."

The Sultan agreed and, turning to Aladdin's mother, said to her, "My good woman, go home and tell your son that I agree to his proposal, but that my daughter cannot marry until the end of three months." Aladdin's mother, overjoyed, rushed home to tell her son, who thought himself the most happy of all men.

When the three-month period had passed, the Grand Vizier had not come up with a richer present. But the Sultan was now having doubts about giving his daughter to a stranger, and he thought of putting Aladdin off by issuing an order that would be impossible to fulfill. So when Aladdin's mother went to the Sultan to remind him of his promise, he said, "My good woman, it is true that Sultans should keep their promises, and I will do so as soon as your son sends me forty trays of gold, each filled with stunning jewels, carried by forty magnificently dressed slaves."

When Aladdin heard of the Sultan's request, he took the lamp and rubbed it and ordered the genie to fetch the desired present as quickly as possible. In a short time the genie returned with forty slaves, each bearing on his head a heavy gold tray filled with pearls, diamonds, rubies, and emeralds, all larger and more beautiful than those already presented to the Sultan.

The forty slaves and the humble mother walked through the streets to the palace. There, the Sultan cast his eyes on what was before him and hesitated no longer. At the sight of such immense riches and Aladdin's quickness in satisfying his demand, he was persuaded that the young man would make a most desirable son-in-law. Therefore he said to Aladdin's mother, "Go and tell your son that I wait with open arms to embrace him."

When Aladdin heard the joyous news, he again summoned the obedient genie. "Genie, provide me with the finest clothing, a magnificent and swift steed, richly clothed slaves to walk by my side, and ten thousand pieces of gold, half of which I will give to the people in the streets. Bring my mother six female attendants, as richly dressed as those of any princess. I would also have you build me a palace near the Sultan's. Build it of the finest marbles of various colors. Let the walls be of gold and silver, and the windows studded with brilliant gems. Let there be a spacious park separating the two palaces. And let there be a carpet of the plushest velvet for the Princess to walk upon, between the two palaces.''

And so the genie granted Aladdin all his wishes, and the marriage between the two young people took place the next day. For several years, the Princess and Aladdin lived happily in peace and contentment. But one day, the African magician became curious to know what had befallen Aladdin after he had left him in the cave. When he learned that Aladdin, instead of having perished miserably, had escaped, had married a princess, was living splendidly, and was in possession of the wonderful lamp, he became enraged.

In less than a day, the magician was at Aladdin's palace, where he was told that Aladdin was on a hunt. The magician then went to a coppersmith's and bought a dozen copper lamps. He placed these in a basket and returned to Aladdin's palace. As he approached, he began crying out, ''Who will change old lamps for new ones?''

Now the Princess, who was in the palace, heard him and remembered the old lamp that Aladdin had. Not knowing the value of the lamp, she had a slave take it and make the exchange.

The magician immediately rubbed the lamp and the genie appeared, saying, "What would you have me do? I will obey you as your slave, and the slave of any who may possess the lamp." "I command you," replied the magician, "to transport me and also the palace that you have built in this city, with all the people in it, to Africa." The genie disappeared, and so too did the magician and the palace.

When the Sultan awoke the next morning, he went to his window to admire Aladdin's palace. But to his great amazement, all he saw was an empty space. He called for his Grand Vizier and demanded, "Tell me, what has become of Aladdin's palace?" "His palace!" exclaimed the Vizier. "Is it not in its usual place?" And when the Vizier went to the window, he too was struck with amazement. "Alas," said the Grand Vizier, "it has vanished completely. I always thought that the building, with all its riches, was the work of magic and a magician!"

At these words the Sultan flew into a great passion. "Where is that imposter, that wicked wretch?" he cried. "Go and bring him to me in chains!" And a detachment of troops met Aladdin as he was returning from the hunt and arrested him. When Aladdin was brought before the Sultan, he said, "I don't know what I have done to lose your favor. What crime have I committed?" "Your crime, you wretch," yelled the Sultan. "Do you not know it? Where is your palace? What has become of my daughter?" Aladdin looked from the window and, seeing the empty spot where his palace had stood, was thrown into confusion.

Finally, he said, "I know not where my palace has vanished. Grant me forty days in which to find out." "Go," said the Sultan. "I give you the forty days you ask for, but if you don't find my daughter, you shall not escape my wrath!"

For many days, Aladdin wandered about the city making inquiries, but all in vain. Finally he wandered into the country and sat down by the bank of a river to rest. Clasping his hands in despair, he accidentally rubbed the ring that the magician had placed upon his finger before he went into the cave. Immediately the same genie appeared who had helped him escape.

Surprised at such good fortune, Aladdin said, "Save my life, genie, by transporting my palace back to where it stood." "What you command is not in my power," answered the genie. "I am only the slave of the ring. You must summon the slave of the lamp." "If that is the case," said Aladdin, "I command you to transport me to the spot where my palace now stands."

Instantly Aladdin found himself in Africa, in his wife's room in the palace. When the Princess saw him standing there, she couldn't believe her eyes. After they had embraced, Aladdin said, "I beg you, dear Princess, tell me what became of an old lamp that I left in my dressing room when I left for the hunt." "Alas, dear husband," answered the Princess, "I was afraid our misfortune might be owing to that lamp, and what grieves me most is that I have been the cause of it." "Princess," replied

Aladdin, ''do not blame yourself, but tell me into whose hands it has fallen.''

The Princess related what had happened, and that the wicked magician visited her each night and tried to persuade her to take him for a husband in place of Aladdin. ''And,'' she added, ''he carries the wonderful lamp with him at all times.''

''Princess,'' said Aladdin, ''I think I have a plan to free ourselves from this perfidious wretch. When he comes to see you tonight, place this powder in a cup of wine and offer it to him. He will esteem it so great a favor from you that he will not refuse.'' With those words Aladdin left her room.

When evening arrived, the magician came at the usual hour. As Aladdin had predicted, he readily drank the wine the Princess offered—and fell to the floor dead. Aladdin then entered and took the lamp and rubbed it. ''Genie,'' said Aladdin, ''transport this palace instantly to where it came from.''

The following morning, the Sultan awoke and wandered over to his window, absorbed in grief. As he cast his eyes toward the spot he expected to find empty, he now saw Aladdin's palace in all its grandeur. He quickly rushed to his daughter's side, and with tears of joy they embraced.

The Sultan was so happy that he held a ten-day festival for the entire city to honor the return of the Princess and Aladdin.

LOOKING AT BOOKS

have you seen **BIRDS?**

"Long-legged tall birds, tiny bug-sized small birds" . . . this colorful picture book introduces birds of all kinds, shapes, and sizes. The lively text, by Joanne Oppenheim, uses clever rhymes to tell about its subject. And the striking illustrations seem ready to fly off the pages—they were modeled in plasticine and then photographed, giving a three-dimensional effect. For her work on the book, the illustrator, Barbara Reid, was awarded a children's literature prize by the Canada Council in 1987.

The Whipping Boy

Spoiled Prince Horace lives up to his nickname—Prince Brat. And it's no wonder that he does: When the prince plays a prank or fails to do his lessons, it's his whipping boy, Jemmy, who must take the punishment. But in this story of suspense and adventure, the haughty young prince and his whipping boy are kidnapped by a pair of villains named Cutwater and Hold-Your-Nose Billy. To trick their captors and escape, they swap identities—and the switch changes both of their lives. This book, written by Sid Fleischman, received the 1987 John Newbery Medal, the highest American award for a book for young people.

HEY, AL

Suppose you were carried off to live on a magical island, where you spent your days sunbathing and flocks of birds waited on you hand and foot. That's what happens to Al, a janitor, and Eddie, his dog, in this fantasy by Arthur Yorinks. But some strange developments convince Al and Eddie that, after all, there's no place like home—even if home is a cramped one-room apartment. With colorful illustrations by Richard Egielski, the book won the 1987 Randolph Caldecott Medal as the best American picture book for children.

How a Book Is Made

Have you ever wondered how books are made? In this book, author and illustrator Aliki explains every step of the process, from an author's first idea to the book's sale in a bookstore. The story is told in comic-strip style, with cats taking the parts of editors, publishers, designers, and the others who work as a team to produce books. You'll learn how an author finds a publisher; the details of how books are edited, illustrated, set in type; and finally how they are printed, bound, and sold.

Author-Artist (Illustrator)

Editor

Publisher

Designer

Copyeditor-Proofreader

Production Director

Color Separator

Printer

Publicity and Promotion Director

Salesperson

THE SHADOWMAKER

In the little town described in this story, nearly everyone is happy —until a mysterious old man driving a red wagon arrives. The stranger is a wizard, of course, and he sells shadows to the townspeople: fantastic shadows of kings, swans, angels, and other creatures. Soon everyone has a new shadow to wear. Then things begin to go wrong. The people find that their new shadows droop, wrinkle, creak, or melt. But an orphan girl named Drizzle spies on the wily wizard and learns his secrets. And with her brother, Soot, she sets out to outwit him. This delightful book was written by Ron Hansen and illustrated by Margot Tomes.

CHERRIES AND CHERRY PITS

Bidemmi is a young girl who loves to draw. And as she creates her pictures with her felt-tipped markers, she makes up stories to go along with them. This book, written and illustrated by Vera B. Williams, presents a string of Bidemmi's tales. Cherries figure in every one of the stories—even a pet parrot eats them. And the charming pictures bring to life Bidemmi's world of apartments, subway stops, and city streets.

Following the Light

In 1874, a group of struggling young artists organized a joint exhibition in an upstairs studio at 35 Boulevard des Capucines in Paris. The group called itself the Anonymous Society of Artists, Painters, Sculptors, Engravers, Etc. Its 30 members included Claude Monet, Auguste Renoir, Edgar Degas, Paul Cézanne, Camille Pissarro, Alfred Sisley, and other now famous names.

For the poor, little-known artists of the Anonymous Society, the 1874 exhibition proved to be a major disappointment. Few people attended, and some laughed out loud at what they saw. Only a handful of paintings were sold, and the prices were meager. Worst of all, the most respected art critics of Paris wrote scathing reviews of the show, mocking the paintings and harshly attacking the artists. The members of the Society closed up the exhibit and went back to their easels. Although they organized other shows in subsequent years, they continued to work in relative poverty and obscurity. It would be another decade or more before any of them gained acceptance with the art world or the general public.

Today, of course, Monet, Renoir, Degas, Cézanne, Pissarro, Sisley, and the others stand out as giants in the history of art. Together they are referred to as the Impressionists, and their paintings are as loved, as richly valued, and as familiar as any in the world—scenes of the streets and cafés of 19th-century Paris, sailboats on the Seine, the woods at Fontainebleau, afternoon light on the face of Chartres Cathedral, lily ponds and poppy fields, ballet classes and horse races, drinkers, bathers, boaters, and mademoiselles in fancy hats.

The hundreds of canvases painted by the Impressionists in the latter half of the 1800's now hang in the great museums of the world. Reproductions decorate living rooms everywhere. Fine art books devoted to the group —with magnificent color plates that many people frame—are constantly being published. And occasionally, when an original canvas from a private collection is auctioned, the bids often reach millions of dollars. In 1986, a work by Édouard Manet called *La Rue Mosnier aux Paveurs* (1878) sold for more than $11 million. The previous year, a small collection of Impressionist works was auctioned for $32.6 million.

The history, artistic influence, and sheer beauty of 19th-century Impressionist painting were given special attention in two noteworthy events of 1986–87. In Paris, the world's largest collection of French Impressionist works was moved from the popular but overcrowded Jeu de Paume museum to the spacious new Musée d'Orsay across the Seine. The new museum was created out of the vast expanses of a former railroad station, and it is dedicated to 19th-century art. Some people consider the Musée d'Orsay to be one of the most spectacular and unique art showplaces anywhere.

The other special event was a major exhibition, held at the National Gallery in Washington, D.C., and the Fine Arts Museum of San Francisco, that reconstructed the first

Impressionist shows of 1874–86. Nearly all the paintings originally shown in Paris—the Monets, Renoirs, Cézannes, and other works that once brought sneers and belly laughs—were re-assembled from museums and private collections throughout the world.

Had the Anonymous Society been told that their first show would be reconstructed a century later—and that their paintings would be worth millions of dollars—they might have had a few laughs of their own. It wasn't that they didn't take their work seriously; it was that nobody else took it seriously. It wasn't that they didn't make enormous sacrifices for their art; it was that their sacrifices never brought the rewards of money or recognition. And it wasn't that their paintings weren't unique or original; it was that the paintings were *too* unique and original. Nobody had seen anything like them before.

In the middle of the 19th century, the paintings considered "respectable" in French art circles were traditional, highly realistic scenes, often from the Bible or classical mythology. Portraits were always elegant and dignified. Still lifes were precise, detailed, photolike renderings. The works were often skillfully executed, but typically they were heavy, somber, and lacking in imagination and creativity. To preserve the traditional style, the powerful Academy of Fine Arts refused to recognize any artist who didn't conform to established standards. If artists were to be successful, they would have to be selected for official Salon showings—regularly held exhibitions governed by the Academy. Any artist with a different vision was considered unworthy and stood little chance of success.

And so, in the staid, placid world of 19th-century art, the so-called Impressionists were nothing less than revolutionaries. They didn't fight with guns or bombs: Their weapons were brushes, paints, canvases, and a complete commitment to a new, freer style of painting. They found their subject matter in the "open air" of forests, rivers, and village lanes. Turning away from classical themes and formal portraits of the wealthy,

they painted ordinary people in everyday settings—mingling in the streets and cafés of Paris, on picnics, in dance halls, at the races. They abandoned the dark, dry, timeworn traditions and brought to the canvas a bright, colorful, new *feeling* for the world around them. In swarms of exuberant brushstrokes, each shimmering with color, they depicted life and nature in an everchanging light. They were fascinated by light—how it enhances images, how it creates moods, how it changes from minute to minute. They studied it, they found inspiration in it, and they struggled to re-create its special qualities on canvas. Against all convention and authority, they truly followed their "own light."

Each of the Impressionist painters, of course, had his or her own style and technique. Monet's paintings were different from Renoir's, Degas', Pissarro's, and Manet's. Perhaps what they had most in common was their strong friendship, their love of painting, and their struggle against the rules, expectations, and strict formality of the established art community. Ridiculed and rejected for more than two decades, they stuck together and continued to follow the light. At times in the 1860's and 1870's, they had little to eat and not enough money even to buy paints. Renoir took bread from his parents' table to feed a starving Monet. Renoir wasn't much better off, unable to answer letters because he couldn't afford postage.

The story that follows is a fictionalized re-creation of how these artists struggled for recognition and a steady livelihood. It is set in and around Paris in 1873–74. There, the group continued to paint—often together—in such places as Argenteuil, a scenic town on the banks of the Seine. As they had for nearly ten years, they also met frequently at the Café Guerbois, a small café in the Montmartre section of Paris. It was a place they gathered to discuss their art and plan their strategies. It was there, most likely, that they first discussed the idea of a joint exhibition. The story tells of how they organized the first show in 1874; of how the public reacted; of how one mocking critic gave them the name "Impressionists"; and of how they clung to a brighter vision.

The glassy, gently rippling surface of the river mirrored a cloud-puffy late-afternoon sky and a blaze of orange, red, and yellow foliage from the tree-lined shores. The point where the water ended and the trees began was lost in glimmering splashes of color that spread from both banks, leaving only a slim channel of blue at midstream. Ahead in the distance, through a parting of the trees, the town of Argenteuil rose up from the water and into the sky, a single church spire and the shimmering outlines of airy, whitewashed houses.

On the deck of a small boat, moored to two wooden poles embedded in the river, Claude Monet stepped back from his easel, scanned the view downstream, looked back again at the easel, and pulled on his thick black beard in frustration. The boat was a kind of floating studio, fitted with a small hut to store his painting materials and, if necessary, to sleep in. The boat-studio gave him a wider choice of river views than he could obtain from

the shore. At midstream he could capture a long perspective and the full depth of color reflection. Since he had settled in Argenteuil three months earlier, Monet had indulged his fascination with water in dozens of paintings of the Seine.

"The devil of it is that the light changes so quickly!" he thought.

As he dabbed the canvas with the last touches of magenta, a voice echoed across the water.

"Claude! Claude! Come quickly! Durand-Ruel! A letter!"

At the edge of the river, against the background of trees, stood Auguste Renoir, waving a white envelope high over his head. A thrill shot up Monet's spine as he made out Renoir's words. Paul Durand-Ruel was an art dealer who had set up a gallery in London and had been buying some of the canvases by Monet, Renoir, and the others. In the last two years, Monet had achieved a modest prosperity and finally could support his wife and young son. Durand-Ruel was a godsend.

Monet quickly packed up his materials, stowed them in the hut, and poled to shore.

"How goes it?" he said cheerily as he secured the boat.

"Not at all bad," said the thin, angular Renoir. "It will prove interesting again to compare how you and I have painted the same scene from our different perspectives. But first," he said, handing Monet the letter, "see what news from Durand-Ruel."

Monet tore open the envelope and began ro read. As his dark, deep-set eyes flitted across the page, his expression of excitement and anticipation changed gradually to one of disappointment. When he came to the bottom of the page, he let out a deep sigh and looked toward the sky. The bright pink-white clouds were rapidly fading to dull steel gray.

"Well," he said finally, pulling on his beard, "already our modest success is proving short-lived. Paul has sold nothing in six weeks. Nothing! Collectors are abandoning him and calling him a crook for passing off our work as art. He is in great debt and plans to close the gallery."

Renoir said nothing. He was stunned. Monet sat on a rock and stared at the ground.

"Well that settles it," said Monet after a long silence. "We cannot go back to the way it was before. We have made too many sacrifices already. Painting is all I know, and I will not do it any other way. We must organize a show. Me, you, Manet, Degas, Cézanne, Sisley, Morisot. Everyone. Forget the Salon! Forget the bourgeois collectors! We will leave it up to the public. And if they don't like it, we will have more shows and more shows until they do!"

"But where will the money come from?" asked Renoir, downcast. "A formal exhibition is very expensive, my friend."

"We will work things out," shot back Monet. "For every painting that is sold, a small percentage will go toward our expenses. Certainly we will sell *some* paintings."

"And if we don't?" replied the gloomy Renoir.

"What's the matter, Auguste? You're the one who always says *I'm* a pessimist! I tell you what. We'll make a bet right now. I'll wager that at least 10,000 people attend the show, and that the sale of paintings will fetch at least 50,000 francs. If neither of those things comes true, I shall take out a full-page ad in the newspaper declaring you the artistic genius of our time. If they do come true, however, you must declare the same of me, in like fashion. A deal?"

"Very well," laughed Renoir. "A deal."

"Very well, then," said Monet, standing up. "Now let's go. My wife is no doubt waiting with a nice supper. Let us at least enjoy our 'riches' while we can. Then tomorrow we can return to Paris and speak with the others."

As the sun dropped slowly behind the trees and the river was cast in shadow, the two artists walked side by side along the water's edge, talking and laughing, toward town.

. . . . .

At 11 Grande rue des Batignolles, a narrow cobblestone street on the hill of Montmartre overlooking Paris, a small crowd gathered in the back room of the Café Guerbois. A single gas lamp in the middle of the ceiling bathed the room in a dull yellow light that flickered each time the door opened and closed. The thin wooden floor creaked and sagged as each person entered, the room gradually filled with smoke, and glasses of ale and absinthe soon covered the long wooden tables.

At the head of one of the tables, surrounded by six or seven other men, Édouard Manet was engaged in his usual animated conversation. Like several of the others, he wore a formal waistcoat, a neatly tied silk cravat, and a full beard. Yet a receding hairline and flecks of gray, along with a supremely self-assured manner, distinguished Manet as the senior figure in the group.

"I still insist open air painting is a mistake," he said. "I share your fascination with light and color, but we must not abandon the masters altogether. Form and composition should always be the key elements."

Paul Cézanne, who was a little stoop-shouldered and had a slight nervous shudder, was the first to respond. Monet had wanted to jump in, but he let Cézanne say his piece.

"Pictures painted in the studio will never be as good as ones done outside," he argued. "Natural light creates contrasts and shadows that *define* form and composition."

Edgar Degas, whose arched eyebrows and high forehead gave him an air of shrewdness, was about to enter the discussion when Monet finally interrupted.

"Excuse me, gentlemen," he said firmly, "but this is a point we have been arguing over for many years. I think we know where everybody stands on the question, and there is a more urgent matter to discuss tonight. Gather round everyone."

When the ten or twelve other artists had found places at the table, Monet, wearing his usual smock and white shirt with frilly cuffs, reported the urgent news. He told of the letter from Durand-Ruel and the dire need for a new source of income.

"We can debate about theory and technique until we are blue in the face," he went on. "We can go to Argenteuil or Louveciennes and paint in the open air, or we can retire to the studio and paint magnificent portraits. As long as we paint in our own way and follow our best instincts, that is what counts. What we can no longer do is cower to the Salon. What we can no longer do is rely on a handful of enlightened dealers. It's high time we take matters into our own hands and appeal directly to the public with a formal group exhibition. This is something we have discussed at various times in the past, but tonight I propose that we give it *serious* consideration. We can collect dues from each artist. We can charge an admission fee from the public. We can each donate a percentage of the paintings we sell. The details can be worked out, but we must make our plans . . . and at once!"

After a brief silence, Camille Pissarro, one of the most respected and best-liked members of the group, spoke up in favor of Monet's proposal. Alfred Sisley, the son of a wealthy English businessman but a longtime member of the Paris circle, also favored a group show separate from the Salon. Berthe Morisot, the most prominent woman artist in the group, agreed enthusiastically. So did Renoir, of course, along with Degas and most of the others.

Only Manet disagreed. Although he had had several paintings accepted by the Salon, he had become a celebrity with the avant-garde for the scandalous subject matter of his work. Later, when some of his paintings were rejected for another official exhibition, Manet defiantly set up his own pavilion. That made him an instant hero with the group of young artists. He became the acknowledged leader of the group and something of a father figure to the younger painters. Now, however, to the shock of everyone, he refused to take part in the group show.

"The Salon is still the only proper place in which to exhibit," he insisted. "We must not abandon the battle. If we are to vindicate ourselves, we must do it through official channels. If we can do that, we will really have won."

Even as he spoke, Manet could see the disappointment in the eyes of his fellow artists. They felt he was abandoning them—and their cause—for personal glory. In that one brief moment, he suffered a loss of respect that would never be fully recovered. In the weeks and months that followed, it was Monet who emerged as the central figure in the group.

There was total silence as Manet got up from the table and put on his overcoat. The floor creaked as he walked across the room, and the gaslight flickered as the door closed behind him.

The meeting continued. Pissarro, who had some experience as an organizer, made several concrete proposals on how the show should be run. The artists would form a kind of joint stock company, with each member buying a share in small monthly installments. It would be like a society of artists with monthly dues. In addition, one franc would be charged for admission to the show. One-tenth of the income from all art sales would go into the common fund. And a catalog of the exhibit would be sold for 50 centimes per copy.

Most of the group was in accord with Pissarro's proposals, and the details were hammered out over the next several weeks. A formal charter was signed in late December and, after considerable debate, the group agreed to call itself the Anonymous Society of Artists, Painters, Sculptors, Engravers, Etc. All that was left was to find a suitable location for the show, recruit as many participants as possible, and mount the exhibit.

The problem of location was quickly solved when the photographer and balloonist Felix Nadar, a longtime friend of the group, offered to lend his studios. The apartment was located on the second and third floors of a building on the Boulevard des Capucines, right in the heart of Paris. It was a series of large, airy rooms with red-brown walls that got plenty of light. It was perfect for the show.

. . . . .

The opening took place on April 15, 1874, just a few days before the official Salon exhibition. The show was to last one month, with hours from ten to six and—as something new—in the evening from eight to ten. A total of 165 works by 30 artists were on display. Among them were twelve Monets, ten Degas, nine Morisots, six Renoirs, five Pissarros, five Sisleys, and three Cézannes.

On the morning of the opening, Monet and Renoir lingered around the fringes of the studio to count heads and listen to the reactions of the viewers. Several other artists wandered through the gallery posing as ordinary visitors. Still others loitered on the sidewalk below to see who entered.

By noon only 47 tickets had been sold. Things picked up in the afternoon, but a deep disappointment gradually etched itself in the face of each artist.

"I don't understand," whispered Monet to Renoir. "We put up posters all over Paris. The newspapers carried announcements. Why is nobody coming? I've hardly even seen any critics."

Their conversation was suddenly interrupted by a burst of laughter from the next room. The two artists looked at each other and closed their eyes. Monet pulled on his long, thick beard. Then came another burst of laughter.

Monet and Renoir walked slowly into the next room, and they merged into the small group of visitors. On the wall in front of them hung three paintings—Pissarro's *Ploughed Field;* Renoir's *Harvesters;* and Monet's *Boulevard des Capucines,* a street scene painted right from Nadar's window. It was hard to tell which one they were laughing at; maybe it was all three. The women covered their mouths with handkerchiefs. The men held their bellies. They all shook their heads and laughed.

"I think I've figured it out!" shouted one well-dressed gentleman, pounding his cane in mirth. "What they do is load a pistol with tubes of paint and fire at the canvas. Then they sign their names and *voilà,* a masterpiece!"

Monet and Renoir both joined in the laughter to look like part of the group. Like the others, they laughed so hard that tears came to their eyes.

By closing time that night, 175 people had attended the show. The first day was always the heaviest, they all knew, and the numbers were certain to dwindle.

"At this rate," sighed Pissarro, "we shall not even draw 5,000."

"Let's not jump to conclusions," said Monet. "One never knows. Let's see what tomorrow brings. Let's see what the critics say. This is only the beginning!"

Despite his outward optimism, Monet knew full well that the show would be a disaster. So did all the others. It wasn't so much the attendance. That could always pick up if a good word got around. It was the laughter. It was the jokes. And what they dreaded most was the reviews.

The first one appeared in *La Presse* a few days later. Monet read it aloud to the group before the doors opened that morning. "The artists fall into a senseless confusion, completely mad, grotesque, and, fortunately, without precedent in the annals of painting. The excesses indulged in by this school are revolting."

Another one appeared in *La Patrie* a week later. "Looking at the first rough works," it read, "you simply shrug your shoulders. Seeing the second set, you burst out laughing. But with the last ones you finally get angry. And you are sorry you did not give the franc you paid to get in to some poor beggar. You wonder if you are not the victim of some hoax."

Of all the reviews, the most damaging in the minds of Monet and Renoir was a piece in the magazine *Le Charivari* by the critic Louis Leroy. The article was called "Exhibition of the Impressionists," and it was a biting satire based on a visit to the show in the company of an artistic master.

"It was a sorry day when I took it upon myself to go to the first exhibition in the Boulevard des Capucines, accompanied by Monsieur Joseph Vincent," the story began.

As the two men proceed through the gallery, the great master is bewildered, then unnerved, and finally rendered delirious by the "smears," "dribbles," and "swish-swash" of the paintings.

Faced with an especially troublesome work by Monet—a red sun seen through the mist over the water at Le Havre—Vincent asks: "What does the canvas depict? Look at the catalog."

" '*Impression, Sunrise*', it is called."

"*Impression*—I was certain of it. I was just telling myself that, since I was impressed, there had to be some impression in it . . . and what freedom, what ease of workmanship! Wallpaper in its embryonic state is more finished than that seascape!"

Monet was deeply hurt by the review, but he said nothing. Renoir, upon finishing it, threw down the magazine and let loose a torrent of anger.

"If they don't like our work, that's one thing," he exploded, "but these critics are mean and vicious. Better they say nothing than take the food out of our mouths! We have been painting the best way we know how and in good faith. Now we have mounted a show with our last centimes, and the only thing we get out of it is a label! Impressionists! How dare he! Now *everyone* will be calling us Impressionists!''

''That is the least of our problems,'' ventured Degas, and several others nodded in agreement.

On the night the show closed, May 15, the artists gathered in Nadar's studio to hear the final accounting. Pissarro had been in charge of the bookkeeping, and he read through a brief financial statement. General expenses for the exhibition came to a total of 9,272 francs. Exactly 3,511 francs had been collected in entrance fees. The sale of paintings totaled 3,600 francs, of which 360 francs (10%) was commission. Along with membership dues, catalog sales, and small gifts, the total receipts added up to 10,221 francs. To the amazement of everyone, they had actually come out ahead by 949 francs!

''Perhaps we should think about another show,'' suggested Monet.

''Perhaps,'' said Berthe Morisot, ''but not right away. I think we all have a desire to get back to our 'impressions.' ''

. . . . .

On a bright summer morning near Argenteuil, four tiny sailboats set off from the grassy banks of the Seine. Their gently billowing sails rose up against a cloudless azure sky, and creamy white silhouettes were cast along the placid blue water. A soft, cool breeze wafted across the surface of the river, rippling the reflections of green grass, creamy canvas, and burnt-red boathouses along the shore.

On the opposite bank of the river, under a shady cluster of elms, the three friends stood side by side in front of three easels, working desperately to capture the moment. They painted in quick, short strokes, adding color and detail with deft rapidity, trying to keep up with the shifts in light.

''What sublime agony!'' declared Monet, finally setting down his brush. ''It is wonderful to be painting again, but the devil of it is that the light changes so quickly!''

''Ah, yes, sublime,'' said Renoir, admiring his friend's work. ''Yet I, for one, do not agonize. It is a magnificent scene, and I take sheer joy in painting. What say you, Édouard?''

Manet was still painting furiously, but he paused a moment to look over at Renoir's easel.

''Perhaps you should agonize a little more, my friend,'' he said with good-natured humor. ''Your work might finally begin to improve!''

Renoir couldn't resist a little jab of his own. ''But Édouard,'' he said, ''you speak like someone with great experience in painting outdoors. Surely it is nothing the *Salon* has demanded of you.''

Manet took no offense, but he put down his brush and answered in a serious tone. ''You are quite right, my friend. I must admit there is much to be learned from painting in the open air. I find it a great challenge and, like you, a great joy. I do not know how you persuaded me, but I am glad you did. As for the Salon, I just hope you realize that my motives in not joining your show were honest and heartfelt. I believed then and I believe now that our final vindication must come through official channels, no matter how hard the fight.''

"Well," interjected Monet, "we may disagree about the Salon, but we hold no grudges about your decision. We know your motives are the same as ours. We know you were in good faith, and our friendship is not shaken in the least.''

Renoir nodded in agreement.

"The most important thing," Monet went on, "is that we continue to paint in our own fashion and not give up. Sooner or later we will be taken seriously. The show was a failure and we are no better off than ten years ago, but none of us has any regrets. I got a letter from Pissarro yesterday. He is flat broke, you know, and living with relatives in Brittany. Let me read part of it to you.''

Monet reached into his knapsack and took out the letter.

"What I suffer at the actual moment is terrible," wrote Pissarro, "much more than when I was young, full of enthusiasm and ardor, convinced as I am now of being lost for the future. Nevertheless, it seems to me that I should not hesitate, if I had to start over again, to follow the same path.''

The thought of their friend, so devoted and so talented, in such destitution saddened the three artists—even though they faced similar circumstances.

"A lamp unto his feet and a light unto his path," said Manet.

A few moments passed before Monet finally spoke. "One last thing," he said cheerfully, breaking the mood. "If I were you, Édouard, I would not criticize Renoir so severely. It appears he has a grand future.''

"What on earth do you mean?" said Manet. Renoir himself looked puzzled.

Monet went to his bag again, this time pulling out a copy of *La Presse*.

"Oh no!" exclaimed Renoir. "Not more reviews! Will they never let us alone?''

"A review of sorts," said Monet cryptically, thumbing through the paper.

Finally he reached the page. He folded back the paper and held it up for the others to see. In heavy bold letters, covering the entire page, were the words "AUGUSTE RENOIR, ARTISTIC GENIUS OF OUR TIME.''

Monet winked at Renoir, and Renoir grinned as he remembered their bet.

"So you see," said Monet to Manet, "you should be careful about criticizing our great friend.''

"Perhaps you are right," laughed Manet, "but he is still just an *Impressionist!*''

JEFFREY H. HACKER
Author, *Carl Sandburg*

POETRY

FROLIC

The children were shouting together
And racing along the sands,
A glimmer of dancing shadows,
A dovelike flutter of hands.

The stars were shouting in heaven,
The sun was chasing the moon:
The game was the same as the children's,
They danced to the self-same tune.
The whole of the world was merry,
One joy from the vale to the height,
Where the blue woods of twilight encircled
The lovely lawns of the light.

        A. E. (G. W. RUSSELL) (1867–1935)

AS THE WORLD TURNS

I'm up and down and round about,
Yet all the world can't find me out.
Though hundreds have employed their leisure,
They never yet could take my measure.
I'm found in almost every garden,
Nay, in the compass of a farthing;
There's not a chariot, coach, nor mill,
Can move an inch except I will.
     (A circle)

        JONATHAN SWIFT (1667–1745)

TO A CRICKET

Voice of summer, keen and shrill,
  Chirping round my winter fire,
  Of thy song I never tire,
Weary others as they will,
For thy song with summer's filled—
  Filled with sunshine, filled with June;
  Firelight echo of that noon
Heard in fields when all is stilled
  In the golden light of May,
  Bringing scents of new-mown hay,
  Bees, and birds, and flowers away,
Prithee, haunt my fireside still,
Voice of summer, keen and shrill.

      WILLIAM COX BENNETT (1820–1895)

FLAME FAIRIES

Knights on golden prancing steeds,
  Elves and goblins leaping higher,
I can see the finest things
  In the dancing fire!

Sometimes dragons twist and curl
  Tails of red and purple light,
Sometimes giants, sometimes gnomes,
  Meet in fearsome fight!

Banners stream above the wood,
  Gaily-painted ships sail past
With a green or yellow flag
  Flying from the mast.

Then they change from this to that,
  Steeds to castles, ships to kings,
And a dragon vanishes
  Into golden rings.

Flames are fairies prisoned fast,
  Long within the logs they lie;
Once they're free they gaily leap
  Upward to the sky!

      RUPERT SARGENT HOLLAND (1878–1952)

CHAIN-MAIL

A chestnut dropped in. A goldfish rose to drink.
Their widening rings of water interlink.

KIJIRÔ (dates unknown)

THE HEIGHT OF THE RIDICULOUS

I wrote some lines once on a time
   In wondrous merry mood,
And thought, as usual, men would say
   They were exceeding good.

They were so queer, so very queer,
   I laughed as I would die;
Albeit, in the general way,
   A sober man am I.

I called my servant, and he came;
   How kind it was of him
To mind the slender man like me,
   He of the mighty limb.

''These to the printer,'' I exclaimed,
   And, in my humorous way,
I added (as a trifling jest),
   ''There'll be the devil to pay.''

He took the paper, and I watched,
   And saw him peep within;
At the first line he read, his face
   Was all upon the grin.

He read the next; the grin grew broad,
   And shot from ear to ear;
He read the third; a chuckling noise
   I now began to hear.

The fourth; he broke into a roar;
   The fifth; his waistband split;
The sixth; he burst five buttons off,
   And tumbled in a fit.

Ten days and nights, with sleepless eye,
   I watched that wretched man,
And since, I never dare to write
   As funny as I can.

OLIVER WENDELL HOLMES (1809–1894)

THE BALD CAVALIER

When periwigs came first in wear,
   Their use was to supply
And cover the bald pate with hair,
   To keep it warm and dry.

For this good end, our Cavalier
   Determined one to buy,
Which did so natural appear
   That it deceived the eye.

But riding out one windy day,
   Behold! a sudden squall
Soon blew his feathered hat away,
   And periwig and all.

He joined the laugh with noddle bare,
   And sang in concert tone,
''How should I save another's hair,
   Who could not keep my own?''

UNKNOWN

THE CAT

Within that porch, across the way,
   I see two naked eyes this night;
Two eyes that neither shut nor blink,
   Searching my face with a green light.

But cats to me are strange, so strange—
   I cannot sleep if one is near;
And though I'm sure I see those eyes
   I'm not so sure a body's there!

WILLIAM HENRY DAVIES (1871–1940)

Around the turn of the century, a journalist named Lyman Frank Baum set out to write a "modern" fairy tale. It would be, he said, a story with the "wonderment and joy" of traditional tales, but without the "heartache and nightmares." Baum's book became one of the most popular children's classics of all time: The Wonderful Wizard of Oz.

The story tells of a girl from Kansas named Dorothy, who, with her dog Toto, is transported by a cyclone to the fantasy land of Oz. (Baum is said to have taken the name from one of his file drawers, which was labeled O–Z.) Dorothy sets off down a yellow brick road to find the Wizard of Oz, who she is told has the power to send her home. She is soon joined by three new friends—the Scarecrow, the Tin Woodman, and the Cowardly Lion—who also believe that the wizard can grant their wishes. Along the way, they share many adventures.

The Wonderful Wizard of Oz was a bestseller from the day it appeared in May, 1900. L. Frank Baum wrote thirteen other Oz books, but the first is still best known. Just as famous as the book is the 1939 film The Wizard of Oz, with music by Harold Arlen. It starred Judy Garland as Dorothy, Ray Bolger as the Scarecrow, Jack Haley as the Tin Man, and Bert Lahr as the Lion.

Here is an excerpt from the book, telling how Dorothy meets her friends.

THE WIZARD OF OZ

She bade her friends good-bye, and again started along the road of yellow brick. When she had gone several miles she thought she would stop to rest, and so climbed to the top of the fence beside the road and sat down. There was a great cornfield beyond the fence, and not far away she saw a Scarecrow, placed high on a pole to keep the birds from the ripe corn.

Dorothy leaned her chin upon her hand and gazed thoughtfully at the Scarecrow. Its head was a small sack stuffed with straw, with eyes, nose, and mouth painted on it to represent a face. An old, pointed blue hat was perched on his head, and the rest of the figure was a blue suit of clothes, worn and faded, which had also been stuffed with straw. On the feet were some old boots, such as every man wore in this country, and the figure was raised above the stalks of corn by means of the pole stuck up its back.

While Dorothy was looking earnestly into the queer, painted face of the Scarecrow, she was surprised to see one of the eyes slowly wink at her. She thought she must have been mistaken at first, for none of the scarecrows in Kansas ever wink; but presently the figure nodded its head to her in a friendly way. Then she climbed down from the fence and walked up to it, while Toto ran around the pole and barked.

"Good day," said the Scarecrow, in a rather husky voice.

"Did you speak?" asked the girl, in wonder.

"Certainly," answered the Scarecrow. "How do you do?"

"I'm pretty well, thank you," replied Dorothy politely. "How do you do?"

"I'm not feeling well," said the Scarecrow, with a smile, "for it is very tedious being perched up here night and day."

"Can't you get down?" asked Dorothy.

"No, for this pole is stuck up my back. If you will please take away the pole I shall be greatly obliged to you."

Dorothy reached up both arms and lifted the figure off the pole, for—being stuffed with straw—it was quite light.

"Thank you very much," said the Scarecrow, when he had been set down on the ground. "I feel like a new man."

Dorothy was puzzled at this, for it sounded queer to hear a stuffed man speak, and to see him bow and walk along beside her.

"Who are you?" asked the Scarecrow when he had stretched himself and yawned. "And where are you going?"

"My name is Dorothy," said the girl, "and I am going to the Emerald City, to ask the Great Oz to send me back to Kansas."

"Where is the Emerald City?" he inquired. "And who is Oz?"

"Why, don't you know?" she returned, in surprise.

"No, indeed. I don't know anything. You see, I am stuffed, so I have no brains at all," he answered sadly.

"Oh," said Dorothy, "I'm awfully sorry for you."

"Do you think," he asked, "if I go to the Emerald City with you, that Oz would give me some brains?"

"I cannot tell," she returned, "but you may come with me, if you like. If Oz will not give you any brains you will be no worse off than you are now."

"That is true," said the Scarecrow. "You see," he continued confidentially, "I don't mind my legs and arms and body being stuffed, because I cannot get hurt. If anyone treads on my toes or sticks a pin into me, it doesn't matter, for I can't feel it. But I do not want people to call me a fool, and if my head stays stuffed with straw instead of with brains, as yours is, how am I ever to know anything?"

"I understand how you feel," said the little girl, who was truly sorry for him. "If you will come with me I'll ask Oz to do all he can for you."

"Thank you," he answered gratefully.

They walked back to the road. Dorothy helped him over the fence, and they started along the path of yellow brick for the Emerald City.

Toto did not like this addition to the party at first. He smelled around the stuffed man as if he suspected there might be a nest of rats in the straw, and he often growled in an unfriendly way.

"Don't mind Toto," said Dorothy to her new friend. "He never bites."

"Oh, I'm not afraid," replied the Scarecrow. "He can't hurt the straw. Do let me carry that basket for you. I shall not mind it, for I can't get tired. I'll tell you a secret," he continued, as he walked along. "There is only one thing in the world I am afraid of."

"What is that?" asked Dorothy. "The farmer who made you?"

"No," answered the Scarecrow. "It's a lighted match."

After a few hours the road began to be rough, and the walking grew so difficult that the Scarecrow often stumbled over the yellow bricks, which were here very uneven. Sometimes, they were broken or missing altogether, leaving holes that Toto jumped across and Dorothy walked around. As for the Scarecrow, having no brains, he walked straight ahead, and so stepped into the holes and fell at full length on the hard bricks. It never hurt him, however, and Dorothy would pick him up and set him upon his feet again, while he joined her in laughing merrily at his own mishap.

The farms were not nearly so well cared for here. There were fewer houses and fewer fruit trees, and the farther they went the more dismal and lonesome the country became.

At noon they sat down by the roadside, near a little brook, and Dorothy opened her basket and got out some bread. She offered a piece to the Scarecrow, but he refused.

"I am never hungry," he said, "and it is a lucky thing I am not, for my mouth is only painted. If I should cut a hole in it so I could eat, the straw I am stuffed with would come out, and that would spoil the shape of my head."

Dorothy saw at once that this was true, so she only nodded and went on eating her bread.

"Tell me something about yourself and the country you came from," said the Scarecrow, when she had finished her dinner. So she told him about Kansas, and how gray everything was there, and how the cyclone had carried her to this queer Land of Oz.

The Scarecrow listened carefully, and said, "I cannot understand why you should wish to leave this beautiful country and go back to the dry, gray place you call Kansas."

"That is because you have no brains," answered the girl.

"No matter how dreary and gray our homes are, we people of flesh and blood would rather live there than in any other country, be it ever so beautiful. There is no place like home."

Toward evening they came to a great forest, where the trees grew so big and close together that their branches met over the road of yellow brick. It was almost dark under the trees, for the branches shut out the daylight; but the travelers did not stop, and went on into the forest.

"If this road goes in, it must come out," said the Scarecrow, "and as the Emerald City is at the other end of the road, we must go wherever it leads us."

"Anyone would know that," said Dorothy.

"Certainly; that is why I know it," returned the Scarecrow. "If it required brains to figure it out, I never should have said it."

After an hour or so the light faded away, and they found themselves stumbling along in the darkness. Dorothy could not see at all, but Toto could, for some dogs see very well in the dark; and the Scarecrow declared he could see as well as by day. So she took hold of his arm and managed to get along fairly well.

"If you see any house, or any place where we can pass the night," she said, "you must tell me; for it is very uncomfortable walking in the dark."

Soon after the Scarecrow stopped.

"I see a little cottage at the right of us," he said, "built of logs and branches. Shall we go there?"

"Yes, indeed," answered the child. "I am all tired out."

So the Scarecrow led her through the trees until they reached the cottage, and Dorothy entered and found a bed of dried leaves in one corner. She lay down, and with Toto beside her soon fell into a sound sleep. The Scarecrow, who was never tired, stood up in another corner and waited patiently until morning came.

When Dorothy awoke the sun was shining through the trees and Toto had long been out chasing birds. There was the Scarecrow, still standing patiently in his corner, waiting for her.

"We must go and search for water," she said to him.

"Why do you want water?" he asked.

"To wash my face clean after the dust of the road, and to drink, so the dry bread will not stick in my throat."

"It must be inconvenient to be made of flesh," said the Scarecrow thoughtfully, "for you must sleep and eat and drink. However, you have brains, and it is worth a lot of bother to be able to think properly."

They left the cottage and walked through the trees until they found a little spring of clear water, where Dorothy drank and bathed and ate her breakfast. She saw there was not much bread left in the basket, and the girl was thankful the Scarecrow did not have to eat anything.

When she had finished her meal, and was about to go back to the road of yellow brick, she was startled to hear a deep groan near by.

"What was that?" she asked timidly.

"I cannot imagine," replied the Scarecrow. "But we can go and see."

Just then another groan reached their ears, and the sound seemed to come from behind them. They turned and walked through the forest a few steps, when Dorothy discovered something shining in a ray of sunshine that fell between the trees. She ran to the place and then stopped short, with a cry of surprise.

One of the big trees had been partly chopped through, and standing beside it, with an uplifted ax in his hands, was a man made entirely of tin. His head and arms and legs were jointed upon his body, but he stood perfectly motionless, as if he could not stir at all.

Dorothy looked at him in amazement, and so did the Scarecrow, while Toto barked sharply and made a snap at the tin legs, which hurt his teeth.

"Did you groan?" asked Dorothy.

"Yes," answered the tin man, "I did. I've been groaning for more than a year, and no one has ever come to help me."

"What can I do for you?" she inquired softly, for she was moved by the sad voice in which the man spoke.

"Get an oilcan and oil my joints," he answered. "They are rusted so badly that I cannot move them at all. If I am well oiled I shall soon be all right. You will find an oilcan in my cottage."

Dorothy at once ran back to the cottage and found the oilcan, and then she returned and asked anxiously, "Where are your joints?"

"Oil my neck, first," replied the Tin Woodman. So she oiled it, and as it was quite badly rusted the Scarecrow took hold of the tin head and moved it gently from side to side until it worked freely, and then the man could turn it himself.

"Now oil the joints in my arms," he said. And Dorothy oiled them and the Scarecrow bent them carefully until they were quite free from rust and as good as new.

The Tin Woodman gave a sigh of satisfaction and lowered his ax, which he leaned against the tree.

"This is a great comfort," he said. "I have been holding that ax in the air ever since I rusted, and I'm glad to be able to put it down at last. Now, if you will oil the joints of my legs, I shall be all right once more."

So they oiled his legs until he could move them freely; and he thanked them again and again for his release, for he seemed a very polite creature, and very grateful.

"I might have stood there always if you had not come along," he said; "so you have certainly saved my life. How did you happen to be here?"

"We are on our way to the Emerald City to see the Great Oz," she answered, "and we stopped at your cottage to pass the night."

"Why do you wish to see Oz?" he asked.

"I want him to send me back to Kansas, and the Scarecrow wants him to put a few brains into his head," she replied.

The Tin Woodman appeared to think deeply for a moment. Then he said: "Do you suppose Oz could give me a heart?"

"Why, I guess so," Dorothy answered. "It would be as easy as to give the Scarecrow brains."

"True," the Tin Woodman returned. "So, if you will allow me to join your party, I will also ask Oz to help me."

"Come along," said the Scarecrow heartily, and Dorothy added that she would be pleased to have his company. So the Tin Woodman shouldered his ax and they all passed through the forest until they came to the road that was paved with yellow brick.

The Tin Woodman had asked Dorothy to put the oilcan in her basket. "For," he said, "if I should get caught in the rain, and rust again, I would need the oilcan badly."

It was a bit of good luck to have their new comrade join the party, for soon after they had begun their journey again they came to a place where the trees and branches grew so thick over the road that the travelers could not pass. But the Tin Woodman set to work with his ax and chopped so well that soon he cleared a passage for the entire party.

Dorothy was thinking so earnestly as they walked along that she did not notice when the Scarecrow stumbled into a hole and rolled over to the side of the road. Indeed, he was obliged to call to her to help him up again.

"Why didn't you walk around the hole?" asked the Tin Woodman.

"I don't know enough," replied the Scarecrow cheerfully. "My head is stuffed with straw, you know, and that is why I am going to Oz to ask him for some brains."

"Oh, I see," said the Tin Woodman. "But, after all, brains are not the best things in the world."

"Have you any?" inquired the Scarecrow.

"No, my head is quite empty," answered the Woodman. "But once I had brains, and a heart also. So, having tried them both, I should much rather have a heart."

"All the same," said the Scarecrow, "I shall ask for brains instead of a heart; for a fool would not know what to do with a heart if he had one."

"I shall take the heart," returned the Tin Woodman; "for brains do not make one happy, and happiness is the best thing in the world."

Dorothy did not say anything, for she was puzzled to know which of her two friends was right, and she decided if she could only get back to Kansas and Aunt Em it did not matter so much whether the Woodman had no brains and the Scarecrow no heart.

What worried her most was that the bread was nearly gone, and another meal for herself and Toto would empty the basket. To be sure, neither the Woodman nor the Scarecrow ever ate anything, but she was not made of tin or straw, and could not live unless she was fed.

All this time Dorothy and her companions had been walking through the thick woods. The road was still paved with yellow bricks, but these were much covered by dried branches and dead leaves from the trees, and the walking was not at all good.

There were few birds in this part of the forest, for birds love the open country where there is plenty of sunshine. But now and then there came a deep growl from some wild animal hidden among the trees. These sounds made the little girl's heart beat fast, for she did not know what made them; but Toto knew, and he walked close to Dorothy's side, and did not even bark in return.

"How long will it be," the child asked of the Tin Woodman, "before we are out of the forest?"

"I cannot tell," was the answer, "for I have never been to the Emerald City. But my father was there once, when I was a boy, and he said it was a long journey through a dangerous country, although nearer to the city where Oz dwells the country is beautiful. But I am not afraid so long as I have my oilcan, and nothing can hurt the Scarecrow, while you bear upon your forehead the mark of the Good Witch's kiss, and that will protect you from harm."

Just as he spoke there came from the forest a terrible roar, and the next moment a great Lion bounded into the road. With one blow of his paw he sent the Scarecrow spinning over and over to the edge of the road, and then he struck at the Tin Woodman with his sharp claws. But, to the Lion's surprise, he could make no impression on the tin, although the Woodman fell over in the road and lay still.

Little Toto ran barking toward the Lion, and the great beast had opened his mouth to bite the dog, when Dorothy, fearing Toto would be killed, rushed forward and slapped the Lion upon

his nose as hard as she could, while she cried out:

"Don't you dare to bite Toto! You ought to be ashamed of yourself, a big beast like you, to bite a poor little dog."

"I didn't bite him," said the Lion, as he rubbed his nose with his paw where Dorothy had hit him.

"No, but you tried to," she retorted. "You are nothing but a big coward."

"I know it," said the Lion, hanging his head in shame. "I've always known it. But how can I help it?"

"I don't know, I'm sure. To think of your striking a stuffed man, like the poor Scarecrow."

"Is he stuffed?" asked the Lion in surprise, as he watched her pick up the Scarecrow and set him upon his feet, while she patted him into shape again.

"Of course he's stuffed," replied Dorothy, who was still angry.

"That's why he fell so easily," remarked the Lion. "It astonished me to see him whirl about so. Is the other one stuffed also?"

"No," said Dorothy, "he's made of tin." And she helped the Woodman up again.

"That's why he nearly blunted my claws," said the Lion. "When they scratched against the tin it made a cold shiver run down my back. What is that little animal you are so tender of?"

"He is my dog, Toto," answered Dorothy.

"Is he made of tin, or stuffed?" asked the Lion.

"Neither. He's a-a-a meat dog," said the girl.

"Oh! He's a curious animal and seems remarkably small, now that I look at him. No one would think of biting such a little thing except a coward like me," continued the Lion sadly.

"What makes you a coward?" asked Dorothy, looking at the great beast in wonder, for he was as big as a small horse.

"It's a mystery," replied the Lion. "I suppose I was born that way. All the other animals in the forest naturally expect me to be brave, for the Lion is everywhere thought to be the King of Beasts. I learned that if I roared very loudly every living thing was frightened and got out of my way. Whenever I've met a man I've been awfully scared. But I just roared at him, and he has always run away as fast as he could go. If the elephants and the tigers and the bears had ever tried to fight me, I should have run myself—I'm such a coward; but just as soon as they hear me roar they all try to get away from me, and of course I let them go."

"But that isn't right. The King of Beasts shouldn't be a coward," said the Scarecrow.

"I know it," returned the Lion, wiping a tear from his eye with the tip of his paw. "It is my great sorrow, and makes my life very unhappy. But whenever there is danger, my heart begins to beat fast."

"Perhaps you have heart disease," said the Tin Woodman.

"It may be," said the Lion.

"If you have," continued the Tin Woodman, "you ought to be glad, for it proves you have a heart. For my part, I have no heart, so I cannot have heart disease."

"Perhaps," said the Lion thoughtfully, "if I had no heart I should not be a coward."

"Have you brains?" asked the Scarecrow.

"I suppose so. I've never looked to see," replied the Lion.

"I am going to the Great Oz to ask him to give me some," remarked the Scarecrow, "for my head is stuffed with straw."

"And I am going to ask him to give me a heart," said the Woodman.

"And I am going to ask him to send Toto and me back to Kansas," added Dorothy.

"Do you think Oz could give me courage?" asked the Lion.

"Just as easily as he could give me brains," said the Scarecrow.

"Or give me a heart," said the Tin Woodman.

"Or send me back to Kansas," said Dorothy.

"Then, if you don't mind, I'll go with you," said the Lion, "for my life is simply unbearable without a bit of courage."

"You will be very welcome," answered Dorothy, "for you will help to keep away the other wild beasts. It seems to me they must be more cowardly than you are if they allow you to scare them so easily."

"They really are," said the Lion, "but that doesn't make me any braver, and as long as I know myself to be a coward I shall be unhappy."

So once more the little company set off upon the journey, the Lion walking with stately strides at Dorothy's side. Toto did not approve this new comrade at first, for he could not forget how nearly he had been crushed between the Lion's great jaws. But after a time he became more at ease, and presently Toto and the Cowardly Lion had grown to be good friends.

THE NEW BOOK OF KNOWLEDGE
1988

The following articles are from the 1988 edition of
The New Book of Knowledge. They are included
here to help you keep your encyclopedia up to date.

CRUSTACEANS

What do a shrimp on your dinner plate, a tiny water flea in a pond, a barnacle on the hull of a fishing boat, and a sow bug hiding under a log have in common? They are all crustaceans, a type of **invertebrate,** or animal without a backbone. Crustaceans are for the most part aquatic animals. They have an **exoskeleton** (hard outer covering), jointed legs, and a body made up of several segments.

About 25,000 different kinds, or species, of crustaceans are known. They range in size from the water flea, which is difficult to see without a magnifying glass, to the giant spider crab, which may grow to be 12 feet (3.7 meters) from the tip of one outstretched claw to the other.

Crustaceans can be found in all the oceans of the world. Many live along ocean shorelines. Some species are found in freshwater rivers, lakes, or ponds. A few kinds live on land.

Many kinds of environments can support at least one kind of crustacean. Krill, small shrimplike animals, can survive in the icy

waters of the Antarctic Ocean. Other crustaceans live in the hot tropics—sometimes a crab can be found on top of a palm tree! Hot springs deep in the ocean are home to large white crabs with no eyes. Even a very salty environment, such as the Great Salt Lake in Utah where few animals can survive, is home to a crustacean called a brine shrimp.

▶ KINDS OF CRUSTACEANS

The crustaceans best known to most people are those that are often used for food. These are the **decapods,** crustaceans with ten legs. They include the familiar shrimps, lobsters, crabs, and crayfish. Decapods can be recognized by their relatively large size, their one or more pairs of claws, their large eyes, and their antennae, which are used for sensing their surroundings.

Less well known but very important to marine life are the many kinds of smaller crustaceans known as **copepods.** These animals are just barely visible to the eye—about ⅛ of an inch (0.25 centimeter) in length. They are found in very large numbers—as many as 100,000 tiny animals in 10 square feet (about 1 square meter) of water. Copepods make up much of the **plankton** in the sea, the drifting and floating plants and animals that provide food for larger marine life.

If you turn over a rock or a log in your backyard, you may see flat, shiny **isopods** running about. Many of the animals in this crustacean group live on land.

▶ PHYSICAL DESCRIPTION

The most noticeable characteristic of crustaceans is their exoskeleton, which is also called a **cuticle.** The exoskeleton is made of a hard material called **chitin** (pronounced KI-tin). It cannot stretch the way our own skin does when we grow, so a growing crustacean must shed its exoskeleton in a process called **molting.** Underneath is a new body covering that soon hardens into a stiff exoskeleton. A crustacean that has just molted is quite soft for a day or two and is likely to be injured or eaten by other animals.

A crustacean's three main body parts are the head, thorax, and abdomen. Each of these parts is made up of several segments, and each includes at least one pair of jointed limbs, or **appendages.** The appendages can

Crustaceans have no internal skeleton as people do. They are supported by a hard outer covering, called an exoskeleton. Three of the many kinds of crustaceans are goose barnacles (*top left*), a Japanese spider crab (*top right*), and a krill, a tiny shrimplike animal (*left*).

be used for sensing the environment, catching or crushing food, breathing, walking, swimming, or carrying eggs—depending on where they are located on the body.

If a crustacean loses one of its walking legs or claws, it can grow a new one. This process is called **regeneration.** The new limb starts to grow within a few days, and after several weeks a tiny, complete new leg or claw is formed. After two or three molts, the regenerated limb catches up to normal size.

▶ DIET

Many crustaceans, both large and small, eat particles of plants, bacteria, or other animals. They scrape the particles off the ocean floor or trap them from the water. Crustaceans that spend most of their lives swimming use their appendages to filter water and extract food. This is called **filter feeding.** Barnacles are filter feeders. They extend their many legs to form a net that traps food.

Some crustaceans are predators—they catch and eat other animals. Many lobsters and crabs are equipped with strong claws for cutting and crushing their prey. Their diet includes smaller crustaceans, worms, snails, and clams. Even some of the tiny copepods are predators. They have mouthparts that can be extended to grab onto smaller animals such as young fish or shrimps.

▶ LIFE CYCLE

Crustaceans reproduce by laying eggs. The eggs may be shed directly into the water or carried by the female, either in a special sac called a **brood pouch** or attached to her swimming legs. The number and size of the eggs produced by the female depend on her size, her food supply, the temperature, and many other factors. A large crab or lobster may carry several thousand eggs on her swimming legs until they hatch several weeks or up to a year later, depending on the species.

Some kinds of young crustaceans, such as crayfish, hatch from their eggs looking very much like their parents. Most crustaceans, especially those in the ocean, hatch as tiny larvae. The larva, called a **nauplius,** has just three pairs of appendages that beat the water to help it swim and a single eye in the center

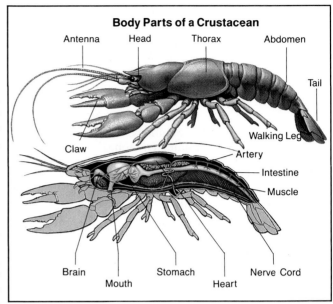

Body Parts of a Crustacean

Antenna · Head · Thorax · Abdomen · Tail · Walking Leg · Claw · Artery · Intestine · Muscle · Brain · Mouth · Stomach · Heart · Nerve Cord

of its head. A nauplius does not resemble its parents; it will molt several times and change its appearance before it finally looks like the adults.

The life spans of crustaceans are varied. A fairy shrimp may live for only a few months in a seasonal pond. A giant lobster may live deep in the ocean for more than 40 years. The life span of most crustaceans is between one and three years if the animals can avoid being captured by predators.

▶ CRUSTACEANS AND PEOPLE

Commercial fishing for crustaceans is an important industry. Shrimps, lobsters, crabs, and crayfish are the main types harvested for food. Scientists are also experimenting with ways to raise these animals in special ponds on aquatic farms.

Crustaceans can sometimes be harmful. Too many barnacles attached to the bottom of a boat can slow it down in the water. Some land-dwelling crabs and crayfish may burrow into the soil and prevent crops from taking root. They may also feed on the plant's tender young shoots. Some isopods bore, or dig holes, in wooden docks, causing them to decay sooner than usual.

LINDA H. MANTEL
City College of New York
Co-editor, *The Biology of Crustacea*

325

COMPOSITIONS

A composition is a written work in which the writer communicates ideas to a reader. It can be based on factual information, or it can be fictional.

A factual composition can be in the form of a report, in which the writer communicates information collected from books, magazines, and other outside sources. It can also be in the form of an essay, in which the material comes from personal experience. In a fictional composition, the writer uses his or her imagination to create events that never took place.

Although it is always important, whenever you communicate, to choose your words with care, it is especially important to do so when you write. Because you are not present to clear up misunderstandings, your composition must do all your explaining for you. It must answer questions that your readers might ask, and it must be organized in a way that allows your readers to follow your train of thought.

▶ REPORTS

Writing a factual report involves five steps: (1) choosing the reference material, (2) taking notes, (3) organizing the notes according to subject matter, (4) arranging the subjects into a logical order, and (5) translating the notes into clear, understandable prose.

Choosing the Reference Material. Let us suppose you are assigned a report on honeybees. Your best source of information on this subject will be in the library. There you will find encyclopedia articles, pamphlets, magazine articles, and nature books, all dealing with the subject of bees. Use as many of these references as possible. Eliminate only those that repeat information you have already collected.

Taking Notes. Taking notes will enable you to remember and organize your information and later to write it out in your own words.

As you read, write down every important fact, in as few words as possible, on a separate index card. Do not copy out whole sentences from the book. For example, suppose you consulted the following paragraphs from the article BEES in *The New Book of Knowledge:*

An average honeybee colony has about 30,000 bees, but there may be up to 80,000 in one hive. There are three different kinds of bees in the hive: a queen, several hundred drones, and thousands of worker bees.

The colony is headed by the queen bee. She is a big female who lays all the eggs in the colony. She starts to lay them during the first warm days of spring and continues to lay them every day until the end of the summer. At the height of the season, the queen bee may lay as many as 1,000 to 2,000 eggs a day. Since she lives about 5 years, she may lay up to 1,000,000 eggs in her lifetime.

Here is what you might put down on your index cards: 30,000–80,000 in colony / Mostly workers, some drones, one queen / Queen heads colony, lays all eggs / Lays eggs in spring and summer / Up to 2,000 a day.

Organizing the Notes. Soon you will discover that the facts you collect can be grouped into separate categories according to subject matter. All your material on the queen, the workers, and the drones, for example, can be included in a category called "The Colony." Facts about how a bee develops from an egg into an adult can go under the heading "Life Cycle," and facts about the function of the stinger and the antennae can be headed "Parts of the Body." Other subject titles might be "The Honeycomb," "How Bees Communicate," and "How Honey is Manufactured."

The world is full of ideas for writing stories. Many ideas originate when a writer wonders, "What if *this* happened, or *that*?" The writer can build on these beginnings to create an entire story. Here are some "What if ..." ideas that you can turn into stories of your own:

What if one day it snowed something that was not snow — like butterflies or feathers, diamonds or peas? What would the world look like? What would everybody do? What would you do?

Arranging the Subjects. Once your information is organized, you will need to arrange your subjects into an order that will make sense to your reader. It is best to put broad, general subjects first and narrow, more specific subjects later. Facts about the habitat, for example, apply to all honeybees and should come before those dealing with only the queen bee or the drones.

Remember, too, that readers must be told certain facts before they can understand others. In explaining how a bee builds a honeycomb out of wax, for instance, you should first define those parts of the bee's body that produce wax. The heading ''Parts of the Body,'' therefore, should come before ''The Honeycomb.''

Translating the Notes. Your next step will be to write out all your information in paragraph form. The rules for writing and arranging paragraphs are the same as for organizing the entire report: Begin with a general or main idea and then follow with more specific details.

Before you begin to write, put all your reference books aside. Consult only your index cards, so that your report will be written in your words and not in those of some other author. The first sentence of each paragraph should state what the whole paragraph is about. Here is how you might translate your notes on bee colonies into readable prose:

''Honeybees do not live alone or in small family groups. Instead, they live in huge colonies containing anywhere from 30,000 to 80,000 bees.

''Every colony is ruled by a queen bee, who produces all the colony's eggs. She begins to lay them in the spring and keeps laying them all summer. Sometimes she lays 2,000 in one day.'' Following paragraphs would define the roles of the drones and the worker bees.

Vary your sentences so that they do not sound repetitious. Make some of them long, others short. Begin some with nouns, others with different parts of speech. A good report is not only informative, but pleasing to the ear.

▶ ESSAYS

In preparing a composition based on your own experience, you will not have to depend on books or magazines for your material. Everything you need will be in your own head.

Whether you write about an event of long ago or an observation of your surroundings here and now, your task will be to describe the

What if animals and people changed places with each other, so that monkeys and rabbits lived in houses like yours and went to work and school each day, while people lived in the jungle or underground? What would such a world be like?

What if everything big traded places with everything small, so that elephants were the size of insects and ants were 10 feet tall? What would your town look like then?

What if you discovered an old map in the cellar of your house that described the way to a hidden treasure? Tell about the adventures you might have as you search your neighborhood or town, following the clues on the map.

What if your pet suddenly began to talk? What kind of conversations might you have with your dog, cat, bird, or fish? What do you think your pet would like to tell you?

What if you were a football, a dandelion, a refrigerator, or a flight of stairs? Tell about a day, a season, a year, or just one moment in your life.

What if you were transported to another era — to prehistoric times, colonial America, or ancient Rome, for example? What would you see and do? What if someone from those days were transported to your neighborhood today? What would he or she see and do?

What if some object you owned — a marble, a glove, a ring, or a pair of skates — suddenly developed magic powers? How would you use it?

What if *you* suddenly developed magic powers? Suppose you could make people invisible or cause everything you pointed at to change color? Describe what might happen.

visions of your mind in such a way as to create similar visions in the minds of your readers.

Those visions are based on what you observe of the world around you. The more carefully you take notice of that world, the more you will be able to tell about it and about yourself as well.

Try, for example, to describe a potato without looking at one. Chances are you will say it is round and brown, hard and dusty. You might add that it has eyes. While such a description is accurate, it does not say anything new or unusual about the potato or about you as its observer.

Now pick up an actual potato and examine it for features you have never paid attention to before. Look at its tiny, smooth speckles and the web of slender lines across its skin. Think back now into your own past. What else have you seen that has speckles or lines like that? Somebody's face? An elephant's ear? Run your fingers along the potato eyes. Do they remind you of something else? Write down what you observe. Remember that no one sees your world exactly as you do, and it is this special awareness that makes your writing different from everyone else's.

Writers must take notice not only with their eyes but with their other senses as well. Close your eyes for a moment, and listen for clues that tell you where you are or what the weather is or the time of day. Now close your ears, too. What can you taste or smell or feel that reveals your surroundings?

You can apply your skills of observation to people as well as to things, and to past as well as to present experiences. Let us say you have chosen to write a composition about a visit last year to your grandmother. Try to recall special details of her behavior. Did she wrinkle her nose a lot or put her hands on her hips? What was her living room like? Some items in it were probably old, some new; some messy, some neat. Without using any of those words, describe her furnishings in exact detail. Mention things like careful stacks of magazines, worn sofa pillows, and smudges on the pages of her photograph album.

Your essay should follow some logical order, but it is not necessary to plan out that order right away. Put down your memories as they occur to you. Along the way, you may decide that your subject should really be the photograph album. In that case, your opening sentence might read, ''What I like best when I visit my grandmother is looking through her photo album.'' Go on from there to describe how you settle on the sofa next to your grandmother and turn the pages of her album.

▶ FICTION

Composing a work of fiction is like playing a game of make-believe, except that you write down what you make up, rather than act it out.

Fiction can be either realistic or a fantasy. In realistic fiction, the events could have taken place; in a fantasy, they could not have. Tall tales, myths, fairy tales, and science fiction are examples of fantasy.

Fiction need not be long. To get started, you might simply tell a tall tale, which is an absurd exaggeration. Describe what some enormously tall—or extremely tiny—person can do. Later, try rewriting a traditional myth or fairy tale, placing all the characters in up-to-date situations and in familiar settings such as your hometown.

One kind of myth is the how-and-why tale, where a fanciful explanation is given for some occurrence in nature. Using this form, tell why leaves change their color in the fall, or why the snake sheds its skin.

Science fiction is frequently based on imaginary machines. Dream up a machine that can perform impossible tasks, or pick some everyday machine around the house and give it extraordinary powers.

When you attempt a longer story, your make-believe events should have a shape from beginning to end. This is called a plot. In most stories, the characters face some sort of problem, and the plot is formed around the development of the problem and its solution.

Do not expect the entire plot to reveal itself to you all at once. As with most compositions, stories are created little by little with an idea here and an idea there. Write them down, even if they do not seem to lead to anything at the time.

Once you have done so, you will discover that ideas are all around you. It is only when you begin to write that you will recognize them for what they are.

SYLVIA CASSEDY
Author, *In Your Own Words:*
A Beginner's Guide to Writing

The oldest artistic traditions in Canada are those of native peoples. Above: An Inuit soapstone carving depicts a camp scene with an attacking polar bear. Left: The colorful embroidery on this bag is characteristic of the decorative art of native Indian tribes.

CANADIAN ART AND ARCHITECTURE

The art and architecture of Canada consists of two separate traditions: the art of native peoples, who have lived in the country for thousands of years; and the art of descendants of Europeans, who began arriving about 400 years ago.

▶ NATIVE ART AND ARCHITECTURE

Canada's native peoples—both Indian and Inuit (formerly called Eskimos)—divide into several tribal groups, which differ in language, customs, and environment. As a result, there are many native artistic traditions.

Indian Art. Prehistoric rock carvings and paintings are the earliest surviving examples of native Indian art. The exact meaning of these simple images is unknown. Later Indian art showed great variety in design and materials. Colorful geometric and floral patterns embroidered on clothing were common to native tribes across Canada. Drums, masks, and other objects used in religious ceremonies or to mark special events also were richly decorated. Among the most dramatic of all Indian art forms were the carved totem poles of the Northwest Coast Indians.

In the 19th century, native Indian art was produced mainly for tourists, but the last half of the 20th century saw a revival of traditional forms such as carving. In addition, new forms emerged among the eastern woodland tribes, such as the Ojibwa and Cree, who began to illustrate their legends with striking paintings. Other Indian artists who do not work in the traditions of native art seek acceptance in the wider artistic world.

Inuit Art. The earliest examples of Inuit art are delicate carvings made from bone, ivory, or antler in the shapes of faces, figures, and birds. Later, traditional art forms were neglected during centuries of producing objects for trade with Europeans. Today, carving in soapstone and ivory as well as newer art forms such as drawing and printmaking show the delicacy, simplicity, and reverence for nature that characterize Inuit art.

Architecture. Traditional native cultures also produced notable buildings. The longhouse of the Iroquois, the tipi (teepee) of the Plains Indians, and the Arctic Inuit's igloo were all well suited to each tribe's particular life-style and environment. Today, however, most traditional native dwellings have been replaced by conventional modern houses.

Château Richer, near Quebec City, was built in the late 1600's, during the French colonial period. Its design is based on building traditions imported from Europe.

▶ FRENCH COLONIAL PERIOD

Permanent French settlements were founded in Canada in the early 1600's, and Canada became a colony of France in 1663. For the next century the art and architecture of the colony was dependent on styles imported from France.

Almost all early artists were French-born clergymen who specialized in religious works. They decorated local churches with paintings and wooden sculpture in the baroque style. By the mid-1700's, merchants in Montreal and Quebec City had grown wealthy enough to purchase works of art, creating a small market for portraits and landscape paintings.

The two most common building types in French Canada were the homestead and the parish church. They were built in the French medieval and baroque styles.

▶ BRITISH COLONIAL PERIOD

After 1760, when Canada became a British colony, the main source for styles in art and architecture shifted from France to England.

While sculpture continued to be mainly decorative works carved in wood, painting underwent several new developments. British officers stationed at forts throughout eastern Canada sought to accurately depict the Canadian landscape in detailed watercolor paintings. More imaginative paintings of nature were produced by immigrant British watercolor artists.

The works of two mid-19th-century artists are landmarks of Canadian art. Paul Kane traveled across the country recording the life-style of Canada's Indians in sketches and paintings. Cornelius Krieghoff is best known for his scenes of life in rural Quebec.

Architecture of the period, especially for public buildings, was greatly influenced by the Georgian style then popular in England. The early 1800's also saw a revival of the medieval Gothic style for both churches and public buildings.

▶ THE NEW NATION

The modern Canadian nation was founded in 1867, and artists were inspired by a new sense of national pride. Landscape artists such as Lucius O'Brien and John Fraser, painting in the romantic style, celebrated the country's dramatic natural features.

A close connection with Europe persisted at the turn of the century. Many of the best painters of the time, including Paul Peel, Robert Harris, and William Brymner, trained in Paris and returned to introduce Canadians to various current styles, such as impressionism and post-impressionism. James Wilson Morrice and Horatio Walker gained wide international reputations.

New sculptural techniques and the use of materials such as plaster and bronze allowed artists to portray subjects with greater realism. Quebec sculptors, including Marc-Aurèle Suzor-Coté and Philippe Hébert,

The Man That Always Rides (1849–55) is one of many Indian portraits by Paul Kane. The artist worked from sketches he made on journeys through Canada's Indian country, and his paintings form a record of a vanishing culture.

J. E. H. MacDonald, one of the Group of Seven, conveys the majesty of Canada's rugged northland in *The Solemn Land* (1921).

The detailed and brightly colored *Végétaux Marins* (1964), by Alfred Pellan, is a surrealistic rendering of sea vegetation.

expressed their pride in French Canadian history by producing public monuments.

In architecture the Gothic revival continued its popularity, along with revivals of other styles of the past.

▶ THE MODERN ERA

Painting in the 1920's was dominated by the Toronto-based artists known as the Group of Seven. Dedicated to producing a truly nationalist art, they concentrated on portraying Canada's rugged northern wilderness. Important contributions were also made by Tom Thomson, whose landscapes inspired the Group of Seven; Emily Carr; and David Milne.

In 1939, John Lyman founded the Contemporary Arts Society, which encouraged the development of a modern art. The principles of surrealism were brought to Canada in the 1940's by a group of artists—notably Paul-Emile Borduas and Jean-Paul Riopelle—who came to be called the Automatistes. In the 1950's, Toronto was introduced to abstract expressionism and other modernist styles with the works of Painters Eleven. After 1960, Canadian painters continued to work in a variety of styles. But painting ceased to be as dominant in Canadian art as it had been in the past.

Notable sculptors working after 1920 included Albert Laliberté, Suzor-Coté, and Elizabeth Wyn Wood. In the early 1950's the modernist styles of cubism and constructivism appeared in the sculptures of Anne Kahane and Louis Archambault. Great diversity in style, material, and subject marks contemporary Canadian sculpture. Sculptors work in plastic, neon, and fiberglass as well as traditional materials.

Canada's earliest skyscrapers, built in Toronto and Montreal in the 1920's and 1930's, were among the first buildings to display the curved lines and reduced details of art deco, a style that remained popular until World War II. After 1945, many factories, schools, and offices were built in the international style, which uses simple shapes and modern materials such as steel, glass, and concrete. Later, postmodernist designs, which combine elements of past architectural styles, began to appear in major cities.

KEN DEWAR
Education Services, Art Gallery of Ontario

CANADIAN LITERATURE

Canadian literature is written in English and French, the country's two official languages. This reflects the fact that Canada was a colony first of France (from 1663 to 1760) and then of England (from 1760 to 1867). After 1760, when France surrendered Canada to English control, the French people living in Canada preserved their heritage despite English dominance. Thus, a literature in the French language, centered in Quebec, thrived along with the literature of the English majority.

After Confederation in 1867, the new nation slowly began to develop its own literature, distinct from that of Europe and of Canada's neighbor, the United States. Canadian literature found its own voice in the early 20th century. Today, Canadian writers have a world audience.

► EARLY WRITING

The earliest examples of Canadian literature were written by explorers, traders, and others who opened up the Canadian wilderness. Their writings are mainly journals that describe the natural wealth of the newfound land and the hardships and rewards of pioneer life.

The works of early 19th century writers were mainly descriptive, focusing on the land itself and on life in the pioneer settlements and growing towns. An interesting writer of this period was Susanna Moodie (1803–85), who moved to Canada from En-

Roger Lemelin's critically acclaimed novel *Au pied de la pente douce (The Town Below)* pioneered a trend toward social realism in modern French Canadian literature.

Margaret Atwood's numerous works of fiction, poetry, and criticism have established her as one of Canada's major contemporary authors writing in English.

gland in 1832. Her autobiographical book *Roughing It in the Bush* (1852) offers a revealing account of the pioneer experience.

Many poets and novelists of this period responded to the Canadian scene using the literary styles and techniques of Europe. For example, early Canadian poets writing in English were influenced by the romantic and Victorian poetry then popular in England. Similarly, novelists writing in French imitated the novels of Victor Hugo and other French romantics. Often, these styles were not well suited to describing the new world.

► 1867 TO WORLD WAR I

The modern Canadian nation was founded in 1867. As more provinces joined the confederacy, that nation stretched across the continent from sea to sea. These events created a sense of national pride and encouraged the development of a Canadian literature.

Four writers have come to be known as the "Poets of the Confederation": Charles G. D. Roberts (1860–1943), Bliss Carman (1861–1929), Archibald Lampman (1861–1899), and Duncan Campbell Scott (1862–1947). Their poetry captured the beauty and variety of the Canadian landscape.

Among the most important fictional works of the period were the animal stories of Charles G. D. Roberts and Ernest Thompson Seton (1860–1946). These stories, with their close observation of nature, marked the beginning of a realistic Canadian fiction.

Many writers of this period used Canada's small villages and towns as the settings for their books. This technique, called **regionalism,** was to become an important element in later Canadian literature. The country's huge size forced writers to focus on small regions that were familiar to them. And, in the course of writing about life in these local settings, writers could often express ideas and themes of universal importance.

Two early regional writers were Ralph Connor (1860–1937), whose real name was Charles William Gordon, and Lucy Maud Montgomery (1874–1942). Connor, a minister, used his fiction to present moral lessons. Montgomery's popular first novel, *Anne of Green Gables* (1908), tells the story of an imaginative young orphan growing up on Prince Edward Island. This book and its many sequels vividly portray the dreams of youth.

Top left: An illustration from L. M. Montgomery's *Anne of Green Gables*, showing the young orphan's arrival at her new home. Above: "Sugar Making," a scene from *Roughing It in the Bush*, Susanna Moodie's account of pioneer life. Left: The title character of *Red Fox*, an animal story by Charles G. D. Roberts.

French Canadian fiction continued the traditions of the romantic rural novel, which had begun in 1846 with *La Terre paternelle (The Homestead)* by Patrice Lacombe (1807–63). This form of regional novel usually depicted the peaceful life of the small Quebec village.

▶ MODERN TIMES

While earlier Canadian literature depicted the immense landscape of the country, later writers focused on the individual human being within that landscape.

Modern Quebec literature began with two novels that portrayed life in the city rather than in small villages. *Au pied de la pente douce* (1944: *The Town Below*) by Roger Lemelin (1919–) was set in one of Quebec City's poor sections. *Bonheur d'occasion* (1945; *The Tin Flute*) by Gabrielle Roy (1909–83) took place in a poor neighborhood of Montreal. These works were among the first to examine the lives of the urban working class.

English Canadian fiction entered the modern period with the publication of *The Double Hook* (1959) by Sheila Watson (1909–), an openly anti-regional novel set in rural British Columbia.

The 1960's saw an explosion of fiction, poetry, and drama in both English and French. The major figure of the decade was Margaret Laurence (1926–87), a novelist, short-story writer, and essayist. In the fic-

tional prairie town of Manawaka, the setting for five of her books, she created a regional world that was universal in its depiction of human life.

The playwright, fiction writer, and translator Michel Tremblay (1942–) focused on the alienated working class of urban Quebec. His plays have brought international attention to a growing Quebec theater. Contemporary Quebec literature has also been enlivened by the haunting short stories of Roch Carrier (1937–) and the feminist writings of Nicole Brossard (1943–).

Modern English Canadian literature is dominated by Margaret Atwood (1939–), some of whose numerous works present the Canadian individual confronting the modern world. Her contemporaries include Robert Kroetsch (1927–), whose fiction and poetry explore the Canadian west; Alice Munro (1931–), noted for her short stories of rural life; and Michael Ondaatje (1943–), whose works portray the disorder of contemporary life.

DAVID STAINES
University of Ottawa

BOTANICAL GARDENS

Botanical gardens are museums that maintain collections of living plants for scientific purposes and for public display. **Botanists** (scientists who study plants) carry out research in the laboratories and test-plots of botanical gardens to learn more about how plants grow, how new plants can be developed, and how plants can be used as a source of food and other products.

Sharing knowledge of plants with the public is one of the most important functions of botanical gardens. Visitors will find all the plants labeled with both their scientific and common names. Botanical gardens may also have information services and may publish books and pamphlets on botanical subjects. School classes might visit local botanical gardens for guided tours or workshops.

Carefully arranged and labeled gardens offer an opportunity to study as well as to enjoy plants in a natural setting. The Royal Botanical Gardens in Hamilton, Ontario, is known for its late-blooming tulip collection.

Sometimes students are even allowed to tend small garden plots there to learn about plants.

Most large botanical gardens include greenhouses or conservatories—glass buildings where temperature, humidity, and light can be controlled. These artificial environments can copy natural ones, making it possible to grow plants from many different regions and climates of the world. In one room a tropical rain forest might be created; in another, desert plants can grow in a sunny, dry climate; and yet another room can display the conditions found in a marshy bog.

In the tropical environment, one might see orchids and other beautiful flowers, as well as some of the tropical plants that provide useful products. There may be cacao trees, whose beans are processed into chocolate, and cinchona trees whose bark is the source of quinine used to treat malaria.

In the desert display will be cacti and other plants that store water to survive with little or no rainfall. For example, there may be lithops, called "living stones" because they look so much like rocks that they are protected from animals that would eat them for the water stored inside.

In a marshy bog display the soil is wet and spongy, with layers of dead plant material. There may be interesting insect-eating plants like the Venus's-flytrap, with a leaf that closes when an insect crawls into it, or the pitcher plant, which traps insects in a digestive liquid. These plants get from insects the nutrients that are not available to them from the soil and water of a bog.

Some botanical gardens have theme gardens, such as a fragrance garden with scented flowers and leaves or a butterfly garden with flowers that attract those insects. A Japanese garden would have the plants arranged in typical Japanese fashion. A Shakespeare garden would have plants mentioned in Shakespeare's plays and sonnets. There is often an herb garden and an herbarium—a place where dried plants are preserved and cataloged for study. Collections of trees and shrubs are called **arboretums.**

▶ HISTORY

As early as 2000 B.C. the ancient Assyrians created formal parks displaying many vari-

Top: The Royal Botanic Gardens, Kew, near London, England, was founded in 1757. More than 25,000 different types of plants are on display there. *Center:* The New York Botanical Garden's 230-acre site makes it the largest such facility in the United States. Its herbarium and research laboratories are outstanding. *Bottom:* The Brooklyn Botanic Garden, also in New York, dates from 1910. It is known for its extensive educational programs.

eties of plants. In 612 B.C., Nebuchadnezzar built one of the seven wonders of the world, the Hanging Gardens of Babylon. Legend says he used plants from Persia, the native country of his bride. The Greek philosopher Aristotle had an herb garden for botanical studies in 350 B.C.

The earliest European botanical gardens were for scientists, especiaily physicians, who were often botanists, too, because they used many plants for medicines. Monasteries and universities kept herb gardens, sometimes called physic gardens.

One of the most interesting of all botanical gardens is in Uppsala, Sweden, home of Carolus Linnaeus. This great 18th-century botanist devised a system of classifying and naming plants and animals. He managed the Uppsala Gardens from 1742 to 1777. Today the gardens display plants in beds that Linnaeus himself laid out.

One of the greatest botanical gardens in the world today is Kew Gardens, near London, England, formerly known as the Royal Botanic Gardens. In the 19th century it introduced plants brought back from the voyages of Captain Cook, including coffee, cotton, and cinchona and cinnamon trees.

One of the best-known botanical gardens in the United States is the New York Botanical Garden in the Bronx, New York, which has more than 13,000 species of plants. The Missouri Botanical Gardens in St. Louis is the oldest in the United States. It also has the Climatron, the first climate-controlled greenhouse ever built. The Brooklyn Botanic Garden, in New York City, is a major publisher of handbooks about plants.

Canada has a number of well-known botanical gardens, among them the Montreal Botanical Gardens in Quebec and the Royal Botanical Gardens in Ontario.

LUCY E. JONES
Brooklyn Botanic Gardens

Palace Ladies Tuning the Lute, a Chinese scroll, was painted about 800 by Chou Fang, an artist of the T'ang dynasty. It shows the elegance of life at a Chinese royal court.

CHINESE ART

China has one of the oldest continuous artistic traditions in the world. The beginnings of Chinese art can be traced to 5000 B.C., when Stone Age people made decorated objects of bone, stone, and pottery.

▶ **PAINTING**

The earliest Chinese painting was ornamental, not representational. That is, it consisted of patterns or designs, not pictures. Stone Age pottery was painted with spirals, zigzags, dots, and lines but very rarely with human figures or animals. It was only during the Warring States period (475–221 B.C.) that artists began to represent the world around them.

Figure Painting. Artists from the Han (206 B.C.–A.D. 220) to the T'ang (618–907) dynasty mainly painted the human figure.

Much of what we know of early Chinese figure painting comes from burial sites, where paintings were preserved on silk banners, lacquered objects, and the walls of tombs. Many of these early tomb paintings were meant to protect the dead or help their souls get to paradise. Others illustrated the teachings of the Chinese philosopher Confucius or showed scenes of daily life.

During the Six Dynasties period (265–581), people began to appreciate painting for its own beauty and to write about art. From this time we begin to know about individual artists, such as Ku K'ai-chih. Even when these artists illustrated Confucian moral themes—such as the proper behavior of a wife to her husband or of children to their parents—they tried to make their figures elegant and graceful.

During the T'ang dynasty, figure painting flourished at the royal court. Artists such as Chou Fang showed the splendor of court life in paintings of emperors, ceremonies, beautiful palace ladies, and imperial horses. Figure painting reached the height of elegant realism in the art of the court of the Southern T'ang (943–960).

Most of the T'ang artists outlined figures with fine black lines and used brilliant color and elaborate detail. However, one T'ang artist, the master Wu Tao-tzu, used only black ink and freely painted brushstrokes to create ink paintings that were so exciting that crowds gathered to watch him work. From his time on, ink paintings were no longer thought to be preliminary sketches or outlines to be filled in with color. Instead they were valued as finished works of art.

Figure painting continues to be an important tradition in Chinese art. However, from the Sung dynasty (960–1279) onward, artists increasingly began to paint landscapes.

Landscape. Many critics consider landscape to be the highest form of Chinese painting. The Five Dynasties and Northern Sung period (960–1127) is known as the Great Age of Chinese Landscape. In the north, artists such as Ching Hao, Fan K'uan, and Kuo Hsi painted pictures of towering mountains, using strong black lines, ink wash, and sharp, dotted brushstrokes to suggest the rough stone. In the south, Tung Yüan, Chü Jan, and other artists painted the rolling hills and rivers of their native countryside in peaceful scenes done with softer, rubbed brushwork. These two kinds of scenes and techniques became the two classical styles of Chinese landscape painting.

During the Southern Sung period (1127–1279), court painters such as Ma Yüan and Hsia Kuei used strong black brushstrokes to sketch trees and rocks and pale washes to suggest misty space.

While many artists were attempting to represent three-dimensional objects and to master the illusion of space, another group of painters pursued very different goals. At the end of the Northern Sung period, the famous poet Su Shih and the scholar-officials in his circle became serious amateur painters. They created a new kind of art in which they used their skills in calligraphy (the art of beautiful writing) to make ink paintings. From then on, many painters strove to freely express their feelings and to capture the inner spirit of their subject instead of describing its outward appearance.

During the Yüan dynasty (1271–1368), painters joined the arts of painting, poetry, and calligraphy by inscribing poems on their paintings. These three arts worked together to express the artist's feelings more completely than any one art could do alone.

Some painters of the Ming dynasty (1368–1644) continued the traditions of the Yüan scholar-painters. This group of painters, known as the Wu School, was led by the artist Shen Chou. Another group of painters, known as the Che School, revived and transformed the styles of the Sung court.

During the early Ch'ing dynasty (1644–1911), painters known as Individualists rebelled against many of the traditional rules of painting and found ways to express themselves more directly through free brushwork. In the 18th and 19th centuries, great commercial cities such as Yangchow and Shanghai became

Top: *Clearing Autumn Sky Over Mountains and Valleys,* by Northern Sung artist Kuo Hsi.
Bottom: *Happy Fishermen of the River Village,* by Shen Chou, an artist of the Ming dynasty.

art centers where wealthy merchant-patrons encouraged artists to produce bold new works.

In the late 19th and 20th centuries, Chinese painters were increasingly exposed to the art of Western cultures. Some artists who studied in Europe rejected Chinese painting; others tried to combine the best of both traditions. Perhaps the most beloved modern painter was Ch'i Pai-shih (1863–1957), who began life as a poor peasant and became a great master.

▶ CALLIGRAPHY

Calligraphy, the art of beautiful writing, is considered the highest form of the visual arts in China. Unlike the Western art of oil painting, in which artists can paint over their work many times, the brushstrokes of calligraphy cannot be changed once they are placed on the paper. Thus it is a very direct form of expression, and admirers of Chinese language and writing believe they can understand a calligra-

Left: a jade carving from the 19th century shows a mountainous landscape. Below left: An elaborately designed bronze vessel from the early Chou dynasty (11th century B.C.) was used for ceremonial purposes. Below right: A glazed green ceramic vase, of a kind known as celadon, was made in the 12th century during the Sung dynasty, the classical age of Chinese ceramics.

pher's feelings, taste, and even personal character by looking at his or her work.

The earliest Chinese writing was scratched into pottery, bone, and shell; inscribed in clay; or cut into stone. Later, people used brushes made from animal hair to write with ink on strips of bamboo, silk, or paper. Because the earliest writers used rigid instruments such as a knife, their script had smooth, even lines. But from the Han dynasty on, calligraphers took advantage of the flexible brush tip to produce thickening and thinning lines or flaring strokes. Over time, new kinds of scripts developed that gave the artist more opportunities for expressive movement.

All the different scripts that developed over the centuries remain available to writers. For example, they may use one style of calligraphy for ceremonial or decorative purposes and another to express their feelings in a flash of inspiration.

Calligraphy and painting are considered to be sister arts. The scholar-painters adapted the brushstrokes and structures of writing for painting. They also judged their paintings according to the standards of calligraphy.

▶ DECORATIVE ARTS

The Chinese were masters of bronze, jade, and ceramics. Decorative objects made of these materials are among China's greatest contributions to world art.

Bronze. Bronze metalwork is the greatest art form of ancient China. The Great Bronze Age of China lasted from the Shang (16th–11th century B.C.) to the Han dynasty. During the Shang dynasty, bronzes were used for ritual purposes. Bronze shapes and designs became more and more elaborate, especially those produced at Anyang, the last Shang capital.

During the Chou dynasty (11th century–256 B.C.) bronze vessels increasingly were used as symbols of wealth and status. But during the Han dynasty, other kinds of luxury goods began to be more desirable than bronze.

Jade. Jade is a hard, beautiful stone that is highly valued by the Chinese. Jade ornaments and sculptures are found at many early burial sites. Because jade is brittle and difficult to work with, the earliest jades are very simply carved. During the Eastern Chou period (770–256 B.C.) improved tools allowed artists to produce exquisite jades with complicated shapes and curved, complex patterns. Jade working

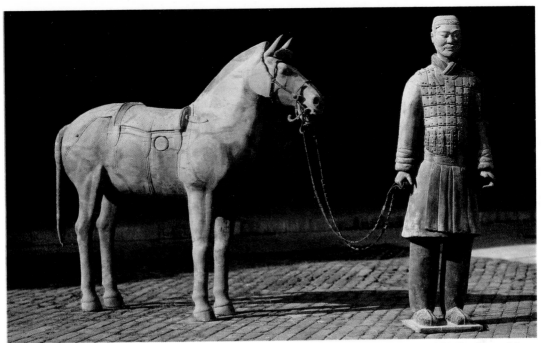

This soldier and saddle horse are part of an "army" of some 7,000 life-size sculptures that were unearthed near the tomb of Ch'in Shih-huang-ti, the first emperor of China.

continues to be one of the main handicraft traditions of modern China.

Ceramics. Over many centuries, Chinese potters learned to control the temperatures of their kilns (special ovens for firing pottery), to refine clays, and to perfect glazes—the glassy coat that helps make ceramics waterproof and enhances their appearance. These techniques enabled them to produce ceramics that were admired throughout the world.

The classical age of Chinese ceramics is the Sung dynasty, when beautiful wares were produced for the royal court. Among the most valued ceramics are a group glazed in different shades of green, which are known in the West as "celadons." The blue and white wares of the Ming dynasty are also admired worldwide.

▶ **SCULPTURE**

Some of the earliest known examples of Chinese sculpture are objects made to be buried with the dead. The most impressive collection of burial sculptures was found near the tomb of Ch'in Shih-huang-ti, the first emperor of China (reigned 221–206 B.C.). Pits near the tomb contained some 7,000 life-size clay sculptures of foot soldiers, charioteers, officers, and horses. The sculptures were intended to protect the emperor after death.

During the Han and T'ang dynasties sculptors made small clay models of dancers, servants, fierce guardians, farmyards, towers, dogs, and horses. All were designed to accompany the dead in the spirit world.

In addition to burial sculptures, monumental stone sculptures were placed above ground along the "Spirit Road" leading to the tombs of important people. Among the most outstanding of these sculptures are the stone lions that guard the Liang tombs near Nanking.

The great tradition of Buddhist sculpture is seen in massive figures cut into the stone of huge cave temples. The first cave temples were made in the 4th century, and as Buddhism flourished, many others were carved. Buddhist monasteries and temples were fitted with magnificent sculptures carved in wood and painted, as well as with gilt-bronze figures of the Buddha and his attendants.

Many critics believe the T'ang dynasty was the golden age of Buddhist sculpture. Later sculptors continued to follow the traditions of both Buddhist and nonreligious sculpture. During the 20th century, Western realistic styles were used in sculptures honoring important persons and events.

MAGGIE BICKFORD
Art Historian

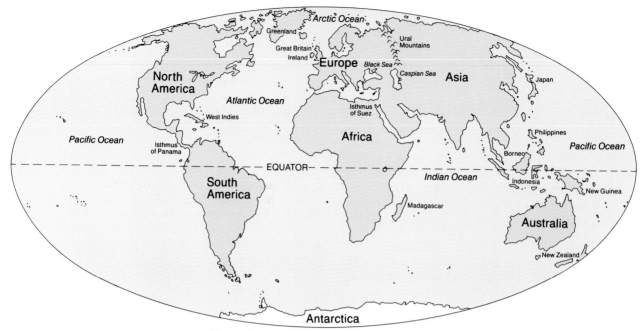

The traditionally recognized continents are Asia, Africa, North America, South America, Antarctica, Europe, and Australia. Europe and Asia are sometimes considered as a single landmass called Eurasia. Each continent's landmass includes its adjacent islands.

CONTINENTS

A continent is a large, continuous landmass located on the surface of the earth. Seven continents are generally recognized. They are Asia, Africa, North America, South America, Antarctica, Europe, and Australia. In some cases, Europe and Asia are viewed as a single continent—Eurasia. The continents of Asia, Europe, and Africa form what is known as the Old World. North America and South America make up the New World.

The strict definition that every continent is a single landmass bounded by the sea is rarely used. In practice, every continent not only includes its own landmass, but nearby islands as well. For example, Greenland is usually thought of as part of North America.

Altogether, the earth's seven continents cover 29 percent of the surface area of the globe. Oceans and other bodies of water cover the remaining 71 percent.

▶ SIZE AND SHAPE

The continents vary considerably in size. Asia, the largest continent, has almost 30 percent of the world's total land surface. After Asia, the continents in order of area are Africa, North America, South America, Antarctica, Europe, and Australia. Australia, the smallest continent, is less than one fifth the size of Asia, and has less than 6 percent of the world's land surface.

The continents also vary significantly in shape. Africa is the most compact continent and has the most regular coastline. Its ratio of length of coastline to total area is the lowest of any continent. Europe has the longest coastline of any continent and the highest ratio of coastline to total land area.

Two continents—Australia and Antarctica—are islands. The other five continents are connected to another landmass. North America and South America are connected at the Isthmus of Panama. (An isthmus is a narrow strip of land that connects two larger bodies of land.) Africa is joined to Asia at the Isthmus of Suez. Europe is actually a peninsula of Asia.

When Europe is treated as a separate continent, the boundary between Europe and Asia lies almost entirely within the Union of Soviet Socialist Republics (U.S.S.R.), which occupies land in both continents. This boundary runs along the eastern edge of the Ural Mountains, southwest to the shore of the Caspian Sea, westward along the Caspian's northern coast to the Caucasus Mountains, and along the crest of the Caucasus to the northern coast of the Black Sea.

▶ POPULATION

Asia, the largest continent in area, also has the greatest number of people. Including the Asian part of the U.S.S.R., it is home to about 60 percent of the world's population. Europe, although only sixth in area, is the most densely populated continent. Counting the European part of the U.S.S.R., it ranks second in population, with more than 14 percent of the world total. When the populations of Europe and Asia are combined, Eurasia has almost three quarters of humanity.

The inhabited continents, in order of population after Asia and Europe, are Africa, North America, South America, and Australia. Antarctica has no inhabitants, except for the scientists who come to study this desolate, ice-covered continent.

▶ DISTRIBUTION

North and South. The continents are irregularly, but not randomly, distributed on the surface of the earth. With the exception of Antarctica, all the continents are broader in the north than in the south. They taper toward the south. Partly as a result of this, approximately two thirds of the world's land surface lies in the Northern Hemisphere—that part of the globe north of the equator (0° latitude).

Land and Water Hemispheres. Because of this uneven distribution of landmasses, geographers sometimes divide the world into land and water hemispheres. The land hemisphere is that half of the earth with the most land. The water hemisphere is that half of the world with the most water. The geographic center of the land hemisphere lies in northwestern Europe near the city of London in the United Kingdom. The geographic center of the water hemisphere is located in the southern Pacific Ocean, southeast of New Zealand.

▶ SOME CONTINENTAL COMPARISONS

Land Surfaces. The land surfaces of the continents have some degree of similarity. In general, interior plateaus and plains are bordered by mountains on one or more sides. The Rocky Mountains of North America and the Andes of South America rim the western edges of these continents. The Pyrenees mountains and the Alps form the southern boundary of Europe. The Ural Mountains and the Himalayas mark Asia's western and southern borders. Antarctica is ringed with high mountains of ice.

By contrast, the continents of Africa and Australia tend to have central plateaus that cover their land areas and extend from coast to coast.

Lowest and Highest Continents. Australia is the lowest as well as the flattest continent. Its average elevation is only 800 feet (244 meters) above sea level. Africa, North America, and South America have average elevations that are very close to the world average of 2,100 feet (640 meters). Asia, due largely to the great peaks of the Himalayas, has an average elevation of 3,200 feet (975 meters). Antarctica has the highest average elevation—6,500 feet (2,000) meters, or twice that of any other continental landmass.

PAUL W. ENGLISH
Chairman, Department of Geography
The University of Texas at Austin

CONTINENTS IN ORDER OF POPULATION	
	POPULATION ESTIMATE
Asia [1]	2,902,000,000
Europe [2]	692,000,000
Africa	553,000,000
North America	401,000,000
South America	269,000,000
Australia	15,000,000
Antarctica	no permanent inhabitants

[1] Includes U.S.S.R. in Asia.

[2] Includes U.S.S.R. in Europe and European Turkey.

CONTINENTS IN ORDER OF AREA		
	TOTAL AREA	
	sq mi	(km²)
Asia [1]	17,297,000	(44,780,000)
Africa	11,708,000	(30,324,000)
North America	9,406,000	(24,362,000)
South America	6,883,000	(17,827,000)
Antartica	5,405,000	(14,000,000)
Europe [2]	4,066,000	(10,531,000)
Australia [3]	3,287,000	(8,513,000)

[1] Includes U.S.S.R. in Asia.

[2] Includes U.S.S.R. in Europe and European Turkey.

[3] Includes adjacent islands.

CIRCULATORY SYSTEM

A large, modern city needs a complicated system of streets and roads to link houses, offices, stores, factories, hospitals, and other important places. The human body is even more complicated than a city, and it, too, needs its own system of roadways over which materials can be transported.

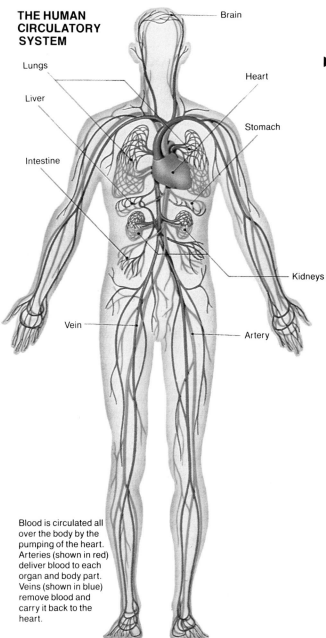

THE HUMAN CIRCULATORY SYSTEM

Brain
Lungs
Heart
Liver
Stomach
Intestine
Kidneys
Vein
Artery

Blood is circulated all over the body by the pumping of the heart. Arteries (shown in red) deliver blood to each organ and body part. Veins (shown in blue) remove blood and carry it back to the heart.

The body's roadways are actually waterways. They are made up of a watery fluid called **blood** flowing through tubes called **blood vessels.** More than 62,000 miles (100,000 kilometers) of blood vessels branch and crisscross through a person's body, linking the cells of the brain, the heart, the lungs, the fingertips, and every other organ and body part into a connected circulatory system. The vessels range from thick, muscular arteries, the largest an inch (2.5 centimeters) in diameter, down to tiny capillaries so thin they cannot be seen without a microscope.

▶ **WHAT THE CIRCULATORY SYSTEM DOES**

The blood vessels of the circulatory system are lifelines for the body's cells. The cells would starve without the food and oxygen brought to them by the flowing blood, and the cells could be poisoned if the blood did not carry away their waste products.

Digested food materials pass into the capillaries around the intestines and then are transported to all parts of the body. Oxygen from the air breathed into the lungs passes into the blood vessels surrounding the lung's tiny air sacs. Carbon dioxide and other waste gases pass from the blood into the air sacs and are sent out of the body with the next exhaled breath. The circulatory system also carries waste products from the body cells to the kidneys. There the wastes pass out of the blood through thin capillary walls and start their one-way trip out of the body in the urine.

Foods, oxygen, and wastes are not the only things carried in the blood. Complicated chemicals called hormones act as chemical messengers and help control and co-ordinate the activities of the body. Other substances called enzymes direct chemical reactions. Blood also contains a sort of chemical repair kit, which can form a solid **clot** to plug up a hole in a damaged blood vessel.

Special kinds of cells travel through the vessels of the circulatory system. Some, the **red blood cells,** are like barges floating along in the bloodstream. They carry loads of oxygen or carbon dioxide. Others, the **white blood cells,** are like migrant workers that travel the body's waterways to get to wherever they are needed. They are the body's defenders, which battle invading viruses and

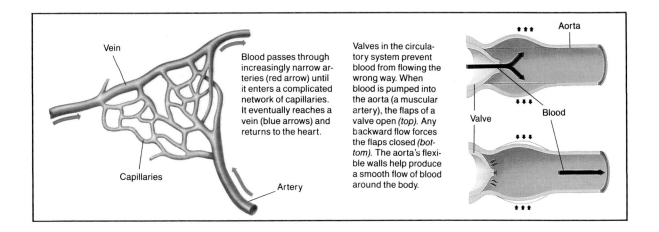

Blood passes through increasingly narrow arteries (red arrow) until it enters a complicated network of capillaries. It eventually reaches a vein (blue arrows) and returns to the heart.

Vein

Capillaries

Artery

Valves in the circulatory system prevent blood from flowing the wrong way. When blood is pumped into the aorta (a muscular artery), the flaps of a valve open *(top)*. Any backward flow forces the flaps closed *(bottom)*. The aorta's flexible walls help produce a smooth flow of blood around the body.

Aorta

Valve

Blood

bacteria. They also clean up old, worn-out cells, and they attack body cells that have changed and might turn into cancer cells.

Even the fluid part of the blood is important. It provides water for the body cells and also helps absorb and carry away excess heat, keeping the body temperature even.

▶ ORGANS OF THE CIRCULATORY SYSTEM

The human circulatory system is a network of tubelike blood vessels that link all parts of the body and are ultimately connected to a central pump, the **heart.** The thick, muscular walls of the heart enclose four **chambers,** which fill with blood and then empty with each heartbeat. To hear the heart at work, roll a piece of paper into a long, thin tube and place one end against a friend's chest. If you put your ear to the other end, you can hear a rhythmic lubb-dup, lubb-dup. The "lubbs" and the "dups" are the sounds of flaps in the heart called **valves** snapping shut. Valves between the compartments of the heart and valves at the outlets into the arteries close with each heartbeat to keep the blood from flowing backward. The diagram above shows how these valves work. The heart keeps on beating steadily, all through a person's lifetime. If it stopped beating, the blood could not flow through the circulatory system.

Blood flowing into the heart enters the two upper chambers, the **atria** (singular, **atrium**). From these receiving chambers it passes down into the **ventricles,** the pumping chambers. The blood collected from all over the body empties into the right atrium. It flows down into the right ventricle, and in the next heartbeat it goes shooting out into blood ves-

sels leading to the lungs. There the blood picks up a fresh supply of oxygen and unloads its waste carbon dioxide. The blood is returned to the heart by blood vessels emptying into the left atrium. This oxygen-rich blood flows down into the left ventricle, and in the next heartbeat it is pumped out into a thick-walled artery called the **aorta.** This is the largest artery in the whole body. From the heart it loops up, over, and down, branching as it goes into smaller and smaller blood vessels that eventually supply all parts of the body.

The blood vessels that carry blood away from the heart are arteries. They have thick, muscular walls. The rhythm of the heartbeat can be felt in the artery walls in various parts of the body where the arteries pass close to the surface. For example, this rhythmic **pulse** can be felt at the wrists and the temples. As the arteries branch again and again, they form smaller and smaller blood vessels. The smallest are called **capillaries.** These are very narrow, thin-walled tubes, too small to be seen without a microscope and so thin that the red blood cells have to travel through them in single file. The capillaries may be tiny, but there are so many of them that they make up 99 percent of the length of all the blood vessels. They are the part of the circulatory system that services the individual body cells.

Eventually the capillaries combine into larger blood vessels, forming the **veins** that carry blood back to the heart. Veins are larger than capillaries, but their walls are not as thick and muscular as those of arteries. The veins are equipped with valves, flaps set up in a one-way arrangement that keeps the blood from flowing backward, even when it is going upward against the pull of gravity.

The heart beats steadily on its own, at a rhythm set by a structure called the **pacemaker.** This is a specialized portion of the heart muscle, located in the wall of the right atrium. Hormones and nerve messages can speed up or slow down the heart and widen or narrow the arteries, adjusting the blood flow to the body's needs. When you get excited, your heart beats faster. More blood flows to your muscles, providing the extra food and oxygen they will need in case you have to fight or run away. But when you are sitting quietly after a meal, extra blood flows to your stomach and intestines, to help you digest your food. When it is very cold, the tiny blood vessels near the surface of your body narrow, conserving body heat. But when it is hot, these blood vessels widen and radiate out the excess heat. Various systems of the body cooperate in coordinating the work of the heart and blood vessels.

The arteries, capillaries, and veins of the circulatory system are organized into two closed loops. Each one begins and ends at the heart. The smaller loop is called the **pulmonary circulation.** The larger loop, which leads through branching networks to all parts of the body and supplies all the organs and body systems, is called the **systemic circulation.** If you were to follow a drop of blood through both loops of the circulatory system, the whole trip would take less than a minute!

The body has still a third system of circulation, but this system does not carry blood. It carries a fluid called **lymph** and is called the **lymphatic system.** Lymph is formed from the watery part of the blood, together with dissolved chemicals and white blood cells. The walls of the blood capillaries are so thin that fluid leaks out of them into the tissues. The fluid drains into tiny open-ended lymph capillaries, which combine to form larger vessels called **lymphatics.** The lymphatics are very similar to veins. They empty into two large lymphatic ducts, which in turn drain into large veins that return blood to the heart.

▶ **OPEN CIRCULATORY SYSTEMS**

All vertebrates (animals with backbones, including human beings) have a **closed circu-** latory system, meaning the blood is enclosed in vessels. Many invertebrates (animals without backbones, such as insects, clams, snails, and lobsters) have a different sort of circulation. Theirs is an **open circulatory system,** because the blood flows only part of the way in blood vessels. It empties out of the aorta into large, open spaces in the animal's body, called **sinuses.** Blood moves slowly through the sinuses, past various organs, and finally empties back into the heart.

▶ **DISORDERS OF THE CIRCULATORY SYSTEM**

Cardiovascular disease—disease of the heart and blood vessels—is the number-one cause of death in the United States, Canada, and other developed countries.

One common kind of cardiovascular disease is **arteriosclerosis,** often called "hardening of the arteries." This occurs when fatty deposits form along the inner walls of the arteries and narrow the channel through which the blood flows. Sometimes the artery even becomes plugged up completely. When this happens in an artery leading to the brain, brain cells starve and die, and the person suffers a **stroke.** When the coronary arteries that supply the heart become blocked, a portion of the heart muscle dies, and the person suffers a **heart attack. Hypertension,** or high blood pressure, is another condition that can lead to a heart attack or stroke.

Drugs can help treat high blood pressure, clogged arteries, and even an irregular heartbeat. Various surgical techniques, including the implanting of artificial pacemakers and the opening or replacing of blocked or damaged arteries, can also be used to keep a damaged cardiovascular system working. These medical advances are helping to bring down the number of heart disease deaths. But medical experts believe that changes in life-style are even more helpful. Getting enough exercise and eating a balanced diet low in salt, saturated fat, and cholesterol can help to keep the arteries clear, the blood pressure low, and the heart strong and healthy.

ALVIN SILVERSTEIN
VIRGINIA SILVERSTEIN
Co-authors, *Circulatory Systems*
and *Heart Disease: America's #1 Killer*

CREDIT CARDS

A credit card is a form of identification that enables the cardholder to buy goods or services and pay for them at a later date. About 70 percent of families in the United States and Canada have at least one credit card.

Types of Credit Cards. Some large department stores, retail chain stores, and oil companies issue "charge cards" that can only be used in their own stores or service stations. But the most popular cards are the all-purpose cards issued by banks—such as MasterCard and VISA—or by corporations such as American Express and Diner's Club. These can be used for almost any kind of purchase in large and small stores, hotels, and restaurants and for services like airline tickets, rental cars, club memberships, and even medical services.

How Credit Cards Work. Any adult may apply for a credit card by providing information about income, place and length of employment, money owed, savings, and other assets such as a home. The credit card company uses this information to decide if the person is a good credit risk, that is, likely to pay his or her debts. This information also helps the company decide the maximum amount the customer may charge. If the application is approved, the person is issued a card.

To use a credit card, the cardholder presents it to the merchant, who puts it into a machine or cash register that transfers the information on the card to a three-copy form. The amount of the purchase is written on the form, and the customer signs it to verify that the amount is correct. The merchant may call the credit card company to make sure the charge will be accepted. Electronic cash registers provide credit information instantly.

The customer and the merchant each receive a copy of the form. The master form is sent to the credit card company, which will give to the merchant's account the amount of the purchase minus a charge. This charge, usually 3 percent of the purchase, is kept by the credit card company as a service fee. The consumer is billed monthly for all purchases made during the month and for any part of the previous month's bill that was not paid. Some cards, such as American Express and Diner's Club, require that the full amount due be paid each month. Most bank cards offer the customer the option of paying the total amount due or paying only a portion. The customer will be charged interest on the unpaid balance. Customers must remember that the unpaid credit card bill is a loan and that interest charges make the real cost of their purchases higher.

Companies issuing credit cards make money on service charges to merchants and on interest charged cardholders for unpaid balances. Most credit card companies also charge users an annual fee of about $25 to $50.

Many merchants use the credit card service instead of requiring cash because they feel people will buy more if they do not have to pay immediately. Many customers find it convenient to pay later, and many prefer not to carry much cash.

Stolen and Counterfeited Credit Cards. Large numbers of credit cards have been stolen and counterfeited, so new ways are being devised to stop this. One way is to put a hologram (a three-dimensional picture) on the card. Holograms are very difficult to counterfeit. Another way is to make what is called a "smart card." The card contains a microchip that has information about the cardholder that must match the information in the credit card company's computer. Someday that microchip might hold a voice print, a computerized recording of the cardholder's voice, or a video image. These will be almost impossible to counterfeit because the recorded voice or image will not match those of a credit card thief.

DONALD BADDERS
National Foundation for Consumer Credit, Inc.

URANUS

Uranus is the seventh planet in our solar system, positioned 19 times farther away from the sun than the Earth. At that great distance, Uranus reflects little of the sun's light. Even though it is one of the giant planets, it appears dim in our night sky. If you have sharp eyes and know exactly where and when to look, you can just barely see Uranus without a telescope.

For years astronomers thought Uranus was a star. The first person to realize that it could not be a star was William Herschel, who was then an organist in Bath, England, and an amateur astronomer. While studying the constellation Gemini in 1781, he found what he at first thought was a comet. It turned out to be a blue-green planet, which was named Uranus after the Greek god of the heavens.

Because it is very dim, Uranus has been hard to study from Earth. Astronomers could calculate that the planet takes 84 Earth years to circle the sun, but they could not tell how long it took to rotate. This is because Uranus' blue-green atmosphere showed no features that they could track with time.

The false color in this photograph of Uranus (which is actually blue-green) brings out details such as a cloud, which is seen as a bright streak at the upper right.

Astronomers also knew that Uranus has an oddly tilted axis—the imaginary line about which it rotates. The planet seems to be lying on its side. No one is sure why this is so. Perhaps when Uranus was young, it collided with an object the size of Earth and was knocked onto its side.

Astronomers had counted five moons circling Uranus. They had also discovered that the planet had a set of nine rings, which was inside the orbit of the moons. But until the mid-1980's they did not know much more than this.

▶ A VISIT BY VOYAGER 2

The year 1986 was an important one for scientists studying Uranus. In that year the United States space probe Voyager 2 flew by the planet. The probe provided astronomers with a great deal of information about this distant member of our solar system. Some of the things they learned from Voyager's visit are described below.

Around its rocky core, Uranus has a dense and icy atmosphere of water, ammonia, and methane topped by a thin atmosphere of hydrogen with a little helium and neon. The dense inner atmosphere may be the remains of comets that crashed into Uranus when it was very young.

The interior of Uranus rotates once every 17.24 hours. Bands of clouds in the atmo-

---

URANUS FACTS AND FIGURES

POSITION IN SOLAR SYSTEM: Seventh planet out from the sun

AVERAGE DISTANCE FROM SUN: 1,783,000,000 miles (2,870,000,000 kilometers)

AVERAGE DIAMETER: 32,300 miles (51,800 kilometers)

MASS: 14.5 times Earth's

GRAVITY: 1.17 of Earth's

KNOWN MOONS: 15

LENGTH OF DAY: 17.24 Earth hours

LENGTH OF YEAR: 84 Earth years

AVERAGE SPEED IN ORBIT: 15,300 miles per hour (24,620 kilometers per hour)

TILT OF AXIS: 98°

ATMOSPHERE: Icy gases of water, ammonia, and methane; also hydrogen, helium, and neon

TEMPERATURE IN UPPER ATMOSPHERE: −355°F (−215°C)

COLOR: Blue-green

sphere rotate faster—once every 14 hours at the poles. The clouds are probably driven by winds similar to Earth's jet streams.

Uranus has a strange magnetic field. On Earth and other planets, the magnetic poles are close to the geographic poles. On Uranus they are not. So far scientists cannot explain this. One idea is that Voyager flew by when the magnetic poles were reversing themselves, as happens from time to time on Earth.

The set of rings is made up of the nine known rings plus two more that could not be seen from Earth. Unlike Saturn's broad, bright rings, these rings are narrow and dark. The material in them is as black as coal. It may be made of chunks of ice with a dark coating.

▶ MOONS

Uranus has at least 15 moons—five that can be seen from Earth and ten tiny moons that Voyager photographed. Two of the newly discovered moons are what scientists call shepherding satellites. Just as shepherds keep their sheep together, these two moons seem to keep material within one of Uranus' rings.

Oberon, the outermost moon, has an icy surface covered with craters. It also has a fault, or crack, that runs across its southern hemisphere. The crack suggests that movement has taken place in the moon's crust.

Titania, the largest moon, is surprisingly smooth. It shows no signs of big, ancient craters. Most likely the moon had enough internal heat to melt its icy surface and erase the craters. Later, a new, smooth surface formed.

Umbriel appears entirely dark except for a small bright mark near its equator. Scientists think that most of Umbriel has a thick, dark crust that meteorites could not break through. Ariel has huge faults, which suggest large crust movements early in the moon's history.

Miranda, the smallest and innermost of the five large moons, was the biggest surprise of all. Miranda looks like nothing else in the solar system. It has two big ovals made of ridges and faults that look like racetracks. Near the equator is a huge cliff. Still other parts of Miranda look like parts of Earth's moon. Scientists think that occasional collisions with comets and other large objects broke Miranda into pieces several times. Each time, the pieces came back together, forming the strange patterns we see. Scientists will be working on this puzzle and others for years to come.

NEPTUNE

Neptune is one of the four giant planets in our solar system. It is the fourth and last of the giants, orbiting far beyond the other three—Jupiter, Saturn, and Uranus. Neptune receives and reflects so little of the sun's light that it cannot be seen from Earth without a telescope. For this reason it was the last of the four giant planets to be discovered.

Even the best Earth-based telescopes and other instruments do not tell us much about Neptune. We know that this planet is 30 times as far from the sun as the Earth is. We know that its diameter is nearly four times that of Earth. Astronomers have learned that Neptune takes nearly 165 Earth years to complete one orbit. They have seen bands and other markings in its atmosphere. By tracking these markings, they have come to believe that Neptune spins, or rotates, once every 18 hours.

In color, size, and atmosphere, Neptune is like Uranus. Both planets have clouds of methane gas and appear blue-green in color. Scientists have been able to measure the temperature of Neptune's outer, or upper, atmosphere. This turned out to be the same as the temperature of Uranus, even though Neptune receives less than half the sunlight Uranus does. The most likely explanation is that there is some kind of heat source inside Neptune.

▶ MOONS

Neptune has two known moons, or satellites. Both have unusual orbits. Most moons circle their planets around the equator, but Neptune's moons do not. Their orbits lie between the equator and the poles.

The smaller moon is named Nereid, after a sea nymph in Greek mythology. It is a tiny moon, with an orbit that has the shape of an oval, called an ellipse. Nereid has the most elliptical orbit of any known moon. (The orbits of others moons are more like circles.)

Neptune's larger moon is Triton, named for a Greek god of the sea. It is about the size of Earth's moon and is the only large moon that orbits its planet backward. All other large moons orbit in the same direction in which their planets spin. Some scientists think the reason Triton is different is that it may once have been a planet. It may have formed at the same time as the planet Pluto but was then captured by Neptune's gravity.

Triton has a thin atmosphere. Its surface seems to be covered with methane ice and by lakes or seas of liquid nitrogen.

▶ DISCOVERY AND EXPLORATION

The planet Uranus is in a way responsible for the discovery of the planet Neptune. As astronomers studied Uranus, they tried to plot its path around the sun using the same rules they had worked out for all the other planets. By the early 1800's they realized that something was wrong. Uranus was not always where they had predicted it would be in its orbit. Some wondered if gravity from an unknown planet was affecting its orbit.

Two scientists decided to find out. One was John Couch Adams, a graduate student at Cambridge University in England. The other was Urbain Leverrier, a French astronomer.

Neither man knew of the other's work, but each calculated that there must be a planet beyond Uranus.

Both Adams and Leverrier then asked their fellow astronomers for help in searching for the planet. German astronomers found it in September, 1846, just where Adams and Leverrier had predicted. Perhaps because the newly discovered planet was blue-green in color, it was named Neptune, after the Roman god of the sea.

Astronomers may soon know a great deal more about this distant planet and its moons. Triton is a major target for the United States space probe Voyager 2, which is scheduled to reach the planet Neptune during the summer of 1989.

If all goes well, scientists will get their first good look at this large, unusual moon. They will also find out whether Neptune has rings or parts of rings. Scientists will learn about the planet's atmosphere and what lies beneath it. They will finally see and be able to study the giant planet that telescopes now show only as a dim blur traveling through the cold and dark of space.

PATRICIA LAUBER
Author, *Journey to the Planets*

Neptune, the eighth planet from the sun, is too far away to be seen without a telescope. Its blue-green color comes from methane gas in its atmosphere.

NEPTUNE FACTS AND FIGURES

POSITION IN SOLAR SYSTEM: Eighth planet out from the sun, except for periods such as 1979—1999, when Pluto's orbit brings that planet inside Neptune's

AVERAGE DISTANCE FROM SUN: 2,794,000 miles (4,497,000,000 kilometers)

AVERAGE DIAMETER: 30,800 miles (49,500 kilometers)

MASS: 17 times Earth's

GRAVITY: 1.19 times Earth's

KNOWN MOONS: 2

LENGTH OF DAY: 18 Earth hours (?)

LENGTH OF YEAR: Nearly 165 Earth years

AVERAGE SPEED IN ORBIT: 10,125 miles per hour (16,200 kilometers per hour)

TILT OF AXIS: 29°

ATMOSPHERE: Methane, probably water and ammonia; also hydrogen and helium

TEMPERATURE IN UPPER ATMOSPHERE: −355°F (−215°C)

COLOR: Blue-green

INTERNATIONAL STATISTICAL SUPPLEMENT

Independent Nations of the World

The United States

    Senate

    House of Representatives

    Supreme Court

    State Governors

Canada and Its Provinces and Territories

INDEPENDENT NATIONS OF THE WORLD

NATION	CAPITAL	AREA (in sq mi)	POPULATION (estimate)	GOVERNMENT
Afghanistan	Kabul	250,000	18,600,000	Najibullah—communist party secretary
Albania	Tirana	11,100	3,000,000	Ramiz Alia—communist party secretary and president Adil Carcani—premier
Algeria	Algiers	919,595	22,400,000	Chadli Benjedid—president
Angola	Luanda	481,354	9,000,000	José Eduardo dos Santos—president
Antigua and Barbuda	St. John's	171	81,000	Vere Bird—prime minister
Argentina	Buenos Aires	1,068,297	31,000,000	Raúl Alfonsín—president
Australia	Canberra	2,967,895	16,000,000	Robert Hawke—prime minister
Austria	Vienna	32,374	7,600,000	Kurt Waldheim—president Franz Vranitzky—chancellor
Bahamas	Nassau	5,380	240,000	Lynden O. Pindling—prime minister
Bahrain	Manama	240	420,000	Isa ibn Sulman al-Khalifa—head of government
Bangladesh	Dhaka	55,598	100,600,000	Hussain Mohammad Ershad—president
Barbados	Bridgetown	168	254,000	Erskine Sandiford—prime minister
Belgium	Brussels	11,781	9,900,000	Baudouin I—king Wilfried Martens—premier
Belize	Belmopan	8,867	171,000	Manuel Esquivel—prime minister
Benin (Dahomey)	Porto-Novo	43,484	4,000,000	Mathieu Kerekou—president
Bhutan	Thimbu	18,147	1,400,000	Jigme Singye Wangchuk—king
Bolivia	La Paz Sucre	424,165	6,500,000	Victor Paz Estenssoro—president
Botswana	Gaborone	231,804	1,100,000	Quett Masire—president
Brazil	Brasília	3,286,478	138,500,000	José Sarney—president
Brunei Darussalam	Bandar Seri Begawan	2,226	270,000	Sultan Muda Hassanal Bolkiah—head of government
Bulgaria	Sofia	42,823	9,000,000	Todor Zhivkov—communist party secretary Georgi Atanasov—premier
Burkina Faso (Upper Volta)	Ouagadougou	105,869	7,900,000	Blaise Compaore—president
Burma	Rangoon	261,218	39,400,000	U San Yu—president U Maung Maung Kha—prime minister
Burundi	Bujumbura	10,747	4,900,000	Pierre Buyoya—head of government
Cambodia (Kampuchea)	Pnompenh	69,898	7,500,000	Heng Samrin—communist party secretary
Cameroon	Yaoundé	183,569	10,400,000	Paul Biya—president

NATION	CAPITAL	AREA (in sq mi)	POPULATION (estimate)	GOVERNMENT
Canada	Ottawa	3,851,809	25,400,000	Martin Brian Mulroney—prime minister
Cape Verde	Praia	1,557	340,000	Aristides Pereira—president
Central African Republic	Bangui	240,535	2,700,000	André Kolingba—president
Chad	N'Djemena	495,754	5,100,000	Hissen Habré—president
Chile	Santiago	292,257	12,500,000	Augusto Pinochet Ugarte—president
China	Peking	3,705,390	1,072,000,000	Zhao Ziyang—communist party secretary Li Peng—premier
Colombia	Bogotá	439,736	28,000,000	Virgilio Barco Vargas—president
Comoros	Moroni	838	480,000	Ahmed Abdallah—president
Congo	Brazzaville	132,047	1,800,000	Denis Sassou-Nguessou—president
Costa Rica	San José	19,575	2,600,000	Oscar Arias Sánchez—president
Cuba	Havana	44,218	10,300,000	Fidel Castro—president
Cyprus	Nicosia	3,572	670,000	Spyros Kyprianou—president
Czechoslovakia	Prague	49,370	15,500,000	Milos Jakes—communist party secretary Lubomir Štrougal—premier
Denmark	Copenhagen	16,629	5,100,000	Margrethe II—queen Poul Schlüter—premier
Djibouti	Djibouti	8,494	460,000	Hassan Gouled Aptidon—president
Dominica	Roseau	290	85,000	Mary Eugenia Charles—prime minister
Dominican Republic	Santo Domingo	18,816	6,400,000	Joaquín Balaguer—president
Ecuador	Quito	109,483	9,600,000	León Febres Cordero Rivadeneira—president
Egypt	Cairo	386,660	50,000,000	Muhammad Hosni Mubarak—president Atef Sedki—premier
El Salvador	San Salvador	8,124	4,900,000	José Napoleón Duarte—president
Equatorial Guinea	Malabo	10,831	400,000	Obiang Nguema Mbasogo—president
Ethiopia	Addis Ababa	471,777	45,000,000	Mengistu Haile Mariam—head of government
Fiji	Suva	7,055	720,000	Ratu Sir Penaia Ganilau—president
Finland	Helsinki	130,120	4,900,000	Mauno Koivisto—president Harri Holkeri—premier
France	Paris	211,207	55,400,000	François Mitterrand—president Jacques Chirac—premier
Gabon	Libreville	103,346	1,200,000	Omar Bongo—president
Gambia	Banjul	4,361	700,000	Sir Dauda K. Jawara—president
Germany (East)	East Berlin	41,768	16,600,000	Erich Honecker—communist party secretary Willi Stoph—premier
Germany (West)	Bonn	95,976	61,000,000	Richard von Weizsäcker—president Helmut Kohl—chancellor

NATION	CAPITAL	AREA (in sq mi)	POPULATION (estimate)	GOVERNMENT
Ghana	Accra	92,099	14,000,000	Jerry Rawlings—head of government
Greece	Athens	50,944	10,000,000	Christos Sartzetakis—president Andreas Papandreou—premier
Grenada	St. George's	133	110,000	Herbert A. Blaize—prime minister
Guatemala	Guatemala City	42,042	8,200,000	Marco Vinicio Cerezo Arévalo—president
Guinea	Conakry	94,926	6,200,000	Lansana Conté—president
Guinea-Bissau	Bissau	13,948	900,000	João Bernardo Vieira—president
Guyana	Georgetown	83,000	800,000	Desmond Hoyte—president
Haiti	Port-au-Prince	10,714	5,400,000	Henri Namphy—head of government
Honduras	Tegucigalpa	43,277	4,500,000	José Azcona Hoyo—president
Hungary	Budapest	35,919	10,600,000	János Kádár—communist party secretary Karoly Grosz—premier
Iceland	Reykjavik	39,768	240,000	Vigdis Finnbogadottir—president Thorsteinn Palsson—prime minister
India	New Delhi	1,269,340	766,000,000	Ramaswamy Venkataraman—president Rajiv Gandhi—prime minister
Indonesia	Jakarta	735,358	167,000,000	Suharto—president
Iran	Teheran	636,294	46,000,000	Ruhollah Khomeini—religious leader Hojatolislam Ali Khamenei—president Mir Hussein Moussavi—premier
Iraq	Baghdad	167,925	16,400,000	Saddam Hussein—president
Ireland	Dublin	27,136	3,600,000	Patrick Hillery—president Charles J. Haughey—prime minister
Israel	Jerusalem	8,019	4,300,000	Chaim Herzog—president Yitzhak Shamir—prime minister
Italy	Rome	116,303	57,200,000	Francesco Cossiga—president Giovanni Goria—premier
Ivory Coast	Yamoussoukro	124,503	10,100,000	Félix Houphouët-Boigny—president
Jamaica	Kingston	4,244	2,400,000	Edward P. G. Seaga—prime minister
Japan	Tokyo	143,751	121,500,000	Hirohito—emperor Noboru Takeshita—premier
Jordan	Amman	37,738	3,700,000	Hussein I—king Zaid Rifai—premier
Kenya	Nairobi	224,959	21,200,000	Daniel arap Moi—president
Kiribati	Tarawa	264	64,000	Ieremia Tabai—president
Korea (North)	Pyongyang	46,540	20,900,000	Kim Il Sung—president Li Gun Mo—premier
Korea (South)	Seoul	38,025	41,600,000	Roh Tae Woo—president-elect Kim Chung Yul—premier
Kuwait	Kuwait	6,880	1,800,000	Jabir al-Ahmad al-Sabah—head of state
Laos	Vientiane	91,429	3,600,000	Phoumi Vongvichit—president Kaysone Phomvihan—premier
Lebanon	Beirut	4,015	2,700,000	Amin Gemayal—president Selim al-Hoss—premier

NATION	CAPITAL	AREA (in sq mi)	POPULATION (estimate)	GOVERNMENT
Lesotho	Maseru	11,720	1,600,000	Moshoeshoe II—king Justin Lekhanya—prime minister
Liberia	Monrovia	43,000	2,200,000	Samuel K. Doe—president
Libya	Tripoli	679,362	3,700,000	Muammar el-Qaddafi—head of government
Liechtenstein	Vaduz	61	27,000	Francis Joseph II—prince
Luxembourg	Luxembourg	999	370,000	Jean—grand duke Jacques Santer—premier
Madagascar	Antananarivo	226,657	10,300,000	Didier Ratsiraka—president
Malawi	Lilongwe	45,747	7,300,000	H. Kamuzu Banda—president
Malaysia	Kuala Lumpur	127,317	16,100,000	Sultan Mahmood Iskandar—king Mahathir Mohammad—prime minister
Maldives	Male	115	189,000	Maumoon Abdul Gayoom—president
Mali	Bamako	478,765	8,400,000	Moussa Traoré—president
Malta	Valletta	122	380,000	Paul Xuereb—president Eddie Fenech Adami—prime minister
Mauritania	Nouakchott	397,954	1,900,000	Maouya Ould Sidi Ahmed Taya—president
Mauritius	Port Louis	790	1,100,000	Aneerood Jugnauth—prime minister
Mexico	Mexico City	761,602	80,000,000	Miguel de la Madrid Hurtado—president
Monaco	Monaco-Ville	0.6	27,000	Rainier III—prince
Mongolia	Ulan Bator	604,248	2,000,000	Dzhambiin Batmunkh—communist party secretary
Morocco	Rabat	172,413	22,500,000	Hassan II—king Azzeddine Laraki—premier
Mozambique	Maputo	309,494	14,200,000	Joaquím A. Chissano—president
Nauru	Yaren District	8	8,000	Hammer DeRoburt—president
Nepal	Katmandu	54,362	17,100,000	Birendra Bir Bikram Shah Deva—king Marish Man Singh Shrestha—prime minister
Netherlands	Amsterdam	15,770	14,500,000	Beatrix—queen Ruud Lubbers—premier
New Zealand	Wellington	103,736	3,300,000	David Lange—prime minister
Nicaragua	Managua	50,193	3,400,000	Daniel Ortega Saavedra—president
Niger	Niamey	489,190	6,700,000	Ali Seybou—president
Nigeria	Lagos	356,667	98,500,000	Ibrahim Babangida—president
Norway	Oslo	125,181	4,200,000	Olav V—king Gro Harlem Brundtland—premier
Oman	Muscat	82,030	2,000,000	Qabus ibn Said—sultan
Pakistan	Islamabad	310,404	99,200,000	Mohammed Zia ul-Haq—president
Panama	Panama City	29,761	2,200,000	Manuel Antonio Noriega—military leader Eric Arturo Delvalle—president

NATION	CAPITAL	AREA (in sq mi)	POPULATION (estimate)	GOVERNMENT
Papua New Guinea	Port Moresby	178,260	3,400,000	Paias Wingti—prime minister
Paraguay	Asunción	157,047	3,800,000	Alfredo Stroessner—president
Peru	Lima	496,222	20,200,000	Alan García Pérez—president
Philippines	Manila	115,830	56,000,000	Corazon C. Aquino—president Salvador H. Laurel—vice-president
Poland	Warsaw	120,725	37,600,000	Wojciech Jaruzelski—communist party secretary and president Zbigniew Messner—premier
Portugal	Lisbon	35,553	10,300,000	Mário Soares—president Anibal Cavaço Silva—premier
Qatar	Doha	4,247	340,000	Khalifa ibn Hamad al-Thani—head of government
Rumania	Bucharest	91,700	23,200,000	Nicolae Ceauşescu—communist party secretary Constantin Dascalescu—premier
Rwanda	Kigali	10,169	6,300,000	Juvénal Habyarimana—president
St. Christopher and Nevis	Basseterre	105	47,000	Kennedy Simmonds—prime minister
St. Lucia	Castries	238	134,000	John Compton—prime minister
St. Vincent and the Grenadines	Kingstown	150	120,000	James Mitchell—prime minister
São Tomé and Príncipe	São Tomé	372	110,000	Manuel Pinto da Costa—president
Saudi Arabia	Riyadh	830,000	12,000,000	Fahd ibn Abdul-Aziz—king
Senegal	Dakar	75,750	6,600,000	Abdou Diouf—president
Seychelles	Victoria	107	66,000	France Albert René—president
Sierra Leone	Freetown	27,700	3,700,000	Joseph Saidu Momoh—president
Singapore	Singapore	224	2,600,000	Wee Kim Wee—president Lee Kuan Yew—prime minister
Solomon Islands	Honiara	10,983	280,000	Peter Kenilorea—prime minister
Somalia	Mogadishu	246,200	5,000,000	Mohammed Siad Barre—president
South Africa	Pretoria Cape Town Bloemfontein	471,444	33,200,000	Pieter W. Botha—president
Spain	Madrid	194,897	38,700,000	Juan Carlos I—king Felipe González Márquez—premier
Sri Lanka (Ceylon)	Colombo	25,332	16,100,000	Junius R. Jayewardene—president Ranasinghe Premadasa—prime minister
Sudan	Khartoum	967,500	22,200,000	Sadiq al-Mahdi—prime minister
Suriname	Paramaribo	63,037	400,000	Désiré Bouterse—military leader
Swaziland	Mbabane	6,704	680,000	Mswati III—king
Sweden	Stockholm	173,731	8,400,000	Carl XVI Gustaf—king Ingvar Carlsson—premier

NATION	CAPITAL	AREA (in sq mi)	POPULATION (estimate)	GOVERNMENT
Switzerland	Bern	15,941	6,500,000	Otto Stich—president
Syria	Damascus	71,498	10,600,000	Hafez al-Assad—president Mahmoud Zubi—premier
Taiwan	Taipei	13,885	19,000,000	Chiang Ching-kwo—president Yu Kuo-hwa—premier
Tanzania	Dar es Salaam	364,898	22,500,000	Ali Hassan Mwinyi—president
Thailand	Bangkok	198,457	52,100,000	Bhumibol Adulyadej—king Prem Tinsulanonda—premier
Togo	Lomé	21,622	3,100,000	Gnassingbe Eyadema—president
Tonga	Nuku'alofa	270	100,000	Taufa'ahau Tupou IV—king Prince Tu'ipelehake—prime minister
Trinidad & Tobago	Port of Spain	1,980	1,200,000	Noor Hassanali—president A.N.R. Robinson—prime minister
Tunisia	Tunis	63,170	7,300,000	Zine el-Abidine Ben Ali—president
Turkey	Ankara	301,381	50,300,000	Kenan Evren—president Turgut Ozal—prime minister
Tuvalu	Funafuti	10	8,000	Tomasi Puapua—prime minister
Uganda	Kampala	91,134	16,000,000	Yoweri Museveni—president
U.S.S.R.	Moscow	8,649,512	280,000,000	Mikhail S. Gorbachev—communist party secretary Andrei A. Gromyko—president Nikolai I. Ryzhkov—premier
United Arab Emirates	Abu Dhabi	32,278	1,400,000	Zayd ibn Sultan al-Nuhayan—president
United Kingdom	London	94,226	56,800,000	Elizabeth II—queen Margaret Thatcher—prime minister
United States	Washington, D.C.	3,618,467	243,000,000	Ronald W. Reagan—president George H. Bush—vice-president
Uruguay	Montevideo	68,037	3,000,000	Julio María Sanguinetti—president
Vanuatu	Vila	5,700	142,000	Walter Lini—prime minister
Venezuela	Caracas	352,143	17,800,000	Jaime Lusinchi—president
Vietnam	Hanoi	128,402	61,000,000	Nguyen Van Linh—communist party secretary Pham Hung—premier
Western Samoa	Apia	1,097	164,000	Malietoa Tanumafili II—head of state
Yemen (Aden)	Madinat al-Shaab	128,559	2,400,000	Haider Abu Bakr al-Attas—president
Yemen (Sana)	Sana	75,290	9,300,000	Ali Abdullah Saleh al-Hasani—president
Yugoslavia	Belgrade	98,766	23,300,000	Lazar Mojsov—president Branko Mikulic—premier
Zaïre	Kinshasa	905,565	30,900,000	Mobutu Sese Seko—president
Zambia	Lusaka	290,585	6,900,000	Kenneth D. Kaunda—president
Zimbabwe	Harare	150,333	8,400,000	Canaan Banana—president Robert Mugabe—prime minister

THE CONGRESS OF THE UNITED STATES

UNITED STATES SENATE

(54 Democrats, 46 Republicans)

Alabama
Howell T. Heflin (D)
Richard C. Shelby (D)

Alaska
Ted Stevens (R)
Frank H. Murkowski (R)

Arizona
Dennis DeConcini (D)
John McCain (R)

Arkansas
Dale Bumpers (D)
David H. Pryor (D)

California
Alan Cranston (D)
Pete Wilson (R)

Colorado
William L. Armstrong (R)
Timothy E. Wirth (D)

Connecticut
Lowell P. Weicker, Jr. (R)
Christopher J. Dodd (D)

Delaware
William V. Roth, Jr. (R)
Joseph R. Biden, Jr. (D)

Florida
Lawton Chiles, Jr. (D)
Bob Graham (D)

Georgia
Sam Nunn (D)
Wyche Fowler, Jr. (D)

Hawaii
Daniel K. Inouye (D)
Spark M. Matsunaga (D)

Idaho
James A. McClure (R)
Steve Symms (R)

Illinois
Alan J. Dixon (D)
Paul Simon (D)

Indiana
Richard G. Lugar (R)
Dan Quayle (R)

Iowa
Charles E. Grassley (R)
Thomas R. Harkin (D)

Kansas
Robert J. Dole (R)
Nancy Landon Kassebaum (R)

Kentucky
Wendell H. Ford (D)
Mitch McConnell (R)

Louisiana
J. Bennett Johnston (D)
John B. Breaux (D)

Maine
William S. Cohen (R)
George J. Mitchell (D)

Maryland
Paul S. Sarbanes (D)
Barbara A. Mikulski (D)

Massachusetts
Edward M. Kennedy (D)
John F. Kerry (D)

Michigan
Donald W. Riegle, Jr. (D)
Carl Levin (D)

Minnesota
David F. Durenberger (R)
Rudy Boschwitz (R)

Mississippi
John C. Stennis (D)
Thad Cochran (R)

Missouri
John C. Danforth (R)
Christopher S. Bond (R)

Montana
John Melcher (D)
Max Baucus (D)

Nebraska
David Karnes (R)*
J. James Exon, Jr. (D)

Nevada
Chic Hecht (R)
Harry Reid (D)

New Hampshire
Gordon J. Humphrey (R)
Warren B. Rudman (R)

New Jersey
Bill Bradley (D)
Frank R. Lautenberg (D)

New Mexico
Pete V. Domenici (R)
Jeff Bingaman (D)

New York
Daniel P. Moynihan (D)
Alfonse M. D'Amato (R)

North Carolina
Jesse Helms (R)
Terry Sanford (D)

North Dakota
Quentin N. Burdick (D)
Kent Conrad (D)

Ohio
John H. Glenn, Jr. (D)
Howard M. Metzenbaum (D)

Oklahoma
David L. Boren (D)
Donald L. Nickles (R)

Oregon
Mark O. Hatfield (R)
Bob Packwood (R)

Pennsylvania
John Heinz (R)
Arlen Specter (R)

Rhode Island
Claiborne Pell (D)
John H. Chafee (R)

South Carolina
Strom Thurmond (R)
Ernest F. Hollings (D)

South Dakota
Larry Pressler (R)
Thomas A. Daschle (D)

Tennessee
James R. Sasser (D)
Albert Gore, Jr. (D)

Texas
Lloyd Bentsen (D)
Phil Gramm (R)

Utah
Jake Garn (R)
Orrin G. Hatch (R)

Vermont
Robert T. Stafford (R)
Patrick J. Leahy (D)

Virginia
John W. Warner (R)
Paul S. Trible, Jr. (R)

Washington
Daniel J. Evans (R)
Brock Adams (D)

West Virginia
Robert C. Byrd (D)
John D. Rockefeller IV (D)

Wisconsin
William Proxmire (D)
Robert W. Kasten, Jr. (R)

Wyoming
Malcolm Wallop (R)
Alan K. Simpson (R)

(D) Democrat
(R) Republican

*was named in 1987 to
replace Edward Zorinsky

UNITED STATES HOUSE OF REPRESENTATIVES

(257 Democrats, 177 Republicans, 1 vacancy)

Alabama
1. H. L. Callahan (R)
2. W. L. Dickinson (R)
3. W. Nichols (D)
4. T. Bevill (D)
5. R. G. Flippo (D)
6. B. Erdreich (D)
7. C. Harris (D)

Alaska
D. Young (R)

Arizona
1. J. J. Rhodes III (R)
2. M. K. Udall (D)
3. B. Stump (R)
4. J. Kyl (R)
5. J. Kolbe (R)

Arkansas
1. W. V. Alexander, Jr. (D)
2. T. F. Robinson (D)
3. J. P. Hammerschmidt (R)
4. B. F. Anthony, Jr. (D)

California
1. D. H. Bosco (D)
2. W. Herger (R)
3. R. T. Matsui (D)
4. V. Fazio (D)
5. N. Pelosi (D)*
6. B. Boxer (D)
7. G. Miller (D)
8. R. V. Dellums (D)
9. F. H. Stark, Jr. (D)
10. D. Edwards (D)
11. T. P. Lantos (D)
12. E. L. Konnyu (R)
13. N. Y. Mineta (D)
14. N. D. Shumway (R)
15. T. Coelho (D)
16. L. E. Panetta (D)
17. C. Pashayan, Jr. (R)
18. R. H. Lehman (D)
19. R. J. Lagomarsino (R)
20. W. M. Thomas (R)
21. E. Gallegly (R)
22. C. J. Moorhead (R)
23. A. C. Beilenson (D)
24. H. A. Waxman (D)
25. E. R. Roybal (D)
26. H. L. Berman (D)
27. M. Levine (D)
28. J. C. Dixon (D)
29. A. F. Hawkins (D)
30. M. G. Martinez, Jr. (D)
31. M. M. Dymally (D)
32. G. M. Anderson (D)
33. D. Dreier (R)
34. E. E. Torres (D)
35. J. Lewis (R)
36. G. E. Brown, Jr. (D)
37. A. A. McCandless (R)
38. R. K. Dornan (R)
39. W. E. Dannemeyer (R)
40. R. E. Badham (R)
41. W. D. Lowery (R)

42. D. E. Lungren (R)
43. R. Packard (R)
44. J. Bates (D)
45. D. L. Hunter (R)

Colorado
1. P. Schroeder (D)
2. D. Skaggs (D)
3. B. N. Campbell (D)
4. H. Brown (R)
5. J. Hefley (R)
6. D. Schaefer (R)

Connecticut
1. B. B. Kennelly (D)
2. S. Gejdenson (D)
3. B. A. Morrison (D)
4. C. Shays (R)*
5. J. G. Rowland (R)
6. N. L. Johnson (R)

Delaware
T. R. Carper (D)

Florida
1. E. Hutto (D)
2. B. Grant (D)
3. C. E. Bennett (D)
4. W. V. Chappell, Jr. (D)
5. B. McCollum, Jr. (R)
6. K. H. MacKay (D)
7. S. M. Gibbons (D)
8. C. W. B. Young (R)
9. M. Bilirakis (R)
10. A. Ireland (R)
11. B. Nelson (D)
12. T. Lewis (R)
13. C. Mack III (R)
14. D. A. Mica (D)
15. E. C. Shaw, Jr. (R)
16. L. J. Smith (D)
17. W. Lehman (D)
18. C. D. Pepper (D)
19. D. B. Fascell (D)

Georgia
1. R. L. Thomas (D)
2. C. F. Hatcher (D)
3. R. B. Ray (D)
4. P. L. Swindall (R)
5. J. Lewis (D)
6. N. Gingrich (R)
7. G. B. Darden (D)
8. J. R. Rowland, Jr. (D)
9. E. L. Jenkins (D)
10. D. Barnard, Jr. (D)

Hawaii
1. P. Saiki (R)
2. D. K. Akaka (D)

Idaho
1. L. E. Craig (R)
2. R. H. Stallings (D)

Illinois
1. C. A. Hayes (D)
2. G. Savage (D)
3. M. Russo (D)
4. J. Davis (R)
5. W. O. Lipinski (D)
6. H. J. Hyde (R)
7. C. Collins (D)
8. D. Rostenkowski (D)
9. S. R. Yates (D)
10. J. E. Porter (R)
11. F. Annunzio (D)
12. P. M. Crane (R)
13. H. W. Fawell (R)
14. J. D. Hastert (R)
15. E. R. Madigan (R)
16. L. M. Martin (R)
17. L. Evans (D)
18. R. H. Michel (R)
19. T. L. Bruce (D)
20. R. Durbin (D)
21. C. M. Price (D)
22. K. J. Gray (D)

Indiana
1. P. J. Visclosky (D)
2. P. R. Sharp (D)
3. J. P. Hiler (R)
4. D. R. Coats (R)
5. J. Jontz (D)
6. D. L. Burton (R)
7. J. T. Myers (R)
8. F. McCloskey (D)
9. L. H. Hamilton (D)
10. A. Jacobs, Jr. (D)

Iowa
1. J. Leach (R)
2. T. J. Tauke (R)
3. D. R. Nagle (D)
4. N. Smith (D)
5. J. R. Lightfoot (R)
6. F. Grandy (R)

Kansas
1. C. P. Roberts (R)
2. J. C. Slattery (D)
3. J. Meyers (R)
4. D. Glickman (D)
5. B. Whittaker (R)

Kentucky
1. C. Hubbard, Jr. (D)
2. W. H. Natcher (D)
3. R. L. Mazzoli (D)
4. J. Bunning (R)
5. H. D. Rogers (R)
6. L. J. Hopkins (R)
7. C. C. Perkins (D)

Louisiana
1. R. L. Livingston, Jr. (R)
2. C. C. Boggs (D)
3. W. J. Tauzin (D)
4. C. E. Roemer III (D)**
5. T. J. Huckaby (D)

6. R. Baker (R)
7. J. Hayes (D)
8. C. Holloway (R)

Maine
1. J. Brennan (D)
2. O. J. Snowe (R)

Maryland
1. R. P. Dyson (D)
2. H. Delich Bentley (R)
3. B. L. Cardin (D)
4. T. McMillen (D)
5. S. H. Hoyer (D)
6. B. Butcher Byron (D)
7. K. Mfume (D)
8. C. A. Morella (R)

Massachusetts
1. S. O. Conte (R)
2. E. P. Boland (D)
3. J. D. Early (D)
4. B. Frank (D)
5. C. G. Atkins (D)
6. N. Mavroules (D)
7. E. J. Markey (D)
8. J. P. Kennedy II (D)
9. J. J. Moakley (D)
10. G. E. Studds (D)
11. B. J. Donnelly (D)

Michigan
1. J. Conyers, Jr. (D)
2. C. D. Pursell (R)
3. H. E. Wolpe (D)
4. F. Upton (R)
5. P. B. Henry (R)
6. B. Carr (D)
7. D. E. Kildee (D)
8. B. Traxler (D)
9. G. Vander Jagt (R)
10. B. Schuette (R)
11. R. W. Davis (R)
12. D. E. Bonior (D)
13. G. W. Crockett, Jr. (D)
14. D. M. Hertel (D)
15. W. D. Ford (D)
16. J. D. Dingell (D)
17. S. M. Levin (D)
18. W. S. Broomfield (R)

Minnesota
1. T. J. Penny (D)
2. V. Weber (R)
3. B. Frenzel (R)
4. B. F. Vento (D)
5. M. O. Sabo (D)
6. G. Sikorski (D)
7. A. Stangeland (R)
8. J. L. Oberstar (D)

Mississippi
1. J. L. Whitten (D)
2. M. Espy (D)
3. G. V. Montgomery (D)

4. W. Dowdy (D)
5. T. Lott (R)

Missouri
1. W. L. Clay (D)
2. J. Buechner (R)
3. R. A. Gephardt (D)
4. I. Skelton (D)
5. A. D. Wheat (D)
6. E. T. Coleman (R)
7. G. Taylor (R)
8. W. Emerson (R)
9. H. L. Volkmer (D)

Montana
1. P. Williams (D)
2. R. C. Marlenee (R)

Nebraska
1. D. Bereuter (R)
2. H. Daub (R)
3. V. Smith (R)

Nevada
1. J. Bilbray (D)
2. B. Farrell Vucanovich (R)

New Hampshire
1. R. C. Smith (R)
2. J. Gregg (R)

New Jersey
1. J. J. Florio (D)
2. W. J. Hughes (D)
3. J. J. Howard (D)
4. C. H. Smith (R)
5. M. S. Roukema (R)
6. B. J. Dwyer (D)
7. M. J. Rinaldo (R)
8. R. A. Roe (D)
9. R. G. Torricelli (D)
10. P. W. Rodino, Jr. (D)
11. D. A. Gallo (R)
12. J. Courter (R)
13. H. J. Saxton (R)
14. F. J. Guarini (D)

New Mexico
1. M. Lujan, Jr. (R)
2. J. R. Skeen (R)
3. W. B. Richardson (D)

New York
1. G. J. Hochbrueckner (D)
2. T. J. Downey (D)
3. R. J. Mrazek (D)
4. N. F. Lent (R)
5. R. J. McGrath (R)
6. F. H. Flake (D)
7. G. L. Ackerman (D)
8. J. H. Scheuer (D)
9. T. J. Manton (D)
10. C. E. Schumer (D)
11. E. Towns (D)
12. M. R. O. Owens (D)
13. S. J. Solarz (D)
14. G. V. Molinari (R)
15. B. Green (R)
16. C. B. Rangel (D)
17. T. Weiss (D)

18. R. Garcia (D)
19. M. Biaggi (D)
20. J. J. DioGuardi (R)
21. H. Fish, Jr. (R)
22. B. A. Gilman (R)
23. S. S. Stratton (D)
24. G. B. Solomon (R)
25. S. L. Boehlert (R)
26. D. O. Martin (R)
27. G. C. Wortley (R)
28. M. F. McHugh (D)
29. F. Horton (R)
30. L. M. Slaughter (D)
31. J. Kemp (R)
32. J. J. LaFalce (D)
33. H. J. Nowak (D)
34. A. Houghton, Jr. (R)

North Carolina
1. W. B. Jones (D)
2. T. Valentine (D)
3. M. Lancaster (D)
4. D. E. Price (D)
5. S. L. Neal (D)
6. H. Coble (R)
7. C. Rose (D)
8. W. G. Hefner (D)
9. J. A. McMillan III (R)
10. C. Ballenger (R)
11. J. McC. Clarke (D)

North Dakota
B. L. Dorgan (D)

Ohio
1. T. A. Luken (D)
2. W. D. Gradison, Jr. (R)
3. T. P. Hall (D)
4. M. G. Oxley (R)
5. D. L. Latta (R)
6. B. McEwen (R)
7. M. DeWine (R)
8. D. Lukens (R)
9. M. C. Kaptur (D)
10. C. E. Miller (R)
11. D. E. Eckart (D)
12. J. R. Kasich (R)
13. D. J. Pease (D)
14. T. C. Sawyer (D)
15. C. P. Wylie (R)
16. R. Regula (R)
17. J. A. Traficant, Jr. (D)
18. D. Applegate (D)
19. E. F. Feighan (D)
20. M. R. Oakar (D)
21. L. Stokes (D)

Oklahoma
1. J. M. Inhofe (R)
2. M. Synar (D)
3. W. W. Watkins (D)
4. D. McCurdy (D)
5. M. H. Edwards (R)
6. G. English (D)

Oregon
1. L. AuCoin (D)
2. R. F. Smith (R)
3. R. L. Wyden (D)
4. P. A. DeFazio (D)
5. D. Smith (R)

Pennsylvania
1. T. M. Foglietta (D)
2. W. H. Gray III (D)
3. R. A. Borski, Jr. (D)
4. J. P. Kolter (D)
5. R. T. Schulze (R)
6. G. Yatron (D)
7. C. Weldon (R)
8. P. H. Kostmayer (D)
9. B. Shuster (R)
10. J. M. McDade (R)
11. P. E. Kanjorski (D)
12. J. P. Murtha (D)
13. L. Coughlin (R)
14. W. J. Coyne (D)
15. D. L. Ritter (R)
16. R. S. Walker (R)
17. G. W. Gekas (R)
18. D. Walgren (D)
19. W. F. Goodling (R)
20. J. M. Gaydos (D)
21. T. J. Ridge (R)
22. A. J. Murphy (D)
23. W. F. Clinger, Jr. (R)

Rhode Island
1. F. J. St. Germain (D)
2. C. Schneider (R)

South Carolina
1. A. Ravenel, Jr. (R)
2. F. D. Spence (R)
3. B. C. Derrick, Jr. (D)
4. L. J. Patterson (D)
5. J. M. Spratt, Jr. (D)
6. R. M. Tallon (D)

South Dakota
T. Johnson (D)

Tennessee
1. J. H. Quillen (R)
2. J. J. Duncan (R)
3. M. Lloyd (D)
4. J. H. S. Cooper (D)
5. vacant
6. B. J. Gordon (D)
7. D. K. Sundquist (R)
8. E. Jones (D)
9. H. Ford (D)

Texas
1. J. Chapman (D)
2. C. Wilson (D)
3. S. Bartlett (R)
4. R. M. Hall (D)
5. J. W. Bryant (D)
6. J. L. Barton (R)
7. B. Archer (R)
8. J. M. Fields (R)
9. J. Brooks (D)
10. J. J. Pickle (D)
11. J. M. Leath (D)
12. J. C. Wright, Jr. (D)
13. E. B. Boulter (R)
14. D. McC. Sweeney (R)
15. E. de la Garza (D)
16. R. D. Coleman (D)
17. C. W. Stenholm (D)
18. M. Leland (D)
19. L. E. Combest (R)

20. H. B. Gonzalez (D)
21. L. Smith (R)
22. T. D. DeLay (R)
23. A. G. Bustamante (D)
24. M. Frost (D)
25. M. A. Andrews (D)
26. R. K. Armey (R)
27. S. P. Ortiz (D)

Utah
1. J. V. Hansen (R)
2. W. Owens (D)
3. H. C. Nielson (R)

Vermont
J. M. Jeffords (R)

Virginia
1. H. H. Bateman (R)
2. O. B. Pickett (D)
3. T. J. Bliley, Jr. (R)
4. N. Sisisky (D)
5. D. Daniel (D)
6. J. R. Olin (D)
7. D. F. Slaughter, Jr. (R)
8. S. Parris (R)
9. F. C. Boucher (D)
10. F. R. Wolf (R)

Washington
1. J. R. Miller (R)
2. A. Swift (D)
3. D. L. Bonker (D)
4. S. W. Morrison (R)
5. T. S. Foley (D)
6. N. D. Dicks (D)
7. M. Lowry (D)
8. R. Chandler (R)

West Virginia
1. A. B. Mollohan (D)
2. H. O. Staggers, Jr. (D)
3. R. E. Wise, Jr. (D)
4. N. J. Rahall II (D)

Wisconsin
1. L. Aspin (D)
2. R. W. Kastenmeier (D)
3. S. C. Gunderson (R)
4. G. D. Kleczka (D)
5. J. Moody (D)
6. T. E. Petri (R)
7. D. R. Obey (D)
8. T. Roth (R)
9. F. J. Sensenbrenner, Jr. (R)

Wyoming
D. Cheney (R)

*elected in 1987
**elected Governor of Louisiana,
  effective March, 1988

UNITED STATES SUPREME COURT

Chief Justice: William H. Rehnquist (1986)

Associate Justices:
William J. Brennan, Jr. (1956)
Byron R. White (1962)
Thurgood Marshall (1967)
Harry A. Blackmun (1970)
John Paul Stevens (1975)
Sandra Day O'Connor (1981)
Antonin Scalia (1986)
Anthony M. Kennedy (nominated, 1987)

UNITED STATES CABINET

Secretary of Agriculture: Richard E. Lyng
Attorney General: Edwin Meese III
Secretary of Commerce: C. William Verity, Jr.
Secretary of Defense: Frank C. Carlucci
Secretary of Education: William J. Bennett
Secretary of Energy: John S. Herrington
Secretary of Health and Human Services:
Otis R. Bowen
Secretary of Housing and Urban Development:
Samuel R. Pierce, Jr.
Secretary of the Interior: Donald P. Hodel
Secretary of Labor: Ann Dore McLaughlin
Secretary of State: George P. Shultz
Secretary of Transportation: James H. Burnley IV
Secretary of the Treasury: James A. Baker III

Anthony M. Kennedy was named an Associate Justice of the Supreme Court, to replace Lewis F. Powell, Jr.

STATE GOVERNORS

Alabama	Guy Hunt (R)	Montana	Ted Schwinden (D)
Alaska	Steve Cowper (D)	Nebraska	Kay A. Orr (R)
Arizona	Evan Mecham (R)	Nevada	Richard H. Bryan (D)
Arkansas	Bill Clinton (D)	New Hampshire	John H. Sununu (R)
California	George Deukmejian (R)	New Jersey	Thomas H. Kean (R)
Colorado	Roy Romer (D)	New Mexico	Garrey E. Carruthers (R)
Connecticut	William A. O'Neill (D)	New York	Mario M. Cuomo (D)
Delaware	Michael N. Castle (R)	North Carolina	James G. Martin (R)
Florida	Bob Martinez (R)	North Dakota	George Sinner (D)
Georgia	Joe Frank Harris (D)	Ohio	Richard F. Celeste (D)
Hawaii	John Waihee (D)	Oklahoma	Henry Bellmon (R)
Idaho	Cecil D. Andrus (D)	Oregon	Neil Goldschmidt (D)
Illinois	James R. Thompson (R)	Pennsylvania	Bob Casey (D)
Indiana	Robert D. Orr (R)	Rhode Island	Edward D. DiPrete (R)
Iowa	Terry E. Branstad (R)	South Carolina	Carroll A. Campbell, Jr. (R)
Kansas	Mike Hayden (R)	South Dakota	George S. Mickelson (R)
Kentucky	Wallace Wilkinson (D)*	Tennessee	Ned R. McWherter (D)
Louisiana	Charles E. Roemer III (D)*	Texas	William Clements (R)
Maine	John R. McKernan, Jr. (R)	Utah	Norman Bangerter (R)
Maryland	William Donald Schaefer (D)	Vermont	Madeleine Kunin (D)
Massachusetts	Michael S. Dukakis (D)	Virginia	Gerald L. Baliles (D)
Michigan	James J. Blanchard (D)	Washington	Booth Gardner (D)
Minnesota	Rudy Perpich (D)	West Virginia	Arch Moore (R)
Mississippi	Ray Maybus (D)*	Wisconsin	Tommy G. Thompson (R)
Missouri	John Ashcroft (R)	Wyoming	Mike Sullivan (D)

*elected in 1987

CANADA

Capital: Ottawa
Head of State: Queen Elizabeth II
Governor General: Jeanne Sauvé
Prime Minister: Martin Brian Mulroney (Progressive Conservative)
Leader of the Opposition: John Turner (Liberal)
Population: 25,400,000
Area: 3,851,809 sq mi (9,976,185 km²)

PROVINCES AND TERRITORIES

Alberta
Capital: Edmonton
Lieutenant Governor: W. Helen Hunley
Premier: Donald R. Getty (Progressive Conservative)
Leader of the Opposition: Ray Martin (New Democratic Party)
Entered Confederation: Sept. 1, 1905
Population: 2,375,300
Area: 255,285 sq mi (661,188 km²)

British Columbia
Capital: Victoria
Lieutenant Governor: Robert G. Rogers
Premier: William N. Vander Zalm (Social Credit)
Leader of the Opposition: Michael F. Harcourt (New Democratic Party)
Entered Confederation: July 20, 1871
Population: 2,889,200
Area: 366,255 sq mi (948,600 km²)

Manitoba
Capital: Winnipeg
Lieutenant Governor: George Johnson
Premier: Howard R. Pawley (New Democratic Party)
Leader of the Opposition: Gary Filmon (Progressive Conservative)
Entered Confederation: July 15, 1870
Population: 1,071,200
Area: 251,000 sq mi (650,090 km²)

New Brunswick
Capital: Fredericton
Lieutenant Governor: Gilbert Finn
Premier: Frank McKenna (Liberal)
Leader of the Opposition: None
Entered Confederation: July 1, 1867
Population: 710,400
Area: 28,354 sq mi (73,436 km²)

Newfoundland
Capital: St. John's
Lieutenant Governor: James A. McGrath
Premier: A. Brian Peckford (Progressive Conservative)
Leader of the Opposition: Clyde Wells (Liberal)
Entered Confederation: March 31, 1949
Population: 568,300
Area: 156,185 sq mi (404,517 km²)

Nova Scotia
Capital: Halifax
Lieutenant Governor: Alan R. Abraham
Premier: John M. Buchanan (Progressive Conservative)
Leader of the Opposition: Vincent J. MacLean (Liberal)
Entered Confederation: July 1, 1867
Population: 873,200
Area: 21,425 sq mi (55,491 km²)

Ontario
Capital: Toronto
Lieutenant Governor: Lincoln M. Alexander
Premier: David Peterson (Liberal)
Leader of the Opposition: Bob Rae (New Democratic Party)
Entered Confederation: July 1, 1867
Population: 9,113,500
Area: 412,582 sq mi (1,068,582 km²)

Prince Edward Island
Capital: Charlottetown
Lieutenant Governor: Lloyd G.MacPhail
Premier: Joseph A. Ghiz (Liberal)
Leader of the Opposition: Leone Bagnall (Progressive Conservative)
Entered Confederation: July 1, 1873
Population: 126,600
Area: 2,184 sq mi (5,657 km²)

Quebec

Capital: Quebec City
Lieutenant Governor: Gilles Lamontagne
Premier: Robert Bourassa (Liberal)
Leader of the Opposition: Guy Chevrette (Parti Québécois)
Entered Confederation: July 1, 1867
Population: 6,540,300
Area: 594,860 sq mi (1,540,700 km²)

Saskatchewan

Capital: Regina
Lieutenant Governor: F. W. Johnson
Premier: Grant Devine (Progressive Conservative)
Leader of the Opposition: Roy Romanow (New Democratic
  Party)
Entered Confederation: Sept. 1, 1905
Population: 1,010,200
Area: 251,700 sq mi (651,900 km²)

Northwest Territories

Capital: Yellowknife
Commissioner: John H. Parker
Leader of the Elected Executive: Dennis Patterson
Reconstituted as a Territory: September 1, 1905
Population: 52,300
Area: 1,304,896 sq mi (3,379,684 km²)

Yukon Territory

Capital: Whitehorse
Commissioner: J. Kenneth McKinnon
Government Leader: Tony Penikett (New
  Democratic Party)
Leader of the Opposition: Willard Phelps
  (Progressive Conservative)
Organized as a Territory: June 13, 1898
Population: 23,500
Area: 186,299 sq mi (482,515 km²)

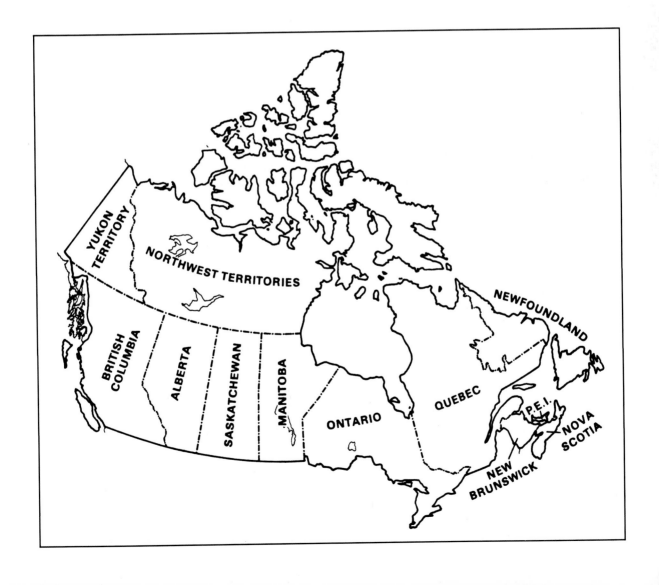

INDEX

A

H

Italy 352
    fans 251
    general elections 29
    minesweeping in Persian Gulf 47
    World Track and Field Championships 163
Ivory Coast 352

J

Jackson, Bo, American athlete, picture 175
Jackson, Michael, American singer 262–63
Jager, Tom, American athlete, picture 181
Jakes, Milos, Czech leader 39
Jamaica 352
Japan 352
    chrysanthemum 217
    exports to United States, tariffs on 52
    fans 250–51, 254
    Jackson, Michael, popularity of 263
    maglev (magnetic levitation) trains 105
    Mt. Fuji climbed by American, picture 65
    stock market 50
    Takeshita, Noboru, elected premier 37
Jefferson, Thomas, president of the United States
    193
Jewish people
    Soviet Union, emigration from 56
Jobs
    Soviet Union 54
    teenagers 230–31; pictures 224–25
John Paul II, pope 32, 33
Johnson, Ben, Canadian athlete, picture 183
Johnson, Earvin (Magic), American athlete 172–73
Johnson, Scott, American athlete 185
Jones, James Earl, American actor 229
Jordan 352
    Arab-Israeli peace plan 49
Joyner-Kersee, Jackie, American athlete 185; picture
    162–63
Jupiter, planet 117
    computer simulation of magnetic field, picture
    242

K

Kahane, Anne, Canadian sculptor 331
Kampuchea see Cambodia
Kane, Paul, Canadian artist, picture 330
Kansas
    Brown versus *Board of Education of Topeka,* Supreme
    Court case 196
Karami, Rashid, premier of Lebanon 26, 48
Kassem, Abdel Raouf al-, premier of Syria 36
Kaye, Danny, American comedian 20

Kea, bird 72
Keene, Carolyn, pen name of writers of *Nancy Drew*
    books 234
Keillor, Garrison, American radio commentator and
    writer, picture 282
Kelp, plant 95–96
Kennedy, Anthony M., American Supreme Court Justice
    nominee 37; picture 359
Kenya 352
Key Largo, Florida
    underwater lodge, picture 279
Khomeini, Ayatollah Ruhollah, religious leader of Iran
    48; pictures 12–13, 49
Kidnappings
    Lebanon 41, 49, 64
Kim Chung Yul, premier of Republic of Korea 29
King, B. B., American musician 237
Kiribati 352
Koala, animal 228
    albino, picture 90
Komodo dragon, reptile 199
Kookaburra III, Australian racing yacht 18, 165–66
Korea, Democratic People's Republic of (North Korea)
    352
    Communist takeover 44
Korea, Republic of (South Korea) 44–45, 352
    commemorative coins 157; pictures 156
    leadership 29
    1988 Olympic Games 82, 189
Kountche, Seyni, president of Niger 37
Kremlin, Moscow, Union of Soviet Socialist Republics,
    picture 67
Krieghoff, Cornelius, Canadian artist 330
Krill, crustacean 324
Kroetsch, Robert, Canadian writer 333
Kudrna, C. Imbior, American writer and illustrator
    To Bathe a Boa, book, picture 284–85
Kuwait 352
    Iran-Iraq war 47
Kvant, Soviet space research module 115

L

La Bamba, motion picture
    Valens, Ritchie 266
Lacombe, Patrice, Canadian writer 333
Lady's slipper orchid, flower, picture 111
Lahr, Bert, American actor 314
Lake Okeechobee, Florida 113
Lake Wobegon Days, novel by Garrison Keillor 282
L.A. Law, television program, picture 269
Laliberté, Albert, Canadian sculptor 331
Lampman, Archibald, Canadian writer 332
Laos 352
Larroquette, John, American actor 268
La Rue Mosnier aux Paveurs, painting by Édouard Manet
    300
Las Campanas Observatory, Chile 117
    Supernova 1987A, discovery of 119
Lasky, Jesse L., American filmmaker 208

M

McEnroe, John, American athlete 182
McFarlane, Robert C., American public official 41
McLaughlin, Ann Dore, American public official 34
Mecca, Saudi Arabia 31
    riots during Muslim pilgrimage 31, 47–48
Medicine and health
    biological rhythms 100
    CD-ROM, hospitals' use of 126
    circulatory disorders 344
    disease carried by birds 73
    hay fever 219–20
Mellencamp, John Cougar, American musician 265
Memphis, Tennessee
    tenth anniversary of Elvis Presley's death 266–67
Merriman, Mike, American photography program winner,
    picture 244
Mexico, 353
    marigolds 220
Michigan
    commemorative postage stamp 144
    Northwest airlines plane crash, Detroit 31
Middle East 46–49
    see also specific countries of the Middle East
Milenkovic, Stefan, Yugoslavian violinist, picture
    233
Milky Way, galaxy 118
Milne, David, Canadian artist 331
Minnelli, Liza, American actress 229
Mir, Soviet space station 39, 115
Miranda, Carmen, Portuguese singer
    hot-air balloon, picture 271
Missiles, nuclear
    U.S.-U.S.S.R. treaty 39
Missouri
    botanical garden, St. Louis 335
Mize, Larry, American athlete, picture 177
Mole, animal 89
Monaco 353
Monet, Claude, French artist 300–01, 307–11
Mongolia 353
Monkey, animal 88–89; picture 87
    Yerosha, Soviet space monkey 115
Monroe, Marilyn, American actress 211
    commemorative postage stamp 147
Montana
    dinosaurs 79
Monterey Bay, off California coast 94–97
Montgomery, Lucy Maud, Canadian writer
    Anne of Green Gables novel 332; picture 333
Montreal, Quebec, Canada
    art of French colonial period 330
    styles of architecture 331
Moodie, Susanna, Canadian writer
    Roughing It in the Bush 332; picture 333
Moonlighting, television program, picture 269
Moons
    Neptune and Uranus 347–48
Morisot, Berthe, French artist 304, 306–07, 310
Morocco 353
Morrice, James Wilson, Canadian artist 330
Morris, Gouverneur, American statesman 194
Moscow, Union of Soviet Socialist Republics
    Kremlin, picture 67
    U.S. Embassy, security concerns of 30–31
Moses, Edwin, American athlete 189
Mosquito, insect 108
Moss, plant 110; pictures 111, 112

Moth, insect 123
    pollination of plants 102, 123
Motion pictures
    Academy awards 256–57
    Astaire, Fred, death of 26; picture 27
    Bolger, Ray, death of 17
    CD-ROM, future use of 127
    Color Purple, The 283
    commemorative postage stamps 147
    Hayworth, Rita, death of 25
    Hollywood, California 208–13
    Huston, John, death of 31
    Matlin, Marlee, picture 278
    Snow White and the Seven Dwarfs 258–59
Mt. Fuji, Japan 65
Mozambique 353
Mshana, Pamela, American playwright 236
Mueller, Louis, American craftsman 274
Müller, K. Alex, Swiss physicist 35
Mulroney, Brian, prime minister of Canada
    Quebec's special identity, protection of 26
    summit meeting in Ottawa, Canada 22
Munro, Alice, Canadian writer 333
Musée d'Orsay, Paris, France 300
Museum of Science, Boston, Massachusetts 120
Music 262–67
    Chrisley, John, picture 237
    commemorative postage stamps 147
    Heifetz, Jascha, death of 38
    Liberace, death of 18
    motion pictures 212
    Segovia, Andrés, death of 26
    Snow White and the Seven Dwarfs 259
Mussel, mollusk 95, 96–97
My Fair Lady, motion picture
    cockney accent 214
    Hepburn, Audrey, costume, picture 213

N

Nakasone, Yasuhiro, premier of Japan 37
Narcissus, flower 220–21
National Gallery, Washington, D.C. 300–01
National Museum of Women in the Arts, Washington,
    D.C., picture 282
National Security Council (NSC) 40–41, 43
Nauru 353
Navratilova, Martina, Czech-American athlete 182
Nazi war crimes
    Hess, Rudolf, death of 30
    Waldheim, Kurt, suspected involvement of 22
Neff, Debra, American playwright 236
Nelson, Willie, American musician 237
Nepal 353
Neptune, planet 347–48
Netherlands 353
Nevada
    Great Basin National Park 30
Newbery Medal, American award for young people's
    literature 295
New Brunswick, province, Canada 360

O

P

Q

T

U

V

Z

ILLUSTRATION CREDITS AND ACKNOWLEDGMENTS

The following list credits or acknowledges, by page, the source of illustrations and text excerpts used in this work. Illustration credits are listed illustration by illustration—left to right, top to bottom. When two or more illustrations appear on one page, their credits are separated by semicolons. When both the photographer or artist and an agency or other source are given for an illustration, they are usually separated by a dash. Excerpts from previously published works are listed by inclusive page numbers.

176 UPI/Bettmann Newsphotos
177 Focus on Sports
178 David Klutho—*Sports Illustrated* © Time Inc.
180 © Jean-Marc Barey—All-Sport; Focus on Sports
181 © Otto Greule—Focus West
182 © Adam J. Stoltman—Duomo
183 Canapress Photo Service
184 © Mitchell Reibel—Sportschrome
185 Richard Mackson—*Sports Illustrated* © Time Inc.; Focus on Sports
186 © Jose Azel—Contact Press Images
187 © Donald Dietz—Stock Boston
188 © *The Christian Science Monitor*—Neal Menschel
189 OCO '88
190– The Architect of the Capitol
191
192 The Granger Collection
194 Courtesy, Chicago Historical Society; © Brad Trent—DOT; © Brad Trent—DOT; © Brad Trent—DOT
195 © Brad Bower—Picture Group
196– Artist, Frank Senyk
197
198– Artist, Michèle A. McLean
203
204 The Granger Collection
205 The Sir Arthur Conan Doyle Foundation
207 Bettmann Archive
208 © Mark Gordon—Preferred Stock
209 Bruce Torrence Historical Collection
210– Hollywood stars pictured: Paul Newman
211 (Phototeque), Charlie Chaplin (The Museum of Modern Art/Film Stills Archive), Humphrey Bogart (The Kobal Collection), Cary Grant (Phototeque), Rudolph Valentino (The Museum of Modern Art/Film Stills Archive), Clark Gable (Phototeque), Katharine Hepburn (Phototeque), Marilyn Monroe (The Kobal Collection), Shirley Temple (The Kobal Collection), Elizabeth Taylor (Phototeque), Mary Pickford (The Kobal Collection), Bette Davis (Phototeque)
213 Collection of Dr. Gary Milan; National Film Archive, London; Kenneth Anger Collection; © 1939 Selznick International Pictures, Inc. Ren. 1967 by Metro-Goldwyn-Mayer Inc.
214 From *Fletcher's Book of Rhyming Slang* by Ronnie Parker. Reprinted by permission of Pan Books
216 © Jerry Howard—PHOTO/NATS; © Dr. E. R. Degginger
217 © Peter B. Kaplan—Photo Researchers, Inc.
218 © Farrell Grehan—Photo Researchers, Inc.; © David M. Stone—PHOTO/NATS
219 © Greg Crisci—PHOTO/NATS; © Robert Bornemann—Photo Researchers, Inc.
220 © Harry Haralambou—Peter Arnold, Inc.; © Mary Nemeth—PHOTO/NATS
221 © Farrell Grehan—Photo Researchers, Inc.
222 Bettmann Archive
223 Courtesy, Seaver Center for Western History Research, Natural History Museum of Los Angeles County
224– © Mark Richards—Picture Group
225
226– Children's Television Workshop
227
228 Nigel Dickson—Owl TV
229 Showtime
230 © Steve Hansen—Stock Boston
231 © Brent Jones
232 Peter Serling—*People* weekly, © 1987 Time Inc.; © Mitchell B. Reibel—Sportschrome
233 Barry Staver—*People* weekly, © 1987 Time Inc.; © Robert McElroy—Woodfin Camp & Associates
234 Courtesy, Pocket Books, Simon & Schuster; Courtesy, Pocket Books, Simon & Schuster
235 Girl Scouts of the USA
236 © Martha Swope
237 Michael Zaganis—*People* weekly, © 1987 Time Inc.; Courtesy, Westinghouse
238 © Jim Pickerell
239 General Electric Research & Development Center
240 © Jim Pickerell
241 Courtesy, Grolier Educational Corporation
242 NASA—JPL
243 Cranston—Csuri Productions; Paul V. Xander
244– Courtesy, Scholastic Photography Awards,
247 conducted by Scholastic Magazines, Inc. and sponsored by Eastman Kodak Company
248– Courtesy, Cooper-Hewitt Museum,
249 Smithsonian Institution—Art Resource
250 Bettmann Archive
251– Courtesy, Cooper-Hewitt Museum,
255 Smithsonian Institution—Art Resource
256 © Phototeque
257 © Ron Phillips—Sygma; © Phototeque
258 © 1937 The Walt Disney Company
259 © Mario Ruiz—Picture Group
260– From *The Shopping Bag: Portable Art* by
261 Stephen C. Wagner & Michael Closen. Reprinted by permission of Crown Publishers Inc. © 1986 by Stephen C. Wagner & Michael Closen
262– Courtesy, Island Records/Atlantic
263
263 © MJJ Productions
264 © Chris V. D. Vooren—Retna Ltd.
265 © Scott Weiner—Retna Ltd.
266 Courtesy, Capitol Records
267 © Scott Weiner—Retna Ltd.
268 Phototeque
269 Phototeque; NBC
270 © Ann Purcell; © Alain Guillou
271 © Carl Purcell; © Ann Purcell
272– From "Craft Today: Poetry of the Physical,"
277 American Craft Museum, New York, 1986. Photographer: George Erml. (*Tri-Color Arch*— courtesy, Rhona Hoffman Gallery, Chicago, IL; *Chest of Drawers*—collection of Ronald and Anne Abramson, Rockville, MD; *Lamp*— courtesy Helen Drutt Gallery, Philadelphia,PA; *Face Goblets*—courtesy, Maurine Littleton Gallery, Washington, D.C.)
278 Phototeque; © Mario Ruiz—Picture Group
279 Clemens Kalischer; © Robert Holland—The Waterhouse
280 © Lester Sloan—Woodfin Camp & Associates; Michael Leshnov
281 Scala/Art Resource; © Botti/Sygma
282 © Brad Markel—Gamma/Liaison; © Jean Pieri —St. Paul Pioneer Press & Dispatch
283 © Harry Benson—Rogers & Cowan Inc.
284– From *To Bathe A Boa* by C. Imbior Kudrna.
285 © 1986 by Carolrhoda Books, Minneapolis, Minn.
286– Artist, Laurie Jordan
293
294 From *Have You Seen Birds?*, by Joanne Oppenheim and illustrated by Barbara Reid.
Reprinted by permission of Scholastic-TAB Publications Ltd.
295 From *The Whipping Boy*, by Sid Fleischmann and illustrated by Peter Sis. © 1986 by Sid Fleischmann. Illustrations © 1986 by Peter Sis. Reprinted by permission of Greenwillow Books (a division of William Morrow & Co.)
296 From *Hey Al*, by Arthur Yorinks. © 1986 by Arthur Yorinks. Illustrations © by Richard Egielski. Reprinted by permission of Farrar, Straus and Giroux
297 From *How a Book is Made*, © 1986 by Aliki Brandenburg. Reprinted by permission of Harper & Row
298 From *The Shadowmaker*, © 1987 by Ron Hansen. Illustrations © 1987 by Margot Tomes. Reprinted by permission of Harper & Row
299 From *Cherries and Cherry Pits*, © 1986 by Vera B. Williams. Reprinted by permission of Greenwillow Books (a division of William Morrow & Co.)
302 Courtauld Institute Galleries, University of London
302– Artist, Kevin Conklin
311
314– Artist, David Wenzel
322
324 © Animals Animals/Oxford Scientific Films; © Tom McHugh—Photo Researchers, Inc.; © Bill Curtsinger—Photo Researchers, Inc.
325 Aretê Publishing Company
326– Artist, Steven Schindler
327
329 Indian Art Center—Indian and Northern Affairs Canada; Indian Art Center—Indian and Northern Affairs Canada; © Yves Tessier— Reflection
330 Courtesy, Royal Ontario Museum, Toronto, Canada
331 National Gallery of Canada, Ottawa; Agnes Etherington Art Centre—Queen's University
332 Courtesy, McClennan & Stewart; © Graeme Gibson—McClennan & Stewart
333 Illustration by M.A. and W.A.J. Claus from *Anne of Green Gables*, by L. M. Montgomery. © L. C. Page & Company, 1908; Illustration by R. A. Stewart from *Roughing It in the Bush*, by Susanna Moodie. © Bell & Cockburn, Toronto, 1913; Illustration by Charles Livingston Bull from *Red Fox*, by Charles G. D. Roberts. © L. C. Page & Company, 1905
334 © W. Griebeling—Miller Services
335 © Nigel Cameron—Photo Researchers, Inc. © Dana Hyde—Photo Researchers, Inc.; © Catherine Ursillo—Photo Researchers, Inc.
336 The Nelson-Atkins Museum of Art (Nelson Fund), Kansas City, MO
337 Courtesy, Freer Gallery of Art, Smithsonian Institution, Washington, D.C.; Courtesy, Freer Gallery of Art, Smithsonian Institution, Washington, D.C.
338 Sotheby Park-Bernet—Art Resource; Courtesy, Freer Gallery of Art, Smithsonian Institution, Washington, D.C.; Courtesy, Freer Gallery of Art, Smithsonian Institution, Washington, D.C.
339 The People's Republic of China
340 J.A.K.
345 © Paul Conklin
346 JPL-NASA
348 NASA
359 UPI/Bettmann Newsphotos